PHILIP'S

DRIVER'S ATLAS
Britain

Contents

www.philips-maps.co.uk

First published in 2006 by Philip's
a division of Octopus Publishing Group Ltd,
Endeavour House, 189 Shaftesbury Avenue
London WC2H 8JY
www.octopus-publishing.co.uk
An Hachette UK company
www.hachette.co.uk

Sixth edition 2011
First impression 2011

ISBN 978-1-84907-159-8

Cartography by Philip's
Copyright © 2011 Philip's

Data for the speed cameras provided by **PocketGPSWorld.com** Ltd.

Information for National Parks, Areas of Outstanding Natural Beauty, National Trails and
Country Parks in Wales supplied by the Countryside Council for Wales.

Information for National Parks, Areas of Outstanding Natural Beauty, National Trails and Country
Parks in England supplied by Natural England. Data for Regional Parks, Long Distance Footpaths
and Country Parks in Scotland provided by Scottish Natural Heritage.

Gaelic name forms used in the Western Isles provided by Comhairle nan Eilean.

Data for the National Nature Reserves in England provided by Natural England. Data for the
National Nature Reserves in Wales provided by Countryside Council for Wales. Darparwyd data'n
ymwneud â Gwarchodfeydd Natur Cenedlaethol Cymru gan Gyngor Cefn Gwlad Cymru.

Information on the location of National Nature Reserves in Scotland was provided by
Scottish Natural Heritage.

Data for National Scenic Areas in Scotland provided by the Scottish Executive Office.
Crown copyright material is reproduced with the permission of the Controller of HMSO and the
Queen's Printer for Scotland. Licence number C02W0003960.

Printed in China

Route-finding system

Town names printed in yellow on a green background are those used on Britain's signposts to indicate primary destinations. To find your route quickly and easily, simply follow the signs to the primary destination immediately beyond the place you require.
Below Driving from St Ives to Camborne, follow the signs to Redruth, the first primary destination beyond Camborne. These will indicate the most direct main route to the side turning for Camborne.

Speed Cameras

Fixed camera locations are shown using the ⑭ symbol.

In congested areas the ⑭ symbol is used to show that there are two or more cameras on the road indicated.

Due to the restrictions of scale the camera locations are only approximate and cannot indicate the operating direction of the camera.

Mobile camera sites, and cameras located on roads not included on the mapping are not shown. Where two or more cameras are shown on the same road, drivers are warned that this may indicate that a SPEC system is in operation. These cameras use the time taken to drive between the two camera positions to calculate the speed of the vehicle.

Road map symbols

M6	Motorway, toll motorway
④ ⑤	Motorway junction – full, restricted access
Ⓢ Ⓢ	Motorway service area – full, restricted access
= = =	Motorway under construction
A453	Primary route – dual, single carriageway
Ⓢ ✳ ○	Service area, roundabout, multi-level junction
④ ⑤	Numbered junction – full, restricted access
	Primary route under construction
	Narrow primary route
Derby	Primary destination
A34	A road – dual, single carriageway
	A road under construction, narrow A road
B2135	B road – dual, single carriageway
	B road under construction, narrow B road
	Minor road – over 4 metres, under 4 metres wide
	Minor road with restricted access
2	Distance in miles
	Scenic route
⑭ ⑭	Speed camera – single, multiple
TOLL	Toll, steep gradient – arrow points downhill
	Tunnel
	National trail – England and Wales
	Long distance footpath – Scotland
	Railway with station
✕)–(	Level crossing, tunnel
	Preserved railway with station
	National boundary
	County / unitary authority boundary
	Car ferry, catamaran
	Passenger ferry, catamaran
	Hovercraft
CALAIS 1:30	Ferry destination, journey time – hrs : mins
Ferry	Car ferry – river crossing
✈ ✈	Principal airport, other airport
	National park
	Area of Outstanding Natural Beauty – England and Wales National Scenic Area – Scotland forest park / regional park / national forest
	Woodland
	Beach
■ ■ ■	Linear antiquity
– – – –	Roman road
⬚ ✕1066	Hillfort, battlefield – with date
⋇ 🍁 ▲795	Viewpoint, nature reserve, spot height – in metres
⚑ ▲ ◎	Golf course, youth hostel, sporting venue
⋏ 🚐 ⬚	Camp site, caravan site, camping and caravan site
🛒 P&R	Shopping village, park and ride
29	Adjoining page number – road maps

Tourist information

✝ Abbey / cathedral / priory	⛵ Historic ship	ℹ Tourist information centre – open all year
🏛 Ancient monument	🏠 House	ℹ Tourist information centre – open seasonally
⚓ Aquarium	🏡 House and garden	
🏛 Art gallery	🏁 Motor racing circuit	🐾 Zoo
🦅 Bird collection / aviary	🏛 Museum	✦ Other place of interest
🏰 Castle	◎ Picnic area	
⛪ Church	🚂 Preserved railway	
🏕 Country park – England and Wales	🏇 Race course	
🏕 Country park – Scotland	🏛 Roman antiquity	
🐑 Farm park	⚘ Safari park	
✿ Garden	🎢 Theme park	

Road map scale: 1: 265 320, 4.2 miles to 1 inch

0 1 2 3 4 5 6 7 8 9 miles
0 1 2 3 4 5 6 7 8 9 10 11 12 13 14 15km

Relief

Feet	metres
3000	914
2600	792
2200	671
1800	549
1400	427
1000	305
0	0

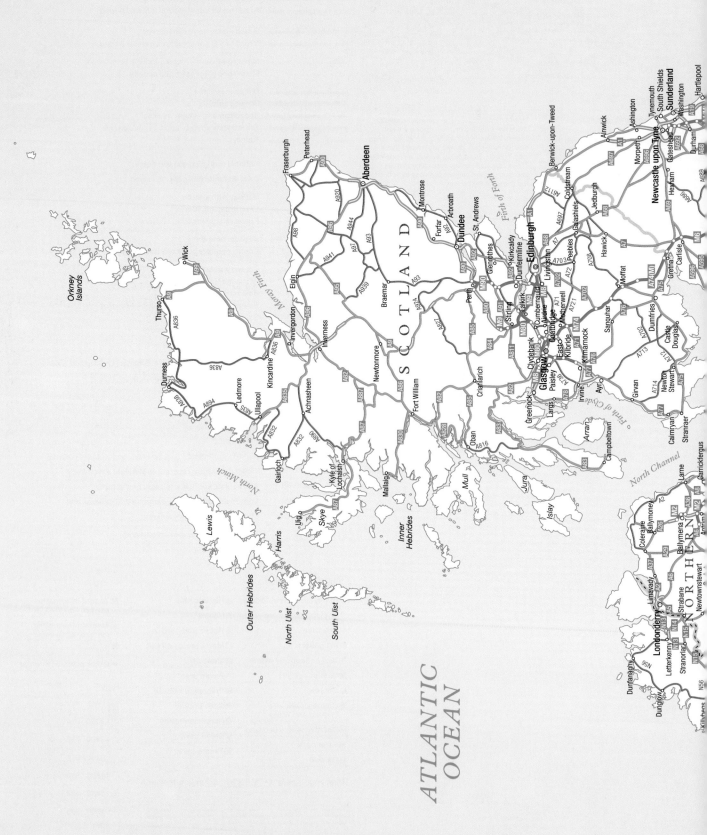

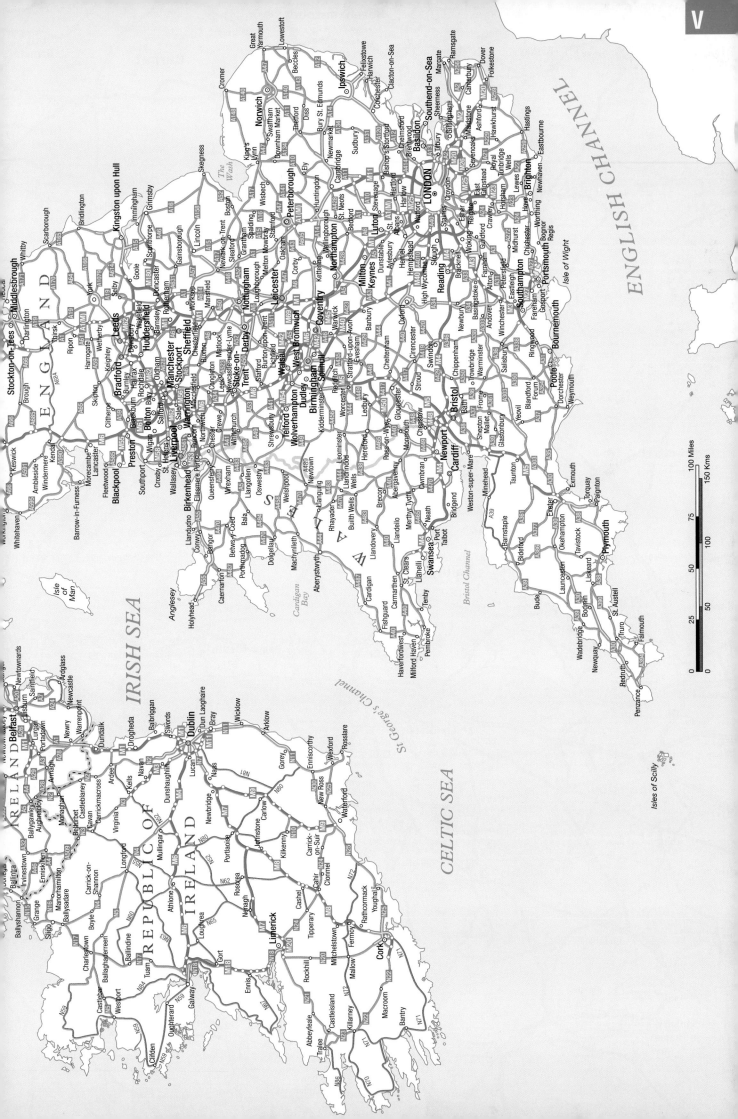

Distance table

How to use this table

Distances are shown in miles and, in *italics*, kilometres.
For example, the distance between Aberdeen and Bournemouth is 564 miles or *908* kilometres.

Supporting

THINK!

Travel safe – Don't drive tired

Distances are given in **miles** and, in *italics*, **kilometres**.

- **London**
- **Aberdeen:** 517 / *832*
- **Aberystwyth:** 445 211 / *716 340*
- **Ayr:** 317 183 / *510 295 634*
- **Berwick-upon-Tweed:** 134 311 182 352 / *216 501 293 567*
- **Birmingham:** 274 289 114 420 117 / *441 465 183 676 188*
- **Blackpool:** 123 181 180 153 308 226 / *198 291 290 246 496 364*
- **Bournemouth:** 270 147 412 436 207 564 107 / *435 237 663 702 333 908 172*
- **Braemar:** 524 281 385 148 143 405 59 482 / *843 452 620 238 230 652 95 776*
- **Brighton:** 534 92 286 163 409 446 253 573 52 / *859 148 460 262 658 718 407 922 84*
- **Bristol:** 147 477 81 362 370 125 493 122 / *237 768 132 328 130 583 595 201 793 196*
- **Cambridge:** 169 116 438 154 208 100 306 357 214 471 54 / *272 187 705 248 335 161 493 575 344 758 87*
- **Cardiff:** 190 45 182 483 117 209 103 368 382 105 505 157 / *306 72 293 778 188 336 166 592 615 169 813 253*
- **Carlisle:** 289 264 277 370 196 343 87 196 87 93 224 221 161 / *465 425 446 596 316 552 140 315 140 150 360 356 484*
- **Doncaster:** 142 209 116 236 310 235 94 184 235 176 344 171 / *229 336 187 282 380 499 378 151 151 296 378 283 554 275*
- **Dover:** 242 389 238 125 202 82 553 174 312 194 424 478 297 588 71 / *390 626 383 201 325 132 890 280 502 312 683 769 478 947 114*
- **Dundee:** 523 275 247 52 495 239 349 113 117 376 67 448 109 / *842 443 245 710 654 692 832 84 797 385 562 182 188 605 108 721*
- **Edinburgh:** 56 462 219 96 385 345 373 456 91 439 183 292 57 73 320 125 180 / *90 744 352 154 620 555 600 734 146 707 295 470 92 117 515 201 628*
- **Exeter:** 450 518 248 353 121 249 76 184 201 569 157 428 446 201 569 181 / *724 834 399 404 568 195 401 122 296 885 132 454 253 689 718 323 916 291*
- **Fishguard:** 230 399 460 331 247 297 112 270 154 291 493 222 209 170 371 373 56 504 260 / *370 642 740 533 398 478 180 435 248 468 794 357 336 274 597 600 90 811 418*
- **Fort William:** 486 560 144 127 596 357 125 539 296 392 190 133 430 149 510 / *782 901 232 204 959 575 332 781 771 782 926 201 867 476 631 306 214 692 240 821*
- **Glasgow:** 101 376 449 44 83 488 249 96 385 372 373 468 110 439 183 292 101 33 320 145 367 / *163 605 723 71 134 786 401 154 620 599 600 753 177 707 295 470 163 53 515 233 639*
- **Gloucester:** 346 454 153 111 349 410 191 150 247 56 318 330 102 468 109 / *557 731 246 179 562 660 307 241 398 90 198 56 256 713 159 280 90 512 531 164 765*
- **Great Yarmouth:** 225 419 527 366 335 386 484 185 167 320 284 82 275 180 477 240 252 180 345 402 294 517 128 / *362 674 848 589 539 621 779 298 269 515 457 132 443 290 768 386 406 290 555 647 473 832 206*
- **Harwich:** 82 196 432 543 337 279 413 469 125 194 336 246 67 217 128 74 206 185 275 167 372 425 281 535 76 / *132 316 695 874 542 449 665 755 201 312 541 396 108 349 206 811 301 443 269 599 684 452 861 122*
- **Holyhead:** 349 334 191 330 438 167 282 333 394 360 181 231 216 270 206 334 426 288 141 148 311 305 111 439 269 / *562 538 307 531 705 269 454 536 634 580 291 372 348 435 332 538 686 463 227 238 501 491 179 707 433*
- **Inverness:** 474 569 553 504 166 66 542 618 158 132 622 383 262 549 505 617 75 132 215 223 364 184 / *763 916 890 811 267 106 872 995 254 212 1001 617 422 884 813 867 993 121 961 560 737 346 320 782 169 885*
- **John o' Groats:** 129 603 693 677 628 295 195 671 744 285 259 746 507 391 680 630 668 741 202 724 478 574 342 328 601 232 663 / *208 970 1116 1090 1011 475 314 1080 1197 459 417 1201 816 629 1094 1014 1075 1193 325 1165 769 924 550 528 967 373 1067*
- **Kingston upon Hull:** 518 394 231 196 207 169 254 369 280 309 295 256 412 76 254 393 224 375 394 526 425 204 216 298 404 359 586 / *834 634 372 316 333 272 409 594 451 497 377 412 76 254 393 224 375 394 526 425 204 216 298 404 359 586 296*
- **Kyle of Lochalsh:** 445 189 84 514 611 602 528 179 79 567 628 216 186 671 432 276 564 555 552 651 159 618 372 471 263 212 499 189 586 / *716 304 135 827 983 969 850 288 127 913 1011 348 299 1080 695 443 908 893 888 1048 256 995 599 758 423 341 803 304 943*
- **Land's End:** 763 421 868 741 405 398 264 235 573 686 353 123 574 642 381 374 643 361 361 602 322 496 1070 330 652 452 888 917 504 1114 478 / *1228 678 1397 1193 652 628 718 378 922 1104 568 198 924 1033 613 602 768 394 602 322 496 1070 330 652 452 888 917 504 1114 478*
- **Leeds:** 405 394 55 487 360 176 223 196 174 215 329 237 270 202 258 260 29 119 232 145 194 260 255 72 113 156 212 169 327 189 / *652 634 89 784 579 283 359 315 280 346 530 381 435 325 415 418 47 192 373 233 312 419 472 410 116 182 251 341 272 526 304*
- **Leicester:** 95 320 500 102 588 461 190 147 140 85 314 422 209 166 389 158 140 92 206 185 74 206 74 113 117 414 97 / *153 515 805 164 947 742 306 237 225 137 505 679 336 315 476 562 298 119 332 248 109 193 267 626 254 225 406 481 246 666 156*
- **Lincoln:** 51 68 371 476 44 554 427 216 155 128 159 291 399 272 247 258 314 202 39 191 208 85 183 197 357 209 128 90 224 274 199 133 131 / *82 109 597 766 71 892 687 348 249 206 256 468 642 438 398 415 505 325 63 307 335 137 295 317 575 336 206 145 360 441 320 616 211*
- **Liverpool:** 129 130 75 361 407 130 511 382 102 265 240 140 210 169 146 221 132 34 181 272 318 202 / *208 209 121 581 655 209 822 615 164 427 386 225 348 530 257 381 348 460 481 138 193 272 512 325 267 581 512 377 79 150 352 343 167 549 325*
- **Manchester:** 35 84 92 40 361 406 95 500 373 124 228 212 126 215 329 146 215 276 61 119 183 165 161 257 318 227 48 80 196 212 129 340 185 / *56 135 148 64 581 654 153 805 600 200 367 341 203 346 530 317 380 346 459 444 98 192 295 266 259 414 512 365 77 129 315 341 208 547 298*
- **Newcastle upon Tyne:** 132 168 159 187 92 498 318 130 395 268 281 366 188 266 148 255 299 86 152 57 321 241 299 352 201 347 129 207 64 149 257 235 286 / *212 270 256 301 148 802 512 212 636 431 438 496 452 428 238 407 529 586 177 267 576 183 92 523 388 431 323 568 208 333 103 240 414 378 460*
- **Norwich:** 261 185 220 105 119 176 421 502 149 654 529 311 73 20 204 385 504 343 308 366 422 174 147 289 262 62 252 175 457 214 232 166 328 382 276 496 114 / *425 298 354 169 192 283 678 937 240 1053 852 501 117 32 328 620 811 552 496 589 679 280 237 465 422 100 406 282 735 344 373 267 528 615 444 798 183*
- **Nottingham:** 130 157 73 98 35 25 70 345 479 90 557 430 175 53 110 249 403 400 147 183 111 145 193 183 111 50 221 274 164 393 122 / *209 253 118 158 56 40 113 555 771 145 896 692 298 241 246 177 472 646 354 356 442 179 80 356 441 264 633 196*
- **Oban:** 390 492 233 307 308 387 419 307 665 128 346 244 117 427 524 515 441 92 49 481 549 123 117 585 346 180 477 468 465 565 141 530 285 384 180 94 412 178 499 / *628 792 375 494 496 623 674 494 1070 206 557 393 188 687 843 829 710 148 79 774 884 198 188 942 557 303 768 753 748 910 227 853 459 618 290 151 663 286 803*
- **Oxford:** 462 109 145 260 144 172 137 73 168 274 550 192 556 52 259 633 205 156 372 433 141 145 260 108 83 74 108 465 90 187 64 324 353 154 483 57 / *744 175 233 418 232 277 221 117 270 441 885 309 1056 856 383 233 322 84 573 760 330 251 418 174 134 119 174 749 145 301 103 521 568 248 778 92*
- **Plymouth:** 199 587 267 343 410 283 283 293 242 316 89 674 355 790 664 328 309 365 157 495 595 264 46 496 552 300 297 399 217 293 122 224 587 128 328 203 474 492 237 615 218 / *320 945 430 552 660 455 455 472 389 509 143 1085 571 1271 1069 528 497 588 253 797 958 425 74 798 888 483 478 642 269 472 196 361 945 206 528 327 763 792 382 990 351*
- **Portsmouth:** 176 77 545 191 207 337 236 254 201 162 527 259 633 289 409 322 261 414 417 433 130 234 348 142 144 97 48 547 51 264 141 401 430 222 560 70 / *283 124 877 307 333 542 380 409 323 261 414 417 1019 433 1186 987 501 267 356 192 721 893 404 217 729 827 209 377 560 229 232 156 77 547 56 264 141 401 430 222 560 70 113*
- **Sheffield:** 230 283 135 339 37 146 125 38 72 46 62 33 361 427 65 520 393 168 187 166 126 248 348 215 237 235 291 245 86 76 190 245 159 260 / *370 455 217 546 60 235 201 61 116 74 100 53 581 687 105 837 632 270 301 267 203 399 560 346 381 378 468 394 29 245 312 193 259 364 515 348 138 122 306 394 256 579 296*
- **Shrewsbury:** 82 207 225 106 364 93 265 37 146 125 38 72 46 62 33 361 427 65 520 77 272 382 145 179 274 330 251 109 176 111 159 103 226 311 185 98 45 265 269 77 399 160 / *132 333 362 171 586 150 330 323 171 69 58 133 84 93 214 135 175 488 726 272 912 705 182 386 542 332 451 160 441 510 288 441 501 274 852 412 72 426 433 242 646 258*
- **Southampton:** 185 199 21 151 64 530 176 206 324 221 239 204 137 322 228 618 723 598 293 164 220 105 433 541 233 105 438 500 143 209 324 121 148 76 532 31 251 128 388 417 201 547 77 / *298 320 34 243 103 853 283 332 521 356 385 328 220 373 367 995 412 1164 963 472 264 354 169 697 871 375 169 705 805 230 336 521 195 238 122 98 856 50 404 206 624 671 323 880 124*
- **Stranraer:** 445 277 263 461 500 379 148 500 403 158 220 221 298 330 220 259 356 480 531 354 942 423 410 610 421 628 610 468 463 78 427 250 336 463 463 195 392 454 124 167 496 257 101 390 379 378 615 194 444 188 297 170 51 325 228 402 / *716 446 423 742 805 610 238 467 649 254 354 356 480 531 354 417 610 731 200 266 258 262 338 410 426 343 84 195 392 454 124 167 496 257 101 390 379 378 615 194 444 188 297 170 51 325 228 402 647*
- **Swansea:** 417 161 118 217 182 506 141 506 192 301 347 187 195 233 177 248 285 594 264 696 572 184 89 409 496 67 161 412 473 274 232 227 85 222 505 167 216 119 383 73 507 194 / *671 259 190 349 293 322 227 815 309 485 559 301 314 375 285 399 459 956 425 1120 921 296 143 658 798 108 259 663 761 441 373 497 66 365 137 357 813 269 348 192 616 610 117 816 312*
- **York:** 272 222 258 133 52 278 333 181 309 77 181 84 64 99 75 108 24 411 407 37 479 352 204 228 201 189 217 330 261 287 194 250 282 34 121 244 165 222 275 269 96 130 214 195 319 207 / *438 357 415 214 84 448 536 291 497 124 291 135 103 159 121 174 39 661 655 60 771 566 328 367 323 304 349 531 420 462 312 402 454 55 195 393 266 357 443 459 433 154 209 238 344 314 513 333*

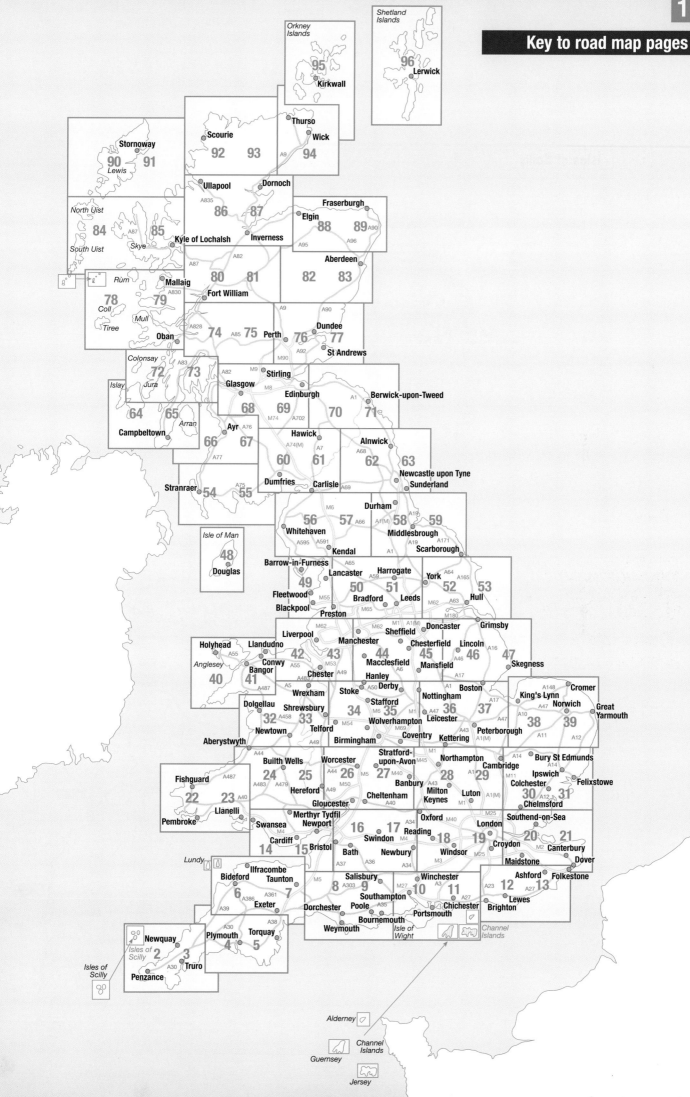

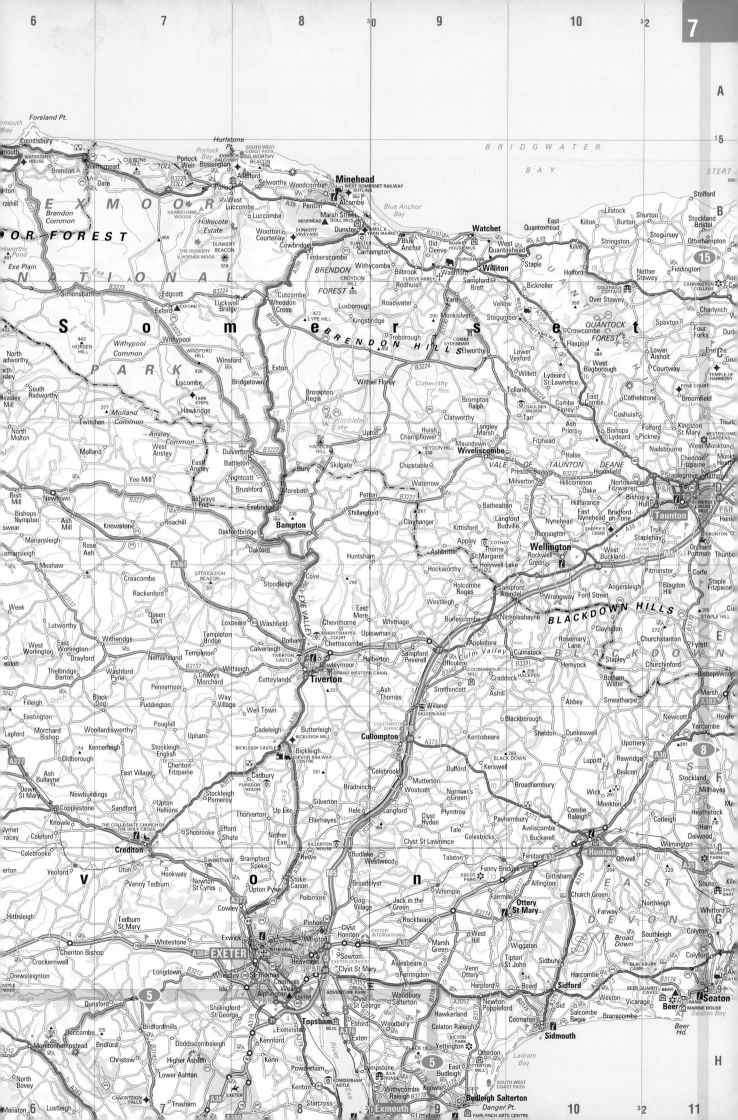

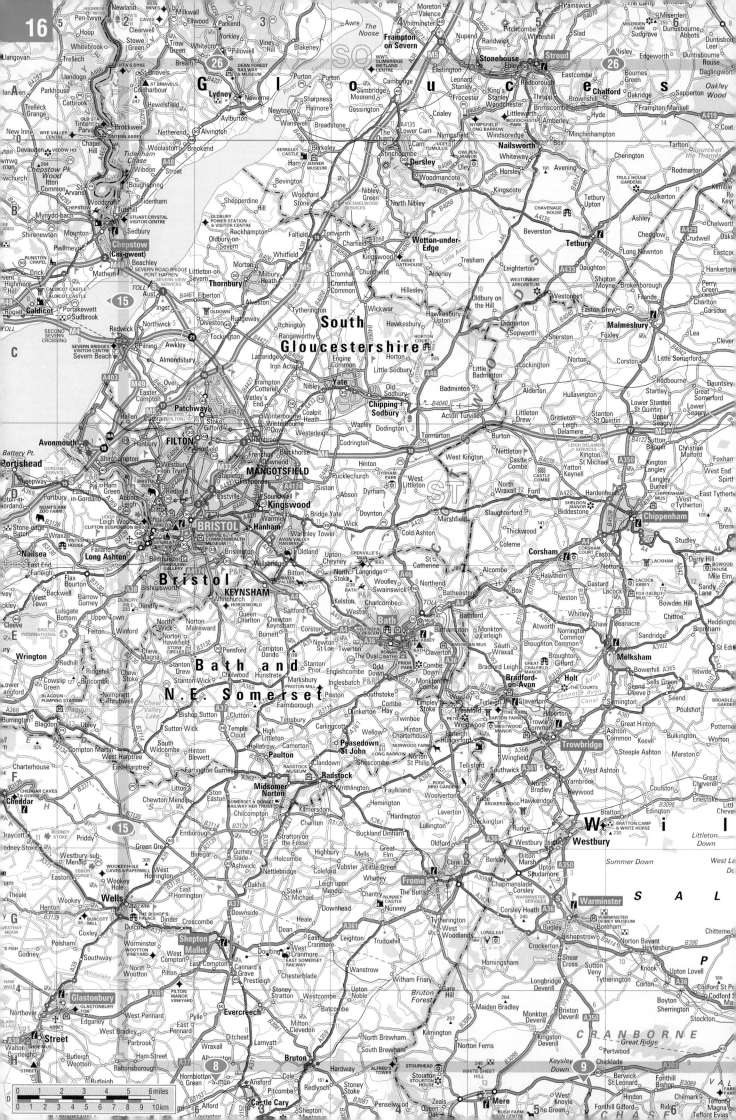

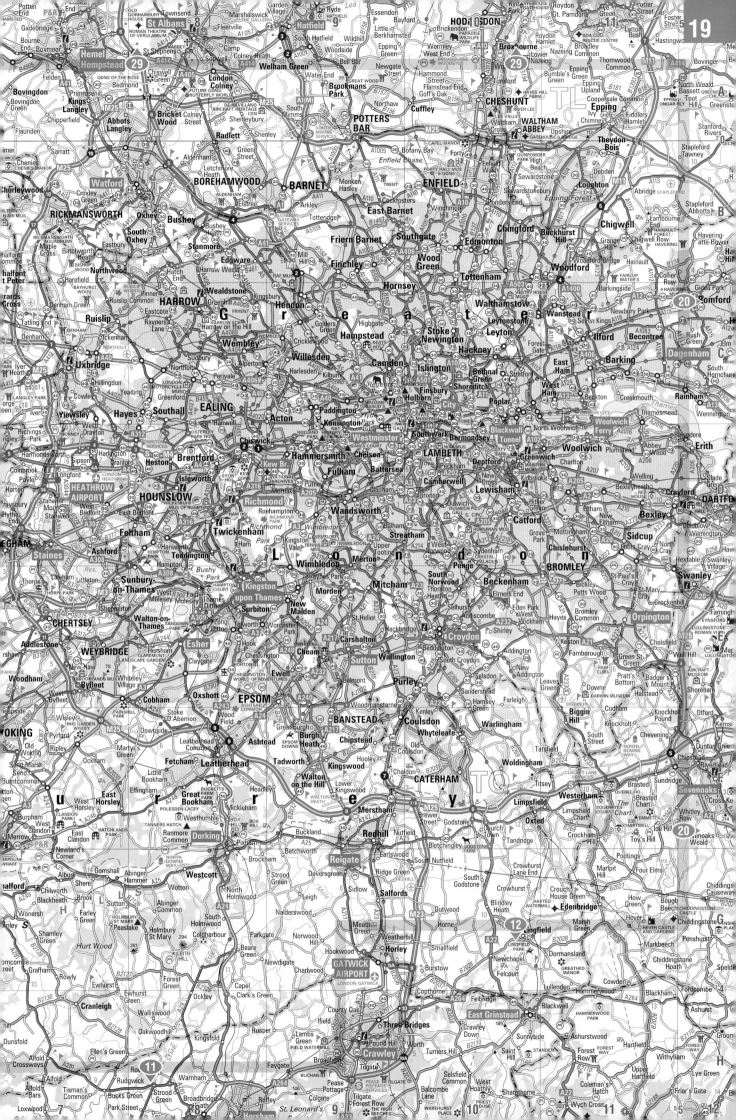

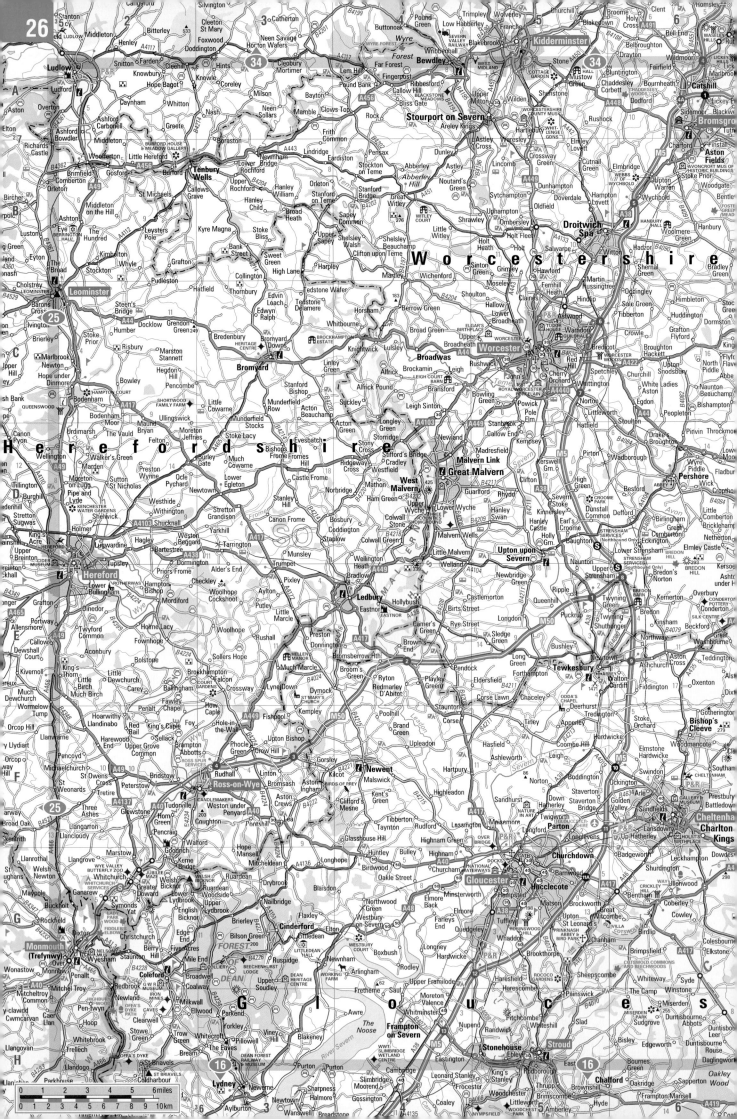

Warwick
Oxford
Coventry
Kenilworth
Royal Leamington Spa
Warwick
Stratford-upon-Avon
Redditch
Rugby
Evesham
Banbury
Southam
Alcester
Studley
Shipston-on-Stour
Moreton-in-Marsh
Stow-on-the-Wold
Chipping Norton
Woodstock
Kidlington
Witney
Burford
Carterton
Charlbury
Broadway
Middleton Cheney
Vale of Evesham
Cotswolds
M40
M42
M45
A46
A44
A40
A429
A3400
35
28
17

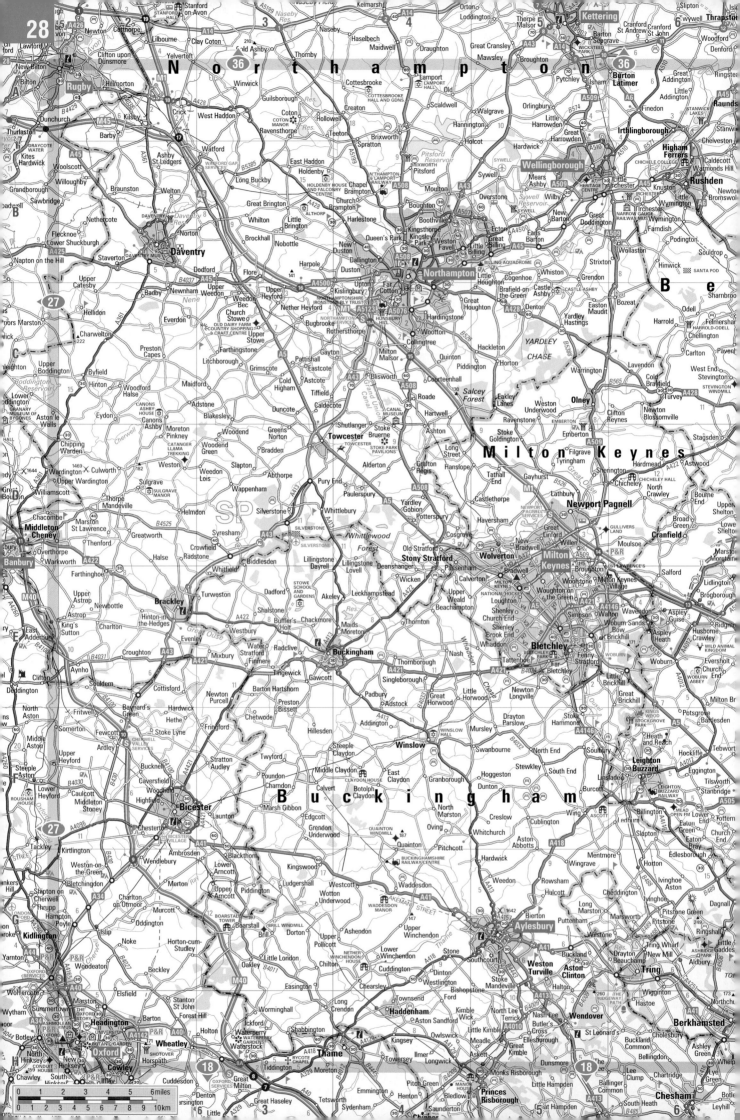

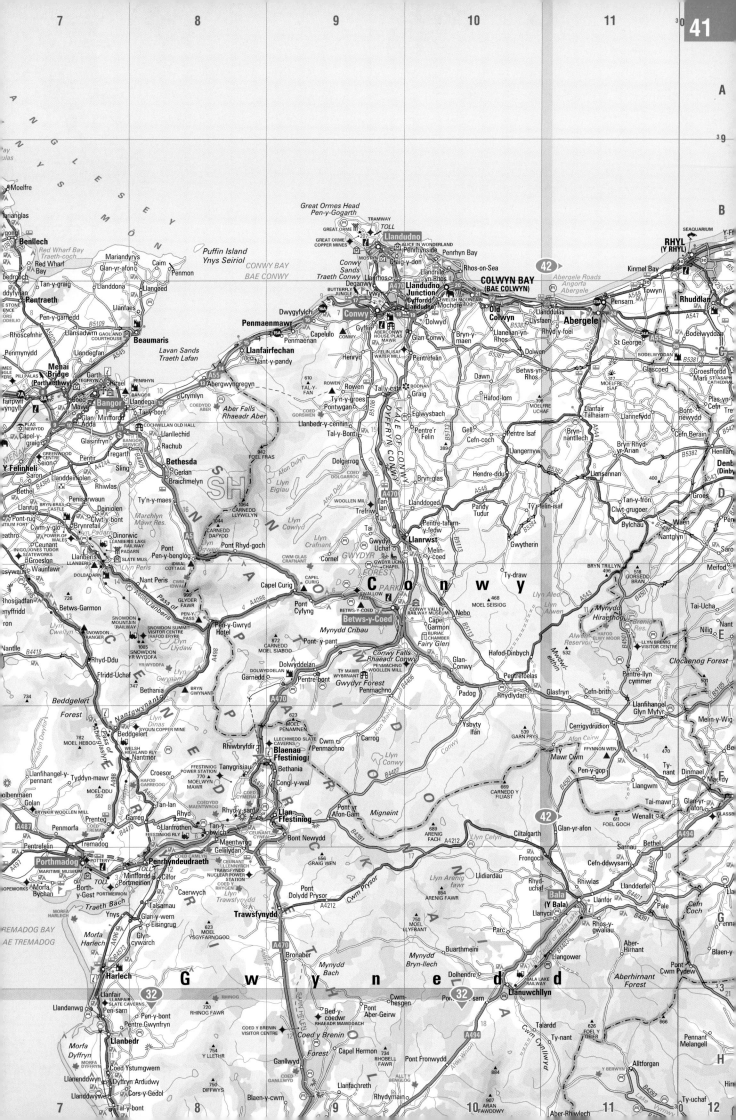

7 8 9 10 11

A

B

C

D

E

F

G

Skeffling
Kilsea
53
SPURN
SPURN
HEAD
ROTTERDAM 10:15
ZEEBRUGGE 12:15

TA

CLEETHORPES
CLEETHORPES COAST LIGHT RAILWAY
PLEASURE ISLAND THEME PARK
CLEETHORPES
Humberston

MOUTH OF THE HUMBER

Tetney Lock
North Cotes
Tetney
Marshchapel
Eskham
Wragholme
Grainthorpe
Fulstow
LINCOLNSHIRE WOLDS RLY
Covenham St Bartholomew
Conisholme
Covenham St Mary
Utterby
Yarburgh
Skidbrooke
South Somercotes
Fotherby
Little Grimsby
ALVINGHAM MILL
Alvingham
North Cockerington
RUSHMOOR
South Cockerington
Louth
ST JAMES
Stewton
Keddington
Grimoldby
Manby
Legbourne
Little Carlton
Great Carlton
South Reston
Gayton le Marsh
North Reston
Strubby
Thorpe
Muckton
Tothill
Authorpe
Maltby le Marsh
Beesby
Woodthorpe
CLAYTHORPE WATER MILL AND WILDFOWL GARDENS
Saleby
Markby
Hannah
Belleau
Aby
Swaby
South Thoresby
ALFORD WINDMILL
Bilsby
Asserby
Huttoft
ALFORD MANOR HOUSE
Rigsby
Alford
Farlesthorpe
Mumby
Anderby
ON YOUR MARQUES
Authorpe Row
Well
Cumberworth
Helsey
Chapel St Leonards
Bonthorpe
Hogsthorpe
Ulceby
Willoughby
Sloothby
Claxby
HARDY'S ANIMAL FARM
Ingoldmells
FANTASY ISLAND
CHILDREN'S PLAYDROME & THE MILLENNIUM ROLLERCOASTER
FUNCOAST WORLD

North Somercotes
DONNA NOOK
Skidbrooke North End
Saltfleet
SALTFLEETBY THEDDLETHORPE
Saltfleetby St Clements
Saltfleetby All Saints
Saltfleetby St Peter
Theddlethorpe St Helen
Theddlethorpe All Saints
Meers Bridge
SEAL SANCTUARY & NATURE CENTRE
Mablethorpe
Trusthorpe
Sutton on Sea
Sandilands

Donna Nook

N O R T H

S E A

Keal Cotes
WOLDS
Tetford
Salmonby
Brinkhill
Somersby
Driby
Calceby
Haugh
Sutterby
Langton
Skendleby
Partney
Scremby
Candlesby
Ashby by Partney
GUNBY HALL
Orby
Orby Marsh
Welton le Marsh
Burgh le Marsh
Winthorpe
Seathorne
NATURELAND SEAL SANCTUARY
Skegness
THE LIFEBOAT STATION
Seacroft
Croft
Croft Marsh
GIBRALTAR POINT

Hagworthingham
afield
Lusby
Mavis Enderby
Hameringham
Raithby
Asgarby
Hundleby
Old Bolingbroke
Spilsby
NORTHCOTE HEAVY HORSE CENTRE
Hareby
BOLINGBROKE
West Keal
East Keal
Toynton All Saints
Halton Holegate
Great Steeping
Toynton St Peter
Irby in the Marsh
Firsby
Little Steeping
Thorpe Culvert
Thorpe St Peter
Wainfleet All Saints
MAGDALEN MUSEUM
Wainfleet St Mary
BURGH LE MARSH WINDMILL
CHURCH FARM MUS

New Bolingbroke
Stickney
Stickford
Midville
New Leake
Eastville
Carrington
Medlam
Northlands
Lade Bank
East Fen
Wrangle Bank
Leake Commonside
Friskney Eaudike
Friskney
Friskney Tofts
Wainfleet Bank
Wainfleet Tofts
Wainfleet Sand

Frithville
Sibsey
SIBSEY TRADER MILL
Wrangle
Hurn's End
Wrangle Lowgate
Friskney Flats

38
BRANCASTER ROADS

boston
Cowbridge
Hill Dyke
Frith Bank
Boston Long Hedges
Leverton
Benington
Leverton Highgate
Leverton Lucasgate
Leverton Outgate

37
GUILDHALL
Skirbeck
Butterwick
Freiston
Scrane End

BOSTON DEEPS

LYNN DEEPS

T H E   W A S H

HOLME BIRD OBSERVATORY
Holme next the Sea
Old Hunstanton
Hunstanton
Thornham
Titchwell
HOLME DUNES
Brancaster
Brancaster Staithe
Burnham Deepdale
SCOLT HEAD ISLAND
Brancaster Bay
Burnham Norton
Westgate
Burnham Market

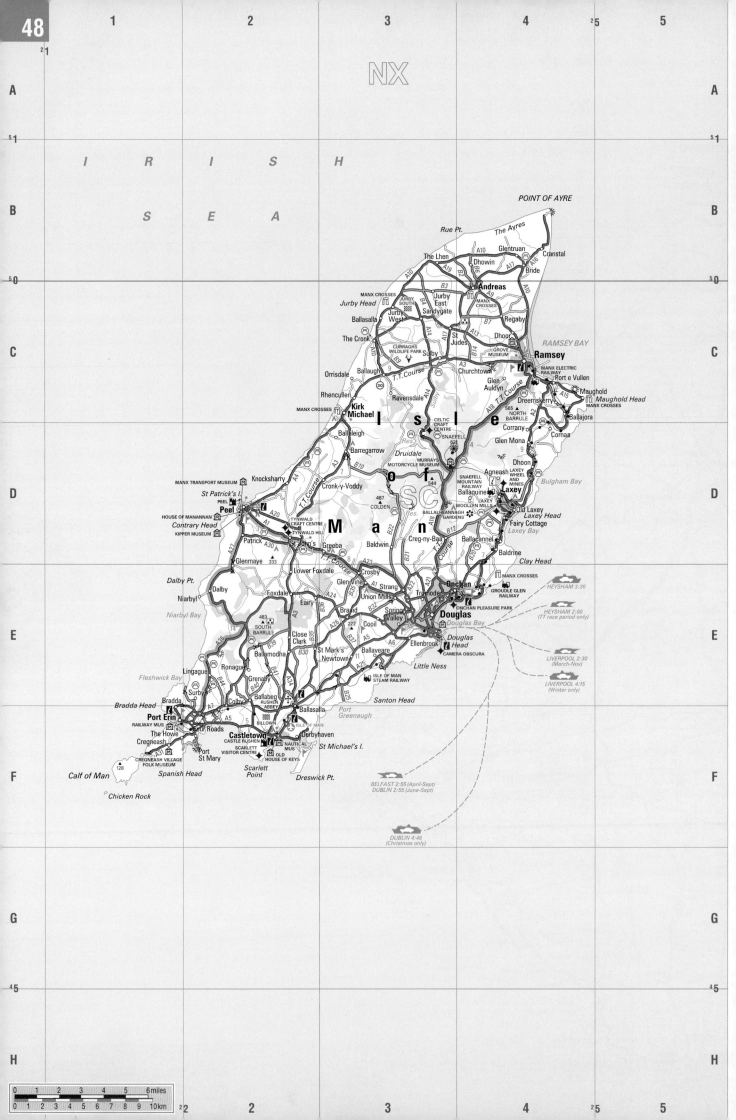

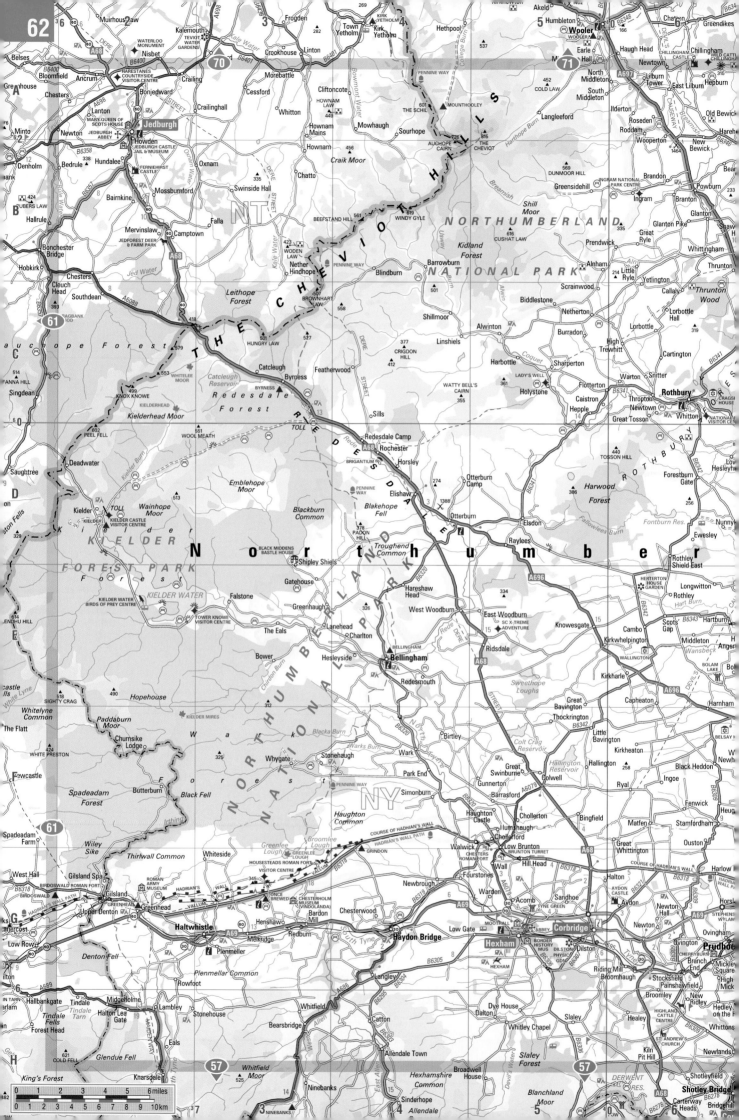

ISLAY

RHINNS
OF
ISLAY

A r g y l l

J U R A
JURA FOREST
PAPS OF JURA

THE OA

NR

N O R T H C H A N N E L

Rubha a'Mhail
COLONSAY 1:10
(Summer only)
Loch an Aircill
439
Loch a Chnuic
Bhric
Corran
785
755
Rubha Bholsa
Nave Island
Ardnave Pt.
364
SGARBH
BREAC
561
Leargybreck
Gleann Astaile
Ardnave
Gortantaoid
Bunnahabhain
BUNNAHABHAIN
DISTILLERY
316
An Clachan
Carraig Bhan
Killinallan
Caol Ila
Keils
Sanaigmore
Leckgruinart
CAOL ILA DISTILLERY
Port Askaig
Braigo
Ardnave
FINLAGGAN
CENTRE
Feolin Ferry
Craighouse
ISLE OF JURA
DISTILLERY
Ballinaby
Carnduncan
Ballygrant
Keills
342
BRAT BHEINN
Ballinaby
Aoradh
Craigens
Ballygrant
Kilmeny
Cabrach
Saligo Bay
Loch
Gorm
Sunderland
Blackrock
Redhouses
Daill
267
BEINN DUBH
JURA HOUSE
WALLED GARDEN
Machir Bay
Kilchoman
Conisby
Bridgend
Sorn
Am Fraoch
Eilean
Brosdale I.
Rubha na T
Kilchiaran Bay
Kilchiaran
Bruichladdich
Bowmore
BOWMORE
ROUND
CHURCH
Mulindry
McArthur's Hd.
ISLAY LIFE
MUSEUM
Tormisdale
RHINNS
ISLAY
Kilennan
Lossit Pt.
Lossit
232
Port
Charlotte
15
Duich
471
BEINN BHAN
491
BEINN
BHEIGEIR
Carraig Mhór
Nerabus
Laggan
Pt.
Laggan
13
Loch Beinn
Uraraidh
Ardtalla
Claggain
Bay
Rubha na Faing
Portnahaven
Port Wemyss
Orsay
Rinns Pt.
LAGGAN
BAY
Glenegedale
B8016
Leorin
347
BEINN SHOLUM
Kintour
Ardmore Pt.
KILDALTON CHURCH
AND CROSSES
Eilean Craobhach
Port Alsaig
Rubha Mór
Kintra
Cornabus
Imeraval
Port Ellen
Lagavulin
ARDBEG
DISTILLERY
Ardbeg
LAGAVULIN DISTILLERY
Eilean Imersay
Eilean a'Chuirn
Eilean Bhride
Dùn Mór Ghil
Lower Cragabus
152
Laphroaig
LAPHROAIG
DISTILLERY
Texa
Lower
Killeyan
Risabus
AMERICAN MONUMENT
Mull of Oa
Inerval
202
Rubha nan Leacan
Rathlin Island

A
B
C
D
E
F
G
H

1   2   3   4   5   6

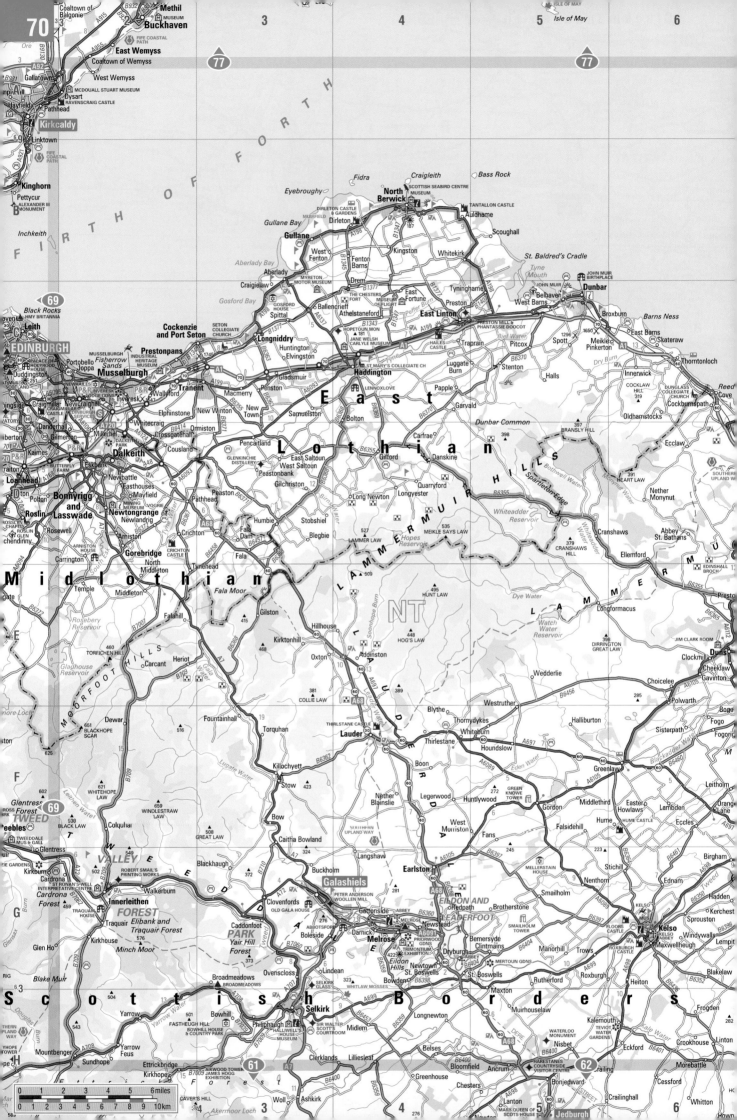

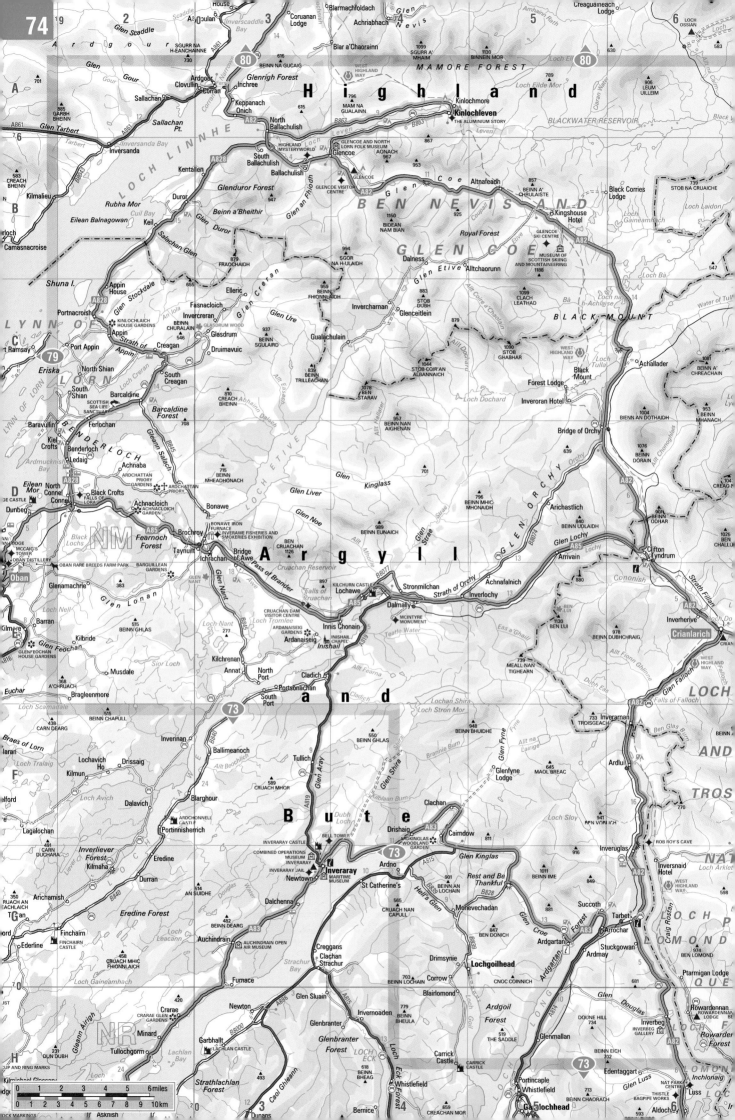

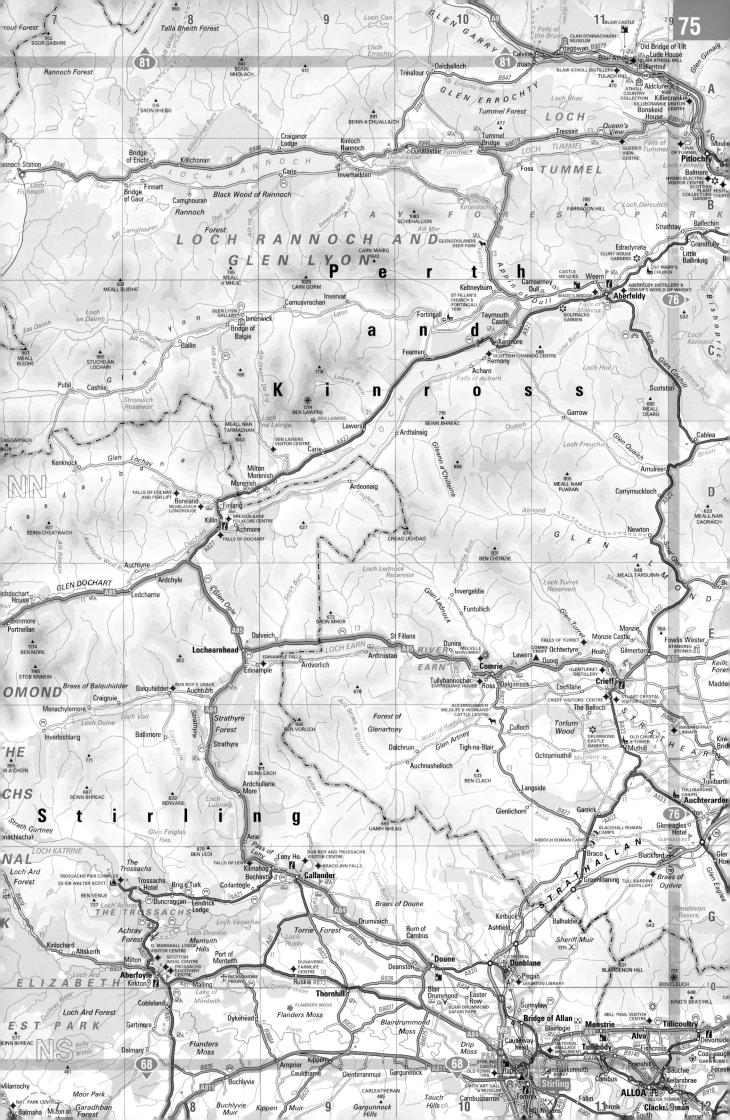

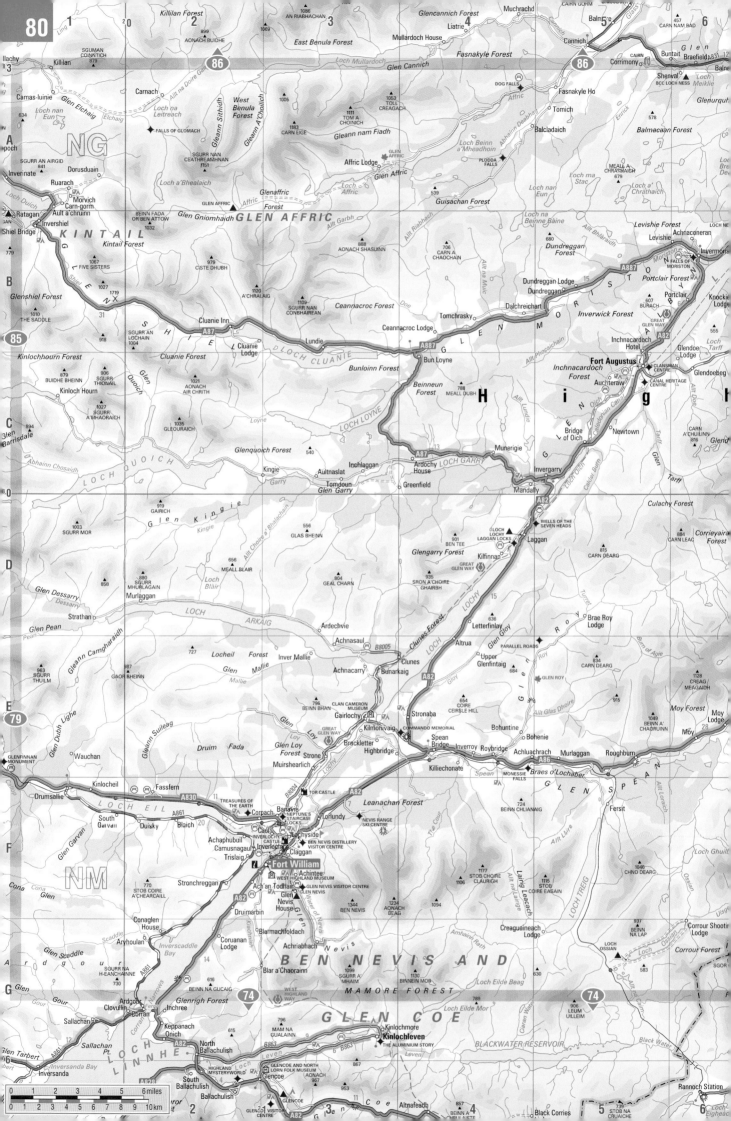

Ling 1   20   Killilan Forest   2   1086 AN RIABHACHAN   3   Glencannich Forest   Muchrachd   Cairn Gorm   Baln   5'e   Glass   Carn Nam Bad   6

East Benula Forest   899 AONACH BUIDHE   1069   1005   Liatrie   Cannich   86   Buntait   A831   Balne   Braefield   86

Killilan Forest   SGUMAN COINNTICH   879   Carnach   West Benula Forest   Loch Mullardoch   Glen Cannich   Fasnakyle Forest   DOG FALLS   CAIRN   Corrimony   Shenval   BCC LOCH NESS   Loch   Meiklie

Killilan   Mullardoch House   1053   TOLL CREAGACH   Affric   Fasnakyle Ho   Tomich   Glenurqu

Camas-luinie   Glen Elchaig   Elchaig   Loch na Leitreach   West Benula Forest   1111 TOM A CHOINICH   Balcladaich   Balmacaan Forest

634   FALLS OF GLOMACH   1183 CARN EIGE   Gleann nam Fiadh   539   578

A   NG   Carn-gorm   SGURR NAN CEATHREAMHNAN 1151   Affric Lodge   GLEN AFFRIC   Loch Beinn a'Mheadhoin   PLODDA FALLS   Loch ma Stac   MEALL A' CHRATHAICH 679   Loch a' Chrathaich

Inverinate   841   Dorusduain   Affric   Glenaffric   Guisachan Forest   Loch nan Eun   Glen   De

Ault a'chruinn   Morvich   BEINN FADA OR BEN ATTOW 1032   Forest   Glen Gniomhaidh   GLEN AFFRIC   Allt Garbh   Loch na Beinne Baine   Levishie Forest   LOCH NE

Ratagan   Invershiel   KINTAIL   Kintail Forest   AONACH SHASUINN   CARN A CHAOCHAIN   706   680   Dundreggan Forest   Levishie   Achnaconeran   Invermoriston

Shiel Bridge   779   FIVE SISTERS   1067   979 CISTE DHUBH   888   A887   Dundreggan Lodge   15   Portclair Forest   FALLS OF MORISTON

B   Glenshiel Forest   1027   1719   1120 A'CHRALAIG   Ceannacroc Forest   Doe   Dundreggan   607 BURACH   Portclair   Knockie Lodge

THE SADDLE   31   1109 SGURR NAN CONBHAIREAN   Tomchrasky   Dalchreichart   Inverwick Forest   GREAT GLEN WAY   A82

Cluanie Inn   A87   Lundie   Ceannacroc Lodge   A887   Inchnacardoch Hotel   Glendoe Lodge

85   SGURR AN LOCHAIN 1004   918   Cluanie Lodge   DLOCH CLUANIE   Bun Loyne   Fort Augustus   555   Loch Tarff

Kinlochhourn Forest   SGURR THIONAIL   Cluanie Forest   Bunloinn Forest   Beinneun Forest   788 MEALL DUBH   H   Inchnacardoch Forest   CLANSMAN CENTRE   Glendoebeg

879 BUIDHE BHEINN   906 SGURR   1021 AONACH AIR CHRITH   i   g   CANAL HERITAGE CENTRE   CARN A'CHUILINN 816   Glend

C   Kinloch Hourn   Glen Quoich   1035 GLEOURAICH   540   Glen   Auchteraw   Newtown

894   1027 SGURR A'MHAORAICH   Loyne   LOCH LOYNE   H   i   g   Bridge of Oich   CARN DEARG

Glen Barrisdale   Abhainn Chosaidh   LOCH QUOICH   Kingie   Glenquoich Forest   A87   13   Ardochy House   LOCH GARRY   Munerigie   Invergarry   Tarff   Glend

Kingie   Garry   Inchlaggan   Greenfield   Mandally   A82   Culachy Forest

919 GAIRICH   Glen Kingie   Aultnaslat   Tomdoun   Glen Garry   WELLS OF THE SEVEN HEADS   884 CARN LEAC   Corrieyaira Forest

D   1003 SGURR MOR   Kingie   556 GLAS BHEINN   LOCH LOCHY LAGGAN LOCKS   Laggan   815 CARN DEARG

656 MEALL BLAIR   901 BEN TEE   GREAT GLEN WAY   Kilfinnan   Glengarry Forest   Corrieyaira Forest

880 SGURR MHURLAGAIN   858   804 GEAL CHARN   935 SRON A'CHOIRE GHAIRBH   Letterfinlay   636   Brae Roy Lodge

Glen Dessarry   Murlaggan   Loch Blàir   LOCH LOCHY   15   Glen Gloy   1128 CREAG MEAGAIDH

E   79   Strathan   Glen Pean   Pean   LOCH ARKAIG   Ardechvie   Altrua   Upper Glenfintaig   684   834 CARN DEARG

963 SGURR THUILM   Gleann Camgharaidh   987 GAOR BHEINN   727   Locheil Forest   Achnasaul   Clunes   Clunes Forest   PARALLEL ROADS   GLEN ROY   915   Moy Forest

Inver Mallie   B8005   Bunarkaig   Gloy   654 COIRE CEIRSLE HILL   1049 BEINN A' CHAORUINN   Moy

Glen   Mallie   Achnacarry   796 BEINN BHAN   CLAN CAMERON MUSEUM   Stronaba   Bohuntine   Moy Lodge

Glen Dubh Lighe   Gairlochy   Kilmonivaig   COMMANDO MEMORIAL   Bohenie   28

F   GLENFINNAN MONUMENT   Wauchan   GREAT GLEN WAY   Brackletter   Highbridge   Spean Bridge   Inverroy   Roybridge   Achluachrach   Murlaggan   Roughburn   Allt Loraich

Kinlocheil   Fassfern   Glen Loy   Glen Loy Forest   Strone   Killiechonate   MONESSIE FALLS   Braes o'Lochaber   GLEN SPEAN

Drumsallie   Loch Eil   A861   A830   TREASURES OF THE EARTH   Corpach   Muirshearlich   Spean   Allt Lèire   Fersit

South Garvan   Duisky   Blaich   20   Banavie   Torlundy   Leanachan Forest   789   Laggan

NM   Achaphubuil   Camusnagaul   INVERLOCHY CASTLE   Caol   NEVIS RANGE SKI CENTRE   BEINN CHLIANAIG   STOB CHOIRE CLAURIGH   LOCH TREIG   1046 CHNO DEARG

Trislaig   Lochyside   Inverlochy   Claggan   BEN NEVIS DISTILLERY VISITOR CENTRE   1177   1106   1115 STOB COIRE EASAIN

Fort William   WEST HIGHLAND MUSEUM   Achintee   1344 BEN NEVIS   1234 AONACH BEAG   1094   937 BEINN NA LAP   Corrour Shooting Lodge

G   Stronchreggan   Ach'an Todhair   Glen Nevis House   GLEN NEVIS VISITOR CENTRE   Creaguaineach Lodge   Loch Ossian   Corrour Forest

Conaglen House   Druimarbin   Blarmachfoldach   Achriabhach   SGURR A' MHAIM   1130 BINNEIN MOR   Loch Ossian   583

Aryhoulan   Coruanan Lodge   BEN NEVIS AND   630

Glen Scaddle   Inverscaddle Bay   14   MAMORE FOREST   Loch Eilde Beag   906 LEUM UILLEIM   STOB NA CRUAICHE

SGURR NA H-EANCHAINNE   616   WEST HIGHLAND WAY   74   Loch Eilde Mor   Amhainn Rath

Ardour   BEINN NA GUCAIG   730   Glenrigh Forest   GLEN COE   BLACKWATER RESERVOIR

Clovullin   Ardgour   Inchree   MAM NA GUALAINN   615   Kinlochmore   Kinlochleven

Corran   Keppanach   Onich   B863   THE ALUMINIUM STORY   867   739 STOB NA CRUAICHE

Sallachan   Sallachan Pt.   North Ballachulish   GLEN COE   867   STOB CHOIRE EASAIN   Rannoch Station

Inversanda Bay   Inversanda   LOCH LINNHE   A82   South Ballachulish   HIGHLAND MYSTERYWORLD   GLENCOE AND NORTH LORN FOLK MUSEUM   Glencoe   953   Black Corries

0   1   2   3   4   5   6 miles   Ballachulish   GLENCOE VISITOR CENTRE   AONACH   Altnafeadh   STOB CRUAICHE   BEINN EIGHEACH
0   2   4   6   8   10km   GLEN COE   BEINN A' CHRULAISTE

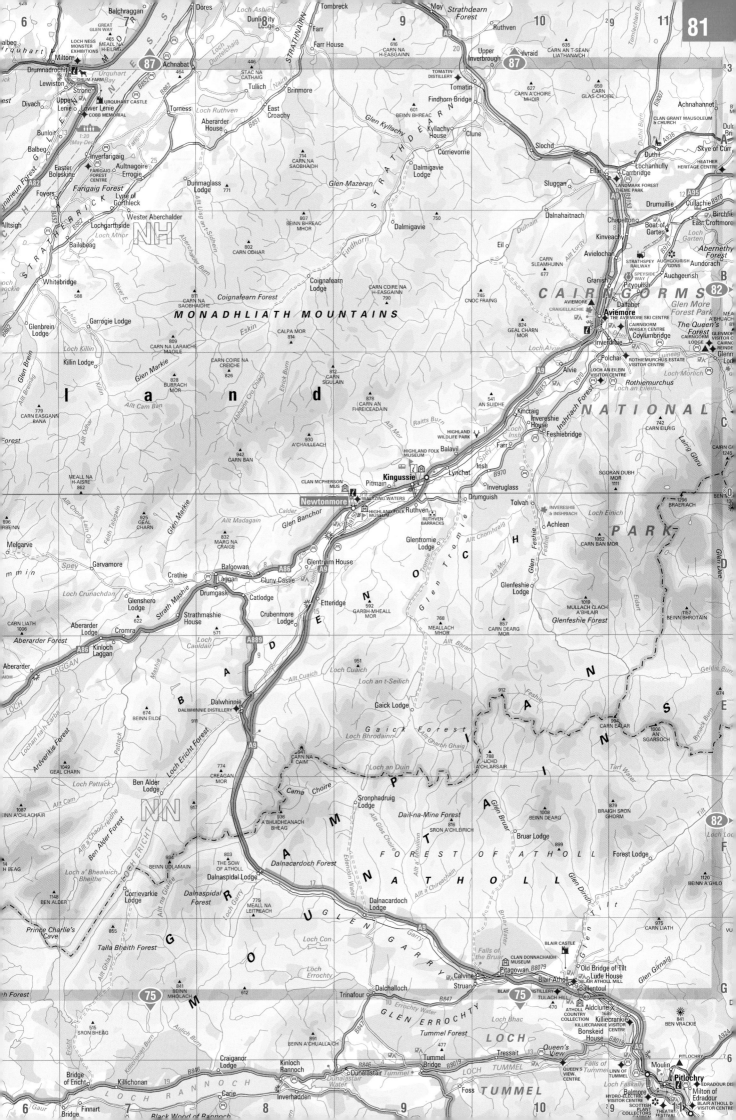

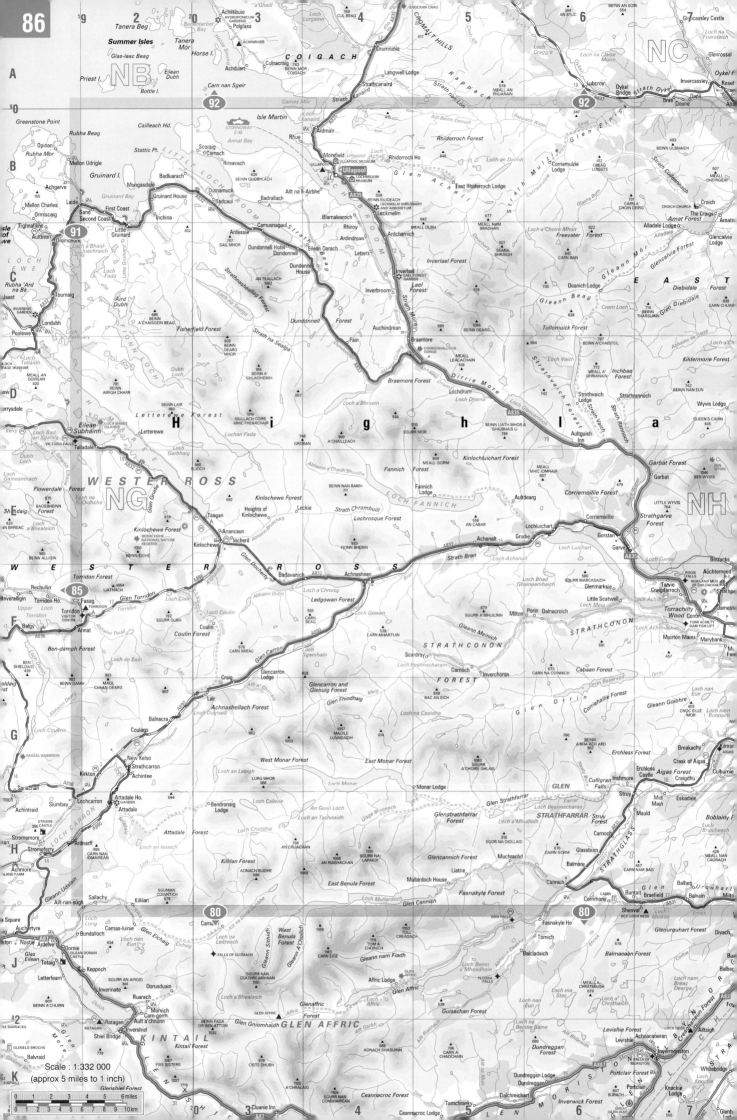

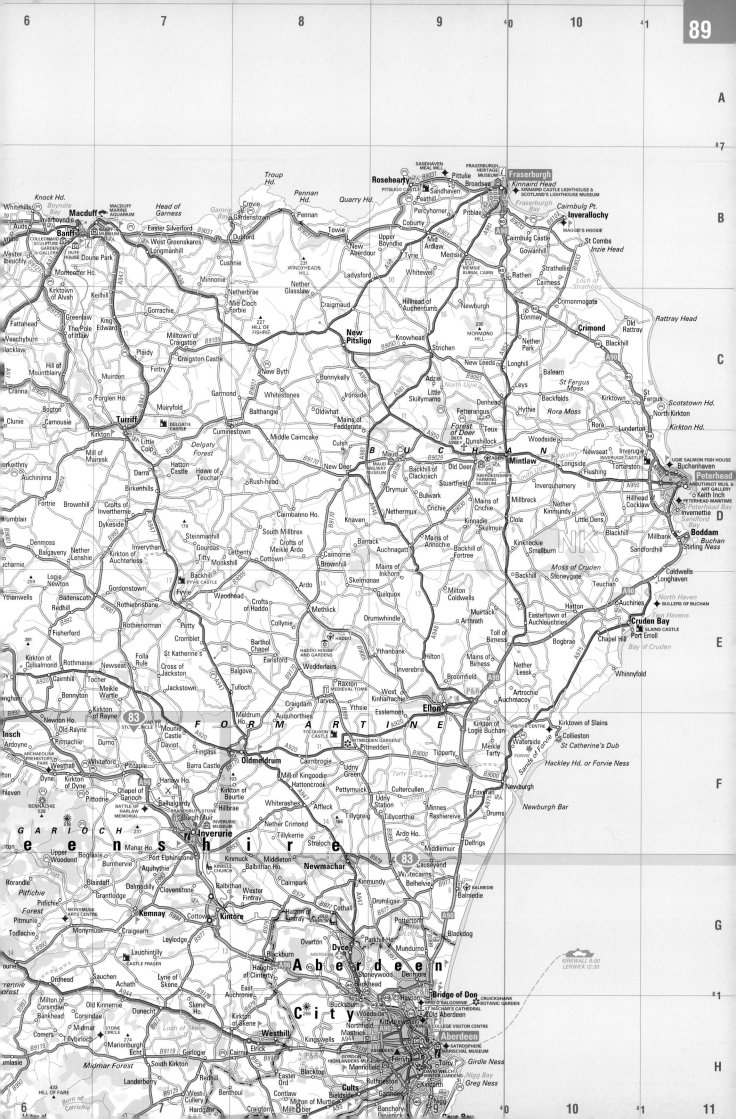

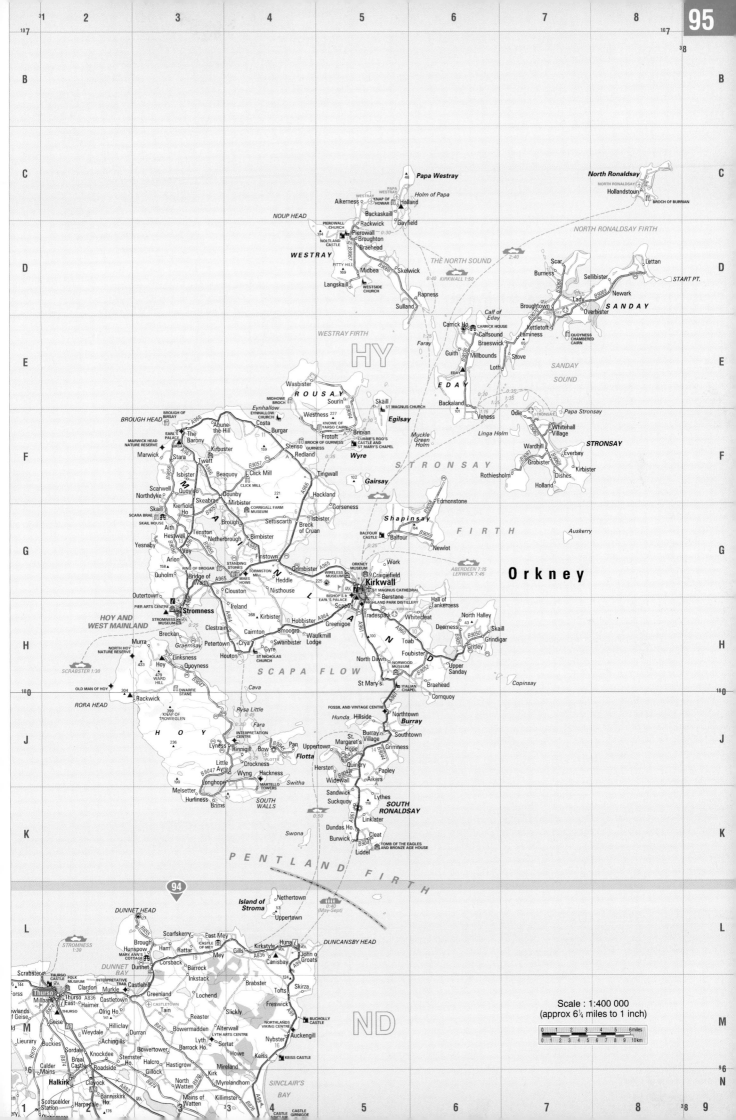

Town plan symbols

Motorway

Primary route – dual, single carriageway

A road – dual, single carriageway

B road – dual, single carriageway

Minor through road

One-way street

Pedestrian roads

Shopping streets

Railway with station

Tramway with station

Underground or Metro station

H Hospital

P Parking

Police, Post Office

Shopmobility

Youth hostel

Bus or railway station building

Shopping precinct or retail park

Park

Congestion charge zone

Abbey or cathedral

Ancient monument

Aquarium

Art gallery

Bird collection or aviary

Building of interest

Castle

Church of interest

Cinema

Garden

Historic ship

House

House and garden

Museum

Preserved railway

Roman antiquity

Safari park

Theatre

Tourist information centre

Zoo

Other place of interest

Aberdeen

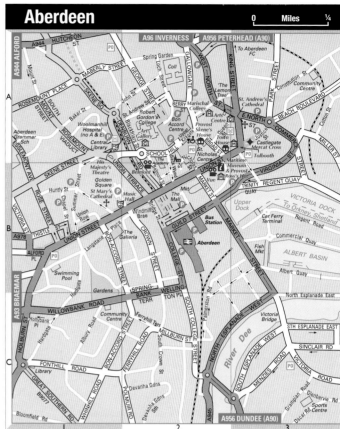

Bath

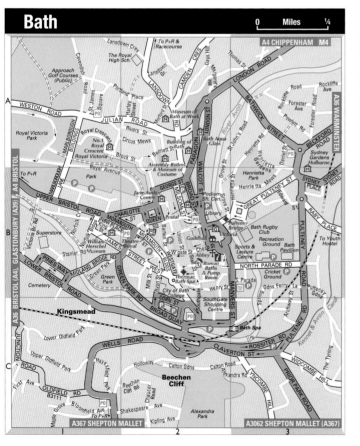

Blackpool

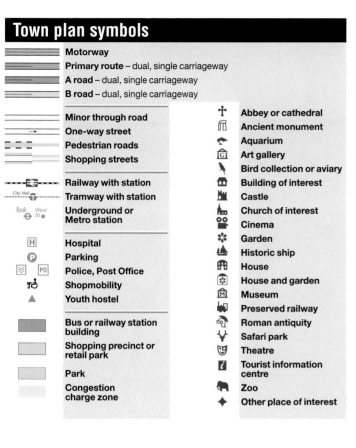

Birmingham

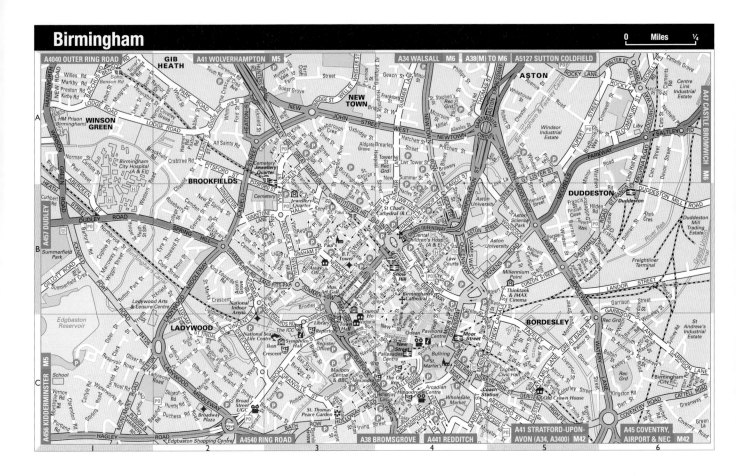

Bournemouth

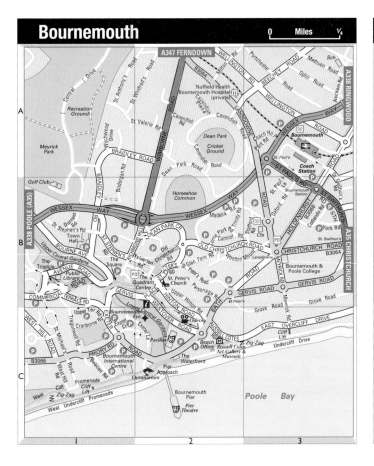

Bradford

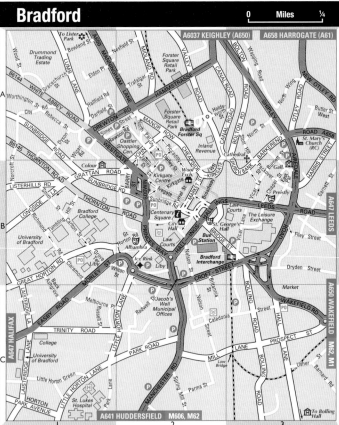

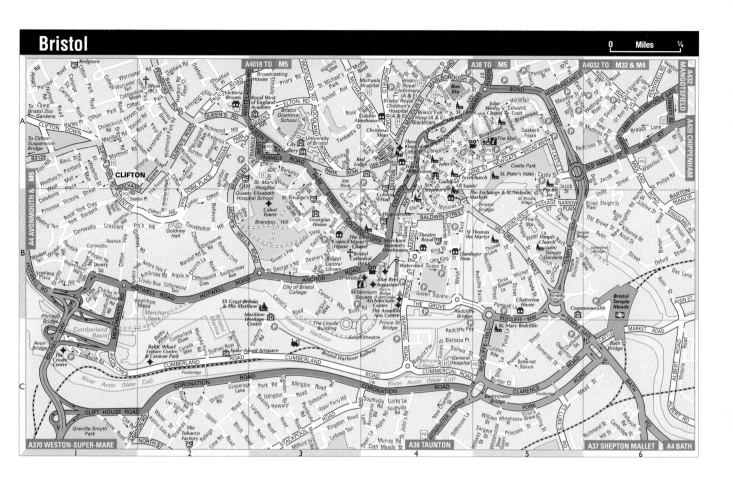

Bristol

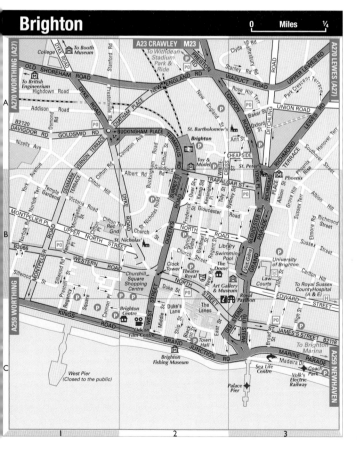

Brighton

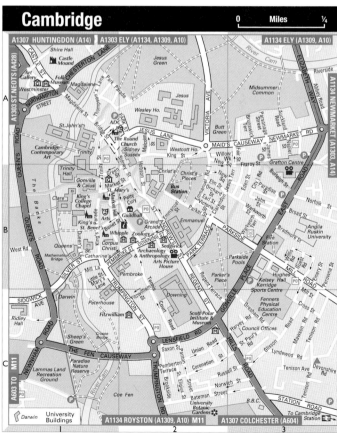

Cambridge

Canterbury

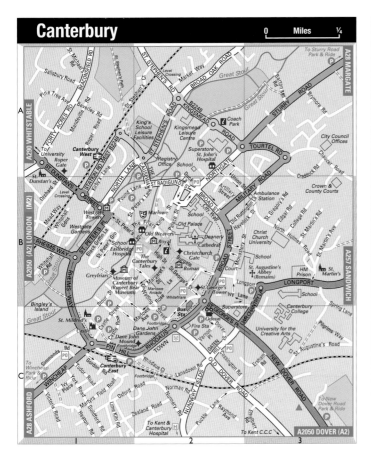

Cardiff / Caerdydd

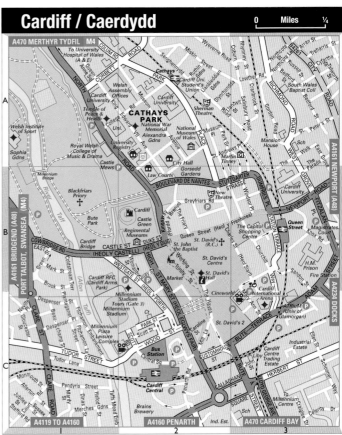

Cheltenham

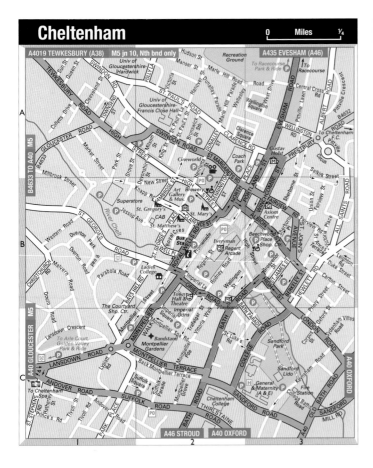

Chester

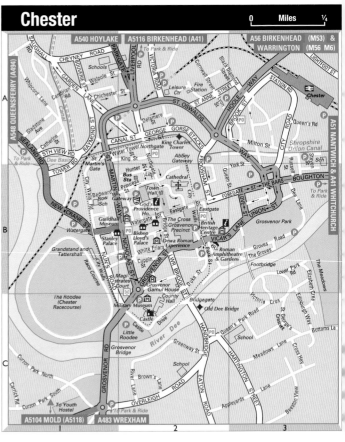

Colchester

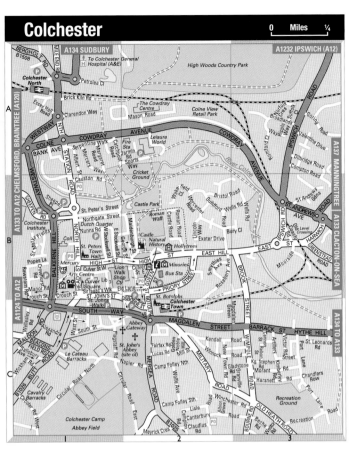

Coventry

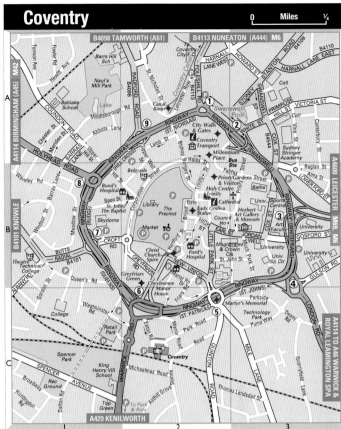

Derby

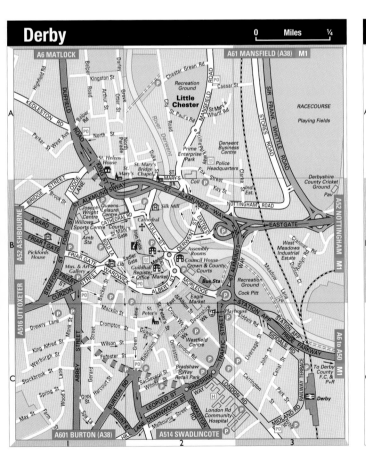

Durham

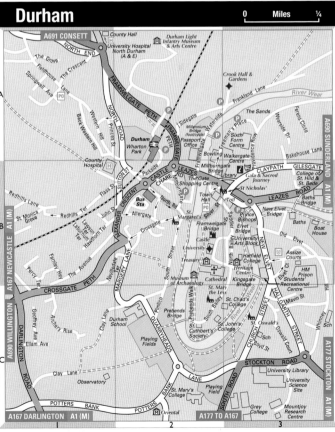

Edinburgh

0　Miles　¼

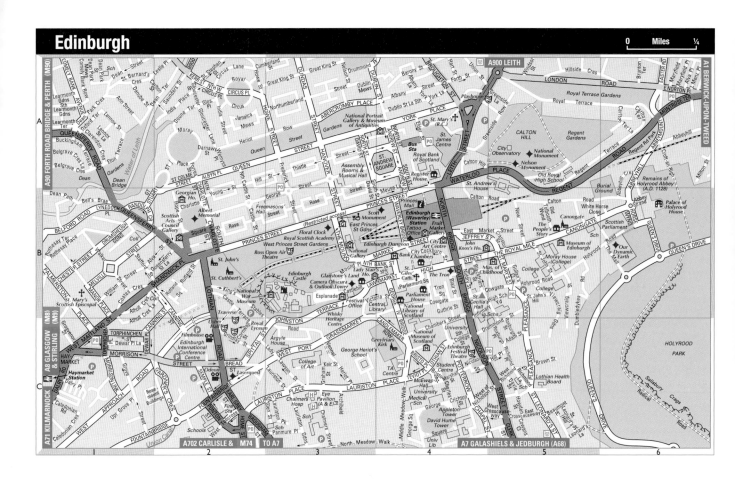

Exeter

0　Miles　¼

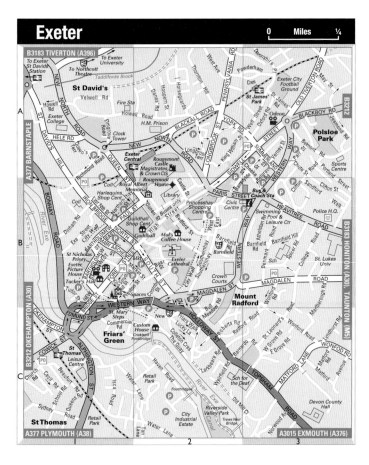

Gloucester

0　Miles　¼

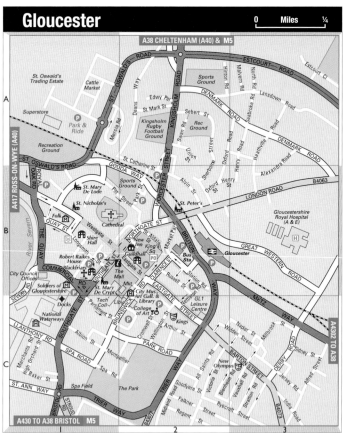

Glasgow

0 Miles ¼

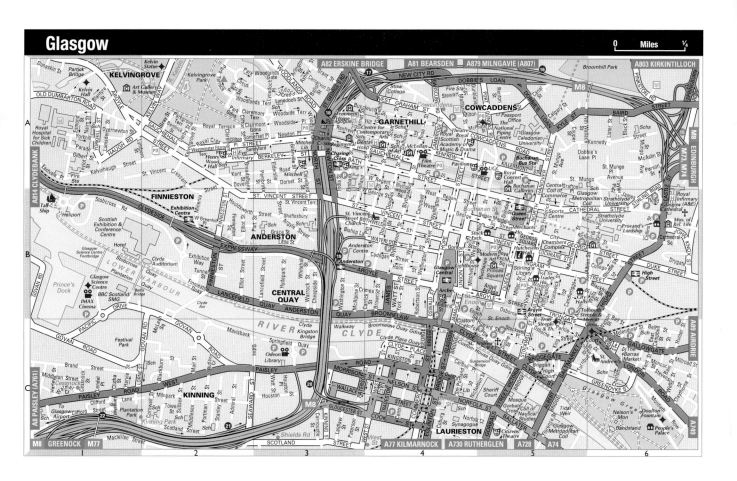

Hull

0 Miles ¼

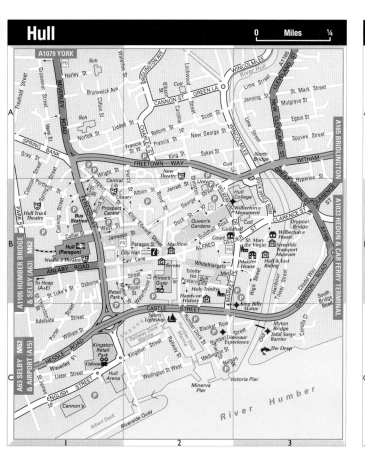

Ipswich

0 Miles ¼

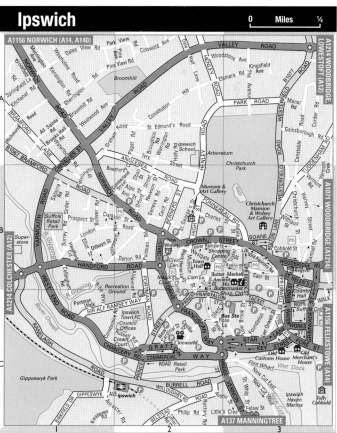

0 ———— Miles ———— ½

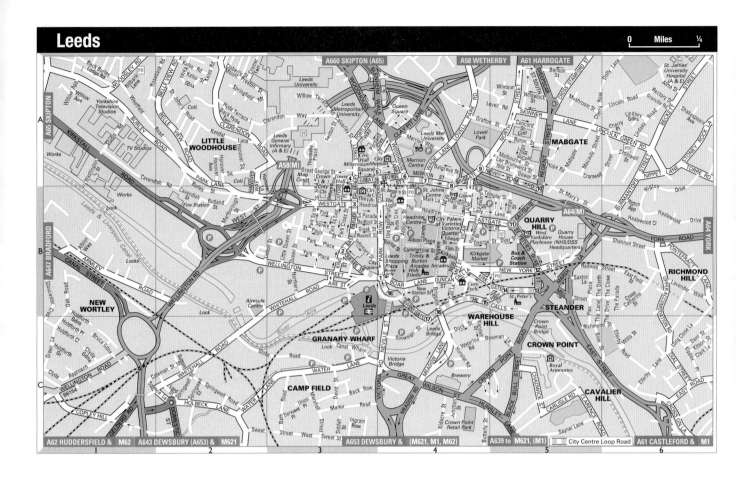

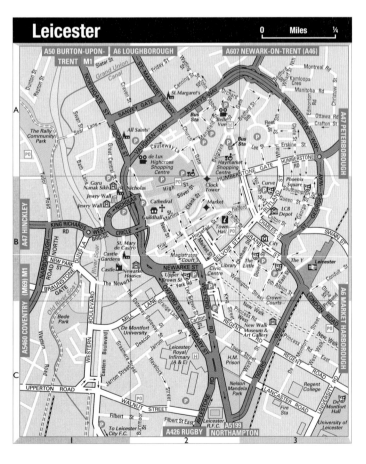

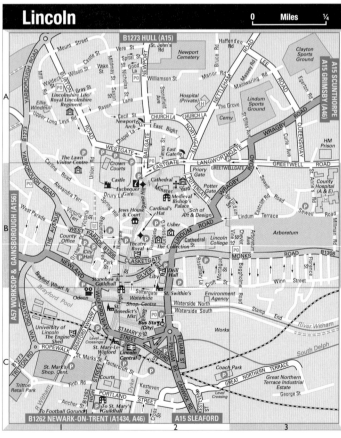

Liverpool

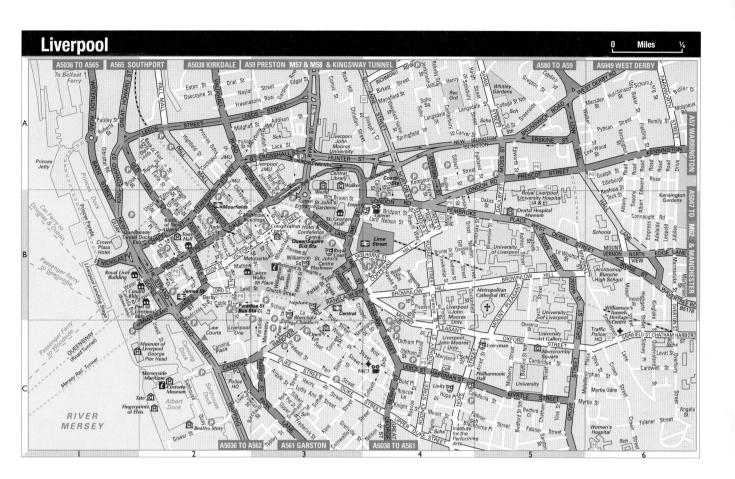

Manchester

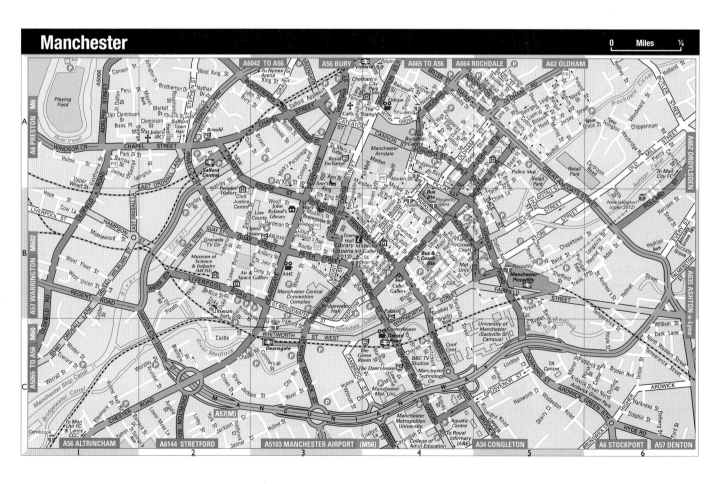

Middlesbrough

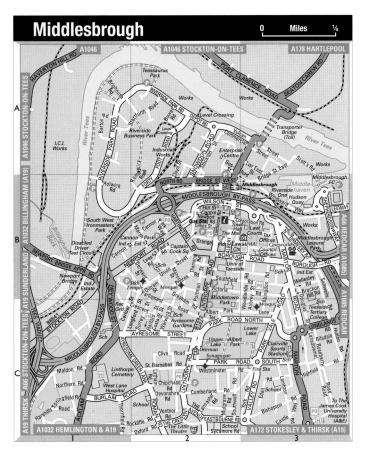

Newcastle upon Tyne

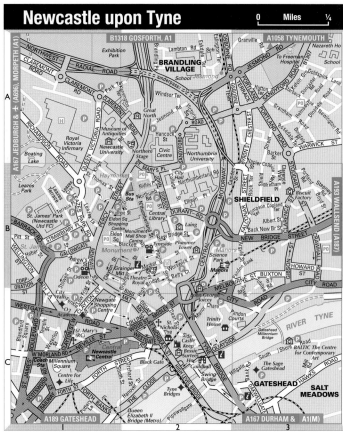

Northampton

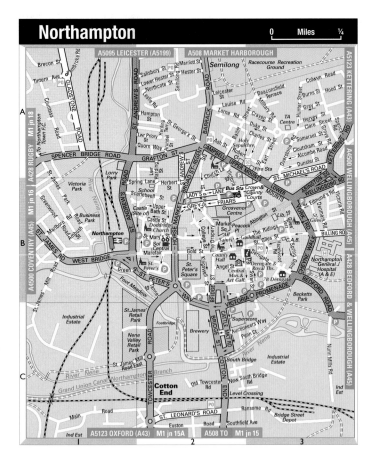

Norwich

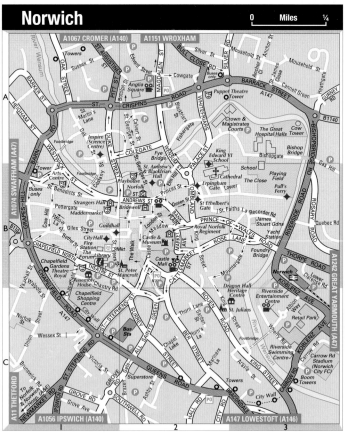

Nottingham

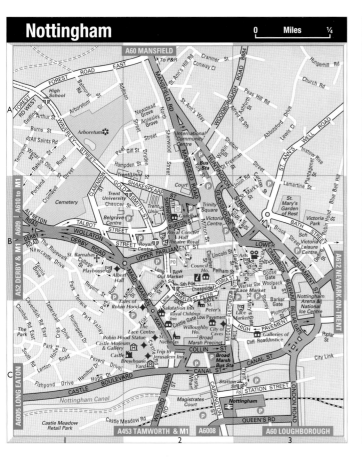

Oxford

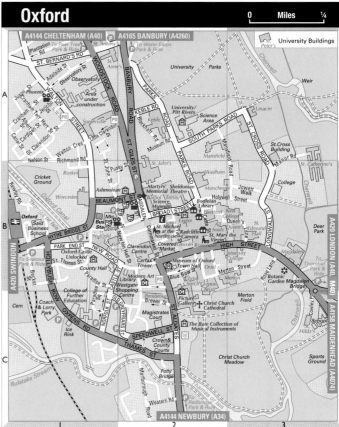

Plymouth

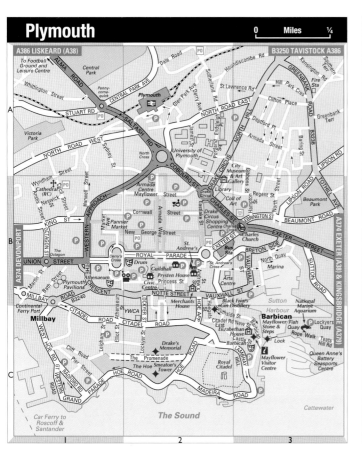

Portsmouth

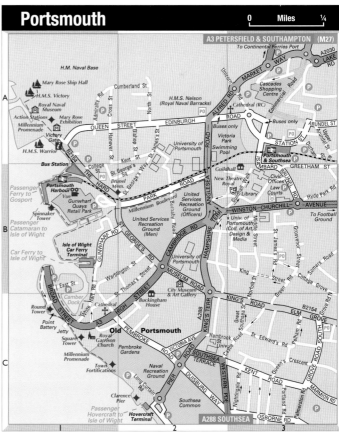

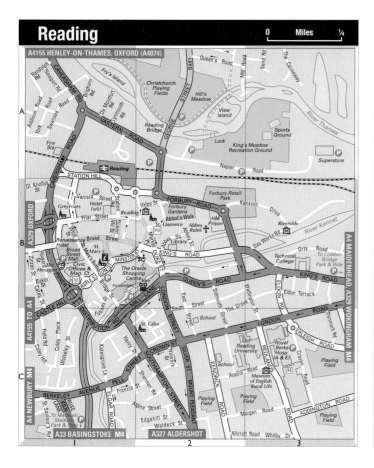

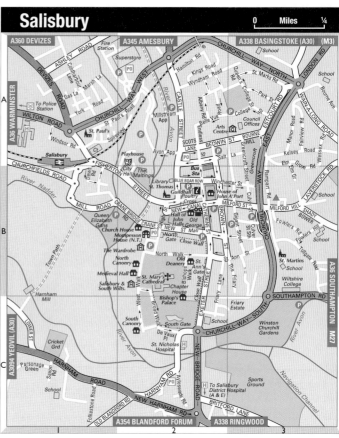

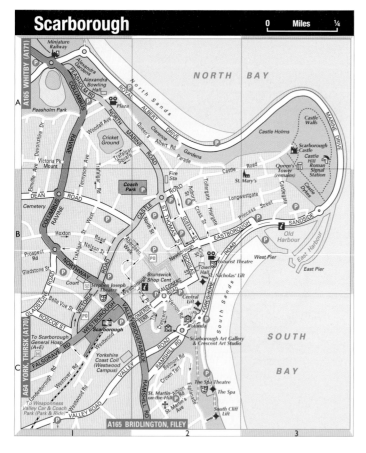

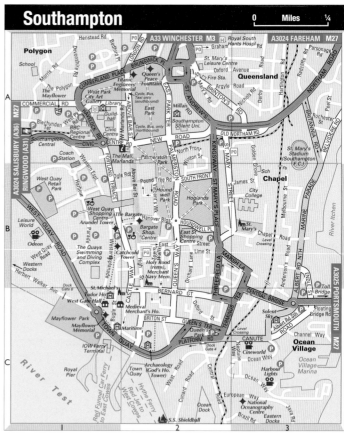

Sheffield

0 Miles ¼

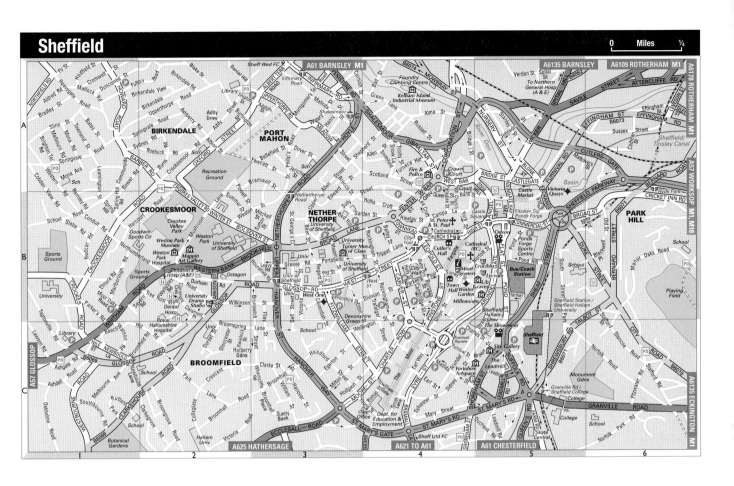

Stratford-upon-Avon

0 Miles ¼

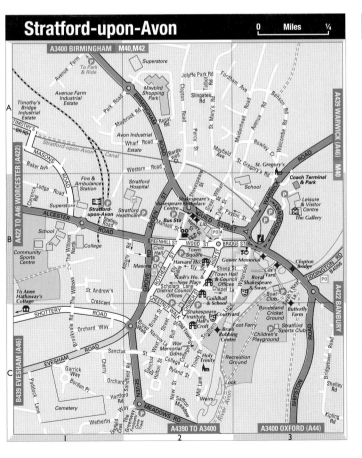

Sunderland

0 Miles ¼

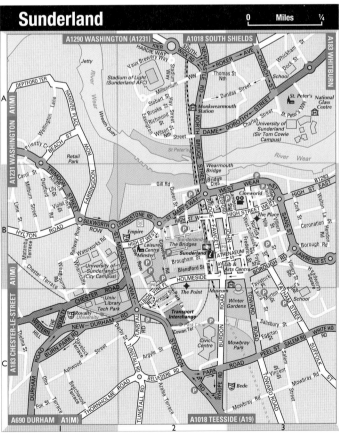

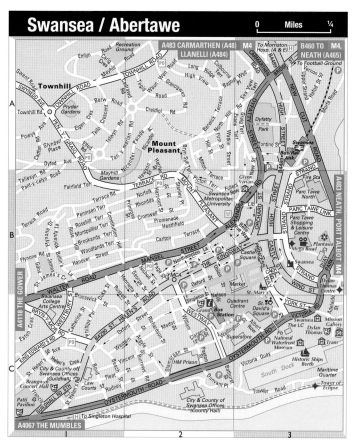

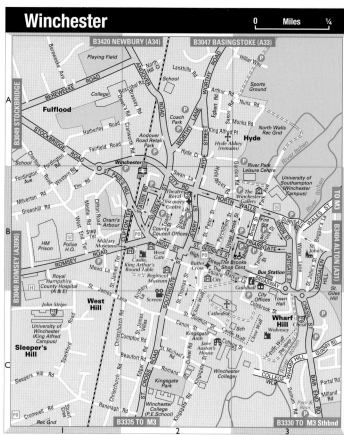

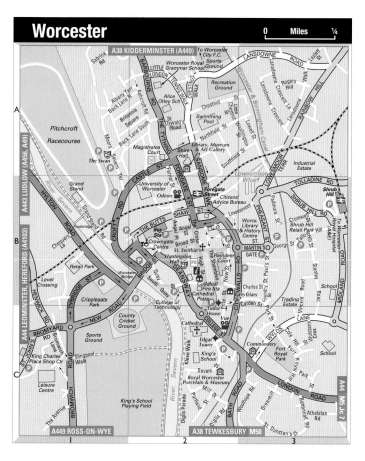

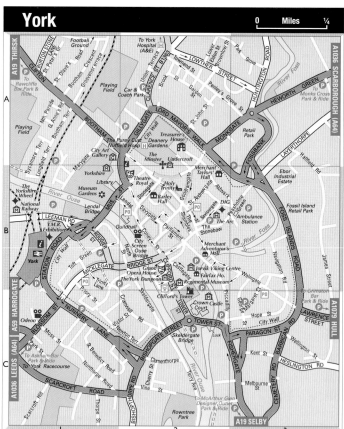

Abbreviations used in the index

Aberdeen **Aberdeen City**
Aberds **Aberdeenshire**
Ald **Alderney**
Anglesey **Isle of Anglesey**
Angus **Angus**
Argyll **Argyll and Bute**
Bath **Bath and North East Somerset**
Bedford **Bedford**
Bl Gwent **Blaenau Gwent**
Blackburn **Blackburn with Darwen**
Blackpool **Blackpool**
Bmouth **Bournemouth**
Borders **Scottish Borders**
Brack **Bracknell**
Bridgend **Bridgend**
Brighton **City of Brighton and Hove**
Bristol **City and County of Bristol**
Bucks **Buckinghamshire**
C Beds **Central Bedfordshire**
Caerph **Caerphilly**
Cambs **Cambridgeshire**
Cardiff **Cardiff**
Carms **Carmarthenshire**
Ceredig **Ceredigion**
Ches E **Cheshire East**
Ches W **Cheshire West and Chester**
Clack **Clackmannanshire**
Conwy **Conwy**
Corn **Cornwall**
Cumb **Cumbria**
Darl **Darlington**
Denb **Denbighshire**
Derby **City of Derby**
Derbys **Derbyshire**
Devon **Devon**
Dorset **Dorset**
Dumfries **Dumfries and Galloway**
Dundee **Dundee City**
Durham **Durham**
E Ayrs **East Ayrshire**
E Dunb **East Dunbartonshire**
E Loth **East Lothian**
E Renf **East Renfrewshire**
E Sus **East Sussex**
E Yorks **East Riding of Yorkshire**
Edin **City of Edinburgh**
Essex **Essex**
Falk **Falkirk**
Fife **Fife**
Flint **Flintshire**
Glasgow **City of Glasgow**
Glos **Gloucestershire**
Gtr Man **Greater Manchester**
Guern **Guernsey**
Gwyn **Gwynedd**
Halton **Halton**
Hants **Hampshire**
Hereford **Herefordshire**
Herts **Hertfordshire**
Highld **Highland**
Hrtlpl **Hartlepool**
Hull **Hull**
IoM **Isle of Man**
IoW **Isle of Wight**
Invclyd **Inverclyde**
Jersey **Jersey**
Kent **Kent**
Lancs **Lancashire**
Leicester **City of Leicester**
Leics **Leicestershire**
Lincs **Lincolnshire**
London **Greater London**
Luton **Luton**
M Keynes **Milton Keynes**
M Tydf **Merthyr Tydfil**
Mbro **Middlesbrough**
Medway **Medway**
Mers **Merseyside**
Midloth **Midlothian**
Mon **Monmouthshire**
Moray **Moray**
N Ayrs **North Ayrshire**
N Lincs **North Lincolnshire**
N Lanark **North Lanarkshire**
N Som **North Somerset**
N Yorks **North Yorkshire**
NE Lincs **North East Lincolnshire**
Neath **Neath Port Talbot**
Newport **City and County of Newport**
Norf **Norfolk**
Northants **Northamptonshire**
Northumb **Northumberland**
Nottingham **City of Nottingham**
Notts **Nottinghamshire**
Orkney **Orkney**
Oxon **Oxfordshire**
Pboro **Peterborough**
Pembs **Pembrokeshire**
Perth **Perth and Kinross**
Plym **Plymouth**
Poole **Poole**
Powys **Powys**
Ptsmth **Portsmouth**
Reading **Reading**
Redcar **Redcar and Cleveland**
Renfs **Renfrewshire**
Rhondda **Rhondda Cynon Taff**
Rutland **Rutland**
S Ayrs **South Ayrshire**
S Glos **South Gloucestershire**
S Lanark **South Lanarkshire**
S Yorks **South Yorkshire**
Scilly **Scilly**
Shetland **Shetland**
Shrops **Shropshire**
Slough **Slough**
Som **Somerset**
Soton **Southampton**
Staffs **Staffordshire**
Southend **Southend-on-Sea**
Stirling **Stirling**
Stockton **Stockton-on-Tees**
Stoke **Stoke-on-Trent**
Suff **Suffolk**
Sur **Surrey**
Swansea **Swansea**
Swindon **Swindon**
T&W **Tyne and Wear**
Telford **Telford and Wrekin**
Thurrock **Thurrock**
Torbay **Torbay**
Torf **Torfaen**
V Glam **The Vale of Glamorgan**
W Berks **West Berkshire**
W Dunb **West Dunbartonshire**
W Isles **Western Isles**
W Loth **West Lothian**
W Mid **West Midlands**
W Sus **West Sussex**
W Yorks **West Yorkshire**
Warks **Warwickshire**
Warr **Warrington**
Wilts **Wiltshire**
Windsor **Windsor and Maidenhead**
Wokingham **Wokingham**
Worcs **Worcestershire**
Wrex **Wrexham**
York **City of York**

How to use the index

Example

Trudoxhill Som **16** G4

- grid square
- page number
- county or unitary authority

Index to road maps of Britain

A

Ab Kettleby Leics 36 C3
Ab Lench Worcs 27 C7
Abbas Combe Som 8 B6
Abberley Worcs 26 B4
Abberton Essex 31 G7
Abberton Worcs 26 C6
Abberwick Northumb 63 B7
Abbess Roding Essex 30 G2
Abbey Devon 7 E10
Abbey-cwm-hir Powys 25 A7
Abbey Dore Hereford 25 E10
Abbey Field Essex 30 F6
Abbey Hulton Stoke 44 H3
Abbey St Bathans Borders 70 D6
Abbey Town Cumb 56 A3
Abbey Village Lancs 50 G2
Abbey Wood London 19 D11
Abbeydale S Yorks 45 D7
Abbeystead Lancs 50 D1
Abbots Bickington Devon 6 E2
Abbots Bromley Staffs 35 C6
Abbots Langley Herts 19 A7
Abbots Leigh N Som 15 D11
Abbots Morton Worcs 27 C7
Abbots Ripton Cambs 37 H8
Abbots Salford Warks 27 C7
Abbotsbury Dorset 8 F4
Abbotsham Devon 6 D3
Abbotskerswell Devon 5 E9
Abbotsley Cambs 29 C9
Abbotswood Hants 10 B2
Abbotts Ann Hants 17 G10
Abcott Shrops 33 H9
Abdon Shrops 34 G1
Aber Ceredig 23 B9
Aber-Arad Carms 23 C8
Aber-banc Ceredig 23 B8
Aber Cowarch Gwyn 32 D4
Aber-Giâr Carms 23 B10
Aber-gwynfi Neath 14 B4
Aber-Hirnant Gwyn 32 B5
Aber-nant Rhondda 14 A6
Aber-Rhiwlech Gwyn 32 C5
Aber-Village Powys 25 F8
Aberaeron Ceredig 24 B1
Aberaman Rhondda 14 A6
Aberangell Gwyn 32 D4
Aberarder Highld 81 E6
Aberarder House Highld 81 A8
Aberarder Lodge Highld 81 E7
Aberargie Perth 76 F4
Aberarth Ceredig 24 B1
Aberavon Neath 14 B3
Aberbeeg Bl Gwent 15 A8
Abercanaid M Tydf 14 A6
Abercarn Caerph 15 B8
Abercastle Pembs 22 C3
Abercegir Powys 32 E4
Aberchirder Aberds 88 C6
Abercraf Powys 24 G5
Abercrombie Fife 77 G8
Abercych Pembs 23 B7
Abercynafon Powys 25 G7
Abercynon Rhondda 14 B6
Aberdâr = Aberdare Rhondda 14 A5
Aberdalgie Perth 76 E3
Aberdare = Aberdâr Rhondda 14 A5
Aberdaron Gwyn 40 H3
Aberdaugleddau = Milford Haven Pembs 22 F4
Aberdeen Aberdeen 83 C11
Aberdesach Gwyn 40 E6
Aberdour Fife 69 B10
Aberdovey Gwyn 32 F2
Aberdulais Neath 14 A3
Aberedw Powys 25 D7
Abereiddy Pembs 22 C2
Abererch Gwyn 40 G5
Aberfan M Tydf 14 A6
Aberfeldy Perth 75 C11
Aberffraw Anglesey 40 D5
Aberffrwd Ceredig 32 H2
Aberford W Yorks 51 F10
Aberfoyle Stirling 75 G8
Abergavenny = Y Fenni Mon 25 G9
Abergele Conwy 42 E2
Aberglorlech Carms 23 C10
Abergwaun = Fishguard Pembs 22 C4
Abergwesyn Powys 24 C5
Abergwili Carms 23 D9
Abergwynant Gwyn 32 D2
Abergwyngregyn Gwyn 41 C8
Abergynolwyn Gwyn 32 E2
Aberhonddu = Brecon Powys 25 F7
Aberhosan Powys 32 F4
Aberkenfig Bridgend 14 C4
Aberlady E Loth 70 B3
Aberlemno Angus 77 B8
Aberllefenni Gwyn 32 E3
Abermagwr Ceredig 24 A3
Abermaw = Barmouth Gwyn 32 D2
Abermeurig Ceredig 23 A10
Abermule Powys 33 F7
Abernaint Powys 33 C7
Abernant Carms 23 D8
Abernethy Perth 76 F4
Abernyte Perth 76 D5
Aberpennar = Mountain Ash Rhondda 14 B6
Aberporth Ceredig 23 A7
Abersoch Gwyn 40 H5
Abersychan Torf 15 A8
Abertawe = Swansea Swansea 14 B2
Aberteifi = Cardigan Ceredig 22 B6
Aberthin V Glam 14 D6
Abertillery = Abertyleri Bl Gwent 15 A8
Abertridwr Caerph 15 C7
Abertridwr Powys 32 D6
Abertyleri = Abertillery Bl Gwent 15 A8
Abertysswg Caerph 25 H8
Aberuthven Perth 76 F2
Aberyscir Powys 24 F6
Aberystwyth Ceredig 32 G1
Abhainn Suidhe W Isles 90 G5
Abingdon Oxon 17 B11
Abinger Common Sur 19 G8
Abinger Hammer Sur 19 G7
Abington S Lanark 60 A5
Abington Pigotts Cambs 29 D10
Ablington Glos 27 H8
Ablington Wilts 17 G8
Abney Derbys 44 E5
Aboyne Aberds 83 D7
Abram Gtr Man 43 B9
Abriachan Highld 87 H8
Abridge Essex 19 B11
Abronhill N Lanark 68 C6
Abson S Glos 16 D4
Abthorpe Northants 28 D3
Abune-the-Hill Orkney 95 F3
Aby Lincs 47 E8
Acaster Malbis York 52 E1
Acaster Selby N Yorks 52 E1
Accrington Lancs 50 G3
Acha Argyll 78 F4
Acha Mor W Isles 91 E8
Achabraid Argyll 73 E7
Achachork Highld 85 D9
Achafolla Argyll 72 B6
Achagary Highld 93 D10
Achahoish Argyll 72 F6
Achalader Perth 76 C4
Achallader Argyll 74 C6
Ach'an Todhair Highld 80 F2
Achanalt Highld 86 E5
Achanamara Argyll 72 E6
Achandunie Highld 87 D9
Achany Highld 93 J8
Achaphubuil Highld 80 F2
Acharacle Highld 79 E9
Acharn Highld 79 F10
Acharn Perth 75 C10
Acharole Highld 94 E4
Achath Aberds 83 B9
Achavanich Highld 94 F3
Achavraat Highld 87 G12
Achddu Carms 23 F9
Achduart Highld 92 J3
Achentoul Highld 93 F11
Achfary Highld 92 F5
Achgarve Highld 91 H13
Achiemore Highld 92 C6
Achiemore Highld 93 D11
A'Chill Highld 84 H7
Achiltibuie Highld 92 J3
Achina Highld 93 C10
Achinduich Highld 93 J8
Achinduin Argyll 79 H11
Achingills Highld 94 D3
Achintee Highld 80 F3
Achintee Highld 86 G2
Achintraid Highld 85 E13
Achlean Highld 81 D10
Achleck Argyll 78 G7
Achluachrach Highld 80 E4
Achlyness Highld 92 D5
Achmelvich Highld 92 G3
Achmore Highld 85 E13
Achmore Stirling 75 D8
Achnaba Argyll 73 E8
Achnaba Argyll 74 D2
Achnabat Highld 87 H8
Achnacarnin Highld 92 F3
Achnacarry Highld 80 E3
Achnacloich Argyll 74 D2
Achnacloich Highld 85 H10
Achnaconeran Highld 80 B6
Achnacraig Argyll 78 G7
Achnacroish Argyll 79 G11
Achnadrish Argyll 78 F7
Achnafalnich Argyll 74 E5
Achnagarron Highld 87 E9
Achnaha Highld 78 E7
Achnahanat Highld 87 B8
Achnahannet Highld 82 A1
Achnairn Highld 93 H8
Achnaluachrach Highld 93 J9
Achnasaul Highld 80 E3
Achnasheen Highld 86 F4
Achosnich Highld 78 E7
Achranich Highld 79 G10
Achreamie Highld 93 C13
Achriabhach Highld 80 G3
Achriesgill Highld 92 D5
Achrimsdale Highld 93 J12
Achtoty Highld 93 C9
Achurch Northants 36 G6
Achuvoldrach Highld 93 D8
Achvaich Highld 87 B10
Achvarasdal Highld 93 C12
Ackergill Highld 94 E5
Acklam Mbro 58 E5
Acklam N Yorks 52 C3
Ackleton Shrops 34 F3
Acklington Northumb 63 C8
Ackton W Yorks 51 G10
Ackworth Moor Top W Yorks 51 H10
Acle Norf 39 D10
Acock's Green W Mid 35 G7
Acol Kent 21 E10
Acomb Northumb 62 G5
Acomb York 52 D1
Aconbury Hereford 26 E2
Acre Lancs 50 G3
Acre Street W Sus 11 E6
Acrefair Wrex 33 A8
Acton Ches E 43 G9
Acton Dorset 9 G8
Acton London 19 C9
Acton Shrops 33 G9
Acton Suff 30 D5
Acton Wrex 42 G6
Acton Beauchamp Hereford 26 C3
Acton Bridge Ches W 43 E8
Acton Burnell Shrops 33 E11
Acton Green Hereford 26 C3
Acton Pigott Shrops 33 E11
Acton Round Shrops 34 F2
Acton Scott Shrops 33 G10
Acton Trussell Staffs 34 D5
Acton Turville S Glos 16 C5
Adbaston Staffs 34 C3
Adber Dorset 8 B4
Adderley Shrops 34 A2
Adderstone Northumb 71 G10
Addiewell W Loth 69 D8
Addingham W Yorks 51 E6
Addington Bucks 28 F4
Addington Kent 20 F3
Addington London 19 E10
Addinston Borders 70 E4
Addiscombe London 19 E10
Addlestone Sur 19 E7
Addlethorpe Lincs 47 F9
Adel W Yorks 51 F8
Adeney Telford 34 D3
Adfa Powys 33 E6
Adforton Hereford 25 A11
Adisham Kent 21 F9
Adlestrop Glos 27 F9
Adlingfleet E Yorks 52 G4
Adlington Lancs 43 A9
Admaston Staffs 34 C6
Admaston Telford 34 D2
Admington Warks 27 D9
Adstock Bucks 28 E4
Adstone Northants 28 C2
Adversane W Sus 11 B9
Advie Highld 88 E1
Adwalton W Yorks 51 G8
Adwell Oxon 18 B3
Adwick le Street S Yorks 45 B9
Adwick upon Dearne S Yorks 45 B8
Adziel Aberds 89 C9
Ae Village Dumfries 60 E5
Affleck Aberds 89 F8
Affpuddle Dorset 9 E7
Affric Lodge Highld 80 A3
Afon-wen Flint 42 E4
Afton IoW 10 F2
Agglethorpe N Yorks 58 H1
Agneash IoM 48 D4
Aigburth Mers 43 D6
Aiginis W Isles 91 D9
Aike E Yorks 52 E6
Aikerness Orkney 95 C5
Aikers Orkney 95 J5
Aiketgate Cumb 57 B6
Aikton Cumb 56 A4
Ailey Hereford 25 D10
Ailstone Warks 27 C9
Ailsworth Pboro 37 F7
Ainderby Quernhow N Yorks 51 A9
Ainderby Steeple N Yorks 58 G4
Aingers Green Essex 31 F8
Ainsdale Mers 42 A6
Ainsdale-on-Sea Mers 42 A6
Ainstable Cumb 57 B7
Ainsworth Gtr Man 43 A10
Ainthorpe N Yorks 59 F8
Aintree Mers 43 C6
Aird Argyll 72 C6
Aird Dumfries 54 C3
Aird Highld 85 A12
Aird W Isles 91 D10
Aird a Mhachair W Isles 84 D2
Aird a' Mhulaidh W Isles 90 F6
Aird Asaig W Isles 90 G6
Aird Dhail W Isles 91 A9
Aird Mhidhinis W Isles 84 H2
Aird Mhighe W Isles 90 H6
Aird Mhighe W Isles 90 J5
Aird Mhor W Isles 84 H2
Aird of Sleat Highld 85 H10
Aird Thunga W Isles 91 D9
Aird Uig W Isles 90 D5
Airdens Highld 87 B9
Airdrie N Lanark 68 D6
Airdtorrisdale Highld 93 C9
Airidh a Bhruaich W Isles 90 F7
Airieland Dumfries 55 D10
Airmyn E Yorks 52 G3
Airntully Perth 76 D3
Airor Highld 85 H12
Airth Falk 69 B7
Airton N Yorks 50 D5
Airyhassen Dumfries 54 E6
Aisby Lincs 36 B6
Aisby Lincs 46 C2
Aisgernis W Isles 84 F2
Aiskew N Yorks 58 H3
Aislaby N Yorks 59 F9
Aislaby N Yorks 59 H8
Aislaby Stockton 58 E5
Aisthorpe Lincs 46 D3
Aith Orkney 95 G3
Aith Shetland 96 D8
Aith Shetland 96 H5
Aithsetter Shetland 96 K6
Aitkenhead S Ayrs 66 F6
Aitnoch Highld 87 H12
Akeld Northumb 71 H8
Akeley Bucks 28 E4
Akenham Suff 31 D8
Albaston Corn 4 D5
Alberbury Shrops 33 D9
Albourne W Sus 12 E1
Albrighton Shrops 33 D10
Albrighton Shrops 34 E4
Alburgh Norf 39 G8
Albury Herts 29 F11
Albury Sur 19 G7
Albury End Herts 29 F11
Alby Hill Norf 39 B7
Alcaig Highld 87 F8
Alcaston Shrops 33 G10
Alcester Warks 27 C7
Alciston E Sus 12 F4
Alcombe Som 7 B8
Alcombe Wilts 16 E5
Alconbury Cambs 37 H7
Alconbury Weston Cambs 37 H7
Aldbar Castle Angus 77 B8
Aldborough N Yorks 51 C10
Aldborough Norf 39 B7
Aldbourne Wilts 17 D9
Aldbrough E Yorks 53 F8
Aldbrough St John N Yorks 58 E3
Aldbury Herts 28 G6
Aldcliffe Lancs 49 C4
Aldclune Perth 76 A2
Aldeburgh Suff 31 C11
Aldeby Norf 39 F10
Aldenham Herts 19 B8
Alderbury Wilts 9 B10
Aldercar Derbys 45 H8
Alderford Norf 39 D7
Alderholt Dorset 9 C10
Alderley Glos 16 B4
Alderley Edge Ches E 44 E2
Aldermaston W Berks 18 E2
Aldermaston Wharf W Berks 18 E3
Alderminster Warks 27 D9
Alder's End Hereford 26 D3
Aldersey Green Ches W 43 G7
Aldershot Hants 18 F5
Alderton Glos 27 E7
Alderton Northants 28 D4
Alderton Shrops 33 C10
Alderton Suff 31 D10
Alderton Wilts 16 C5
Alderwasley Derbys 45 G7
Aldfield N Yorks 51 C8
Aldford Ches W 43 G7
Aldham Essex 30 F6
Aldham Suff 31 D7
Aldie Highld 87 C10
Aldingbourne W Sus 11 D8
Aldingham Cumb 49 B2
Aldington Kent 13 C9
Aldington Worcs 27 D7
Aldington Frith Kent 13 C9
Aldochlay Argyll 68 A2
Aldreth Cambs 29 A11
Aldridge W Mid 35 E6
Aldringham Suff 31 B11
Aldsworth Glos 27 G8
Aldunie Moray 82 A5
Aldwark Derbys 44 G6
Aldwark N Yorks 51 C10
Aldwick W Sus 11 E8
Aldwincle Northants 36 G6
Aldworth W Berks 18 D2
Alexandria W Dunb 68 C2
Alfardisworthy Devon 6 E1
Alfington Devon 7 G10
Alfold Sur 11 A9
Alfold Bars W Sus 11 A9
Alfold Crossways Sur 19 H7
Alford Aberds 83 B7
Alford Lincs 47 E8
Alford Som 8 A5
Alfreton Derbys 45 G8
Alfrick Worcs 26 C4
Alfrick Pound Worcs 26 C4
Alfriston E Sus 12 F4
Algaltraig Argyll 73 F9
Algarkirk Lincs 37 B8
Alhampton Som 8 A5
Aline Lodge W Isles 90 F6
Alisary Highld 79 D10
Alkborough N Lincs 52 G4
Alkerton Oxon 27 D10
Alkham Kent 21 G9
Alkington Shrops 33 B11
Alkmonton Derbys 35 B7
All Cannings Wilts 17 E7
All Saints South Elmham Suff 39 G9
All Stretton Shrops 33 F10
Alladale Lodge Highld 86 C7
Allaleigh Devon 5 F9
Allanaquoich Aberds 82 D3
Allangrange Mains Highld 87 F9
Allanton Borders 71 E7
Allanton N Lanark 69 E7
Allathasdal W Isles 84 H1
Allendale Town Northumb 62 H4
Allenheads Northumb 57 B10
Allens Green Herts 29 G11
Allensford Durham 58 A1
Allensmore Hereford 25 E11
Allenton Derby 35 B9
Aller Som 8 B3
Allerby Cumb 56 C2
Allerford Som 7 B8
Allerston N Yorks 52 A4
Allerthorpe E Yorks 52 E3
Allerton Mers 43 D7
Allerton W Yorks 51 F7
Allerton Bywater W Yorks 51 G10
Allerton Mauleverer N Yorks 51 D10
Allesley W Mid 35 G9
Allestree Derby 35 B9
Allet Corn 3 E6
Allexton Leics 36 E4
Allgreave Ches E 44 F3
Allhallows Medway 20 D5
Allhallows-on-Sea Medway 20 D5
Alligin Shuas Highld 85 C13
Allimore Green Staffs 34 D4
Allington Lincs 36 A4
Allington Wilts 17 E7
Allington Wilts 17 H9
Allithwaite Cumb 49 B3
Alloa Clack 69 A7
Allonby Cumb 56 B2
Alloway S Ayrs 66 E6
Allt Carms 23 F10
Allt na h-Airbhe Highld 86 B4
Allt-nan-sùgh Highld 85 F14
Alltchaorunn Highld 74 B4
Alltforgan Powys 32 C5
Alltmawr Powys 25 D7
Alltnacaillich Highld 92 E7
Alltsigh Highld 81 B6
Alltwalis Carms 23 C9
Alltwen Neath 14 A3
Alltyblaca Ceredig 23 B10
Allwood Green Suff 31 A7
Almeley Hereford 25 C10
Almer Dorset 9 E8
Almholme S Yorks 45 B9
Almington Staffs 34 B3
Alminstone Cross Devon 6 D2
Almondbank Perth 76 E3
Almondbury W Yorks 51 H7
Almondsbury S Glos 16 C3
Alne N Yorks 51 C10
Alness Highld 87 E9
Alnham Northumb 62 B5
Alnmouth Northumb 63 B8
Alnwick Northumb 63 B7
Alperton London 19 C8
Alphamstone Essex 30 E5
Alpheton Suff 30 C5
Alphington Devon 7 G8
Alport Derbys 44 F6
Alpraham Ches E 43 G8
Alresford Essex 31 F7
Alrewas Staffs 35 D7
Alsager Ches E 43 G10
Alsagers Bank Staffs 44 H2
Alsop en le Dale Derbys 44 G5
Alston Cumb 57 B9
Alston Devon 8 D2
Alstone Glos 26 E6
Alstonefield Staffs 44 G5
Alswear Devon 7 D6
Altandhu Highld 92 H2
Altanduin Highld 93 G11
Altarnun Corn 4 C3
Altass Highld 92 J7
Alterwall Highld 94 D4
Altham Lancs 50 F3
Althorne Essex 20 B6
Althorpe N Lincs 46 B2
Alticry Dumfries 54 D5
Altnabreac Station Highld 93 E13
Altnacealgach Hotel Highld 92 H5
Altnacraig Argyll 79 J11
Altnafeadh Highld 74 B5
Altnaharra Highld 93 F8
Altofts W Yorks 51 G9
Alton Derbys 45 F7
Alton Hants 18 H4
Alton Staffs 35 A6
Alton Pancras Dorset 8 D6
Alton Priors Wilts 17 E8
Altrincham Gtr Man 43 D10
Altrua Highld 80 E4
Altskeith Stirling 75 G7
Altyre Ho. Moray 87 F13
Alva Clack 75 H11
Alvanley Ches W 43 E7
Alvaston Derby 35 B9
Alvechurch Worcs 27 A7
Alvecote Warks 35 E8
Alvediston Wilts 9 B8
Alveley Shrops 34 G3
Alverdiscott Devon 6 D4
Alverstoke Hants 10 E5
Alverstone IoW 10 F4
Alverton Notts 36 A3
Alves Moray 88 B1
Alvescot Oxon 17 A9
Alveston S Glos 16 C3
Alveston Warks 27 C9
Alvie Highld 81 C10
Alvingham Lincs 47 C7
Alvington Glos 16 A3
Alwalton Cambs 37 F7
Alweston Dorset 8 C5
Alwinton Northumb 62 C5
Alwoodley W Yorks 51 E8
Alyth Perth 76 C5
Am Baile W Isles 84 G2
Am Buth Argyll 79 J11
Amatnatua Highld 86 B7
Amber Hill Lincs 46 H6
Ambergate Derbys 45 G7
Amberley Glos 16 A5
Amberley W Sus 11 C9
Amble Northumb 63 C8
Amblecote W Mid 34 G4
Ambler Thorn W Yorks 51 G6
Ambleside Cumb 56 F5
Ambleston Pembs 22 D5
Ambrosden Oxon 28 G3
Amcotts N Lincs 46 A2
Amersham Bucks 18 B6
Amesbury Wilts 17 G8
Amington Staffs 35 E8
Amisfield Dumfries 60 E5
Amlwch Anglesey 40 A6
Amlwch Port Anglesey 40 A6
Ammanford = Rhydaman Carms 24 G3
Amod Argyll 65 E8
Amotherby N Yorks 52 B3
Ampfield Hants 10 B3
Ampleforth N Yorks 52 B1
Ampney Crucis Glos 17 A7
Ampney St Mary Glos 17 A7
Ampney St Peter Glos 17 A7
Amport Hants 17 G9
Ampthill C Beds 29 E7
Ampton Suff 30 A5
Amroth Pembs 22 F6
Amulree Perth 75 D11
An Caol Highld 85 C11
An Cnoc W Isles 91 D9
An Gleann Ur W Isles 91 D9
An t-Ob = Leverburgh W Isles 90 J5
Anagach Highld 82 A2
Anaheilt Highld 79 E11
Anancaun Highld 86 E3
Ancaster Lincs 36 A5
Anchor Shrops 33 G7
Anchorsholme Blackpool 49 E3
Ancroft Northumb 71 F8
Ancrum Borders 62 A2
Anderby Lincs 47 E9
Anderson Dorset 9 E7
Anderton Ches W 43 E9
Andover Hants 17 G10
Andover Down Hants 17 G10
Andoversford Glos 27 G7
Andreas IoM 48 C4
Anfield Mers 43 C6
Angersleigh Som 7 E10
Angle Pembs 22 F3
Angmering W Sus 11 D9
Angram N Yorks 51 E11
Angram N Yorks 57 G10
Anie Stirling 75 F8
Ankerville Highld 87 D11
Anlaby E Yorks 52 G6
Anmer Norf 38 C3
Anna Valley Hants 17 G10
Annan Dumfries 61 G7
Annat Argyll 74 E3
Annat Highld 85 C13
Annbank S Ayrs 67 D7
Annesley Notts 45 G9
Annesley Woodhouse Notts 45 G8
Annfield Plain Durham 58 A2
Annifirth Shetland 96 J3
Annitsford T&W 63 F8
Annscroft Shrops 33 E10
Ansdell Lancs 49 G3
Ansford Som 8 A5
Ansley Warks 35 F8
Anslow Staffs 35 C8
Anslow Gate Staffs 35 C7
Anstey Herts 29 E11
Anstey Leics 35 E11
Anstruther Easter Fife 77 G8

aycliff Cumb 49 B2
aydon Wilts 17 D9
ayford Herts 29 H10
ayford Som 8 B6
ayles Cumb 57 B9
aylham Suff 31 C8
aynard's Green Oxon 28 F2
ayston Hill Shrops 33 E10
aythorn End Essex 30 D4
ayton Worcs 26 A3
each Highld 79 F10
eachampton Bucks 28 E4
eachamwell Norf 38 E3
eachans Moray 87 G13
eacharr Argyll 65 D7
eachborough Kent 21 H8
eachley Glos 16 B2
eacon Devon 7 F10
eacon End Essex 30 F6
eacon Hill Sur 18 H5
eacon's Bottom Bucks 18 B4
eaconsfield Bucks 18 C6
eacrabhaic W Isles 90 H6
eadlam N Yorks 52 A2
eadlow C Beds 29 E8
eadnell Northumb 71 H11
eaford Devon 6 E4
eal N Yorks 51 G11
eal Northumb 71 F9
eamhurst Staffs 35 B6
eaminster Dorset 8 D3
eamish Durham 58 A3
eamsley N Yorks 51 D6
ean Kent 20 D2
eanacre Wilts 16 E6
eanley Northumb 62 B6
eaquoy Orkney 95 F4
ear Cross Bmouth 9 E9
eardwood Blackburn 50 G2
eare Green Sur 19 G8
earley Warks 27 B8
earnus Argyll 78 G6
earpark Durham 58 B3
earsbridge Northumb 62 H3
earsden E Dunb 68 C4
earsted Kent 20 F4
earstone Shrops 34 B3
earwood Hereford 25 C10
earwood Poole 9 E9
earwood W Mid 34 G6
eattock Dumfries 60 C6
eauchamp Roding Essex 30 G2
eauchief S Yorks 45 D7
eaufort Bl Gwent 25 G8
eaufort Castle Highld 87 G8
eaulieu Hants 10 D2
eauly Highld 87 G8
eaumaris Anglesey 41 C8
eaumont Cumb 61 H9
eaumont Essex 31 F8
eaumont Hill Darl 58 E3
eausale Warks 27 A9
eauworth Hants 10 B4
eaworthy Devon 6 G3
eazley End Essex 30 F4
ebington Mers 42 D6
ebside Northumb 63 E8
eccles Suff 39 F10
ecconsall Lancs 49 G4
eck Foot Cumb 57 G8
eck Hole N Yorks 59 F9
eck Row Suff 38 H2
eck Side Cumb 49 A2
eckbury Shrops 34 E3
eckenham London 19 E10
eckermet Cumb 56 F2
eckfoot Cumb 56 B2
eckfoot Cumb 56 F3
eckford Worcs 26 E6
eckhampton Wilts 17 E7
eckingham Lincs 46 G2
eckingham Notts 45 D11
eckington Som 16 F5
eckley E Sus 13 D7
eckley Hants 9 E11
eckley Oxon 28 G2
eckton London 19 C11
eckwithshaw N Yorks 51 D8
econtree London 19 C11
ed-y-coedwr Gwyn 32 C3
edale N Yorks 58 H3
edburn Durham 58 C2
edchester Dorset 9 C7
eddau Rhondda 14 C6
eddgelert Gwyn 41 F7
eddingham E Sus 12 F3
eddington London 19 E10
edfield Suff 31 B9
edford Bedford 29 C7
edham W Sus 11 B9
edhampton Hants 10 D6
edingfield Suff 31 B8
edlam N Yorks 51 C8
edlington Northumb 63 E8
edlington Station Northumb 63 E8
edlinog M Tydf 14 A6
edminster Bristol 16 D2
edmond Herts 19 A7
ednall Staffs 34 D5
edrule Borders 62 B2
edstone Shrops 33 H9
edwas Caerph 15 C7
edworth Warks 35 G9
edworth Heath Warks 35 G9
eeby Leics 36 E2
eech Hants 18 H3
eech Staffs 34 B4
eech Hill Gtr Man 43 B8
eech Hill W Berks 18 E3
eechingstoke Wilts 17 F7
eedon W Berks 17 D11
eeford E Yorks 53 D7
eeley Derbys 44 F6
eelsby NE Lincs 46 B6
eenham W Berks 18 E2
eeny Corn 4 B2
eer Devon 7 H11
eer Hackett Dorset 8 C4
eercrocombe Som 8 B2
eesands Devon 5 G9
eesby Lincs 47 D8
eeson Devon 5 G9
eeston C Beds 29 D8
eeston Ches W 43 G8
eeston Norf 38 D5
eeston Notts 35 B11
eeston W Yorks 51 F8
eeston Regis Norf 39 A7
eeswing Dumfries 55 C11
eetham Cumb 49 B4
eetley Norf 38 D5
egbroke Oxon 27 G11
egelly Pembs 22 F6
eggar's Bush Powys 25 B9
eguildy Powys 33 H7
eighton Norf 39 E9
eighton S Yorks 45 D8
eighton Hill Derbys 44 G6
eith N Ayrs 66 A6
Bekesbourne Kent 21 F8
Belaugh Norf 39 D8
Belbroughton Worcs 34 H5
Belchamp Otten Essex 30 D5
Belchamp St Paul Essex 30 D4
Belchamp Walter Essex 30 D5
Belchford Lincs 46 E6
Belford Northumb 71 G10
Belhaven E Loth 70 C5
Belhelvie Aberds 83 B11
Belhinnie Aberds 82 A6
Bell Bar Herts 29 H9
Bell Busk N Yorks 50 D5
Bell End Worcs 34 H5
Bell o' th' Hill Ches W 43 H8
Bellabeg Aberds 82 B5
Bellamore S Ayrs 66 H5
Bellanoch Argyll 72 D6
Bellaty Angus 76 B5
Belleau Lincs 47 E8
Bellehiglash Moray 88 E1
Bellerby N Yorks 58 G2
Bellever Devon 5 D7
Belliehill Angus 77 A8
Bellingdon Bucks 28 H6
Bellingham Northumb 62 E4
Belloch Argyll 65 E7
Bellochantuy Argyll 65 E7
Bells Yew Green E Sus 12 C5
Bellsbank E Ayrs 67 F7
Bellshill N Lanark 68 D6
Bellshill Northumb 71 G10
Bellspool Borders 69 G10
Bellsquarry W Loth 69 D9
Belmaduthy Highld 87 F9
Belmesthorpe Rutland 36 D6
Belmont Blackburn 50 H2
Belmont London 19 E9
Belmont S Ayrs 66 D6
Belmont Shetland 96 C7
Belnacraig Aberds 82 B5
Belowda Corn 3 C8
Belper Derbys 45 H7
Belper Lane End Derbys 45 H7
Belsay Northumb 63 F7
Belses Borders 70 H4
Belsford Devon 5 F8
Belstead Suff 31 D8
Belston S Ayrs 67 D6
Belstone Devon 6 G5
Belthorn Blackburn 50 G3
Beltinge Kent 21 E8
Beltoft N Lincs 46 B2
Belton Leics 35 C10
Belton Lincs 36 B5
Belton N Lincs 45 B11
Belton Norf 39 E10
Belton in Rutland Rutland 36 E4
Beltring Kent 20 G3
Belts of Collonach Aberds 83 D8
Belvedere London 19 D11
Belvoir Leics 36 B4
Bembridge IoW 10 F5
Bemersyde Borders 70 G4
Bemerton Wilts 9 A10
Bempton E Yorks 53 B7
Ben Alder Lodge Highld 81 F7
Ben Armine Lodge Highld 93 H10
Ben Casgro W Isles 91 E9
Benacre Suff 39 G11
Benbuie Dumfries 60 D3
Benderloch Argyll 74 D2
Bendronaig Lodge Highld 86 H3
Benenden Kent 13 C7
Benfield Dumfries 54 C6
Bengate Norf 39 C9
Bengeworth Worcs 27 D7
Benhall Green Suff 31 B10
Benhall Street Suff 31 B10
Benholm Aberds 83 G10
Beningbrough N Yorks 51 D11
Benington Herts 29 F9
Benington Lincs 47 H7
Benllech Anglesey 41 B7
Benmore Argyll 73 E10
Benmore Stirling 75 E7
Benmore Lodge Highld 92 H6
Bennacott Corn 6 G1
Bennan N Ayrs 66 D2
Benniworth Lincs 46 D6
Benover Kent 20 G4
Bensham T&W 63 G8
Benslie N Ayrs 67 B6
Benson Oxon 18 B3
Bent Aberds 83 F8
Bent Gate Lancs 50 G3
Benthall Northumb 71 H11
Benthall Shrops 34 E2
Bentham Glos 26 G6
Benthoul Aberdeen 83 C10
Bentlawnt Shrops 33 E9
Bentley E Yorks 52 F6
Bentley Hants 18 G4
Bentley S Yorks 45 B9
Bentley Suff 31 E8
Bentley Warks 35 F8
Bentley Worcs 26 B6
Bentley Heath W Mid 35 H7
Benton Devon 6 C5
Bentpath Dumfries 61 D9
Bents W Loth 69 D8
Bentworth Hants 18 G3
Benvie Dundee 76 D6
Benwick Cambs 37 F9
Beoley Worcs 27 B7
Beoraidbeg Highld 79 B9
Bepton W Sus 11 C7
Berden Essex 29 F11
Bere Alston Devon 4 E5
Bere Ferrers Devon 4 E5
Bere Regis Dorset 9 E7
Berepper Corn 2 G5
Bergh Apton Norf 39 E9
Berinsfield Oxon 18 B2
Berkeley Glos 16 B3
Berkhamsted Herts 28 H6
Berkley Som 16 G5
Berkswell W Mid 35 H8
Bermondsey London 19 D10
Bernera Highld 85 F13
Bernice Argyll 73 D10
Bernisdale Highld 85 C9
Berrick Salome Oxon 18 B3
Berriedale Highld 94 H3
Berrier Cumb 56 D5
Berriew Powys 33 E7
Berrington Northumb 71 F9
Berrington Shrops 33 E11
Berrow Som 15 F9
Berrow Green Worcs 26 C4
Berry Down Cross Devon 6 B4
Berry Hill Glos 26 G2
Berry Hill Pembs 22 B5
Berry Pomeroy Devon 5 E9
Berryhillock Moray 88 B5
Berrynarbor Devon 6 B4
Bersham Wrex 42 H6
Berstane Orkney 95 G5
Berwick E Sus 12 F4
Berwick Bassett Wilts 17 D7
Berwick Hill Northumb 63 F7
Berwick St James Wilts 17 H7
Berwick St John Wilts 9 B8
Berwick St Leonard Wilts 9 A8
Berwick-upon-Tweed Northumb 71 E8
Bescar Lancs 43 A6
Besford Worcs 26 D6
Bessacarr S Yorks 45 B10
Bessels Leigh Oxon 17 A11
Bessingby E Yorks 53 C7
Bessingham Norf 39 B7
Bestbeech Hill E Sus 12 C5
Besthorpe Norf 39 F6
Besthorpe Notts 46 F2
Bestwood Nottingham 36 A1
Bestwood Village Notts 45 H9
Beswick E Yorks 52 E6
Betchworth Sur 19 G9
Bethania Ceredig 24 B2
Bethania Gwyn 41 E8
Bethania Gwyn 41 F9
Bethel Anglesey 40 C5
Bethel Gwyn 32 B5
Bethel Gwyn 41 D7
Bethersden Kent 13 B8
Bethesda Gwyn 41 D8
Bethesda Pembs 22 E5
Bethlehem Carms 24 F3
Bethnal Green London 19 C10
Betley Staffs 43 H10
Betsham Kent 20 D3
Betteshanger Kent 21 F10
Bettiscombe Dorset 8 E2
Bettisfield Wrex 33 B10
Betton Shrops 33 E9
Betton Shrops 34 B2
Bettws Bridgend 14 C5
Bettws Mon 25 G9
Bettws Newport 15 B8
Bettws Cedewain Powys 33 F7
Bettws Gwerfil Goch Denb 42 H3
Bettws Ifan Ceredig 23 B8
Bettws Newydd Mon 25 H10
Bettws-y-crwyn Shrops 33 G8
Bettyhill Highld 93 C10
Betws Carms 24 G3
Betws Bledrws Ceredig 23 A10
Betws-Garmon Gwyn 41 E7
Betws-y-Coed Conwy 41 E9
Betws-yn-Rhos Conwy 42 E2
Beulah Ceredig 23 B7
Beulah Powys 24 C6
Bevendean Brighton 12 F2
Bevercotes Notts 45 E10
Beverley E Yorks 52 F6
Beverston Glos 16 B5
Bevington Glos 16 B3
Bewaldeth Cumb 56 C4
Bewcastle Cumb 61 F11
Bewdley Worcs 34 H3
Bewerley N Yorks 51 C7
Bewholme E Yorks 53 D7
Bexhill E Sus 12 F6
Bexley London 19 D11
Bexleyheath London 19 D11
Bexwell Norf 38 E2
Beyton Suff 30 B6
Bhaltos W Isles 90 D5
Bhatarsaigh W Isles 84 J1
Bibury Glos 27 H8
Bicester Oxon 28 F2
Bickenhall Som 8 C1
Bickenhill W Mid 35 G7
Bicker Lincs 37 B8
Bickershaw Gtr Man 43 B9
Bickerstaffe Lancs 43 B7
Bickerton Ches E 43 G8
Bickerton N Yorks 51 D10
Bickington Devon 5 D8
Bickington Devon 6 C4
Bickleigh Devon 4 E6
Bickleigh Devon 7 F8
Bickleton Devon 6 C4
Bickley London 19 E11
Bickley Moss Ches W 43 H8
Bicknacre Essex 20 A4
Bicknoller Som 7 C10
Bicknor Kent 20 F5
Bickton Hants 9 C10
Bicton Shrops 33 D10
Bicton Shrops 33 G8
Bidborough Kent 12 B4
Biddenden Kent 13 C7
Biddenham Bedford 29 D7
Biddestone Wilts 16 D5
Biddisham Som 15 F9
Biddlesden Bucks 28 D3
Biddlestone Northumb 62 C5
Biddulph Staffs 44 G2
Biddulph Moor Staffs 44 G3
Bideford Devon 6 D3
Bidford-on-Avon Warks 27 C8
Bidston Mers 42 C5
Bielby E Yorks 52 E3
Bieldside Aberdeen 83 C10
Bierley IoW 10 G4
Bierley W Yorks 51 F7
Bierton Bucks 28 G5
Big Sand Highld 85 A12
Bigbury Devon 5 G7
Bigbury on Sea Devon 5 G7
Bigby Lincs 46 B4
Biggar Cumb 49 C1
Biggar S Lanark 69 G9
Biggin Derbys 44 G5
Biggin Derbys 44 H6
Biggin N Yorks 51 F11
Biggin Hill London 19 F11
Biggings Shetland 96 G3
Biggleswade C Beds 29 D8
Bighouse Highld 93 C11
Bighton Hants 10 A5
Bignor W Sus 11 C8
Bigton Shetland 96 L5
Bilberry Corn 3 C9
Bilborough Nottingham 35 A11
Bilbrook Som 7 B9
Bilbrough N Yorks 51 E11
Bilbster Highld 94 E4
Bildershaw Durham 58 D3
Bildeston Suff 30 D6
Billericay Essex 20 B3
Billesdon Leics 36 E3
Billesley Warks 27 C8
Billingborough Lincs 37 B7
Billinge Mers 43 B8
Billingford Norf 38 C6
Billingham Stockton 58 D5
Billinghay Lincs 46 G5
Billingley S Yorks 45 B8
Billingshurst W Sus 11 B9
Billingsley Shrops 34 G3
Billington C Beds 28 F6
Billington Lancs 50 F3
Billockby Norf 39 D10
Billy Row Durham 58 C2
Bilsborrow Lancs 49 F5
Bilsby Lincs 47 E8
Bilsham W Sus 11 D8
Bilsington Kent 13 C9
Bilson Green Glos 26 G3
Bilsthorpe Notts 45 F10
Bilsthorpe Moor Notts 45 G10
Bilston Midloth 69 D11
Bilston W Mid 34 F5
Bilstone Leics 35 E9
Bilting Kent 21 G7
Bilton E Yorks 53 F7
Bilton Northumb 63 B8
Bilton Warks 27 A11
Bilton in Ainsty N Yorks 51 E10
Bimbister Orkney 95 G4
Binbrook Lincs 46 C6
Binchester Blocks Durham 58 C3
Bincombe Dorset 8 F5
Bindal Highld 87 C12
Binegar Som 16 G3
Binfield Brack 18 D5
Binfield Hth. Oxon 18 D4
Bingfield Northumb 62 F5
Bingham Notts 36 B3
Bingley W Yorks 51 F7
Bings Heath Shrops 33 D11
Binham Norf 38 B5
Binley Hants 17 F11
Binley W Mid 35 H9
Binley Woods Warks 35 H9
Binniehill Falk 69 C7
Binsoe N Yorks 51 B8
Binstead IoW 10 E4
Binsted Hants 18 G4
Binton Warks 27 C8
Bintree Norf 38 C6
Binweston Shrops 33 E9
Birch Essex 30 G6
Birch Gtr Man 44 B2
Birch Green Essex 30 G6
Birch Heath Ches W 43 F8
Birch Hill Ches W 43 E8
Birch Vale Derbys 44 D4
Bircham Newton Norf 38 B3
Bircham Tofts Norf 38 B3
Birchanger Essex 30 F2
Birchencliffe W Yorks 51 H7
Bircher Hereford 25 B11
Birchgrove Cardiff 15 D7
Birchgrove Swansea 14 B3
Birchington Kent 21 E9
Birchmoor Warks 35 E8
Birchover Derbys 44 F6
Birchwood Lincs 46 F3
Birchwood Warr 43 C9
Bircotes Notts 45 C10
Birdbrook Essex 30 D4
Birdforth N Yorks 51 B10
Birdham W Sus 11 E7
Birdholme Derbys 45 F7
Birdingbury Warks 27 B11
Birdlip Glos 26 G6
Birds Edge W Yorks 44 B6
Birdsall N Yorks 52 C4
Birdsgreen Shrops 34 G3
Birdsmoor Gate Dorset 8 D2
Birdston E Dunb 68 C5
Birdwell S Yorks 45 B7
Birdwood Glos 26 G4
Birgham Borders 70 G6
Birkby N Yorks 58 F4
Birkdale Mers 49 H3
Birkenhead Mers 42 D6
Birkenhills Aberds 89 D7
Birkenshaw N Lanark 68 D5
Birkenshaw W Yorks 51 G8
Birkhall Aberds 82 D5
Birkhill Angus 76 D6
Birkhill Borders 61 B8
Birkholme Lincs 36 C5
Birkin N Yorks 51 G11
Birley Hereford 25 C11
Birling Kent 20 E3
Birling Northumb 63 C8
Birling Gap E Sus 12 G4
Birlingham Worcs 26 D6
Birmingham W Mid 35 G6
Birnam Perth 76 C3
Birse Aberds 83 D7
Birsemore Aberds 83 D7
Birstall Leics 36 E1
Birstall W Yorks 51 G8
Birstwith N Yorks 51 D8
Birthorpe Lincs 37 B7
Birtley Hereford 25 B10
Birtley Northumb 62 F4
Birtley T&W 63 H8
Birts Street Worcs 26 E4
Bisbrooke Rutland 36 F4
Biscathorpe Lincs 46 D6
Biscot Luton 29 F7
Bish Mill Devon 7 D6
Bisham Windsor 18 C5
Bishampton Worcs 26 C6
Bishop Auckland Durham 58 D3
Bishop Burton E Yorks 52 F5
Bishop Middleham Durham 58 C4
Bishop Monkton N Yorks 51 C9
Bishop Norton Lincs 46 C3
Bishop Sutton Bath 16 F2
Bishop Thornton N Yorks 51 C8
Bishop Wilton E Yorks 52 D3
Bishopbridge Lincs 46 C4
Bishopbriggs E Dunb 68 D5
Bishopmill Moray 88 B2
Bishops Cannings Wilts 17 E7
Bishop's Castle Shrops 33 G9
Bishop's Caundle Dorset 8 C5
Bishop's Cleeve Glos 26 F6
Bishops Frome Hereford 26 D3
Bishop's Green Essex 30 G3
Bishop's Hull Som 7 D11
Bishop's Itchington Warks 27 C10
Bishops Lydeard Som 7 D10
Bishops Nympton Devon 7 D6
Bishop's Offley Staffs 34 C3
Bishop'S Stortford Herts 29 F11
Bishop's Sutton Hants 10 A5
Bishop's Tachbrook Warks 27 B10
Bishops Tawton Devon 6 C4
Bishop's Waltham Hants 10 C4
Bishop's Wood Staffs 34 E4
Bishopsbourne Kent 21 F8
Bishopsteignton Devon 5 D10
Bishopstoke Hants 10 C3
Bishopston Swansea 23 H10
Bishopstone Bucks 28 G5
Bishopstone E Sus 12 F3
Bishopstone Hereford 25 D11
Bishopstone Swindon 17 C9
Bishopstone Wilts 9 B9
Bishopstrow Wilts 16 G5
Bishopswood Som 8 C1
Bishopsworth Bristol 16 E2
Bishopthorpe York 52 E1
Bishopton Darl 58 D4
Bishopton Dumfries 55 E7
Bishopton N Yorks 51 B9
Bishopton Renfs 68 C3
Bishopton Warks 27 C8
Bishton Newport 15 C9
Bisley Glos 26 H6
Bisley Sur 18 F6
Bispham Blackpool 49 E3
Bispham Green Lancs 43 A7
Bissoe Corn 3 E6
Bisterne Close Hants 9 D11
Bitchfield Lincs 36 C5
Bittadon Devon 6 B4
Bittaford Devon 5 F7
Bittering Norf 38 D5
Bitterley Shrops 34 H1
Bitterne Soton 10 C3
Bitteswell Leics 35 G11
Bitton S Glos 16 E3
Bix Oxon 18 C4
Bixter Shetland 96 H5
Blaby Leics 36 F1
Black Bourton Oxon 17 A9
Black Callerton T&W 63 G7
Black Clauchrie S Ayrs 54 A5
Black Corries Lodge Highld 74 B5
Black Crofts Argyll 74 D2
Black Dog Devon 7 F7
Black Heddon Northumb 62 F6
Black Lane Gtr Man 43 B10
Black Marsh Shrops 33 F9
Black Mount Argyll 74 C5
Black Notley Essex 30 F4
Black Pill Swansea 14 B2
Black Tar Pembs 22 F4
Black Torrington Devon 6 F3
Blackacre Dumfries 60 D6
Blackadder West Borders 71 E7
Blackawton Devon 5 F9
Blackborough Devon 7 F9
Blackborough End Norf 38 D2
Blackboys E Sus 12 D4
Blackbrook Derbys 45 H7
Blackbrook Mers 43 C8
Blackbrook Staffs 34 B3
Blackburn Aberds 83 B10
Blackburn Aberds 88 E5
Blackburn Blackburn 50 G2
Blackburn W Loth 69 D8
Blackcraig Dumfries 60 E3
Blackden Heath Ches E 43 E10
Blackdog Aberds 83 B11
Blackfell T&W 63 H8
Blackfield Hants 10 D3
Blackford Cumb 61 G9
Blackford Perth 75 G11
Blackford Som 8 B5
Blackford Som 15 G10
Blackfordby Leics 35 D9
Blackgang IoW 10 G3
Blackhall Colliery Durham 58 C5
Blackhall Mill T&W 63 H7
Blackhall Rocks Durham 58 C5
Blackham E Sus 12 C3
Blackhaugh Borders 70 G3
Blackheath Essex 31 F7
Blackheath Suff 31 A11
Blackheath Sur 19 G7
Blackheath W Mid 34 G5
Blackhill Aberds 89 C10
Blackhill Aberds 89 D10
Blackhill Highld 85 C8
Blackhills Highld 87 F12
Blackhills Moray 88 C2
Blackhorse S Glos 16 D3
Blackland Wilts 17 E7
Blacklaw Aberds 89 C6
Blackley Gtr Man 44 B2
Blacklunans Perth 76 A4
Blackmill Bridgend 14 C5
Blackmoor Hants 11 A6
Blackmoor Gate Devon 6 B5
Blackmore Essex 20 A3
Blackmore End Essex 30 E4
Blackmore End Herts 29 G8
Blackness Falk 69 C9
Blacknest Hants 18 G4
Blacko Lancs 50 E4
Blackpool Blackpool 49 F3
Blackpool Devon 5 G9
Blackpool Pembs 22 E5
Blackpool Gate Cumb 61 F11
Blackridge W Loth 69 D7
Blackrock Argyll 64 B4
Blackrock Mon 25 G9
Blackrod Gtr Man 43 A9
Blackshaw Dumfries 60 G6
Blackshaw Head W Yorks 50 G5
Blacksmith's Green Suff 31 B8
Blackstone W Sus 11 C11
Blackthorn Oxon 28 G3
Blackthorpe Suff 30 B6
Blacktoft E Yorks 52 G4
Blacktop Aberdeen 83 C10
Blacktown Newport 15 C8
Blackwall Tunnel London 19 C10
Blackwater Corn 2 E6
Blackwater Hants 18 F5
Blackwater IoW 10 F4
Blackwaterfoot N Ayrs 66 D1
Blackwell Darl 58 E3
Blackwell Derbys 44 E5
Blackwell Derbys 45 G8
Blackwell W Sus 12 C2
Blackwell Warks 27 D9
Blackwell Worcs 26 A6
Blackwood = Coed Duon Caerph 15 B7
Blackwood S Lanark 68 F6
Blackwood Hill Staffs 44 G3
Blacon Ches W 43 F6
Bladnoch Dumfries 55 D7
Bladon Oxon 27 G11
Blaen-gwynfi Neath 14 B4
Blaen-waun Carms 23 D7
Blaen-y-coed Carms 23 D8
Blaen-y-Cwm Denb 32 B6
Blaen-y-cwm Gwyn 32 C3
Blaen-y-cwm Powys 33 C6
Blaenannerch Ceredig 23 B7
Blaenau Ffestiniog Gwyn 41 F9
Blaenavon Torf 25 H9
Blaencelyn Ceredig 23 A8
Blaendyryn Powys 24 E6
Blaenffos Pembs 22 C6
Blaengarw Bridgend 14 B5
Blaengwrach Neath 24 H5
Blaenpennal Ceredig 24 B3
Blaenplwyf Ceredig 32 H1
Blaenporth Ceredig 23 B7
Blaenrhondda Rhondda 14 A5
Blaenycwm Ceredig 32 H4
Blagdon N Som 15 F11
Blagdon Torbay 5 E9
Blagdon Hill Som 7 E11
Blagill Cumb 57 B9
Blaguegate Lancs 43 B7
Blaich Highld 80 F2
Blain Highld 79 E9
Blaina Bl Gwent 25 H9
Blair Atholl Perth 81 G10
Blair Drummond Stirling 75 H10
Blairbeg N Ayrs 66 C3
Blairdaff Aberds 83 B8
Blairglas Argyll 68 B2
Blairgowrie Perth 76 C4
Blairhall Fife 69 B9
Blairingone Perth 76 H2
Blairland N Ayrs 66 B6
Blairlogie Stirling 75 H11
Blairlomond Argyll 74 H4
Blairmore Argyll 73 E10
Blairnamarrow Moray 82 B4
Blairquhosh Stirling 68 B4
Blair's Ferry Argyll 73 G8
Blairskaith E Dunb 68 C4
Blaisdon Glos 26 G4
Blakebrook Worcs 34 H4
Blakedown Worcs 34 H4
Blakelaw Borders 70 G6
Blakeley Staffs 34 F4
Blakeley Lane Staffs 44 H3
Blakemere Hereford 25 D10
Blakeney Glos 26 H3
Blakeney Norf 38 A6
Blakenhall Ches E 43 H10
Blakenhall W Mid 34 F5
Blakeshall Worcs 34 G4
Blakesley Northants 28 C3
Blanchland Northumb 57 A11
Bland Hill N Yorks 51 D8
Blandford Forum Dorset 9 D7
Blandford St Mary Dorset 9 D7
Blanefield Stirling 68 C4
Blankney Lincs 46 F4
Blantyre S Lanark 68 E5
Blar a'Chaorainn Highld 80 G3
Blaran Argyll 73 B7
Blarghour Argyll 73 B8
Blarmachfoldach Highld 80 G2
Blarnalearoch Highld 86 B4
Blashford Hants 9 D10
Blaston Leics 36 F4
Blatherwycke Northants 36 F5
Blawith Cumb 56 H4
Blaxhall Suff 31 C10
Blaxton S Yorks 45 B10
Blaydon T&W 63 G7
Bleadon N Som 15 F9
Bleak Hey Nook Gtr Man 44 B4
Blean Kent 21 E8
Bleasby Lincs 46 D5
Bleasby Notts 45 H11
Bleasdale Lancs 50 E1
Bleatarn Cumb 57 E9
Blebocraigs Fife 77 F7
Bleddfa Powys 25 B9
Bledington Glos 27 F9
Bledlow Bucks 18 A4
Bledlow Ridge Bucks 18 B4
Blegbie E Loth 70 D3
Blencarn Cumb 57 C8
Blencogo Cumb 56 B3
Blendworth Hants 10 C6
Blenheim Park Norf 38 B4
Blennerhasset Cumb 56 B3
Blervie Castle Moray 87 F13
Bletchingdon Oxon 28 G2
Bletchingley Sur 19 F10
Bletchley M Keynes 28 E5
Bletchley Shrops 34 B2
Bletherston Pembs 22 D5
Bletsoe Bedford 29 C7
Blewbury Oxon 18 C2
Blickling Norf 39 C7
Blidworth Notts 45 G9
Blindburn Northumb 62 B4
Blindcrake Cumb 56 C3
Blindley Heath Sur 19 G10
Blisland Corn 4 D2
Bliss Gate Worcs 26 A4
Blissford Hants 9 C10
Blisworth Northants 28 C4
Blithbury Staffs 35 C6
Blitterlees Cumb 56 A3
Blo' Norton Norf 38 H6
Blockley Glos 27 E8
Blofield Norf 39 E9
Blofield Heath Norf 39 D9
Bloomfield Borders 61 A11
Blore Staffs 44 H5
Blount's Green Staffs 35 B6
Blowick Mers 49 H3
Bloxham Oxon 27 E11
Bloxholm Lincs 46 G4
Bloxwich W Mid 34 E5
Bloxworth Dorset 9 E7
Blubberhouses N Yorks 51 D7
Blue Anchor Som 7 B9
Blue Anchor Swansea 23 G10
Blue Row Essex 31 G7
Blundeston Suff 39 F11
Blunham C Beds 29 C8
Blunsdon St Andrew Swindon 17 C8
Bluntington Worcs 26 A5
Bluntisham Cambs 29 A10
Blunts Corn 4 E4
Blyborough Lincs 46 C3
Blyford Suff 39 H10
Blymhill Staffs 34 D4
Blyth Northumb 63 E9
Blyth Notts 45 D10
Blyth Bridge Borders 69 F10
Blythburgh Suff 39 H10
Blythe Borders 70 F4
Blythe Bridge Staffs 34 A5
Blyton Lincs 46 C2
Boarhills Fife 77 F8
Boarhunt Hants 10 D5
Boars Head Gtr Man 43 B8
Boars Hill Oxon 17 A11
Boarshead E Sus 12 C4
Boarstall Bucks 28 G3
Boasley Cross Devon 6 G3
Boat of Garten Highld 81 B11
Boath Highld 87 D8
Bobbing Kent 20 E5
Bobbington Staffs 34 F4
Bobbingworth Essex 30 H2
Bocaddon Corn 4 F2
Bochastle Stirling 75 G9
Bocking Essex 30 F4
Bocking Churchstreet Essex 30 F4
Boddam Aberds 89 D11
Boddam Shetland 96 M5
Boddington Glos 26 F5
Bodedern Anglesey 40 B5
Bodelwyddan Denb 42 E3
Bodenham Hereford 26 C2
Bodenham Wilts 9 B10
Bodenham Moor Hereford 26 C2
Bodermid Gwyn 40 H3
Bodewryd Anglesey 40 A5
Bodfari Denb 42 E3
Bodffordd Anglesey 40 C6
Bodham Norf 39 A7
Bodiam E Sus 13 D6
Bodicote Oxon 27 E11
Bodieve Corn 3 B8
Bodinnick Corn 4 F2
Bodle Street Green E Sus 12 E5
Bodmin Corn 4 E1
Bodney Norf 38 F4
Bodorgan Anglesey 40 D5
Bodsham Kent 21 G8
Boduan Gwyn 40 G5
Bodymoor Heath Warks 35 F7
Bogallan Highld 87 F9
Bogbrae Aberds 89 E10
Bogend Borders 70 F6
Bogend S Ayrs 67 C6
Boghall W Loth 69 D8
Boghead S Lanark 68 F6
Bogmoor Moray 88 B3
Bogniebrae Aberds 88 D5
Bognor Regis W Sus 11 E8
Bograxie Aberds 83 B9
Bogside N Lanark 69 E7
Bogton Aberds 89 C6
Bogue Dumfries 55 A9
Bohenie Highld 80 E4
Bohortha Corn 3 F7
Bohuntine Highld 80 E4
Boirseam W Isles 90 J5
Bojewyan Corn 2 F2
Bolam Durham 58 D2
Bolam Northumb 62 E6
Bolberry Devon 5 H7
Bold Heath Mers 43 D8
Boldon T&W 63 G9
Boldon Colliery T&W 63 G9
Boldre Hants 10 E2
Boldron Durham 58 E1
Bole Notts 45 D11
Bolehill Derbys 44 G6
Boleside Borders 70 G3
Bolham Devon 7 E8
Bolham Water Devon 7 E10
Bolingey Corn 3 D6
Bollington Ches E 44 E3
Bollington Cross Ches E 44 E3
Bolney W Sus 12 D1
Bolnhurst Bedford 29 C7
Bolshan Angus 77 B9
Bolsover Derbys 45 E8
Bolsterstone S Yorks 44 C6
Bolstone Hereford 26 E2
Boltby N Yorks 58 H5
Bolter End Bucks 18 B4
Bolton Cumb 57 D8
Bolton E Loth 70 C4
Bolton E Yorks 52 D3
Bolton Gtr Man 43 B10
Bolton Northumb 63 B7
Bolton Abbey N Yorks 51 D6
Bolton Bridge N Yorks 51 D6
Bolton-by-Bowland Lancs 50 E3
Bolton-le-Sands Lancs 49 C4
Bolton Low Houses Cumb 56 B4
Bolton-on-Swale N Yorks 58 G3
Bolton Percy N Yorks 51 E11
Bolton Town End Lancs 49 C4
Bolton upon Dearne S Yorks 45 B8
Boltonfellend Cumb 61 G10
Boltongate Cumb 56 B4
Bolventor Corn 4 D2
Bomere Heath Shrops 33 D10
Bon-y-maen Swansea 14 B2
Bonar Bridge Highld 87 B9
Bonawe Argyll 74 D3
Bonby N Lincs 52 H6
Boncath Pembs 23 C7
Bonchester Bridge Borders 61 B11
Bonchurch IoW 10 G4
Bondleigh Devon 6 F5
Bonehill Devon 5 D8
Bonehill Staffs 35 E7
Bo'ness Falk 69 B8
Bonhill W Dunb 68 C2
Boningale Shrops 34 E4
Bonjedward Borders 62 A2
Bonkle N Lanark 69 E7
Bonnavoulin Highld 79 F8
Bonnington Edin 69 D10
Bonnington Kent 13 C9
Bonnybank Fife 76 G6
Bonnybridge Falk 69 B7
Bonnykelly Aberds 89 C8
Bonnyrigg and Lasswade Midloth 70 D2
Bonnyton Aberds 89 E6
Bonnyton Angus 76 D6
Bonnyton Angus 77 B9
Bonsall Derbys 44 G6
Bonskeid House Perth 75 A11
Bont Mon 25 G10
Bont-Dolgadfan Powys 32 E4
Bont-goch Ceredig 32 G2
Bont-newydd Conwy 42 E3
Bont Newydd Gwyn 32 C3
Bont Newydd Gwyn 41 F9
Bontddu Gwyn 32 D2
Bonthorpe Lincs 47 E8
Bontnewydd Ceredig 24 B3
Bontnewydd Gwyn 40 E6
Bontuchel Denb 42 G3
Bonvilston V Glam 14 D6
Booker Bucks 18 B5
Boon Borders 70 F4
Boosbeck Redcar 59 E7
Boot Cumb 56 F3
Boot Street Suff 31 D9
Booth W Yorks 50 G6
Booth Wood W Yorks 50 H6
Boothby Graffoe Lincs 46 G3
Boothby Pagnell Lincs 36 B5
Boothen Stoke 34 A4
Boothferry E Yorks 52 G3
Boothville Northants 28 B4
Bootle Cumb 56 H3
Bootle Mers 42 C6
Booton Norf 39 C7
Boquhan Stirling 68 B4
Boraston Shrops 26 A3
Borden Kent 20 E5
Borden W Sus 11 B7
Bordley N Yorks 50 C5
Bordon Hants 18 H5
Bordon Camp Hants 18 H4
Boreham Essex 30 H4
Boreham Wilts 16 G5
Boreham Street E Sus 12 E5
Borehamwood Herts 19 B8
Boreland Dumfries 61 D7
Boreland Stirling 75 D8
Borgh W Isles 84 H1
Borgh W Isles 90 J4
Borghastan W Isles 90 C7
Borgie Highld 93 D9
Borgue Dumfries 55 E9
Borgue Highld 94 H3
Borley Essex 30 D5
Bornais W Isles 84 F2
Bornesketaig Highld 85 A8
Borness Dumfries 55 E9
Borough Green Kent 20 F3
Boroughbridge N Yorks 51 C9
Borras Head Wrex 42 G6
Borreraig Highld 84 C6
Borrobol Lodge Highld 93 G11
Borrowash Derbys 35 B10
Borrowby N Yorks 58 H5
Borrowdale Cumb 56 E4
Borrowfield Aberds 83 D10
Borth Ceredig 32 F2
Borth-y-Gest Gwyn 41 G7
Borthwickbrae Borders 61 B10
Borthwickshiels Borders 61 B10
Borve Highld 85 D9
Borve Lodge W Isles 90 H5
Borwick Lancs 49 B5
Bosavern Corn 2 F2
Bosbury Hereford 26 D3
Boscastle Corn 4 B2
Boscombe Bmouth 9 E10
Boscombe Wilts 17 H9
Boscoppa Corn 3 D9
Bosham W Sus 11 D7
Bosherston Pembs 22 G4
Boskenna Corn 2 G3
Bosley Ches E 44 F3
Bossall N Yorks 52 C3
Bossiney Corn 4 C1
Bossingham Kent 21 G8
Bossington Som 7 B7
Bostock Green Ches W 43 F9
Boston Lincs 37 A9
Boston Long Hedges Lincs 47 H7
Boston Spa W Yorks 51 E10
Boston West Lincs 46 H6
Boswinger Corn 3 E8
Botallack Corn 2 F2
Botany Bay London 19 B9
Botcherby Cumb 61 H10
Botcheston Leics 35 E10
Botesdale Suff 38 H6
Bothal Northumb 63 E8
Bothamsall Notts 45 E10
Bothel Cumb 56 C3
Bothenhampton Dorset 8 E3
Bothwell S Lanark 68 E6
Botley Bucks 18 A6
Botley Hants 10 C4
Botley Oxon 27 H11
Botolph Claydon Bucks 28 F4
Botolphs W Sus 11 D10
Bottacks Highld 86 E7
Bottesford Leics 36 B4
Bottesford N Lincs 46 B2
Bottisham Cambs 30 B2
Bottlesford Wilts 17 F8
Bottom Boat W Yorks 51 G9
Bottom House Staffs 44 G4
Bottom o' th' Moor Gtr Man 43 A9
Bottom of Hutton Lancs 49 G4
Bottomcraig Fife 76 E6
Botusfleming Corn 4 E5
Botwnnog Gwyn 40 G4
Bough Beech Kent 19 G11
Boughrood Powys 25 E8
Boughspring Glos 16 B2
Boughton Norf 38 E2
Boughton Northants 28 B4
Boughton Notts 45 F10
Boughton Aluph Kent 21 G7
Boughton Lees Kent 21 G7
Boughton Malherbe Kent 20 G5
Boughton Monchelsea Kent 20 F4
Boughton Street Kent 21 F7
Boulby Redcar 59 E8
Boulden Shrops 33 G11
Boulmer Northumb 63 B8
Boulston Pembs 22 E4
Boultenstone Aberds 82 B6
Boultham Lincs 46 F3
Bourn Cambs 29 C10
Bourne Lincs 37 C6
Bourne End Bucks 18 C5
Bourne End C Beds 28 D6
Bourne End Herts 29 H7
Bournemouth Bmouth 9 E9
Bournes Green Glos 16 A6
Bournes Green Southend 20 C6
Bournheath Worcs 26 A6
Bournmoor Durham 58 A4
Bournville W Mid 34 G6
Bourton Dorset 9 A6
Bourton N Som 15 E9
Bourton Oxon 17 C9
Bourton Shrops 34 F1
Bourton on Dunsmore Warks 27 A11
Bourton on the Hill Glos 27 E8
Bourton-on-the-Water Glos 27 F8
Bousd Argyll 78 E5
Boustead Hill Cumb 61 H8
Bouth Cumb 56 H5
Bouthwaite N Yorks 51 B7
Boveney Bucks 18 D6
Boverton V Glam 14 E5
Bovey Tracey Devon 5 D9
Bovingdon Herts 19 A7
Bovingdon Green Bucks 18 C5
Bovingdon Green Herts 19 A7
Bovinger Essex 30 H2
Bovington Camp Dorset 9 F7
Bow Borders 70 F3
Bow Devon 6 F6
Bow Orkney 95 J4
Bow Brickhill M Keynes 28 E6
Bow of Fife Fife 76 F6
Bow Street Ceredig 32 G2
Bowbank Durham 57 D11
Bowburn Durham 58 C4
Bowcombe IoW 10 F3
Bowd Devon 7 G10
Bowden Borders 70 G4
Bowden Devon 5 G9
Bowden Hill Wilts 16 E6
Bowderdale Cumb 57 F8
Bowdon Gtr Man 43 D10
Bower Northumb 62 E3
Bower Hinton Som 8 C3
Bowerchalke Wilts 9 B9
Bowerhill Wilts 16 E6
Bowermadden Highld 94 D4
Bowers Gifford Essex 20 C4
Bowershall Fife 69 A9
Bowertower Highld 94 D4
Bowes Durham 57 E11
Bowgreave Lancs 49 E4
Bowgreen Gtr Man 43 D10
Bowhill Borders 70 H3
Bowhouse Dumfries 60 G6
Bowland Bridge Cumb 56 H6
Bowley Hereford 26 C2
Bowlhead Green Sur 18 H6
Bowling W Dunb 68 C3
Bowling W Yorks 51 F7
Bowling Bank Wrex 43 H6
Bowling Green Worcs 26 C5
Bowmanstead Cumb 56 G5
Bowmore Argyll 64 C4
Bowness-on-Solway Cumb 61 G8
Bowness-on-Windermere Cumb 56 G6
Bowsden Northumb 71 F8
Bowside Lodge Highld 93 C11
Bowston Cumb 57 G6
Bowthorpe Norf 39 E7
Box Glos 16 A5
Box Wilts 16 E5
Box End Bedford 29 D7
Boxbush Glos 26 G4
Boxford Suff 30 D6
Boxford W Berks 17 D11
Boxgrove W Sus 11 D8
Boxley Kent 20 F4
Boxmoor Herts 29 H7
Boxted Essex 30 E6
Boxted Suff 30 C5
Boxted Cross Essex 31 E7
Boxted Heath Essex 31 E7
Boxworth Cambs 29 B10
Boxworth End Cambs 29 B10
Boyden Gate Kent 21 E9
Boylestone Derbys 35 B7
Boyndie Aberds 89 B6
Boynton E Yorks 53 C7
Boysack Angus 77 C9
Boyton Corn 6 G2
Boyton Suff 31 D10
Boyton Wilts 16 H6
Boyton Cross Essex 30 H3
Boyton End Suff 30 D4
Bozeat Northants 28 C6
Braaid IoM 48 E3
Braal Castle Highld 94 D3
Brabling Green Suff 31 B9
Brabourne Kent 13 B9
Brabourne Lees Kent 13 B9
Brabster Highld 94 D5
Bracadale Highld 85 E8
Bracara Highld 79 B10
Braceborough Lincs 37 D6
Bracebridge Lincs 46 F3
Bracebridge Heath Lincs 46 F3
Bracebridge Low Fields Lincs 46 F3
Braceby Lincs 36 B6
Bracewell Lancs 50 E4
Brackenfield Derbys 45 G7
Brackenthwaite Cumb 56 B4
Brackenthwaite N Yorks 51 D8
Bracklesham W Sus 11 E7
Brackletter Highld 80 E3
Brackley Argyll 65 D8
Brackley Northants 28 E2
Brackloch Highld 92 G4
Bracknell Brack 18 E5
Braco Perth 75 G11
Bracobrae Moray 88 C5
Bracon Ash Norf 39 F7
Bracorina Highld 79 B10
Bradbourne Derbys 44 G6
Bradbury Durham 58 D4

Bradda IoM 48 F1
Bradden Northants 28 D3
Braddock Corn 4 E2
Bradeley Stoke 44 G2
Bradenham Bucks 18 B5
Bradenham Norf 38 E5
Bradenstoke Wilts 17 D7
Bradfield Essex 31 E8
Bradfield Norf 39 B8
Bradfield W Berks 18 D3
Bradfield Combust Suff 30 C5
Bradfield Green Ches E 43 G9
Bradfield Heath Essex 31 F8
Bradfield St Clare Suff 30 C6
Bradfield St George Suff 30 B6
Bradford Corn 4 D2
Bradford Derbys 44 F6
Bradford Devon 6 F3
Bradford Northumb 71 G10
Bradford W Yorks 51 F7
Bradford Abbas Dorset 8 C4
Bradford Leigh Wilts 16 E5
Bradford-on-Avon Wilts 16 E5
Bradford-on-Tone Som 7 D10
Bradford Peverell Dorset 8 E5
Brading IoW 10 F5
Bradley Derbys 44 H6
Bradley Hants 18 G3
Bradley NE Lincs 46 B6
Bradley Staffs 34 D4
Bradley W Mid 34 F5
Bradley W Yorks 51 G7
Bradley Green Worcs 26 B6
Bradley in the Moors Staffs 35 A6
Bradlow Hereford 26 E4
Bradmore Notts 36 B1
Bradmore W Mid 34 F4
Bradninch Devon 7 F9
Bradnop Staffs 44 G4
Bradpole Dorset 8 E3
Bradshaw Gtr Man 43 A10
Bradshaw W Yorks 44 A4
Bradstone Devon 4 C4
Bradwall Green Ches E 43 F10
Bradway S Yorks 45 D7
Bradwell Derbys 44 D5
Bradwell Essex 30 F5
Bradwell M Keynes 28 E5
Bradwell Norf 39 E11
Bradwell Staffs 44 H2
Bradwell Grove Oxon 27 H9
Bradwell on Sea Essex 31 H7
Bradwell Waterside Essex 30 H6
Bradworthy Devon 6 E2
Bradworthy Cross Devon 6 E2
Brae Dumfries 60 F4
Brae Highld 91 J13
Brae Highld 92 J7
Brae Shetland 96 G5
Brae of Achnahaird Highld 92 H3
Brae Roy Lodge Highld 80 D5
Braeantra Highld 87 D8
Braedownie Angus 82 F4
Braefield Highld 86 H7
Braegrum Perth 76 E3
Braehead Dumfries 55 D7
Braehead Orkney 95 D5
Braehead Orkney 95 H6
Braehead S Lanark 69 E8
Braehead S Lanark 69 G7
Braehead of Lunan Angus 77 B9
Braehoulland Shetland 96 F4
Braehungie Highld 94 G3
Braelangwell Lodge Highld 87 B8
Braemar Aberds 82 D3
Braemore Highld 86 D4
Braemore Highld 94 G2
Braes of Enzie Moray 88 C3
Braeside Invclyd 73 F11
Braeswick Orkney 95 E7
Braewick Shetland 96 H5
Brafferton Darl 58 D3
Brafferton N Yorks 51 B10
Brafield-on-the-Green Northants 28 C5
Bragar W Isles 91 C7
Bragbury End Herts 29 F9
Bragleenmore Argyll 74 E2
Braichmelyn Gwyn 41 D8
Braid Edin 69 D11
Braides Lancs 49 D4
Braidley N Yorks 50 A6
Braidwood S Lanark 69 F7
Braigo Argyll 64 B3
Brailsford Derbys 35 A8
Brainshaugh Northumb 63 C8
Braintree Essex 30 F4
Braiseworth Suff 31 A8
Braishfield Hants 10 B2
Braithwaite Cumb 56 D4
Braithwaite S Yorks 45 A10
Braithwaite W Yorks 50 E6
Braithwell S Yorks 45 C9
Bramber W Sus 11 C10
Bramcote Notts 35 B11
Bramcote Warks 35 G10
Bramdean Hants 10 B5
Bramerton Norf 39 E8
Bramfield Herts 29 G9
Bramfield Suff 31 A10
Bramford Suff 31 D8
Bramhall Gtr Man 44 D2
Bramham W Yorks 51 E10
Bramhope W Yorks 51 E8
Bramley Hants 18 F3
Bramley S Yorks 45 C8
Bramley Sur 19 G7
Bramley W Yorks 51 F8
Bramling Kent 21 F9
Brampford Speke Devon 7 G8
Brampton Cambs 29 A9
Brampton Cumb 57 D8
Brampton Cumb 61 G11
Brampton Derbys 45 E7
Brampton Hereford 25 E11
Brampton Lincs 46 E2
Brampton Norf 39 C8
Brampton S Yorks 45 B8
Brampton Suff 39 G10
Brampton Abbotts Hereford 26 F3
Brampton Ash Northants 36 G3
Brampton Bryan Hereford 25 A10
Brampton en le Morthen S Yorks 45 D8
Bramshall Staffs 35 B6
Bramshaw Hants 10 C1
Bramshill Hants 18 E4
Bramshott Hants 11 A7
Bran End Essex 30 F3
Branault Highld 79 E8
Brancaster Norf 38 A3
Brancaster Staithe Norf 38 A3
Brancepeth Durham 58 C3
Branch End Northumb 62 G6
Branchill Moray 87 F13
Brand Green Glos 26 F4
Branderburgh Moray 88 A2
Brandesburton E Yorks 53 E7
Brandeston Suff 31 B9
Brandhill Shrops 33 H10
Brandis Corner Devon 6 F3
Brandiston Norf 39 C7
Brandon Durham 58 C3
Brandon Lincs 46 H3
Brandon Northumb 62 B6
Brandon Suff 38 G3
Brandon Warks 35 H10
Brandon Bank Cambs 38 G2
Brandon Creek Norf 38 F2
Brandon Parva Norf 39 E6
Brandsby N Yorks 52 B1
Brandy Wharf Lincs 46 C4
Brane Corn 2 G3
Branksome Poole 9 E9
Branksome Park Poole 9 E9
Bransby Lincs 46 E2
Branscombe Devon 7 H10
Bransford Worcs 26 C4
Bransgore Hants 9 E10
Branshill Clack 69 A7
Bransholme Hull 53 F7
Branson's Cross Worcs 27 A7
Branston Leics 36 C4
Branston Lincs 46 F4
Branston Staffs 35 C8
Branston Booths Lincs 46 F4
Branstone IoW 10 F4
Bransty Cumb 56 E1
Brant Broughton Lincs 46 G3
Brantham Suff 31 E8
Branthwaite Cumb 56 C4
Branthwaite Cumb 56 D2
Brantingham E Yorks 52 G5
Branton Northumb 62 B6
Branton S Yorks 45 B10
Branxholm Park Borders 61 B10
Branxholme Borders 61 B10
Branxton Northumb 71 G7
Brassey Green Ches W 43 F8
Brassington Derbys 44 G6
Brasted Kent 19 F11
Brasted Chart Kent 19 F11
Brathens Aberds 83 D8
Bratoft Lincs 47 F8
Brattleby Lincs 46 D3
Bratton Telford 34 D2
Bratton Wilts 16 F6
Bratton Clovelly Devon 6 G3
Bratton Fleming Devon 6 C5
Bratton Seymour Som 8 B5
Braughing Herts 29 F10
Braunston Northants 28 B2
Braunston-in-Rutland Rutland 36 E4
Braunstone Town Leicester 36 E1
Braunton Devon 6 C3
Brawby N Yorks 52 B3
Brawl Highld 93 C11
Brawlbin Highld 94 E2
Bray Windsor 18 D6
Bray Shop Corn 4 D4
Bray Wick Windsor 18 D5
Braybrooke Northants 36 G3
Braye Ald 11
Brayford Devon 6 C5
Braystones Cumb 56 F2
Braythorn N Yorks 51 E8
Brayton N Yorks 52 F2
Brazacott Corn 6 G1
Breach Kent 20 E5
Breachacha Castle Argyll 78 F4
Breachwood Green Herts 29 F8
Breacleit W Isles 90 D6
Breaden Heath Shrops 33 B10
Breadsall Derbys 35 B9
Breadstone Glos 16 A4
Breage Corn 2 G5
Breakachy Highld 86 G7
Bream Glos 26 H3
Breamore Hants 9 C10
Brean Som 15 F8
Breanais W Isles 90 E4
Brearton N Yorks 51 C9
Breascleit W Isles 90 D7
Breaston Derbys 35 B10
Brechfa Carms 23 C10
Brechin Angus 77 A8
Breck of Cruan Orkney 95 G4
Breckan Orkney 95 H3
Breckrey Highld 85 B10
Brecon = Aberhonddu Powys 25 F7
Bredbury Gtr Man 44 C3
Brede E Sus 13 E7
Bredenbury Hereford 26 C3
Bredfield Suff 31 C9
Bredgar Kent 20 E5
Bredhurst Kent 20 E4
Bredicot Worcs 26 C6
Bredon Worcs 26 E6
Bredon's Norton Worcs 26 E6
Bredwardine Hereford 25 D10
Breedon on the Hill Leics 35 C10
Breibhig W Isles 84 J1
Breibhig W Isles 91 D9
Breich W Loth 69 D8
Breightmet Gtr Man 43 B10
Breighton E Yorks 52 F3
Breinton Hereford 25 E11
Breinton Common Hereford 25 D11
Breiwick Shetland 96 J6
Bremhill Wilts 16 D6
Bremirehoull Shetland 96 L6
Brenchley Kent 12 B5
Brendon Devon 7 B6
Brenkley T&W 63 F8
Brent Eleigh Suff 30 D6
Brent Knoll Som 15 F9
Brent Pelham Herts 29 E11
Brentford London 19 D8
Brentingby Leics 36 D3
Brentwood Essex 20 B2
Brenzett Kent 13 D9
Brereton Staffs 35 D6
Brereton Green Ches E 43 F10
Brereton Heath Ches E 44 F2
Bressingham Norf 39 G6
Bretby Derbys 35 C8
Bretford Warks 35 H10
Bretforton Worcs 27 D7
Bretherdale Head Cumb 57 F7
Bretherton Lancs 49 G4
Brettabister Shetland 96 H6
Brettenham Norf 38 G5
Brettenham Suff 30 C6
Bretton Derbys 44 E6
Bretton Flint 42 F6
Brewer Street Sur 19 F10
Brewlands Bridge Angus 76 A4
Brewood Staffs 34 E4
Briach Moray 87 F13
Briants Puddle Dorset 9 E7
Brick End Essex 30 F2
Brickendon Herts 29 H10
Bricket Wood Herts 19 A8
Bricklehampton Worcs 26 D6
Bride IoM 48 B4
Bridekirk Cumb 56 C3
Bridell Pembs 22 B6
Bridestowe Devon 4 C6
Brideswell Aberds 88 E5
Bridford Devon 5 C9
Bridfordmills Devon 5 C9
Bridge Kent 21 F8
Bridge End Lincs 37 B7
Bridge Green Essex 29 E11
Bridge Hewick N Yorks 51 B9
Bridge of Alford Aberds 83 B7
Bridge of Allan Stirling 75 H10
Bridge of Avon Moray 88 E1
Bridge of Awe Argyll 74 E3
Bridge of Balgie Perth 75 C8
Bridge of Cally Perth 76 B4
Bridge of Canny Aberds 83 D8
Bridge of Craigisla Angus 76 B5
Bridge of Dee Dumfries 55 D10
Bridge of Don Aberdeen 83 B11
Bridge of Dun Angus 77 B9
Bridge of Dye Aberds 83 E8
Bridge of Earn Perth 76 F4
Bridge of Ericht Perth 75 B8
Bridge of Feugh Aberds 83 D9
Bridge of Forss Highld 93 C13
Bridge of Gairn Aberds 82 D5
Bridge of Gaur Perth 75 B8
Bridge of Muchalls Aberds 83 D10
Bridge of Oich Highld 80 C5
Bridge of Orchy Argyll 74 D5
Bridge of Waith Orkney 95 G3
Bridge of Walls Shetland 96 H4
Bridge of Weir Renfs 68 D2
Bridge Sollers Hereford 25 D11
Bridge Street Suff 30 D5
Bridge Trafford Ches W 43 E7
Bridge Yate S Glos 16 D3
Bridgefoot Angus 76 D6
Bridgefoot Cumb 56 D2
Bridgehampton Som 8 B4
Bridgehill Durham 58 A1
Bridgemary Hants 10 D4
Bridgemont Derbys 44 D4
Bridgend Aberds 83 B7
Bridgend Aberds 88 E5
Bridgend Angus 83 G7
Bridgend Argyll 64 B4
Bridgend Argyll 65 E8
Bridgend Argyll 73 D7
Bridgend = Pen-y-bont ar Ogwr Bridgend 14 D5
Bridgend Cumb 56 E5
Bridgend Fife 76 F6
Bridgend Moray 88 E3
Bridgend N Lanark 68 C5
Bridgend Pembs 22 B6
Bridgend W Loth 69 C9
Bridgend of Lintrathen Angus 76 B5
Bridgerule Devon 6 F1
Bridges Shrops 33 F9
Bridgeton Glasgow 68 D5
Bridgetown Corn 4 C4
Bridgetown Som 7 C8
Bridgham Norf 38 G5
Bridgnorth Shrops 34 F3
Bridgtown Staffs 34 E5
Bridgwater Som 15 H8
Bridlington E Yorks 53 C7
Bridport Dorset 8 E3
Bridstow Hereford 26 F2
Brierfield Lancs 50 F4
Brierley Glos 26 G3
Brierley Hereford 25 C11
Brierley S Yorks 45 A8
Brierley Hill W Mid 34 G5
Briery Hill Bl Gwent 25 H8
Brig o'Turk Stirling 75 G8
Brigg N Lincs 46 B4
Briggswath N Yorks 59 F9
Brigham Cumb 56 C2
Brigham E Yorks 53 D6
Brighouse W Yorks 51 G7
Brighstone IoW 10 F3
Brightgate Derbys 44 G6
Brighthampton Oxon 17 A10
Brightling E Sus 12 D5
Brightlingsea Essex 31 G7
Brighton Brighton 12 F2
Brighton Corn 3 D8
Brighton Hill Hants 18 G3
Brightons Falk 69 C8
Brightwalton W Berks 17 D11
Brightwell Suff 31 D9
Brightwell Baldwin Oxon 18 B3
Brightwell cum Sotwell Oxon 18 B2
Brignall Durham 58 E1
Brigsley NE Lincs 46 B6
Brigsteer Cumb 57 H6
Brigstock Northants 36 G5
Brill Bucks 28 G3
Brilley Hereford 25 D9
Brimaston Pembs 22 D4
Brimfield Hereford 26 B2
Brimington Derbys 45 E8
Brimley Devon 5 D8
Brimpsfield Glos 26 G6
Brimpton W Berks 18 E2
Brims Orkney 95 K3
Brimscombe Glos 16 A5
Brimstage Mers 42 D6
Brinacory Highld 79 B10
Brind E Yorks 52 F3
Brindister Shetland 96 H4
Brindister Shetland 96 K6
Brindle Lancs 50 G2
Brindley Ford Stoke 44 G2
Brineton Staffs 34 D4
Bringhurst Leics 36 F4
Brington Cambs 37 H6
Brinian Orkney 95 F5
Briningham Norf 38 B6
Brinkhill Lincs 47 E7
Brinkley Cambs 30 C3
Brinklow Warks 35 H10
Brinkworth Wilts 17 C7
Brinmore Highld 81 A8
Brinscall Lancs 50 G2
Brinsea N Som 15 E10
Brinsley Notts 45 H8
Brinsop Hereford 25 D11
Brinsworth S Yorks 45 D8
Brinton Norf 38 B6
Brisco Cumb 56 A6
Brisley Norf 38 C5
Brislington Bristol 16 D3
Bristol Bristol 16 D2
Briston Norf 39 B6
Britannia Lancs 50 G4
Britford Wilts 9 B10
Brithdir Gwyn 32 D3
British Legion Village Kent 20 F4
Briton Ferry Neath 14 B3
Britwell Salome Oxon 18 B3
Brixham Torbay 5 F10
Brixton Devon 5 F6
Brixton London 19 D10
Brixton Deverill Wilts 16 H5
Brixworth Northants 28 A4
Brize Norton Oxon 27 H10
Broad Blunsdon Swindon 17 B8
Broad Campden Glos 27 E8
Broad Chalke Wilts 9 B9
Broad Green C Beds 28 D6
Broad Green Essex 30 F5
Broad Green Worcs 26 C4
Broad Haven Pembs 22 E3
Broad Heath Worcs 26 B3
Broad Hill Cambs 38 H1
Broad Hinton Wilts 17 D8
Broad Laying Hants 17 E11
Broad Marston Worcs 27 D8
Broad Oak Carms 23 D10
Broad Oak Cumb 56 G3
Broad Oak Dorset 8 E3
Broad Oak Dorset 9 C6
Broad Oak E Sus 12 D5
Broad Oak E Sus 13 E7
Broad Oak Hereford 25 F11
Broad Oak Mers 43 C8
Broad Street Kent 20 F5
Broad Street Green Essex 30 H5
Broad Town Wilts 17 D7
Broadbottom Gtr Man 44 C3
Broadbridge W Sus 11 D7
Broadbridge Heath W Sus 11 A10
Broadclyst Devon 7 G8
Broadfield Gtr Man 44 A2
Broadfield Lancs 49 G5
Broadfield Pembs 22 F6
Broadfield W Sus 12 C1
Broadford Highld 85 F11
Broadford Bridge W Sus 11 B9
Broadhaugh Borders 61 C10
Broadhaven Highld 94 E5
Broadheath Gtr Man 43 D10
Broadhembury Devon 7 F10
Broadhempston Devon 5 E9
Broadholme Derbys 45 H7
Broadholme Lincs 46 E2
Broadland Row E Sus 13 E7
Broadlay Carms 23 F8
Broadley Lancs 50 H4
Broadley Moray 88 B3
Broadley Common Essex 29 H11
Broadmayne Dorset 8 F6
Broadmeadows Borders 70 G3
Broadmere Hants 18 G3
Broadmoor Pembs 22 F5
Broadoak Kent 21 E8
Broadrashes Moray 88 C4
Broadsea Aberds 89 B9
Broadstairs Kent 21 E10
Broadstone Poole 9 E9
Broadstone Shrops 33 G11
Broadtown Lane Wilts 17 D7
Broadwas Worcs 26 C4
Broadwater Herts 29 F9
Broadwater W Sus 11 D10
Broadway Carms 23 F7
Broadway Pembs 22 E3
Broadway Som 8 C2
Broadway Suff 39 H9
Broadway Worcs 27 E7
Broadwell Glos 26 G2
Broadwell Glos 27 F9
Broadwell Oxon 17 A9
Broadwell Warks 27 B11
Broadwell House Northumb 57 A11
Broadwey Dorset 8 F5
Broadwindsor Dorset 8 D3
Broadwood Kelly Devon 6 F5
Broadwoodwidger Devon 4 C5
Brobury Hereford 25 D10
Brochel Highld 85 D10
Brochloch Dumfries 67 G8
Brochroy Argyll 74 D3
Brockamin Worcs 26 C4
Brockbridge Hants 10 C5
Brockdam Northumb 63 A7
Brockdish Norf 39 H8
Brockenhurst Hants 10 D2
Brocketsbrae S Lanark 69 G7
Brockford Street Suff 31 B8
Brockhall Northants 28 B3
Brockham Sur 19 G8
Brockhampton Glos 27 F7
Brockhampton Hereford 26 E2
Brockholes W Yorks 44 A5
Brockhurst Derbys 45 F7
Brockhurst Hants 10 D5
Brocklebank Cumb 56 B5
Brocklesby Lincs 46 A5
Brockley N Som 15 E10
Brockley Green Suff 30 C5
Brockleymoor Cumb 57 C6
Brockton Shrops 33 E9
Brockton Shrops 33 G9
Brockton Shrops 34 E3
Brockton Shrops 34 F1
Brockton Telford 34 D3
Brockweir Glos 15 A11
Brockwood Hants 10 B5
Brockworth Glos 26 G5
Brocton Staffs 34 D5
Brodick N Ayrs 66 C3
Brodsworth S Yorks 45 B9
Brogaig Highld 85 B9
Brogborough C Beds 28 E6
Broken Cross Ches E 44 E2
Broken Cross Ches W 43 E9
Brokenborough Wilts 16 C6
Bromborough Mers 42 D6
Brome Suff 39 H7
Brome Street Suff 39 H7
Bromeswell Suff 31 C10
Bromfield Cumb 56 B3
Bromfield Shrops 33 H10
Bromham Bedford 29 C7
Bromham Wilts 16 E6
Bromley London 19 E11
Bromley W Mid 34 G5
Bromley Common London 19 E11
Bromley Green Kent 13 C8
Brompton Medway 20 E4
Brompton N Yorks 52 A5
Brompton N Yorks 58 G4
Brompton-on-Swale N Yorks 58 G3
Brompton Ralph Som 7 C9
Brompton Regis Som 7 C8
Bromsash Hereford 26 F3
Bromsberrow Hth. Glos 26 E4
Bromsgrove Worcs 26 A6
Bromyard Hereford 26 C3
Bromyard Downs Hereford 26 C3
Bronaber Gwyn 41 G9
Brongest Ceredig 23 B8
Bronington Wrex 33 B10
Bronllys Powys 25 E8
Bronnant Ceredig 24 B3
Bronwydd Arms Carms 23 D9
Bronydd Powys 25 D9
Bronygarth Shrops 33 B8
Brook Carms 23 F7
Brook Hants 10 B2
Brook Hants 10 C1
Brook IoW 10 F2
Brook Kent 13 B9
Brook Sur 18 H6
Brook Sur 19 G7
Brook End Bedford 29 B7
Brook Hill Hants 10 C1
Brook Street Kent 13 C8
Brook Street Kent 20 G2
Brook Street W Sus 12 D2
Brooke Norf 39 F8
Brooke Rutland 36 E4
Brookenby Lincs 46 C6
Brookend Glos 16 B2
Brookfield Renfs 68 D3
Brookhouse Lancs 49 C5
Brookhouse Green Ches E 44 F2
Brookland Kent 13 D8
Brooklands Dumfries 60 F4
Brooklands Gtr Man 43 C10
Brooklands Shrops 33 A11
Brookmans Park Herts 19 A9
Brooks Powys 33 F7
Brooks Green W Sus 11 B10
Brookthorpe Glos 26 G5
Brookville Norf 38 F3
Brookwood Sur 18 F6
Broom C Beds 29 D8
Broom S Yorks 45 C8
Broom Warks 27 C7
Broom Worcs 34 H5
Broom Green Norf 38 C5
Broom Hill Dorset 9 D9
Broome Norf 39 F9
Broome Shrops 33 G10
Broome Park Northumb 63 B7
Broomedge Warr 43 D10
Broomer's Corner W Sus 11 B10
Broomfield Aberds 89 E9
Broomfield Essex 30 G4
Broomfield Kent 20 F5
Broomfield Kent 21 E8
Broomfield Som 7 C11
Broomfleet E Yorks 52 G4
Broomhall Ches E 43 H9
Broomhall Windsor 18 E6
Broomhaugh Northumb 62 G6
Broomhill Norf 38 E2
Broomhill Northumb 63 C8
Broomhill S Yorks 45 B8
Broomholm Norf 39 B9
Broomley Northumb 62 G6
Broompark Durham 58 B3
Broom's Green Glos 26 E4
Broomy Lodge Hants 9 C11
Brora Highld 93 J12
Broseley Shrops 34 E2
Brotherhouse Bar Lincs 37 D8
Brotherstone Borders 70 G5
Brothertoft Lincs 46 H6
Brotherton N Yorks 51 G10
Brotton Redcar 59 E7
Broubster Highld 93 C13
Brough Cumb 57 E9
Brough Derbys 44 D5
Brough E Yorks 52 G5
Brough Highld 94 C4
Brough Notts 46 G2
Brough Orkney 95 G4
Brough Shetland 96 F7
Brough Shetland 96 F6
Brough Shetland 96 G7
Brough Shetland 96 H6
Brough Shetland 96 J7
Brough Lodge Shetland 96 D7
Brough Sowerby Cumb 57 E9
Broughall Shrops 34 A1
Broughton Borders 69 G10
Broughton Cambs 37 H8
Broughton Flint 42 F6
Broughton Hants 10 A2
Broughton Lancs 49 F5
Broughton M Keynes 28 D5
Broughton N Lincs 46 B3
Broughton N Yorks 50 D5
Broughton N Yorks 52 B3
Broughton Northants 36 H4
Broughton Orkney 95 D5
Broughton Oxon 27 E11
Broughton V Glam 14 D5
Broughton Astley Leics 35 F11
Broughton Beck Cumb 49 A2
Broughton Common Wilts 16 E5
Broughton Gifford Wilts 16 E5
Broughton Hackett Worcs 26 C6
Broughton in Furness Cumb 56 H4
Broughton Mills Cumb 56 G4
Broughton Moor Cumb 56 C2
Broughton Park Gtr Man 44 B2
Broughton Poggs Oxon 17 A9
Broughtown Orkney 95 D7
Broughty Ferry Dundee 77 D7
Browhouses Dumfries 61 G8
Browland Shetland 96 H4
Brown Candover Hants 18 H2
Brown Edge Lancs 42 A6
Brown Edge Staffs 44 G3
Brown Heath Ches W 43 F7
Brownhill Aberds 89 D8
Brownhill Aberds 89 D6
Brownhill Blackburn 50 F2
Brownhill Shrops 33 C10
Brownhills Fife 77 F8
Brownhills W Mid 34 E6
Brownlow Ches E 44 F2
Brownlow Heath Ches E 44 F2
Brownmuir Aberds 83 F9
Brown's End Glos 26 E4
Brownshill Glos 16 A5
Brownston Devon 5 F7
Brownyside Northumb 63 A7
Broxa N Yorks 59 G10
Broxbourne Herts 29 H10
Broxburn E Loth 70 C5
Broxburn W Loth 69 C9
Broxholme Lincs 46 E3
Broxted Essex 30 F2
Broxton Ches W 43 G7
Broxwood Hereford 25 C10
Broyle Side E Sus 12 E3
Brù W Isles 91 C8
Bruairnis W Isles 84 H2
Bruan Highld 94 G5
Bruar Lodge Perth 81 F10
Brucehill W Dunb 68 C2
Bruera Ches W 43 F7
Bruern Abbey Oxon 27 F9
Bruichladdich Argyll 64 B3
Bruisyard Suff 31 B10
Brumby N Lincs 46 B2
Brund Staffs 44 F5
Brundall Norf 39 E9
Brundish Suff 31 B9
Brundish Street Suff 31 A9
Brunery Highld 79 D10
Brunshaw Lancs 50 F4
Brunswick Village T&W 63 F8
Bruntcliffe W Yorks 51 G8
Bruntingthorpe Leics 36 F2
Brunton Fife 76 E6
Brunton Northumb 63 A8
Brunton Wilts 17 F9
Brushford Devon 6 F5
Brushford Som 7 D8
Bruton Som 8 A5
Bryanston Dorset 9 D7
Brydekirk Dumfries 61 F7
Bryher Scilly 2 C2
Brymbo Wrex 42 G5
Brympton Som 8 C4
Bryn Carms 23 F10
Bryn Gtr Man 43 B8
Bryn Neath 14 B4
Bryn Shrops 33 G8
Bryn-coch Neath 14 B3
Bryn Du Anglesey 40 C5
Bryn Gates Gtr Man 43 B8
Bryn-glas Conwy 41 D10
Bryn Golau Rhondda 14 C5
Bryn-Iwan Carms 23 C8
Bryn-mawr Gwyn 40 G4
Bryn-nantllech Conwy 42 F2
Bryn-penarth Powys 33 E7
Bryn Rhyd-yr-Arian Conwy 42 F2
Bryn Saith Marchog Denb 42 G3
Bryn Sion Gwyn 32 D4
Bryn-y-gwenin Mon 25 G10
Bryn-y-maen Conwy 41 C10
Bryn-yr-eryr Gwyn 40 F6
Brynamman Carms 24 G4
Brynberian Pembs 22 C6
Brynbryddan Neath 14 B3
Brynbuga = Usk Mon 15 A9
Bryncae Rhondda 14 C5
Bryncethin Bridgend 14 C5
Bryncir Gwyn 40 F6
Bryncroes Gwyn 40 G4
Bryncrug Gwyn 32 E2
Bryneglwys Denb 42 H4
Brynford Flint 42 E4
Bryngwran Anglesey 40 C5
Bryngwyn Ceredig 23 B7
Bryngwyn Mon 25 H10
Bryngwyn Powys 25 D8
Brynhenllan Pembs 22 C5
Brynhoffnant Ceredig 23 A8
Brynithel Bl Gwent 15 A8
Brynmawr Bl Gwent 25 G8
Brynmenyn Bridgend 14 C5
Brynmill Swansea 14 B2
Brynna Rhondda 14 C5
Brynrefail Anglesey 40 B6
Brynrefail Gwyn 41 D7
Brynsadler Rhondda 14 C6
Brynsiencyn Anglesey 40 D6
Brynteg Anglesey 40 B6
Brynteg Ceredig 23 B9
Buaile nam Bodach W Isles 84 H2
Bualintur Highld 85 F9
Buarthmeini Gwyn 41 G10
Bubbenhall Warks 27 A10
Bubwith E Yorks 52 F3
Buccleuch Borders 61 B9
Buchanhaven Aberds 89 D11
Buchanty Perth 76 E2
Buchlyvie Stirling 68 A4
Buckabank Cumb 56 B5
Buckden Cambs 29 B8
Buckden N Yorks 50 B5
Buckenham Norf 39 E9
Buckerell Devon 7 F10
Buckfast Devon 5 E8
Buckfastleigh Devon 5 E8
Buckhaven Fife 76 H6
Buckholm Borders 70 G3
Buckholt Mon 26 G2
Buckhorn Weston Dorset 9 B6
Buckhurst Hill Essex 19 B11
Buckie Moray 88 B4
Buckies Highld 94 D3
Buckingham Bucks 28 E3
Buckland Bucks 28 G5
Buckland Devon 5 G7
Buckland Glos 27 E7
Buckland Hants 10 E2
Buckland Herts 29 E10
Buckland Kent 21 G10
Buckland Oxon 17 B10
Buckland Sur 19 F9
Buckland Brewer Devon 6 D3
Buckland Common Bucks 28 H6
Buckland Dinham Som 16 F4
Buckland Filleigh Devon 6 F3
Buckland in the Moor Devon 5 D8
Buckland Monachorum Devon 4 E5
Buckland Newton Dorset 8 D5
Buckland St Mary Som 8 C1
Bucklebury W Berks 18 D2
Bucklegate Lincs 37 B9
Bucklerheads Angus 77 D7
Bucklers Hard Hants 10 E3
Bucklesham Suff 31 D9
Buckley = Bwcle Flint 42 F5
Bucklow Hill Ches E 43 D10
Buckminster Leics 36 C4
Bucknall Lincs 46 F5
Bucknall Stoke 44 H3
Bucknell Oxon 28 F2
Bucknell Shrops 25 A10
Buckpool Moray 88 B4
Buck's Cross Devon 6 D2
Bucks Green W Sus 11 A9
Bucks Horn Oak Hants 18 G5
Buck's Mills Devon 6 D2
Bucksburn Aberdeen 83 C10
Buckskin Hants 18 F3
Buckton E Yorks 53 B7
Buckton Hereford 25 A10
Buckton Northumb 71 G9
Buckworth Cambs 37 H7
Budbrooke Warks 27 B9
Budby Notts 45 F10
Budd's Titson Corn 4 A3
Bude Corn 6 F1
Budlake Devon 7 G8
Budle Northumb 71 G10
Budleigh Salterton Devon 7 H9
Budock Water Corn 3 F6
Buerton Ches E 34 A2
Buffler's Holt Bucks 28 E3
Bugbrooke Northants 28 C3
Buglawton Ches E 44 F2
Bugle Corn 3 D9
Bugley Wilts 16 G5
Bugthorpe E Yorks 52 D3
Buildwas Shrops 34 E2
Builth Road Powys 25 C7
Builth Wells = Llanfair-ym-Muallt Powys 25 C7
Buirgh W Isles 90 H5
Bulby Lincs 37 C6
Bulcote Notts 36 A2
Buldoo Highld 93 C12
Bulford Wilts 17 G8
Bulford Camp Wilts 17 G8
Bulkeley Ches E 43 G8
Bulkington Warks 35 G9
Bulkington Wilts 16 F6
Bulkworthy Devon 6 E2
Bull Hill Hants 10 E2
Bullamoor N Yorks 58 G4
Bullbridge Derbys 45 G7
Bullbrook Brack 18 E5
Bulley Glos 26 G4
Bullgill Cumb 56 C2
Bullington Hants 17 G11
Bullington Lincs 46 E4
Bull's Green Herts 29 G9
Bullwood Argyll 73 F10
Bulmer Essex 30 D5
Bulmer N Yorks 52 C2
Bulmer Tye Essex 30 E5
Bulphan Thurrock 20 C3
Bulverhythe E Sus 13 F6
Bulwark Aberds 89 D9
Bulwell Nottingham 45 H9
Bulwick Northants 36 F5
Bumble's Green Essex 29 H11
Bun Abhainn Eadarra W Isles 90 G6
Bun a'Mhuillin W Isles 84 G2
Bun Loyne Highld 80 C4
Bunacaimb Highld 79 C9
Bunarkaig Highld 80 E3
Bunbury Ches E 43 G8
Bunbury Heath Ches E 43 G8
Bunchrew Highld 87 G9
Bundalloch Highld 85 F13
Buness Shetland 96 C8
Bunessan Argyll 78 J6
Bungay Suff 39 G9
Bunker's Hill Lincs 46 E3
Bunker's Hill Lincs 46 G6
Bunkers Hill Oxon 27 G11
Bunloit Highld 81 A7
Bunnahabhain Argyll 64 A5
Bunny Notts 36 C1
Buntait Highld 86 H6
Buntingford Herts 29 F10
Bunwell Norf 39 F7
Burbage Derbys 44 E4
Burbage Leics 35 F10
Burbage Wilts 17 E9
Burchett's Green Windsor 18 C5
Burcombe Wilts 9 A9
Burcot Oxon 18 B2
Burcott Bucks 28 F5
Burdon T&W 58 A4
Bures Suff 30 E6
Bures Green Suff 30 E6
Burford Ches E 43 G9
Burford Oxon 27 G9
Burford Shrops 26 B2
Burg Argyll 78 G6
Burgar Orkney 95 F4
Burgate Hants 9 C10
Burgate Suff 39 H6
Burgess Hill W Sus 12 E2
Burgh Suff 31 C9
Burgh by Sands Cumb 61 H9
Burgh Castle Norf 39 E10
Burgh Heath Sur 19 F9
Burgh le Marsh Lincs 47 F9
Burgh Muir Aberds 83 A9
Burgh next Aylsham Norf 39 C8
Burgh on Bain Lincs 46 D6
Burgh St Margaret Norf 39 D10
Burgh St Peter Norf 39 F10
Burghclere Hants 17 E11
Burghead Moray 87 E14
Burghfield W Berks 18 E3
Burghfield Common W Berks 18 E3
Burghfield Hill W Berks 18 E3
Burghill Hereford 25 D11
Burghwallis S Yorks 45 A9
Burham Kent 20 E4
Buriton Hants 10 B6
Burland Ches E 43 G9
Burlawn Corn 3 B8
Burleigh Brack 18 E5
Burlescombe Devon 7 E9
Burleston Dorset 9 E6
Burley Hants 9 D11
Burley Rutland 36 D4
Burley W Yorks 51 F8
Burley Gate Hereford 26 D2
Burley in Wharfedale W Yorks 51 E7
Burley Lodge Hants 9 D11
Burley Street Hants 9 D11
Burleydam Ches E 34 A2
Burlingjobb Powys 25 C9
Burlow E Sus 12 E4
Burlton Shrops 33 C10
Burmarsh Kent 13 C9
Burmington Warks 27 E9
Burn N Yorks 52 G1
Burn of Cambus Stirling 75 G10
Burnaston Derbys 35 B8
Burnbank S Lanark 68 E6
Burnby E Yorks 52 E4
Burncross S Yorks 45 C7
Burneside Cumb 57 G7
Burness Orkney 95 D7
Burneston N Yorks 58 H4
Burnett Bath 16 E3
Burnfoot Borders 61 B11
Burnfoot Borders 61 B10
Burnfoot E Ayrs 67 F7
Burnfoot Perth 76 G2
Burnham Bucks 18 C6
Burnham N Lincs 53 H6
Burnham Deepdale Norf 38 A4
Burnham Green Herts 29 G9
Burnham Market Norf 38 A4
Burnham Norton Norf 38 A4
Burnham-on-Crouch Essex 20 B6
Burnham-on-Sea Som 15 G9
Burnham Overy Staithe Norf 38 A4
Burnham Overy Town Norf 38 A4
Burnham Thorpe Norf 38 A4
Burnhead Dumfries 60 D4
Burnhead S Ayrs 66 F5
Burnhervie Aberds 83 B9
Burnhill Green Staffs 34 E3
Burnhope Durham 58 B2
Burnhouse N Ayrs 67 A6
Burniston N Yorks 59 G11
Burnlee W Yorks 44 B5
Burnley Lancs 50 F4
Burnley Lane Lancs 50 F4
Burnmouth Borders 71 D8
Burnopfield Durham 63 H7
Burnsall N Yorks 50 C6
Burnside Angus 77 B8
Burnside E Ayrs 67 E8
Burnside Fife 76 G4
Burnside S Lanark 68 D5
Burnside Shetland 96 F4
Burnside W Loth 69 C9
Burnside of Duntrune Angus 77 D7
Burnswark Dumfries 61 F7
Burnt Heath Derbys 44 E6
Burnt Houses Durham 58 D2
Burnt Yates N Yorks 51 C8
Burntcommon Sur 19 F7
Burnthouse Corn 3 F6
Burntisland Fife 69 B11
Burnton E Ayrs 67 F7
Burntwood Staffs 35 E6
Burnwynd Edin 69 D10
Burpham Sur 19 F7
Burpham W Sus 11 D9
Burradon Northumb 62 C5
Burradon T&W 63 F8
Burrafirth Shetland 96 B8
Burraland Shetland 96 F5
Burraland Shetland 96 J4
Burras Corn 2 F5
Burravoe Shetland 96 F7
Burravoe Shetland 96 G5
Burray Village Orkney 95 J5
Burrells Cumb 57 E8
Burrelton Perth 76 D5
Burridge Devon 6 C4
Burridge Hants 10 C4
Burrill N Yorks 58 H3
Burringham N Lincs 46 B2
Burrington Devon 6 E5
Burrington Hereford 25 A11
Burrington N Som 15 F10
Burrough Green Cambs 30 C3
Burrough on the Hill Leics 36 D3
Burrow-bridge Som 8 B2
Burrowhill Sur 18 E6
Burry Swansea 23 G9
Burry Green Swansea 23 G
Burry Port = Porth Tywyn Carms 23 F
Burscough Lancs 43 A
Burscough Bridge Lancs 43 A
Bursea E Yorks 52 F
Burshill E Yorks 53 E
Bursledon Hants 10 D
Burslem Stoke 44 H
Burstall Suff 31 D
Burstock Dorset 8 D
Burston Norf 39 G
Burston Staffs 34 B
Burstow Sur 12 B
Burstwick E Yorks 53 G
Burtersett N Yorks 57 H1
Burtle Som 15 G
Burton Ches W 42 E
Burton Ches W 43 F
Burton Dorset 9 E1
Burton Lincs 46 E
Burton Northumb 71 G1
Burton Pembs 22 F
Burton Som 7 B
Burton Wilts 16 D
Burton Agnes E Yorks 53 C
Burton Bradstock Dorset 8 F
Burton Dassett Warks 27 C1
Burton Fleming E Yorks 53 B
Burton Green W Mid 35 H
Burton Green Wrex 42 G
Burton Hastings Warks 35 F1
Burton-in-Kendal Cumb 49 B
Burton in Lonsdale N Yorks 50 B
Burton Joyce Notts 36 A
Burton Latimer Northants 28 A
Burton Lazars Leics 36 D
Burton-le-Coggles Lincs 36 C
Burton Leonard N Yorks 51 C
Burton on the Wolds Leics 36 C
Burton Overy Leics 36 F
Burton Pedwardine Lincs 37 A
Burton Pidsea E Yorks 53 F
Burton Salmon N Yorks 51 G1
Burton Stather N Lincs 52 H
Burton upon Stather N Lincs 52 H
Burton upon Trent Staffs 35 C
Burtonwood Warr 43 C
Burwardsley Ches W 43 G
Burwarton Shrops 34 G
Burwash E Sus 12 D
Burwash Common E Sus 12 D
Burwash Weald E Sus 12 D
Burwell Cambs 30 B
Burwell Lincs 47 E
Burwen Anglesey 40 A
Burwick Orkney 95 K
Bury Cambs 37 G
Bury Gtr Man 44 A
Bury Som 7 D
Bury W Sus 11 C
Bury Green Herts 29 F1
Bury St Edmunds Suff 30 B
Burythorpe N Yorks 52 C
Busby E Renf 68 E
Buscot Oxon 17 B
Bush Bank Hereford 25 C
Bush Crathie Aberds 82 D
Bush Green Norf 39 G
Bushbury W Mid 34 E
Bushby Leics 36 E
Bushey Herts 19 B
Bushey Heath Herts 19 B
Bushley Worcs 26 E
Bushton Wilts 17 D
Buslingthorpe Lincs 46 D
Busta Shetland 96 G
Butcher's Cross E Sus 12 D
Butcombe N Som 15 E1
Butetown Cardiff 15 D
Butleigh Som 8 A
Butleigh Wootton Som 15 H1
Butler's Cross Bucks 28 H
Butler's End Warks 35 G
Butlers Marston Warks 27 C1
Butley Suff 31 C1
Butley High Corner Suff 31 D
Butt Green Ches E 43 G
Butterburn Cumb 62 F
Buttercrambe N Yorks 52 D
Butterknowle Durham 58 D
Butterleigh Devon 7 F
Buttermere Cumb 56 E
Buttermere Wilts 17 E1
Buttershaw W Yorks 51 G
Butterstone Perth 76 C
Butterton Staffs 44 G
Butterwick Durham 58 D
Butterwick Lincs 37 A
Butterwick N Yorks 52 B
Butterwick N Yorks 52 B
Buttington Powys 33 E
Buttonoak Worcs 34 H
Butt's Green Hants 10 B
Buttsash Hants 10 D
Buxhall Suff 31 C
Buxhall Fen Street Suff 31 C
Buxley Borders 71 E
Buxted E Sus 12 D
Buxton Derbys 44 E
Buxton Norf 39 C
Buxworth Derbys 44 D
Bwcle = Buckley Flint 42 F
Bwlch Powys 25 F
Bwlch-Llan Ceredig 23 A1
Bwlch-y-cibau Powys 33 D
Bwlch-y-fadfa Ceredig 23 B
Bwlch-y-ffridd Powys 33 F
Bwlch-y-sarnau Powys 25 A
Bwlchgwyn Wrex 42 G
Bwlchnewydd Carms 23 D
Bwlchtocyn Gwyn 40 H

Croes-y-mwyalch Torf 15 B9
Croeserw Neath 14 B4
Croesor Gwyn 41 F8
Croesyceiliog Carms 23 E9
Croesyceiliog Torf 15 B9
Croesywaun Gwyn 41 E7
Croft Leics 35 F11
Croft Lincs 47 F9
Croft Pembs 22 B6
Croft Warr 43 C9
Croft-on-Tees N Yorks 58 F3
Croftamie Stirling 68 B3
Croftmalloch W Loth 69 D8
Crofton W Yorks 51 H9
Crofton Wilts 17 E9
Crofts of Benachielt Highld 94 G3
Crofts of Haddo Aberds 89 E8
Crofts of Inverthernie Aberds 89 D7
Crofts of Meikle Ardo Aberds 89 D8
Crofty Swansea 23 G10
Croggan Argyll 79 J10
Croglin Cumb 57 B7
Croich Highld 86 B7
Crois Dughaill W Isles 84 F2
Cromarty Highld 87 E10
Cromblet Aberds 89 E7
Cromdale Highld 82 A2
Cromer Herts 29 F9
Cromer Norf 39 A8
Cromford Derbys 44 G6
Cromhall S Glos 16 B3
Cromhall Common S Glos 16 C3
Cromor W Isles 91 E9
Cromra Highld 81 D7
Cromwell Notts 45 F11
Cronberry E Ayrs 67 D9
Crondall Hants 18 G4
Cronk-y-Voddy IoM 48 D3
Cronton Mers 43 D7
Crook Cumb 56 G6
Crook Durham 58 C2
Crook of Devon Perth 76 G3
Crookedholm E Ayrs 67 C7
Crookes S Yorks 45 D7
Crookham Northumb 71 G8
Crookham W Berks 18 E2
Crookham Village Hants 18 F4
Crookhaugh Borders 69 H10
Crookhouse Borders 70 H6
Crooklands Cumb 49 A5
Cropredy Oxon 27 D11
Cropston Leics 36 D1
Cropthorne Worcs 26 D6
Cropton N Yorks 59 H8
Cropwell Bishop Notts 36 B2
Cropwell Butler Notts 36 B2
Cros W Isles 91 A10
Crosbost W Isles 91 E8
Crosby Cumb 56 C2
Crosby IoM 48 E3
Crosby N Lincs 46 A2
Crosby Garrett Cumb 57 F9
Crosby Ravensworth Cumb 57 E8
Crosby Villa Cumb 56 C2
Croscombe Som 16 G2
Cross Som 15 F10
Cross Ash Mon 25 G11
Cross-at-Hand Kent 20 G4
Cross Green Devon 4 C4
Cross Green Suff 30 C6
Cross Green Suff 30 C5
Cross Green Warks 27 C10
Cross-hands Carms 22 D6
Cross Hands Carms 23 E10
Cross Hands Pembs 22 E5
Cross Hill Derbys 45 H8
Cross Houses Shrops 33 E11
Cross in Hand E Sus 12 D4
Cross in Hand Leics 35 G11
Cross Inn Ceredig 23 A8
Cross Inn Ceredig 24 B2
Cross Inn Rhondda 14 C6
Cross Keys Kent 20 F2
Cross Lane Head Shrops 34 F3
Cross Lanes Corn 2 G5
Cross Lanes N Yorks 51 C11
Cross Lanes Wrex 43 H6
Cross o' th' hands Derbys 44 H6
Cross Oak Powys 25 F8
Cross of Jackston Aberds 89 E7
Cross Street Suff 39 H7
Cross Trickett's Dorset 9 D9
Crossaig Argyll 65 C9
Crossal Highld 85 E9
Crossapol Argyll 78 G2
Crossburn Falk 69 C7
Crossbush W Sus 11 D9
Crosscanonby Cumb 56 C2
Crossdale Street Norf 39 B8
Crossens Mers 49 H3
Crossflatts W Yorks 51 E7
Crossford Fife 69 B9
Crossford S Lanark 69 F7
Crossgate Lincs 37 C8
Crossgatehall E Loth 70 D2
Crossgates Fife 69 B10
Crossgates Powys 25 B7
Crossgill Lancs 50 C1
Crosshill E Ayrs 67 D7
Crosshill Fife 76 H4
Crosshill S Ayrs 66 F6
Crosshouse E Ayrs 67 C6
Crossings Cumb 61 F11
Crosskeys Caerph 15 B8
Crosskirk Highld 93 B13
Crosslanes Shrops 33 D9
Crosslee Borders 61 B9
Crosslee Renfs 68 D3
Crossmichael Dumfries 55 C10
Crossmoor Lancs 49 F4
Crossroads Aberds 83 D9
Crossroads E Ayrs 67 C7
Crossway Hereford 26 E3
Crossway Mon 25 G11
Crossway Powys 25 C7
Crossway Green Worcs 26 B5
Crossways Dorset 9 F6
Crosswell Pembs 22 C6
Crosswood Ceredig 24 A3
Crosthwaite Cumb 56 G6
Croston Lancs 49 H4
Crostwick Norf 39 D8
Crostwight Norf 39 C9
Crothair W Isles 90 D6
Crouch Kent 20 F3
Crouch Hill Dorset 8 C6
Crouch House Green Kent 19 G11
Croucheston Wilts 9 B9
Croughton Northants 28 E2
Crovie Aberds 89 B8
Crow Edge S Yorks 44 B5
Crow Hill Hereford 26 F3
Crowan Corn 2 F5
Crowborough E Sus 12 C4
Crowcombe Som 7 C10
Crowdecote Derbys 44 F5
Crowden Derbys 44 C4
Crowell Oxon 18 B4
Crowfield Northants 28 D3
Crowfield Suff 31 C8
Crowhurst E Sus 13 E6
Crowhurst Sur 19 G10
Crowhurst Lane End Sur 19 G10
Crowland Lincs 37 D8
Crowlas Corn 2 F4
Crowle N Lincs 45 A11
Crowle Worcs 26 C6
Crowmarsh Gifford Oxon 18 C3
Crown Corner Suff 31 A9
Crownhill Plym 4 F5
Crownland Suff 31 B7
Crownthorpe Norf 39 E6
Crowntown Corn 2 F5
Crows-an-wra Corn 2 G2
Crowshill Norf 38 E5
Crowsnest Shrops 33 E9
Crowthorne Brack 18 E5
Crowton Ches W 43 E8
Croxall Staffs 35 D7
Croxby Lincs 46 C5
Croxdale Durham 58 C3
Croxden Staffs 35 B6
Croxley Green Herts 19 B7
Croxton Cambs 29 B9
Croxton N Lincs 46 A4
Croxton Norf 38 G4
Croxton Staffs 34 B3
Croxton Kerrial Leics 36 C4
Croxtonbank Staffs 34 B3
Croy Highld 87 G10
Croy N Lanark 68 C6
Croyde Devon 6 C3
Croydon Cambs 29 D10
Croydon London 19 E10
Crubenmore Lodge Highld 81 D8
Cruckmeole Shrops 33 E10
Cruckton Shrops 33 D10
Cruden Bay Aberds 89 E10
Crudgington Telford 34 D2
Crudwell Wilts 16 B6
Crug Powys 25 A8
Crugmeer Corn 3 B8
Crugybar Carms 24 E3
Crulabhig W Isles 90 D6
Crumlin = Crymlyn Caerph 15 B8
Crumpsall Gtr Man 44 B2
Crundale Kent 21 G7
Crundale Pembs 22 E4
Cruwys Morchard Devon 7 E7
Crux Easton Hants 17 F11
Crwbin Carms 23 E9
Crya Orkney 95 H4
Cryers Hill Bucks 18 B5
Crymlyn = Crumlin Caerph 15 B8
Crymlyn Gwyn 41 C8
Crymych Pembs 22 C6
Crynant Neath 14 A3
Crynfryn Ceredig 24 B3
Cuaig Highld 85 C12
Cuan Argyll 72 B6
Cubbington Warks 27 B10
Cubeck N Yorks 57 H11
Cubert Corn 3 D6
Cubley S Yorks 44 B6
Cubley Common Derbys 35 B7
Cublington Bucks 28 F5
Cublington Hereford 25 E11
Cuckfield W Sus 12 D2
Cucklington Som 9 B6
Cuckney Notts 45 E9
Cuckoo Hill Notts 45 C11
Cuddesdon Oxon 18 A3
Cuddington Bucks 28 G4
Cuddington Ches W 43 E9
Cuddington Heath Ches W 43 H7
Cuddy Hill Lancs 49 F4
Cudham London 19 F11
Cudliptown Devon 4 D6
Cudworth S Yorks 45 B7
Cudworth Som 8 C2
Cuffley Herts 19 A10
Cuiashader W Isles 91 B10
Cuidhir W Isles 84 H1
Cuidhtinis W Isles 90 J5
Culbo Highld 87 E9
Culbokie Highld 87 F9
Culburnie Highld 86 G7
Culcabock Highld 87 G9
Culcairn Highld 87 E9
Culcharry Highld 87 F11
Culcheth Warr 43 C9
Culdrain Aberds 88 E5
Culduie Highld 85 D12
Culford Suff 30 A5
Culgaith Cumb 57 D8
Culham Oxon 18 B2
Culkein Highld 92 F3
Culkein Drumbeg Highld 92 F4
Culkerton Glos 16 B6
Cullachie Highld 81 A11
Cullen Moray 88 B5
Cullercoats T&W 63 F9
Cullicudden Highld 87 E9
Cullingworth W Yorks 51 F6
Cullipool Argyll 72 B6
Cullivoe Shetland 96 C7
Culloch Perth 75 F10
Culloden Highld 87 G10
Cullompton Devon 7 F9
Culmaily Highld 87 B11
Culmazie Dumfries 54 D6
Culmington Shrops 33 G10
Culmstock Devon 7 E10
Culnacraig Highld 92 J3
Culnaknock Highld 85 B10
Culpho Suff 31 D9
Culrain Highld 87 B8
Culross Fife 69 B8
Culroy S Ayrs 66 E6
Culsh Aberds 82 D5
Culsh Aberds 89 D8
Culshabbin Dumfries 54 D6
Culswick Shetland 96 J4
Cultercullen Aberds 89 F9
Cults Aberdeen 83 C10
Cults Aberds 88 E5
Cults Dumfries 55 E7
Culverstone Green Kent 20 E3
Culverthorpe Lincs 36 A6
Culworth Northants 28 D2
Culzie Lodge Highld 87 D8
Cumbernauld N Lanark 68 C6
Cumbernauld Village N Lanark 68 C6
Cumberworth Lincs 47 E9
Cuminestown Aberds 89 C8
Cumlewick Shetland 96 L6
Cummersdale Cumb 56 A5
Cummertrees Dumfries 61 G7
Cummingston Moray 88 B1
Cumnock E Ayrs 67 D8
Cumnor Oxon 17 A11
Cumrew Cumb 57 A7
Cumwhinton Cumb 56 A6
Cumwhitton Cumb 57 A7
Cundall N Yorks 51 B10
Cunninghamhead N Ayrs 67 B6
Cunnister Shetland 96 D7
Cupar Fife 76 F6
Cupar Muir Fife 76 F6
Cupernham Hants 10 B2
Curbar Derbys 44 E6
Curbridge Hants 10 C4
Curbridge Oxon 27 H10
Curdridge Hants 10 C4
Curdworth Warks 35 F7
Curland Som 8 C1
Curlew Green Suff 31 B10
Currarie S Ayrs 66 G4
Curridge W Berks 17 D11
Currie Edin 69 D10
Curry Mallet Som 8 B2
Curry Rivel Som 8 B2
Curtisden Green Kent 12 B6
Curtisknowle Devon 5 F8
Cury Corn 2 G5
Cushnie Aberds 89 B7
Cushuish Som 7 C10
Cusop Hereford 25 D9
Cutcloy Dumfries 55 F7
Cutcombe Som 7 C8
Cutgate Gtr Man 44 A2
Cutiau Gwyn 32 D2
Cutlers Green Essex 30 E2
Cutnall Green Worcs 26 B5
Cutsdean Glos 27 E7
Cutthorpe Derbys 45 E7
Cutts Shetland 96 K6
Cuxham Oxon 18 B3
Cuxton Medway 20 E4
Cuxwold Lincs 46 B5
Cwm Bl Gwent 25 H8
Cwm Denb 42 E3
Cwm Swansea 14 B2
Cwm-byr Carms 24 E3
Cwm-Cewydd Gwyn 32 D4
Cwm-cou Ceredig 23 B7
Cwm-Dulais Swansea 14 A2
Cwm-felin-fach Caerph 15 B7
Cwm Ffrwd-oer Torf 15 A8
Cwm-hesgen Gwyn 32 C3
Cwm-hwnt Rhondda 24 H6
Cwm Irfon Powys 24 D5
Cwm-Llinau Powys 32 E4
Cwm-mawr Carms 23 E10
Cwm-parc Rhondda 14 B5
Cwm Penmachno Conwy 41 F9
Cwm-y-glo Carms 23 E10
Cwm-y-glo Gwyn 41 D7
Cwmafan Neath 14 B3
Cwmaman Rhondda 14 B6
Cwmann Carms 23 B10
Cwmavon Torf 25 H9
Cwmbach Carms 23 D7
Cwmbach Carms 23 F9
Cwmbach Powys 25 C7
Cwmbach Powys 25 E8
Cwmbach Rhondda 14 A6
Cwmbelan Powys 32 G5
Cwmbrân = Cwmbran Torf 15 B8
Cwmbran = Cwmbrân Torf 15 B8
Cwmbrwyno Ceredig 32 G3
Cwmcarn Caerph 15 B8
Cwmcarvan Mon 25 H11
Cwmcych Carms 23 C7
Cwmdare Rhondda 14 A5
Cwmderwen Powys 32 E5
Cwmdu Carms 24 E3
Cwmdu Powys 25 F8
Cwmdu Swansea 14 B2
Cwmduad Carms 23 C8
Cwmdwr Carms 24 E4
Cwmfelin Bridgend 14 C4
Cwmfelin M Tydf 14 A6
Cwmfelin Boeth Carms 22 E6
Cwmfelin Mynach Carms 23 D7
Cwmffrwd Carms 23 E9
Cwmgiedd Powys 24 G4
Cwmgors Neath 24 G4
Cwmgwili Carms 23 E10
Cwmgwrach Neath 14 A4
Cwmhiraeth Carms 23 C8
Cwmifor Carms 24 F3
Cwmisfael Carms 23 E9
Cwmllynfell Neath 24 G4
Cwmorgan Pembs 23 C7
Cwmpengraig Carms 23 C8
Cwmrhos Powys 25 F8
Cwmsychpant Ceredig 23 B9
Cwmtillery Bl Gwent 25 H9
Cwmwysg Powys 24 F5
Cwmyoy Mon 25 F9
Cwmystwyth Ceredig 24 A4
Cwrt Gwyn 32 E2
Cwrt-newydd Ceredig 23 B9
Cwrt-y-cadno Carms 24 D3
Cwrt-y-gollen Powys 25 G9
Cydweli = Kidwelly Carms 23 F9
Cyffordd Llandudno = Llandudno Junction Conwy 41 C9
Cyffylliog Denb 42 G3
Cyfronydd Powys 33 E7
Cymer Neath 14 B4
Cyncoed Cardiff 15 C7
Cynghordy Carms 24 D5
Cynheidre Carms 23 F9
Cynwyd Denb 33 A6
Cynwyl Elfed Carms 23 D8
Cywarch Gwyn 32 D4

D

Dacre Cumb 56 D6
Dacre N Yorks 51 C7
Dacre Banks N Yorks 51 C7
Daddry Shield Durham 57 C10
Dadford Bucks 28 E3
Dadlington Leics 35 F10
Dafarn Faig Gwyn 40 F6
Dafen Carms 23 F10
Daffy Green Norf 38 E5
Dagenham London 19 C11
Daglingworth Glos 26 H6
Dagnall Bucks 28 G6
Dail Beag W Isles 90 C7
Dail bho Dheas W Isles 91 A9
Dail bho Thuath W Isles 91 A9
Dail Mor W Isles 90 C7
Daill Argyll 64 B4
Dailly S Ayrs 66 F5
Dairsie or Osnaburgh Fife 77 F7
Daisy Hill Gtr Man 43 B9
Dalabrog W Isles 84 F2
Dalavich Argyll 73 B8
Dalbeattie Dumfries 55 C11
Dalblair E Ayrs 67 E9
Dalbog Angus 83 F7
Dalbury Derbys 35 B8
Dalby IoM 48 E2
Dalby N Yorks 52 B2
Dalchalloch Perth 75 A10
Dalchalm Highld 93 J12
Dalchenna Argyll 73 C9
Dalchirach Moray 88 E1
Dalchork Highld 93 H8
Dalchreichart Highld 80 B4
Dalchruin Perth 75 F10
Dalderby Lincs 46 F6
Dale Pembs 22 F3
Dale Abbey Derbys 35 B10
Dale Head Cumb 56 E6
Dale of Walls Shetland 96 H3
Dalelia Highld 79 E10
Daless Highld 87 H11
Dalfaber Highld 81 B11
Dalgarven N Ayrs 66 B5
Dalgety Bay Fife 69 B10
Dalginross Perth 75 E10
Dalguise Perth 76 C2
Dalhalvaig Highld 93 D11
Dalham Suff 30 B4
Dalinlongart Argyll 73 E10
Dalkeith Midloth 70 D2
Dallam Warr 43 C8
Dallas Moray 87 F14
Dalleagles E Ayrs 67 E8
Dallinghoo Suff 31 C9
Dallington E Sus 12 E5
Dallington Northants 28 B4
Dallow N Yorks 51 B7
Dalmadilly Aberds 83 B9
Dalmally Argyll 74 E4
Dalmarnock Glasgow 68 D5
Dalmary Stirling 75 H8
Dalmellington E Ayrs 67 F7
Dalmeny Edin 69 C10
Dalmigavie Highld 81 B9
Dalmigavie Lodge Highld 81 A9
Dalmore Highld 87 E9
Dalmuir W Dunb 68 C3
Dalnabreck Highld 79 E9
Dalnacardoch Lodge Perth 81 F9
Dalnacroich Highld 86 F6
Dalnaglar Castle Perth 76 A4
Dalnahaitnach Highld 81 A10
Dalnaspidal Lodge Perth 81 F8
Dalnavaid Perth 76 A3
Dalnavie Highld 87 D9
Dalnawillan Lodge Highld 93 E13
Dalness Highld 74 B4
Dalnessie Highld 93 H9
Dalqueich Perth 76 G3
Dalreavoch Highld 93 J10
Dalry N Ayrs 66 B5
Dalrymple E Ayrs 67 E6
Dalserf S Lanark 69 E7
Dalston Cumb 56 A5
Dalswinton Dumfries 60 E5
Dalton Dumfries 61 F7
Dalton Lancs 43 B7
Dalton N Yorks 51 B10
Dalton N Yorks 58 F2
Dalton Northumb 62 H5
Dalton Northumb 63 F7
Dalton S Yorks 45 C8
Dalton-in-Furness Cumb 49 B2
Dalton-le-Dale Durham 58 B5
Dalton-on-Tees N Yorks 58 F3
Dalton Piercy Hrtlpl 58 C5
Dalveich Stirling 75 E9
Dalvina Lo. Highld 93 E9
Dalwhinnie Highld 81 E8
Dalwood Devon 8 D1
Dalwyne S Ayrs 66 G6
Dam Green Norf 39 G6
Dam Side Lancs 49 E4
Damerham Hants 9 C10
Damgate Norf 39 E10
Damnaglaur Dumfries 54 F4
Damside Borders 69 F10
Danbury Essex 30 H4
Danby N Yorks 59 F8
Danby Wiske N Yorks 58 G4
Dandaleith Moray 88 D2
Danderhall Midloth 70 D2
Dane End Herts 29 F10
Danebridge Ches E 44 F3
Danehill E Sus 12 D3
Danemoor Green Norf 39 E6
Danesford Shrops 34 F3
Daneshill Hants 18 F3
Dangerous Corner Lancs 43 A8
Danskine E Loth 70 D4
Darcy Lever Gtr Man 43 B10
Darenth Kent 20 D2
Daresbury Halton 43 D8
Darfield S Yorks 45 B8
Darfoulds Notts 45 E9
Dargate Kent 21 E7
Darite Corn 4 E3
Darlaston W Mid 34 F5
Darley N Yorks 51 D8
Darley Bridge Derbys 44 F6
Darley Head N Yorks 51 D7
Darlingscott Warks 27 D9
Darlington Darl 58 E3
Darliston Shrops 34 B1
Darlton Notts 45 E11
Darnall S Yorks 45 D7
Darnick Borders 70 G4
Darowen Powys 32 E4
Darra Aberds 89 D7
Darracott Devon 6 C3
Darras Hall Northumb 63 F7
Darrington W Yorks 51 G10
Darsham Suff 31 B11
Dartford Kent 20 D2
Dartford Crossing Kent 20 D2
Dartington Devon 5 E8
Dartmeet Devon 5 D7
Dartmouth Devon 5 F9
Darton S Yorks 45 B7
Darvel E Ayrs 68 G4
Darwell Hole E Sus 12 E5
Darwen Blackburn 50 G2
Datchet Windsor 18 D6
Datchworth Herts 29 G9
Datchworth Green Herts 29 G9
Daubhill Gtr Man 43 B10
Daugh of Kinermony Moray 88 D2
Dauntsey Wilts 16 C6
Dava Moray 87 H13
Davenham Ches W 43 E9
Davenport Green Ches E 44 E2
Daventry Northants 28 B2
David's Well Powys 33 H6
Davidson's Mains Edin 69 C11
Davidstow Corn 4 C2
Davington Dumfries 61 C8
Daviot Aberds 83 A9
Daviot Highld 87 H10
Davoch of Grange Moray 88 C4
Davyhulme Gtr Man 43 C10
Dawley Telford 34 E2
Dawlish Devon 5 D10
Dawlish Warren Devon 5 D10
Dawn Conwy 41 C10
Daws Heath Essex 20 C5
Daw's House Corn 4 C4
Dawsmere Lincs 37 B10
Dayhills Staffs 34 B5
Daylesford Glos 27 F9
Ddôl-Cownwy Powys 32 D6
Ddrydwy Anglesey 40 C5
Deadwater Northumb 62 D2
Deaf Hill Durham 58 C4
Deal Kent 21 F10
Deal Hall Essex 21 B7
Dean Cumb 56 D2
Dean Devon 5 E8
Dean Devon 6 B4
Dean Dorset 9 C8
Dean Hants 10 C4
Dean Som 16 G3
Dean Prior Devon 5 E8
Dean Row Ches E 44 D2
Deanburnhaugh Borders 61 B9
Deane Gtr Man 43 B9
Deane Hants 18 F2
Deanich Lodge Highld 86 C6
Deanland Dorset 9 C8
Deans W Loth 69 D9
Deanscales Cumb 56 D2
Deanshanger Northants 28 E4
Deanston Stirling 75 G10
Dearham Cumb 56 C2
Debach Suff 31 C9
Debden Essex 19 B11
Debden Essex 30 E2
Debden Cross Essex 30 E2
Debenham Suff 31 B8
Dechmont W Loth 69 C9
Deddington Oxon 27 E11
Dedham Essex 31 E7
Dedham Heath Essex 31 E7
Deebank Aberds 83 D8
Deene Northants 36 F5
Deenethorpe Northants 36 F5
Deepcar S Yorks 44 C6
Deepcut Sur 18 F6
Deepdale Cumb 50 A3
Deeping Gate Lincs 37 E7
Deeping St James Lincs 37 E7
Deeping St Nicholas Lincs 37 D8
Deerhill Moray 88 C4
Deerhurst Glos 26 F5
Deerness Orkney 95 H6
Defford Worcs 26 D6
Defynnog Powys 24 F6
Deganwy Conwy 41 C9
Deighton N Yorks 58 F4
Deighton W Yorks 51 H7
Deighton York 52 E2
Deiniolen Gwyn 41 D7
Delabole Corn 4 C1
Delamere Ches W 43 F8
Delfrigs Aberds 89 F9
Dell Lodge Highld 82 B2
Delliefure Highld 87 H13
Delnabo Moray 82 B3
Delnadamph Aberds 82 C4
Delph Gtr Man 44 B3
Delves Durham 58 B2
Delvine Perth 76 C4
Dembleby Lincs 36 B6
Denaby Main S Yorks 45 C8
Denbigh = Dinbych Denb 42 F3
Denbury Devon 5 E9
Denby Derbys 45 H7
Denby Dale W Yorks 44 B6
Denchworth Oxon 17 B10
Dendron Cumb 49 B2
Denel End C Beds 29 E7
Denend Aberds 88 E6
Denford Northants 36 H5
Dengie Essex 20 A6
Denham Bucks 19 C7
Denham Suff 30 B4
Denham Suff 31 A8
Denham Street Suff 31 A8
Denhead Aberds 89 C9
Denhead Fife 77 F7
Denhead of Arbilot Angus 77 C8
Denhead of Gray Dundee 76 D6
Denholm Borders 61 B11
Denholme W Yorks 51 F6
Denholme Clough W Yorks 51 F6
Denio Gwyn 40 G5
Denmead Hants 10 C5
Denmore Aberdeen 83 B11
Denmoss Aberds 89 D6
Dennington Suff 31 B9
Denny Falk 69 B7
Denny Lodge Hants 10 D2
Dennyloanhead Falk 69 B7
Denshaw Gtr Man 44 A3
Denside Aberds 83 D10
Densole Kent 21 G9
Denston Suff 30 C4
Denstone Staffs 35 A7
Dent Cumb 57 H9
Denton Cambs 37 G7
Denton Darl 58 E3
Denton E Sus 12 F3
Denton Gtr Man 44 C3
Denton Kent 21 G9
Denton Lincs 36 B4
Denton N Yorks 51 E7
Denton Norf 39 G8
Denton Northants 28 C5
Denton Oxon 18 A2
Denton's Green Mers 43 C7
Denver Norf 38 E2
Denwick Northumb 63 B8
Deopham Norf 39 E6
Deopham Green Norf 38 F6
Depden Suff 30 C4
Depden Green Suff 30 C4
Deptford London 19 D10
Deptford Wilts 17 H7
Derby Derby 35 B9
Derbyhaven IoM 48 F2
Dereham Norf 38 D5
Deri Caerph 15 A7
Derril Devon 6 F2
Derringstone Kent 21 G9
Derrington Staffs 34 C4
Derriton Devon 6 F2
Derry Hill Wilts 16 D6
Derryguaig Argyll 78 H7
Derrythorpe N Lincs 46 B2
Dersingham Norf 38 B2
Dervaig Argyll 78 F7
Derwen Denb 42 G3
Derwenlas Powys 32 F3
Desborough Northants 36 G4
Desford Leics 35 E10
Detchant Northumb 71 G9
Detling Kent 20 F4
Deuddwr Powys 33 D8
Devauden Mon 15 B10
Devil's Bridge Ceredig 32 H3
Devizes Wilts 17 E7
Devol Invclyd 68 C2
Devonport Plym 4 F5
Devonside Clack 76 H2
Devoran Corn 3 F6
Dewar Borders 70 F2
Dewlish Dorset 9 E6
Dewsbury W Yorks 51 G8
Dewsbury Moor W Yorks 51 G8
Dewshall Court Hereford 25 E11
Dhoon IoM 48 D4
Dhoor IoM 48 C4
Dhowin IoM 48 B4
Dial Post W Sus 11 C10
Dibden Hants 10 D3
Dibden Purlieu Hants 10 D3
Dickleburgh Norf 39 G7
Didbrook Glos 27 E7
Didcot Oxon 18 C2
Diddington Cambs 29 B8
Diddlebury Shrops 33 G11
Didley Hereford 25 E11
Didling W Sus 11 C7
Didmarton Glos 16 C5
Didsbury Gtr Man 44 C2
Didworthy Devon 5 E7
Digby Lincs 46 G4
Digg Highld 85 B9
Diggle Gtr Man 44 B4
Digmoor Lancs 43 B7
Digswell Park Herts 29 G9
Dihewyd Ceredig 23 A9
Dilham Norf 39 C9
Dilhorne Staffs 34 A5
Dillarburn S Lanark 69 F7
Dillington Cambs 29 B8
Dilston Northumb 62 G5
Dilton Marsh Wilts 16 G5
Dilwyn Hereford 25 C11
Dinas Carms 23 C7
Dinas Gwyn 40 G4
Dinas Cross Pembs 22 C5
Dinas Dinlle Gwyn 40 E6
Dinas-Mawddwy Gwyn 32 D4
Dinas Powys V Glam 15 D7
Dinbych = Denbigh Denb 42 F3
Dinbych-y-Pysgod = Tenby Pembs 22 F6
Dinder Som 16 G2
Dinedor Hereford 26 E2
Dingestow Mon 25 G11
Dingle Mers 42 D6
Dingleden Kent 13 C7
Dingley Northants 36 G3
Dingwall Highld 87 F8
Dinlabyre Borders 61 D11
Dinmael Conwy 32 A6
Dinnet Aberds 82 D6
Dinnington S Yorks 45 D9
Dinnington Som 8 C3
Dinnington T&W 63 F8
Dinorwic Gwyn 41 D7
Dinton Bucks 28 G4
Dinton Wilts 9 A9
Dinwoodie Mains Dumfries 61 D7
Dinworthy Devon 6 E2
Dippen N Ayrs 66 D3
Dippenhall Sur 18 G5
Dipple Moray 88 C3
Dipple S Ayrs 66 F5
Diptford Devon 5 F8
Dipton Durham 58 A2
Dirdhu Highld 82 A2
Dirleton E Loth 70 B4
Dirt Pot Northumb 57 B10
Discoed Powys 25 B9
Diseworth Leics 35 C10
Dishes Orkney 95 F7
Dishforth N Yorks 51 B9
Disley Ches E 44 D3
Diss Norf 39 H7
Disserth Powys 25 C7
Distington Cumb 56 D2
Ditchampton Wilts 9 A9
Ditcheat Som 16 H3
Ditchingham Norf 39 F9
Ditchling E Sus 12 E2
Ditherington Shrops 33 D11
Dittisham Devon 5 F9
Ditton Halton 43 D7
Ditton Kent 20 F4
Ditton Green Cambs 30 C3
Ditton Priors Shrops 34 G2
Divach Highld 81 A6
Divlyn Carms 24 E4
Dixton Glos 26 E6
Dixton Mon 26 G2
Dobcross Gtr Man 44 B3
Dobwalls Corn 4 E3
Doc Penfro = Pembroke Dock Pembs 22 F4
Doccombe Devon 5 C8
Dochfour Ho. Highld 87 H9
Dochgarroch Highld 87 G9
Docking Norf 38 B3
Docklow Hereford 26 C2
Dockray Cumb 56 D5
Dockroyd W Yorks 51 F6
Doddinghurst Essex 20 B2
Doddington Cambs 37 F9
Doddington Kent 20 F6
Doddington Lincs 46 E3
Doddington Northumb 71 G8
Doddington Shrops 34 H2
Doddiscombsleigh Devon 5 C9
Dodford Northants 28 B3
Dodford Worcs 26 A6
Dodington S Glos 16 C4
Dodleston Ches W 42 F6
Dods Leigh Staffs 34 B6
Dodworth S Yorks 45 B7
Doe Green Warr 43 D8
Doe Lea Derbys 45 F8
Dog Village Devon 7 G8
Dogdyke Lincs 46 G6
Dogmersfield Hants 18 F4
Dogridge Wilts 17 C7
Dogsthorpe Pboro 37 E7
Dol-fôr Powys 32 E4
Dôl-y-Bont Ceredig 32 G2
Dol-y-cannau Powys 25 D9
Dolanog Powys 33 D6
Dolau Powys 25 B8
Dolau Rhondda 14 C5
Dolbenmaen Gwyn 41 F7
Dolfach Powys 32 E5
Dolfor Powys 33 G7
Dolgarrog Conwy 41 D9
Dolgellau Gwyn 32 D3
Dolgran Carms 23 C9
Dolhendre Gwyn 41 G10
Doll Highld 93 J11
Dollar Clack 76 H2
Dolley Green Powys 25 B9
Dollwen Ceredig 32 G2
Dolphin Flint 42 E4
Dolphinholme Lancs 49 D5
Dolphinton S Lanark 69 F10
Dolton Devon 6 E4
Dolwen Conwy 41 C10
Dolwen Powys 32 E5
Dolwyd Conwy 41 C10
Dolwyddelan Conwy 41 E9
Dolyhir Powys 25 C9
Doncaster S Yorks 45 B9
Dones Green Ches W 43 E9
Donhead St Andrew Wilts 9 B8
Donhead St Mary Wilts 9 B8
Donibristle Fife 69 B10
Donington Lincs 37 B8
Donington on Bain Lincs 46 D6
Donington South Ing Lincs 37 B8
Donisthorpe Leics 35 D9
Donkey Town Sur 18 E6
Donnington Glos 27 F8
Donnington Hereford 26 E4
Donnington Shrops 34 E1
Donnington Telford 34 D3
Donnington W Berks 17 E11
Donnington W Sus 11 D7
Donnington Wood Telford 34 D3
Donyatt Som 8 C2
Doonfoot S Ayrs 66 E6
Dorback Lodge Highld 82 B2
Dorchester Dorset 8 E5
Dorchester Oxon 18 B2
Dordon Warks 35 E8
Dore S Yorks 45 D7
Dores Highld 87 H8
Dorking Sur 19 G8
Dormansland Sur 12 B3
Dormanstown Redcar 59 D6
Dormington Hereford 26 D2
Dormston Worcs 26 C6
Dornal S Ayrs 54 B5
Dorney Bucks 18 D6
Dornie Highld 85 F13
Dornoch Highld 87 C10
Dornock Dumfries 61 G8
Dorrery Highld 94 E2
Dorridge W Mid 35 H7
Dorrington Lincs 46 G4
Dorrington Shrops 33 E10
Dorsington Warks 27 D8
Dorstone Hereford 25 D10
Dorton Bucks 28 G3
Dorusduain Highld 80 A1
Dosthill Staffs 35 F8
Dottery Dorset 8 E3
Doublebois Corn 4 E2
Dougarie N Ayrs 66 C1
Doughton Glos 16 B5
Douglas IoM 48 E3
Douglas S Lanark 69 G7
Douglas & Angus Dundee 77 D7
Douglas Water S Lanark 69 G7
Douglas West S Lanark 69 G7
Douglastown Angus 77 C7
Doulting Som 16 G3
Dounby Orkney 95 F3
Doune Highld 92 J7
Doune Stirling 75 G10
Doune Park Aberds 89 B7
Douneside Aberds 82 C6
Dounie Highld 87 B8
Dounreay Highld 93 C12
Dousland Devon 4 E6
Dovaston Shrops 33 C9
Dove Holes Derbys 44 E4
Dovenby Cumb 56 C2
Dover Kent 21 G10
Dovercourt Essex 31 E9
Doverdale Worcs 26 B5
Doveridge Derbys 35 B7
Doversgreen Sur 19 G9
Dowally Perth 76 C3
Dowbridge Lancs 49 F4
Dowdeswell Glos 26 G6
Dowlais M Tydf 25 H7
Dowland Devon 6 E4
Dowlish Wake Som 8 C2
Down Ampney Glos 17 B8
Down Hatherley Glos 26 F5
Down St Mary Devon 7 F6
Down Thomas Devon 4 F6
Downcraig Ferry N Ayrs 73 H10
Downderry Corn 4 F4
Downe London 19 E11
Downend IoW 10 F4
Downend S Glos 16 D3
Downend W Berks 17 D11
Downfield Dundee 76 D6
Downgate Corn 4 D4
Downham Essex 20 B4
Downham Lancs 50 E3
Downham Northumb 71 G7
Downham Market Norf 38 E2
Downhead Som 16 G3
Downhill Perth 76 D3
Downhill T&W 63 H9
Downholland Cross Lancs 42 B6
Downholme N Yorks 58 G2
Downies Aberds 83 D11
Downley Bucks 18 B5
Downside Som 16 G3
Downside Sur 19 F8
Downton Hants 10 E1
Downton Wilts 9 B10
Downton on the Rock Hereford 25 A11
Dowsby Lincs 37 C7
Dowsdale Lincs 37 D8
Dowthwaitehead Cumb 56 D5
Doxey Staffs 34 C5
Doxford Northumb 63 A7
Doxford Park T&W 58 A4
Doynton S Glos 16 D4
Draffan S Lanark 68 F6
Dragonby N Lincs 46 A3
Drakeland Corner Devon 5 F6
Drakemyre N Ayrs 66 A5
Drake's Broughton Worcs 26 D6
Drakes Cross Worcs 35 H6
Drakewalls Corn 4 D5
Draughton N Yorks 50 D6
Draughton Northants 36 H3
Drax N Yorks 52 G2
Draycote Warks 27 A11
Draycott Derbys 35 B10
Draycott Glos 27 E8
Draycott Som 15 F10
Draycott in the Clay Staffs 35 C7
Draycott in the Moors Staffs 34 A5
Drayford Devon 7 E6
Drayton Leics 36 F4
Drayton Lincs 37 B8
Drayton Norf 39 D7
Drayton Oxon 17 B11
Drayton Oxon 27 D11
Drayton Ptsmth 10 D5
Drayton Som 8 B3
Drayton Worcs 34 H5
Drayton Bassett Staffs 35 E7
Drayton Beauchamp Bucks 28 G6
Drayton Parslow Bucks 28 F5
Drayton St Leonard Oxon 18 B2
Dre-fach Carms 24 G3
Dre-fach Ceredig 23 B10
Drebley N Yorks 51 D6
Dreemskerry IoM 48 C4
Dreenhill Pembs 22 E4
Drefach Carms 23 C8
Drefach Carms 23 E10
Drefelin Carms 23 C8
Dreghorn N Ayrs 67 C6
Drellingore Kent 21 G9
Drem E Loth 70 C4
Dresden Stoke 34 A5
Dreumasdal W Isles 84 E2
Drewsteignton Devon 7 G6
Driby Lincs 47 E7
Driffield E Yorks 52 D6
Driffield Glos 17 B7
Drigg Cumb 56 G2
Drighlington W Yorks 51 G8
Drimnin Highld 79 F8
Drimpton Dorset 8 D3
Drimsynie Argyll 74 G4
Drinisiadar W Isles 90 H6
Drinkstone Suff 30 B6
Drinkstone Green Suff 30 B6
Drishaig Argyll 74 F4
Drissaig Argyll 73 B8
Drochil Borders 69 F10
Drointon Staffs 34 C6
Droitwich Spa Worcs 26 B5
Droman Highld 92 D4
Dron Perth 76 F4
Dronfield Derbys 45 E7
Dronfield Woodhouse Derbys 45 E7
Drongan E Ayrs 67 E7
Dronley Angus 76 D6
Droxford Hants 10 C5
Droylsden Gtr Man 44 C3
Druid Denb 32 A6
Druidston Pembs 22 E3
Druimarbin Highld 80 F2
Druimavuic Argyll 74 C3
Druimdrishaig Argyll 72 F6
Druimindarroch Highld 79 C9
Druimyeon More Argyll 65 C7
Drum Argyll 73 F8
Drum Perth 76 G3
Drumbeg Highld 92 F4
Drumblade Aberds 88 D5
Drumblair Aberds 89 D6
Drumbuie Dumfries 55 A8
Drumbuie Highld 85 E12
Drumburgh Cumb 61 H8
Drumburn Dumfries 60 G5
Drumchapel Glasgow 68 C4
Drumchardine Highld 87 G8
Drumchork Highld 91 J13
Drumclog S Lanark 68 G5
Drumderfit Highld 87 F9
Drumeldrie Fife 77 G7
Drumelzier Borders 69 G10
Drumfearn Highld 85 G11
Drumgask Highld 81 D8
Drumgley Angus 77 B7
Drumguish Highld 81 D9
Drumin Moray 88 E1
Drumlasie Aberds 83 C8
Drumlemble Argyll 65 G7
Drumligair Aberds 83 B11
Drumlithie Aberds 83 E9
Drummoddie Dumfries 54 E6
Drummond Highld 87 E9
Drummore Dumfries 54 F4
Drummuir Moray 88 D3
Drummuir Castle Moray 88 D3
Drumnadrochit Highld 81 A7
Drumnagorrach Moray 88 C5
Drumoak Aberds 83 D9
Drumpark Dumfries 60 E4
Drumphail Dumfries 54 C5
Drumrash Dumfries 55 B9
Drumrunie Highld 92 J4
Drums Aberds 89 F9
Drumsallie Highld 80 F1
Drumstinchall Dumfries 55 D11
Drumsturdy Angus 77 D7
Drumtochty Castle Aberds 83 F8
Drumtroddan Dumfries 54 E6
Drumuie Highld 85 D9
Drumuillie Highld 81 A11
Drumvaich Stirling 75 G9
Drumwhindle Aberds 89 E9
Drunkendub Angus 77 C9
Drury Flint 42 F5
Drury Square Norf 38 D5
Dry Doddington Lincs 46 H2
Dry Drayton Cambs 29 B10
Drybeck Cumb 57 E8
Drybridge Moray 88 B4
Drybridge N Ayrs 67 C6
Drybrook Glos 26 G3
Dryburgh Borders 70 G4
Dryhope Borders 61 A8
Drylaw Edin 69 C11
Drym Corn 2 F5
Drymen Stirling 68 B3
Drymuir Aberds 89 D9
Drynoch Highld 85 E9
Dryslwyn Carms 23 D10
Dryton Shrops 34 E1
Dubford Aberds 89 B8
Dubton Angus 77 B8
Duchally Highld 92 H6
Duchlage Argyll 68 B2
Duck Corner Suff 31 D10
Duckington Ches W 43 G7
Ducklington Oxon 27 H10
Duckmanton Derbys 45 E8
Duck's Cross Bedford 29 C8
Duddenhoe End Essex 29 E11
Duddingston Edin 69 C11
Duddington Northants 36 E5
Duddleswell E Sus 12 D3
Duddo Northumb 71 F8
Duddon Ches W 43 F8
Duddon Bridge Cumb 56 H4
Dudleston Shrops 33 B9
Dudleston Heath Shrops 33 B9
Dudley T&W 63 F8
Dudley W Mid 34 F5
Dudley Port W Mid 34 F5
Duffield Derbys 35 A9
Duffryn Neath 14 B4
Duffryn Newport 15 C8
Dufftown Moray 88 E3
Duffus Moray 88 B1
Dufton Cumb 57 D8
Duggleby N Yorks 52 C4
Duirinish Highld 85 E12
Duisdalemore Highld 85 G12
Duisky Highld 80 F2
Dukestown Bl Gwent 25 G8
Dukinfield Gtr Man 44 C3
Dulas Anglesey 40 B6
Dulcote Som 16 G2
Dulford Devon 7 F9
Dull Perth 75 C11
Dullatur N Lanark 68 C6
Dullingham Cambs 30 C3
Dulnain Bridge Highld 82 A1
Duloe Bedford 29 B8
Duloe Corn 4 F3
Dulsie Highld 87 G12
Dulverton Som 7 D8
Dulwich London 19 D10
Dumbarton W Dunb 68 C2
Dumbleton Glos 27 E7
Dumcrieff Dumfries 61 C7
Dumfries Dumfries 60 F5
Dumgoyne Stirling 68 B4
Dummer Hants 18 G2
Dumpford W Sus 11 B7
Dumpton Kent 21 E10
Dun Angus 77 B9
Dun Charlabhaigh W Isles 90 C6
Dunain Ho. Highld 87 G9
Dunalastair Perth 75 B10
Dunan Highld 85 F10
Dunans Argyll 73 D9
Dunball Som 15 G9
Dunbar E Loth 70 C5
Dunbeath Highld 94 H3
Dunbeg Argyll 79 H11
Dunblane Stirling 75 G10
Dunbog Fife 76 F5
Duncanston Highld 87 F8
Duncanstone Aberds 83 A7
Dunchurch Warks 27 A11
Duncote Northants 28 C3
Duncow Dumfries 60 E5
Duncraggan Stirling 75 G8
Duncrievie Perth 76 G4
Duncton W Sus 11 C8
Dundas Ho. Orkney 95 K5
Dundee Dundee 77 D7
Dundeugh Dumfries 67 H8
Dundon Som 8 A3
Dundonald S Ayrs 67 C6

Dundonnell Highld 86 C3
Dundonnell Hotel Highld 86 C3
Dundonnell House Highld 86 C4
Dundraw Cumb 56 B4
Dundreggan Highld 80 B5
Dundreggan Lodge Highld 80 B5
Dundrennan Dumfries 55 E10
Dundry N Som 16 E2
Dunecht Aberds 83 C9
Dunfermline Fife 69 B9
Dunfield Glos 17 B8
Dunford Bridge S Yorks 44 B5
Dungworth S Yorks 44 D6
Dunham Notts 46 E2
Dunham-on-the-Hill Ches W 43 E7
Dunham Town Gtr Man 43 D10
Dunhampton Worcs 26 B5
Dunholme Lincs 46 E4
Dunino Fife 77 F8
Dunipace Falk 69 B7
Dunira Perth 75 E10
Dunkeld Perth 76 C3
Dunkerton Bath 16 F4
Dunkeswell Devon 7 F10
Dunkeswick N Yorks 51 E9
Dunkirk Kent 21 F7
Dunkirk Norf 39 C8
Dunk's Green Kent 20 F3
Dunlappie Angus 83 G7
Dunley Hants 17 F11
Dunley Worcs 26 B4
Dunlichity Lodge Highld 87 H9
Dunlop E Ayrs 67 B7
Dunmaglass Lodge Highld 81 A7
Dunmore Argyll 72 G6
Dunmore Falk 69 B7
Dunnet Highld 94 C4
Dunnichen Angus 77 C8
Dunninald Angus 77 B10
Dunning Perth 76 F3
Dunnington E Yorks 53 D7
Dunnington Warks 27 C7
Dunnington York 52 D2
Dunnockshaw Lancs 50 G4
Dunollie Argyll 79 H11
Dunoon Argyll 73 F10
Dunragit Dumfries 54 D4
Dunrostan Argyll 72 E6
Duns Borders 70 E6
Duns Tew Oxon 27 F11
Dunsby Lincs 37 C7
Dunscore Dumfries 60 E4
Dunscroft S Yorks 45 B10
Dunsdale Redcar 59 E7
Dunsden Green Oxon 18 D4
Dunsfold Sur 19 H7
Dunsford Devon 5 C9
Dunshalt Fife 76 F5
Dunshillock Aberds 89 D9
Dunskey Ho. Dumfries 54 D3
Dunsley N Yorks 59 E9
Dunsmore Bucks 28 H5
Dunsop Bridge Lancs 50 D2
Dunstable C Beds 29 F7
Dunstall Staffs 35 C7
Dunstall Common Worcs 26 D5
Dunstall Green Suff 30 B4
Dunstan Northumb 63 B8
Dunstan Steads Northumb 63 A8
Dunster Som 7 B8
Dunston Lincs 46 F4
Dunston Norf 39 E8
Dunston Staffs 34 D5
Dunston T&W 63 G8
Dunsville S Yorks 45 B10
Dunswell E Yorks 53 F6
Dunsyre S Lanark 69 F9
Dunterton Devon 4 D4
Duntisbourne Abbots Glos 26 H6
Duntisbourne Leer Glos 26 H6
Duntisbourne Rouse Glos 26 H6
Duntish Dorset 8 D5
Duntocher W Dunb 68 C3
Dunton Bucks 28 F5
Dunton C Beds 29 D9
Dunton Norf 38 B4
Dunton Bassett Leics 35 F11
Dunton Green Kent 20 F2
Dunton Wayletts Essex 20 B3
Duntulm Highld 85 A9
Dunure S Ayrs 66 E5
Dunvant Swansea 23 G10
Dunvegan Highld 84 D7
Dunwich Suff 31 A11
Dunwood Staffs 44 G3
Dupplin Castle Perth 76 F3
Durdar Cumb 56 A6
Durgates E Sus 12 C5
Durham Durham 58 B3
Durisdeer Dumfries 60 C4
Durisdeermill Dumfries 60 C4
Durkar W Yorks 51 H9
Durleigh Som 15 H8
Durley Hants 10 C4
Durley Wilts 17 E9
Durnamuck Highld 86 B3
Durness Highld 92 C7
Durno Aberds 83 A9
Duror Highld 74 B2
Durran Argyll 73 C8
Durran Highld 94 D3
Durrington W Sus 11 D10
Durrington Wilts 17 G8
Dursley Glos 16 B4
Durston Som 8 B1
Durweston Dorset 9 D7
Dury Shetland 96 G6
Duston Northants 28 B4
Duthil Highld 81 A11
Dutlas Powys 33 H8
Duton Hill Essex 30 F3
Dutson Corn 4 C4
Dutton Ches W 43 E8
Duxford Cambs 29 D11
Duxford Oxon 17 B10
Dwygyfylchi Conwy 41 C9
Dwyran Anglesey 40 D6
Dyce Aberdeen 83 B10
Dye House Northumb 62 H5
Dyffryn Bridgend 14 B4
Dyffryn Carms 23 D8
Dyffryn Pembs 22 C4
Dyffryn Ardudwy Gwyn 32 C1
Dyffryn Castell Ceredig 32 G3
Dyffryn Ceidrych Carms 24 F4
Dyffryn Cellwen Neath 24 H5
Dyke Lincs 37 C7
Dyke Moray 87 F12
Dykehead Angus 76 A6
Dykehead N Lanark 69 E7
Dykehead Stirling 75 H8
Dykelands Aberds 83 G9
Dykends Angus 76 B5
Dykeside Aberds 89 D7
Dykesmains N Ayrs 66 B5
Dylife Powys 32 F4
Dymchurch Kent 13 D9
Dymock Glos 26 E4
Dyrham S Glos 16 D4
Dysart Fife 70 A2
Dyserth Denb 42 E3

E

Eachwick Northumb 63 F7
Eadar Dha Fhadhail W Isles 90 D5
Eagland Hill Lancs 49 E4
Eagle Lincs 46 F2
Eagle Barnsdale Lincs 46 F2
Eagle Moor Lincs 46 F2
Eaglescliffe Stockton 58 E5
Eaglesfield Cumb 56 D2
Eaglesfield Dumfries 61 F8
Eaglesham E Renf 68 E4
Eaglethorpe Northants 37 F6
Eairy IoM 48 E2
Eakley Lanes M Keynes 28 C5
Eakring Notts 45 F10
Ealand N Lincs 45 A11
Ealing London 19 C8
Eals Northumb 62 H2
Eamont Bridge Cumb 57 D7
Earby Lancs 50 E5
Earcroft Blackburn 50 G2
Eardington Shrops 34 F3
Eardisland Hereford 25 C11
Eardisley Hereford 25 D10
Eardiston Shrops 33 C9
Eardiston Worcs 26 B3
Earith Cambs 29 A10
Earl Shilton Leics 35 F10
Earl Soham Suff 31 B9
Earl Sterndale Derbys 44 F4
Earl Stonham Suff 31 C8
Earle Northumb 71 H8
Earley Wokingham 18 D4
Earlham Norf 39 E8
Earlish Highld 85 B8
Earls Barton Northants 28 B5
Earls Colne Essex 30 F5
Earl's Croome Worcs 26 D5
Earl's Green Suff 31 B7
Earlsdon W Mid 35 H9
Earlsferry Fife 77 H7
Earlsfield Lincs 36 B5
Earlsford Aberds 89 E8
Earlsheaton W Yorks 51 G8
Earlsmill Moray 87 F12
Earlston Borders 70 G4
Earlston E Ayrs 67 C7
Earlswood Mon 15 B10
Earlswood Sur 19 G9
Earlswood Warks 27 A8
Earnley W Sus 11 E7
Earsairidh W Isles 84 J2
Earsdon T&W 63 F9
Earsham Norf 39 G9
Earswick York 52 D2
Eartham W Sus 11 D8
Easby N Yorks 58 F2
Easby N Yorks 59 F6
Easdale Argyll 72 B6
Easebourne W Sus 11 B7
Easenhall Warks 35 H10
Eashing Sur 18 G6
Easington Bucks 28 G3
Easington Durham 58 B5
Easington E Yorks 53 H9
Easington Northumb 71 G10
Easington Oxon 18 B3
Easington Oxon 27 E11
Easington Redcar 59 E8
Easington Colliery Durham 58 B5
Easington Lane T&W 58 B4
Easingwold N Yorks 51 C11
Easole Street Kent 21 F9
Eassie Angus 76 C6
East Aberthaw V Glam 14 E6
East Adderbury Oxon 27 E11
East Allington Devon 5 G8
East Anstey Devon 7 D7
East Appleton N Yorks 58 G3
East Ardsley W Yorks 51 G9
East Ashling W Sus 11 D7
East Auchronie Aberds 83 C10
East Ayton N Yorks 59 H10
East Bank Bl Gwent 25 H9
East Barkwith Lincs 46 D5
East Barming Kent 20 F4
East Barnby N Yorks 59 E9
East Barnet London 19 B9
East Barns E Loth 70 C6
East Barsham Norf 38 B5
East Beckham Norf 39 B7
East Bedfont London 19 D7
East Bergholt Suff 31 E7
East Bilney Norf 38 D5
East Blatchington E Sus 12 F3
East Boldre Hants 10 D2
East Brent Som 15 F9
East Bridgford Notts 36 A2
East Buckland Devon 6 C5
East Budleigh Devon 7 H9
East Burrafirth Shetland 96 H5
East Burton Dorset 9 F7
East Butsfield Durham 58 B2
East Butterwick N Lincs 46 B2
East Cairnbeg Aberds 83 F9
East Calder W Loth 69 D9
East Carleton Norf 39 E7
East Carlton Northants 36 G4
East Carlton W Yorks 51 E8
East Chaldon Dorset 9 F6
East Challow Oxon 17 C10
East Chiltington E Sus 12 E2
East Chinnock Som 8 C3
East Chisenbury Wilts 17 F8
East Clandon Sur 19 F7
East Claydon Bucks 28 F4
East Clyne Highld 93 J12
East Coker Som 8 C4
East Combe Som 7 C10
East Common N Yorks 52 F2
East Compton Som 16 G3
East Cottingwith E Yorks 52 E3
East Cowes IoW 10 E4
East Cowick E Yorks 52 G2
East Cowton N Yorks 58 F4
East Cramlington Northumb 63 F8
East Cranmore Som 16 G3
East Creech Dorset 9 F8
East Croachy Highld 81 A8
East Croftmore Highld 81 B11
East Curthwaite Cumb 56 B5
East Dean E Sus 12 G4
East Dean Hants 10 B1
East Dean W Sus 11 C8
East Down Devon 6 B5
East Drayton Notts 45 E11
East Ella Hull 53 G6
East End Dorset 9 E8
East End E Yorks 53 G8
East End Hants 10 B5
East End Hants 10 E2
East End Hants 17 E11
East End Herts 29 F11
East End Kent 13 C7
East End N Som 15 D10
East End Oxon 27 G10
East Farleigh Kent 20 F4
East Farndon Northants 36 G3
East Ferry Lincs 46 C2
East Fortune E Loth 70 C4
East Garston W Berks 17 D10
East Ginge Oxon 17 C11
East Goscote Leics 36 D2
East Grafton Wilts 17 E9
East Grimstead Wilts 9 B11
East Grinstead W Sus 12 C2
East Guldeford E Sus 13 D8
East Haddon Northants 28 B3
East Hagbourne Oxon 18 C2
East Halton N Lincs 53 H7
East Ham London 19 C11
East Hanney Oxon 17 B11
East Hanningfield Essex 20 A4
East Hardwick W Yorks 51 H10
East Harling Norf 38 G5
East Harlsey N Yorks 58 G5
East Harnham Wilts 9 B10
East Harptree Bath 16 F2
East Hartford Northumb 63 F8
East Harting W Sus 11 C6
East Hatley Cambs 29 C9
East Hauxwell N Yorks 58 G2
East Haven Angus 77 D8
East Heckington Lincs 37 A7
East Hedleyhope Durham 58 B2
East Hendred Oxon 17 C11
East Herrington T&W 58 A4
East Heslerton N Yorks 52 B5
East Hoathly E Sus 12 E4
East Horrington Som 16 G2
East Horsley Sur 19 F7
East Horton Northumb 71 G9
East Huntspill Som 15 G9
East Hyde C Beds 29 G8
East Ilkerton Devon 6 B6
East Ilsley W Berks 17 C11
East Keal Lincs 47 F7
East Kennett Wilts 17 E8
East Keswick W Yorks 51 E9
East Kilbride S Lanark 68 E5
East Kirkby Lincs 47 F7
East Knapton N Yorks 52 B4
East Knighton Dorset 9 F7
East Knoyle Wilts 9 A7
East Kyloe Northumb 71 G9
East Lambrook Som 8 C3
East Lamington Highld 87 D10
East Langdon Kent 21 G10
East Langton Leics 36 F3
East Langwell Highld 93 J10
East Lavant W Sus 11 D7
East Lavington W Sus 11 C8
East Layton N Yorks 58 F2
East Leake Notts 36 C1
East Learmouth Northumb 71 G7
East Leigh Devon 6 F5
East Lexham Norf 38 D4
East Lilburn Northumb 62 A6
East Linton E Loth 70 C4
East Liss Hants 11 B6
East Looe Corn 4 F3
East Lound N Lincs 45 C11
East Lulworth Dorset 9 F7
East Lutton N Yorks 52 C5
East Lydford Som 8 A4
East Mains Aberds 83 D8
East Malling Kent 20 F4
East March Angus 77 D7
East Marden W Sus 11 C7
East Markham Notts 45 E11
East Marton N Yorks 50 D5
East Meon Hants 10 B5
East Mere Devon 7 E8
East Mersea Essex 31 G7
East Mey Highld 94 C5
East Molesey Sur 19 E8
East Morden Dorset 9 E8
East Morton W Yorks 51 E6
East Ness N Yorks 52 B2
East Newton E Yorks 53 F8
East Norton Leics 36 E3
East Nynehead Som 7 D10
East Oakley Hants 18 F2
East Ogwell Devon 5 D9
East Orchard Dorset 9 C7
East Ord Northumb 71 E8
East Panson Devon 6 G2
East Peckham Kent 20 G3
East Pennard Som 16 H2
East Perry Cambs 29 B8
East Portlemouth Devon 5 H8
East Prawle Devon 5 H8
East Preston W Sus 11 D9
East Putford Devon 6 E2
East Quantoxhead Som 7 B10
East Rainton T&W 58 B4
East Ravendale NE Lincs 46 C6
East Raynham Norf 38 C4
East Rhidorroch Lodge Highld 86 B5
East Rigton W Yorks 51 E9
East Rounton N Yorks 58 F5
East Row N Yorks 59 E9
East Rudham Norf 38 C4
East Runton Norf 39 A7
East Ruston Norf 39 C9
East Saltoun E Loth 70 D3
East Sleekburn Northumb 63 E8
East Somerton Norf 39 D10
East Stockwith Lincs 45 C11
East Stoke Dorset 9 F7
East Stoke Notts 45 H11
East Stour Dorset 9 B7
East Stourmouth Kent 21 E9
East Stowford Devon 6 D5
East Stratton Hants 18 H2
East Studdal Kent 21 G10
East Suisnish Highld 85 E10
East Taphouse Corn 4 E2
East-the-Water Devon 6 D3
East Thirston Northumb 63 D7
East Tilbury Thurrock 20 D3
East Tisted Hants 10 A6
East Torrington Lincs 46 D5
East Tuddenham Norf 39 D6
East Tytherley Hants 10 B1
East Tytherton Wilts 16 D6
East Village Devon 7 F7
East Wall Shrops 33 F11
East Walton Norf 38 D3
East Wellow Hants 10 B2
East Wemyss Fife 76 H6
East Whitburn W Loth 69 D8
East Williamston Pembs 22 F5
East Winch Norf 38 D2
East Winterslow Wilts 9 A11
East Wittering W Sus 11 E6
East Witton N Yorks 58 H2
East Woodburn Northumb 62 E5
East Woodhay Hants 17 E11
East Worldham Hants 18 H4
East Worlington Devon 7 E6
East Worthing W Sus 11 D10
Eastbourne E Sus 12 G5
Eastbridge Suff 31 B11
Eastburn W Yorks 50 E6
Eastbury London 19 B7
Eastbury W Berks 17 D10
Eastby N Yorks 50 D6
Eastchurch Kent 20 D6
Eastcombe Glos 16 A5
Eastcote London 19 C8
Eastcote Northants 28 C3
Eastcote W Mid 35 H7
Eastcott Corn 6 E1
Eastcott Wilts 17 F7
Eastcourt Wilts 16 B6
Eastcourt Wilts 17 E9
Easter Ardross Highld 87 D9
Easter Balmoral Aberds 82 D4
Easter Boleskine Highld 81 A7
Easter Compton S Glos 16 C2
Easter Cringate Stirling 68 B6
Easter Davoch Aberds 82 C6
Easter Earshaig Dumfries 60 C6
Easter Fearn Highld 87 C9
Easter Galcantray Highld 87 G11
Easter Howgate Midloth 69 D11
Easter Howlaws Borders 70 F6
Easter Kinkell Highld 87 F8
Easter Lednathie Angus 76 A6
Easter Milton Highld 87 F12
Easter Moniack Highld 87 G8
Easter Ord Aberdeen 83 C10
Easter Quarff Shetland 96 K6
Easter Rhynd Perth 76 F4
Easter Row Stirling 75 H10
Easter Silverford Aberds 89 B7
Easter Skeld Shetland 96 J5
Easter Whyntie Aberds 88 B6
Eastergate W Sus 11 D8
Easterhouse Glasgow 68 D5
Eastern Green W Mid 35 G8
Easterton Wilts 17 F7
Eastertown Som 15 F9
Eastertown of Auchleuchries Aberds 89 E10
Eastfield N Lanark 69 D7
Eastfield N Yorks 52 A6
Eastfield Hall Northumb 63 C8
Eastgate Durham 57 C11
Eastgate Norf 39 C7
Eastham Mers 42 D6
Eastham Ferry Mers 42 D6
Easthampstead Brack 18 E5
Eastheath Wokingham 18 E5
Easthope Shrops 34 F1
Easthorpe Essex 30 F6
Easthorpe Leics 36 B4
Easthorpe Notts 45 G11
Easthouses Midloth 70 D2
Eastington Devon 7 F6
Eastington Glos 26 H4
Eastington Glos 27 G8
Eastleach Martin Glos 27 H9
Eastleach Turville Glos 27 H8
Eastleigh Devon 6 D3
Eastleigh Hants 10 C3
Eastling Kent 20 F6
Eastmoor Derbys 45 E7
Eastmoor Norf 38 E3
Eastney Ptsmth 10 E5
Eastnor Hereford 26 E4
Eastoft N Lincs 52 H4
Eastoke Hants 10 E6
Easton Cambs 29 A8
Easton Cumb 61 F10
Easton Cumb 61 H8
Easton Devon 5 C8
Easton Dorset 8 G5
Easton Hants 10 A4
Easton Lincs 36 C5
Easton Norf 39 D7
Easton Som 15 G11
Easton Suff 31 C9
Easton Wilts 16 D5
Easton Grey Wilts 16 C5
Easton-in-Gordano N Som 15 D11
Easton Maudit Northants 28 C5
Easton on the Hill Northants 36 E6
Easton Royal Wilts 17 E9
Eastpark Dumfries 60 G6
Eastrea Cambs 37 F8
Eastriggs Dumfries 61 G8
Eastrington E Yorks 52 G3
Eastry Kent 21 F10
Eastville Bristol 16 D3
Eastville Lincs 47 G8
Eastwell Leics 36 C3
Eastwick Herts 29 G11
Eastwick Shetland 96 F5
Eastwood Notts 45 H8
Eastwood Southend 20 C5
Eastwood W Yorks 50 G5
Eathorpe Warks 27 B10
Eaton Ches E 44 F2
Eaton Ches W 43 F8
Eaton Leics 36 C3
Eaton Norf 39 E8
Eaton Notts 45 E11
Eaton Oxon 17 A11
Eaton Shrops 33 G9
Eaton Shrops 33 G11
Eaton Bishop Hereford 25 E11
Eaton Bray C Beds 28 F6
Eaton Constantine Shrops 34 E1
Eaton Green C Beds 28 F6
Eaton Hastings Oxon 17 B9
Eaton on Tern Shrops 34 C2
Eaton Socon Cambs 29 C8
Eavestone N Yorks 51 C8
Ebberston N Yorks 52 A4
Ebbesbourne Wake Wilts 9 B8
Ebbw Vale = Glyn Ebwy Bl Gwent 25 H8
Ebchester Durham 63 H7
Ebford Devon 5 C10
Ebley Glos 26 H5
Ebnal Ches W 43 H7
Ebrington Glos 27 D8
Ecchinswell Hants 17 F11
Ecclaw Borders 70 D6
Ecclefechan Dumfries 61 F7
Eccles Borders 70 F6
Eccles Gtr Man 43 C10
Eccles Kent 20 E4
Eccles on Sea Norf 39 C10
Eccles Road Norf 38 F6
Ecclesall S Yorks 45 D7
Ecclesfield S Yorks 45 C7
Ecclesgreig Aberds 83 G9
Eccleshall Staffs 34 C4
Eccleshill W Yorks 51 F7
Ecclesmachan W Loth 69 C9
Eccleston Ches W 43 F7
Eccleston Lancs 49 H5
Eccleston Mers 43 C7
Eccleston Park Mers 43 C7
Eccup W Yorks 51 E8
Echt Aberds 83 C9
Eckford Borders 70 H6
Eckington Derbys 45 E8
Eckington Worcs 26 D6
Ecton Northants 28 B5
Edale Derbys 44 D5
Edburton W Sus 11 C11
Edderside Cumb 56 B2
Edderton Highld 87 C10
Eddistone Devon 6 D1
Eddleston Borders 69 F11
Eden Park London 19 E10
Edenbridge Kent 19 G11
Edenfield Lancs 50 H3
Edenhall Cumb 57 C7
Edenham Lincs 37 C6
Edensor Derbys 44 F6
Edentaggart Argyll 68 A2
Edenthorpe S Yorks 45 B10
Edentown Cumb 61 H9
Ederline Argyll 73 C7
Edern Gwyn 40 G4
Edgarley Som 15 H11
Edgbaston W Mid 35 G6
Edgcott Bucks 28 F3
Edgcott Som 7 C7
Edge Shrops 33 E9
Edge End Glos 26 G2
Edge Green Ches W 43 G7
Edge Hill Mers 42 C6
Edgebolton Shrops 34 C1
Edgefield Norf 39 B6
Edgefield Street Norf 39 B6
Edgeside Lancs 50 G4
Edgeworth Glos 26 H6
Edgmond Telford 34 D3
Edgmond Marsh Telford 34 C3
Edgton Shrops 33 G9
Edgware London 19 B8
Edgworth Blackburn 50 H3
Edinample Stirling 75 E8
Edinbane Highld 85 C8
Edinburgh Edin 69 C11
Edingale Staffs 35 D8
Edingight Ho. Moray 88 C5
Edingley Notts 45 G10
Edingthorpe Norf 39 B9
Edingthorpe Green Norf 39 B9
Edington Som 15 H9
Edington Wilts 16 F6
Edintore Moray 88 D4
Edith Weston Rutland 36 E5
Edithmead Som 15 G9
Edlesborough Bucks 28 G6
Edlingham Northumb 63 C7
Edlington Lincs 46 E6
Edmondsham Dorset 9 C9
Edmondsley Durham 58 B3
Edmondthorpe Leics 36 D4
Edmonstone Orkney 95 F6
Edmonton London 19 B10
Edmundbyers Durham 58 A1
Ednam Borders 70 G6
Ednaston Derbys 35 A8
Edradynate Perth 75 B11
Edrom Borders 71 E7
Edstaston Shrops 33 B11
Edstone Warks 27 B8
Edvin Loach Hereford 26 C3
Edwalton Notts 36 B1
Edwardstone Suff 30 D6
Edwinsford Carms 24 E3
Edwinstowe Notts 45 F10
Edworth C Beds 29 D9
Edwyn Ralph Hereford 26 C3
Edzell Angus 83 G7
Efail Isaf Rhondda 14 C6
Efailnewydd Gwyn 40 G5
Efailwen Carms 22 D6
Efenechtyd Denb 42 G4
Effingham Sur 19 F8
Effirth Shetland 96 H5
Efford Devon 7 F7
Egdon Worcs 26 C6
Egerton Gtr Man 43 A10
Egerton Kent 20 G6
Egerton Forstal Kent 20 G5
Eggborough N Yorks 52 G1
Eggbuckland Plym 4 F6
Eggington C Beds 28 F6
Egginton Derbys 35 C8
Egglescliffe Stockton 58 E5
Eggleston Durham 57 D11
Egham Sur 19 D7
Egleton Rutland 36 E4
Eglingham Northumb 63 B7
Egloshayle Corn 3 B8
Egloskerry Corn 4 C3
Eglwys-Brewis V Glam 14 E6
Eglwys Cross Wrex 33 A10
Eglwys Fach Ceredig 32 F2
Eglwysbach Conwy 41 C10
Eglwyswen Pembs 22 C6
Eglwyswrw Pembs 22 C6
Egmanton Notts 45 F11
Egremont Cumb 56 E2
Egremont Mers 42 C6
Egton N Yorks 59 F9
Egton Bridge N Yorks 59 F9
Eight Ash Green Essex 30 F6
Eignaig Highld 79 G10
Eil Highld 81 B10
Eilanreach Highld 85 G13
Eilean Darach Highld 86 C4
Eileanach Lodge Highld 87 E8
Einacleite W Isles 90 E6
Eisgean W Isles 91 F8
Eisingrug Gwyn 41 G8
Elan Village Powys 24 B6
Elberton S Glos 16 C3
Elburton Plym 4 F6
Elcho Perth 76 E4
Elcombe Swindon 17 C8
Eldernell Cambs 37 F9
Eldersfield Worcs 26 E5
Elderslie Renfs 68 D3
Eldon Durham 58 D3
Eldrick S Ayrs 54 A5
Eldroth N Yorks 50 C3
Eldwick W Yorks 51 E7
Elfhowe Cumb 56 G6
Elford Northumb 71 G10
Elford Staffs 35 D7
Elgin Moray 88 B2
Elgol Highld 85 G10
Elham Kent 21 G8
Elie Fife 77 G7
Elim Anglesey 40 B5
Eling Hants 10 C2
Elishader Highld 85 B10
Elishaw Northumb 62 D4
Elkesley Notts 45 E10
Elkstone Glos 26 G6
Ellan Highld 81 A10
Elland W Yorks 51 G7
Ellary Argyll 72 F6
Ellastone Staffs 35 A7
Ellemford Borders 70 D6
Ellenbrook IoM 48 E3
Ellenhall Staffs 34 C4
Ellen's Green Sur 19 H7
Ellerbeck N Yorks 58 G5
Ellerburn N Yorks 52 A4
Ellerby N Yorks 59 E8
Ellerdine Heath Telford 34 C2
Ellerhayes Devon 7 F8
Elleric Argyll 74 C3
Ellerker E Yorks 52 G5
Ellerton E Yorks 52 F3
Ellerton Shrops 34 C3
Ellesborough Bucks 28 H5
Ellesmere Shrops 33 B10
Ellesmere Port Ches W 43 E7
Ellingham Norf 39 F9
Ellingham Northumb 71 H10
Ellingstring N Yorks 51 A7
Ellington Cambs 29 A8
Ellington Northumb 63 D8
Elliot Angus 77 D9
Ellisfield Hants 18 G3
Ellistown Leics 35 D10
Ellon Aberds 89 E9
Ellonby Cumb 56 C6
Ellough Suff 39 G10
Elloughton E Yorks 52 G5
Ellwood Glos 26 H2
Elm Cambs 37 E10
Elm Hill Dorset 9 B7
Elm Park London 20 C2
Elmbridge Worcs 26 B6
Elmdon Essex 29 E11
Elmdon W Mid 35 G7
Elmdon Heath W Mid 35 G7
Elmers End London 19 E10
Elmesthorpe Leics 35 F10
Elmfield IoW 10 E5
Elmhurst Staffs 35 D7
Elmley Castle Worcs 26 D6
Elmley Lovett Worcs 26 B5
Elmore Glos 26 G4
Elmore Back Glos 26 G4
Elmscott Devon 6 D1
Elmsett Suff 31 D7
Elmstead Market Essex 31 F7
Elmsted Kent 13 B10
Elmstone Kent 21 E9
Elmstone Hardwicke Glos 26 F6
Elmswell E Yorks 52 D5
Elmswell Suff 30 B6
Elmton Derbys 45 E9
Elphin Highld 92 H5
Elphinstone E Loth 70 C2
Elrick Aberds 83 C10
Elrig Dumfries 54 E6
Elsdon Northumb 62 D5
Elsecar S Yorks 45 C7
Elsenham Essex 30 F2
Elsfield Oxon 28 G2
Elsham N Lincs 46 A4
Elsing Norf 39 D6
Elslack N Yorks 50 E5
Elson Shrops 33 B9
Elsrickle S Lanark 69 F9
Elstead Sur 18 G6
Elsted W Sus 11 C7
Elsthorpe Lincs 37 C6
Elstob Durham 58 D4
Elston Notts 45 H11
Elston Wilts 17 G7
Elstone Devon 6 E5
Elstow Bedford 29 D7
Elstree Herts 19 B8
Elstronwick E Yorks 53 F8
Elswick Lancs 49 F4
Elsworth Cambs 29 B10
Elterwater Cumb 56 F5
Eltham London 19 D11
Eltisley Cambs 29 C9
Elton Cambs 37 F6
Elton Ches W 43 E7
Elton Derbys 44 F6
Elton Glos 26 G4
Elton Hereford 25 A11
Elton Notts 36 B3
Elton Stockton 58 E5
Elton Green Ches W 43 E7
Elvanfoot S Lanark 60 B5
Elvaston Derbys 35 B10
Elveden Suff 38 H4
Elvingston E Loth 70 C3
Elvington Kent 21 F9
Elvington York 52 E2
Elwick Hrtlpl 58 C5
Elwick Northumb 71 G10
Elworth Ches E 43 F10
Elworthy Som 7 C9
Ely Cambs 37 G11
Ely Cardiff 15 D7
Emberton M Keynes 28 D5
Embleton Cumb 56 C3
Embleton Northumb 63 A8
Embo Highld 87 B11
Embo Street Highld 87 B11
Emborough Som 16 F3
Embsay N Yorks 50 D6
Emery Down Hants 10 D1
Emley W Yorks 44 A6
Emmbrook Wokingham 18 E4
Emmer Green Reading 18 D4
Emmington Oxon 18 A4
Emneth Norf 37 E10
Emneth Hungate Norf 37 E11
Empingham Rutland 36 E5
Empshott Hants 11 A6
Emstrey Shrops 33 D11
Emsworth Hants 10 D6
Enborne W Berks 17 E11
Enchmarsh Shrops 33 F11
Enderby Leics 35 F11
Endmoor Cumb 49 A5
Endon Staffs 44 G3
Endon Bank Staffs 44 G3
Enfield London 19 B10
Enfield Wash London 19 B10
Enford Wilts 17 F8
Engamoor Shetland 96 H4
Engine Common S Glos 16 C3
Englefield W Berks 18 D3
Englefield Green Sur 18 D6
Englesea-brook Ches E 43 G10
English Bicknor Glos 26 G2
English Frankton Shrops 33 C10
Englishcombe Bath 16 E4
Enham Alamein Hants 17 G10
Enmore Som 8 A1
Ennerdale Bridge Cumb 56 E2
Enoch Dumfries 60 C4
Enochdhu Perth 76 A3
Ensay Argyll 78 G6
Ensbury Bmouth 9 E9
Ensdon Shrops 33 D10
Ensis Devon 6 D4
Enstone Oxon 27 F10
Enterkinfoot Dumfries 60 C4
Enterpen N Yorks 58 F5
Enville Staffs 34 G4
Eolaigearraidh W Isles 84 H2
Eorabus Argyll 78 J6
Eòropaidh W Isles 91 A10
Epperstone Notts 45 H10
Epping Essex 19 A11
Epping Green Essex 29 H11
Epping Green Herts 29 H9
Epping Upland Essex 19 A11
Eppleby N Yorks 58 E2
Eppleworth E Yorks 52 F6
Epsom Sur 19 E9
Epwell Oxon 27 D10
Epworth N Lincs 45 B11
Epworth Turbary N Lincs 45 B11
Erbistock Wrex 33 A9
Erbusaig Highld 85 F12
Erchless Castle Highld 86 G7
Erdington W Mid 35 F7
Eredine Argyll 73 C8
Eriboll Highld 92 D7
Ericstane Dumfries 60 B6
Eridge Green E Sus 12 C4
Erines Argyll 73 F7
Eriswell Suff 38 H3
Erith London 20 D2
Erlestoke Wilts 16 F6
Ermine Lincs 46 E3
Ermington Devon 5 F7
Erpingham Norf 39 B7
Errogie Highld 81 A7
Errol Perth 76 E5
Erskine Renfs 68 C3
Erskine Bridge Renfs 68 C3
Ervie Dumfries 54 C3
Erwarton Suff 31 E9
Erwood Powys 25 D7
Eryholme N Yorks 58 F4
Eryrys Denb 42 G5
Escomb Durham 58 D2
Escrick N Yorks 52 E2
Esgairdawe Carms 24 D3
Esgairgeiliog Powys 32 E3
Esh Durham 58 B2
Esh Winning Durham 58 B2
Esher Sur 19 E8
Esholt W Yorks 51 E7
Eshott Northumb 63 D8
Eshton N Yorks 50 D5
Esk Valley N Yorks 59 F9
Eskadale Highld 86 H7
Eskbank Midloth 70 D2
Eskdale Green Cumb 56 F3
Eskdalemuir Dumfries 61 D8
Eske E Yorks 53 E6
Eskham Lincs 47 C7
Esprick Lancs 49 F4
Essendine Rutland 36 D6
Essendon Herts 29 H9
Essich Highld 87 H9
Essington Staffs 34 E5
Esslemont Aberds 89 F9
Eston Redcar 59 E6
Eswick Shetland 96 H6
Etal Northumb 71 G8
Etchilhampton Wilts 17 E7
Etchingham E Sus 12 D6
Etchinghill Kent 21 H8
Etchinghill Staffs 34 D6
Ethie Castle Angus 77 C9
Ethie Mains Angus 77 C9
Etling Green Norf 38 D6
Eton Windsor 18 D6
Eton Wick Windsor 18 D6
Etteridge Highld 81 D8
Ettersgill Durham 57 D10
Ettingshall W Mid 34 F5
Ettington Warks 27 D9
Etton E Yorks 52 E5
Etton Pboro 37 E7
Ettrick Borders 61 B8
Ettrickbridge Borders 61 A9
Ettrickhill Borders 61 B8
Etwall Derbys 35 B8
Euston Suff 38 H4
Euximoor Drove Cambs 37 F10
Euxton Lancs 50 H1
Evanstown Bridgend 14 C5
Evanton Highld 87 E9
Evedon Lincs 46 H4
Evelix Highld 87 B10
Evenjobb Powys 25 B9
Evenley Northants 28 E2
Evenlode Glos 27 F9
Evenwood Durham 58 D2
Evenwood Gate Durham 58 D2
Everbay Orkney 95 F7
Evercreech Som 16 H3
Everdon Northants 28 C2
Everingham E Yorks 52 E4
Everleigh Wilts 17 F9
Everley N Yorks 59 H10
Eversholt C Beds 28 E6
Evershot Dorset 8 D4
Eversley Hants 18 E4
Eversley Cross Hants 18 E4
Everthorpe E Yorks 52 F5
Everton C Beds 29 C9
Everton Hants 10 E1
Everton Mers 42 C6
Everton Notts 45 C10
Evertown Dumfries 61 F9
Evesbatch Hereford 26 D3
Evesham Worcs 27 D7
Evington Leicester 36 E2
Ewden Village S Yorks 44 C6
Ewell Sur 19 E9
Ewell Minnis Kent 21 G9
Ewelme Oxon 18 B3
Ewen Glos 17 B7
Ewenny V Glam 14 D5
Ewerby Lincs 46 H5
Ewerby Thorpe Lincs 46 H5
Ewes Dumfries 61 D9
Ewesley Northumb 62 D6
Ewhurst Sur 19 G7
Ewhurst Green E Sus 13 D6
Ewhurst Green Sur 19 H7
Ewloe Flint 42 F6
Ewloe Green Flint 42 F5
Ewood Blackburn 50 G2
Eworthy Devon 6 G3
Ewshot Hants 18 G5
Ewyas Harold Hereford 25 F10
Exbourne Devon 6 F5
Exbury Hants 10 E3
Exebridge Devon 7 D8
Exelby N Yorks 58 H3
Exeter Devon 7 G8
Exford Som 7 C7
Exhall Warks 27 C8
Exley Head W Yorks 50 F6
Exminster Devon 5 C10
Exmouth Devon 5 C11
Exnaboe Shetland 96 M5
Exning Suff 30 B3
Exton Devon 5 C10
Exton Hants 10 B5
Exton Rutland 36 D5
Exton Som 7 C8
Exwick Devon 7 G8
Eyam Derbys 44 E6
Eydon Northants 28 C2
Eye Hereford 25 B11
Eye Pboro 37 E8
Eye Suff 31 A8
Eye Green Pboro 37 E8
Eyemouth Borders 71 D8
Eyeworth C Beds 29 D9
Eyhorne Street Kent 20 F5
Eyke Suff 31 C10
Eynesbury Cambs 29 C8
Eynort Highld 85 F8
Eynsford Kent 20 E2
Eynsham Oxon 27 H11
Eype Dorset 8 E3
Eyre Highld 85 C9
Eyre Highld 85 E10
Eythorne Kent 21 G9
Eyton Hereford 25 B11
Eyton Shrops 33 G9
Eyton Wrex 33 A9
Eyton upon the Weald Moors Telford 34 D2

F

Faccombe Hants 17 F10
Faceby N Yorks 58 F5
Facit Lancs 50 H4
Faddiley Ches E 43 G8
Fadmoor N Yorks 59 H7
Faerdre Swansea 14 A2
Failand N Som 15 D1
Failford S Ayrs 67 D
Failsworth Gtr Man 44 B
Fain Highld 86 D
Fair Green Norf 38 D
Fair Hill Cumb 57 C
Fair Oak Hants 10 C
Fair Oak Green Hants 18 E
Fairbourne Gwyn 32 D
Fairburn N Yorks 51 G1
Fairfield Derbys 44 E
Fairfield Stockton 58 E
Fairfield Worcs 27 D
Fairfield Worcs 34 H
Fairford Glos 17 A
Fairhaven Lancs 49 G
Fairlie N Ayrs 73 H1
Fairlight E Sus 13 E
Fairlight Cove E Sus 13 E
Fairmile Devon 7 G
Fairmilehead Edin 69 D1
Fairoak Staffs 34 B
Fairseat Kent 20 E
Fairstead Essex 30 G
Fairstead Norf 38 D
Fairwarp E Sus 12 D
Fairy Cottage IoM 48 D
Fairy Cross Devon 6 D
Fakenham Norf 38 C
Fakenham Magna Suff 38 H
Fala Midloth 70 D
Fala Dam Midloth 70 D
Falahill Borders 70 E
Falcon Hereford 26 E
Faldingworth Lincs 46 D
Falfield S Glos 16 B
Falkenham Suff 31 E
Falkirk Falk 69 C
Falkland Fife 76 G
Falla Borders 62 B
Fallgate Derbys 45 F
Fallin Stirling 69 A
Fallowfield Gtr Man 44 C
Fallsidehill Borders 70 F
Falmer E Sus 12 F
Falmouth Corn 3 F
Falsgrave N Yorks 59 H1
Falstone Northumb 62 E
Fanagmore Highld 92 E
Fangdale Beck N Yorks 59 G
Fangfoss E Yorks 52 D
Fankerton Falk 68 B
Fanmore Argyll 78 G
Fannich Lodge Highld 86 E
Fans Borders 70 F
Far Bank S Yorks 45 A1
Far Bletchley M Keynes 28 E
Far Cotton Northants 28 C
Far Forest Worcs 26 A
Far Laund Derbys 45 H
Far Sawrey Cumb 56 G
Farcet Cambs 37 F
Farden Shrops 34 H
Fareham Hants 10 D
Farewell Staffs 35 D
Farforth Lincs 47 E
Faringdon Oxon 17 B
Farington Lancs 49 G
Farlam Cumb 61 H1
Farlary Highld 93 J1
Farleigh N Som 15 E1
Farleigh Sur 19 E1
Farleigh Hungerford Som 16 F
Farleigh Wallop Hants 18 G
Farlesthorpe Lincs 47 E
Farleton Cumb 49 A
Farleton Lancs 50 C
Farley Shrops 33 E
Farley Staffs 35 A
Farley Wilts 9 B1
Farley Green Sur 19 G
Farley Hill Luton 29 F
Farley Hill Wokingham 18 E
Farleys End Glos 26 G
Farlington N Yorks 52 C
Farlow Shrops 34 G
Farmborough Bath 16 E
Farmcote Glos 27 F
Farmcote Shrops 34 F
Farmington Glos 27 G
Farmoor Oxon 27 H1
Farmtown Moray 88 C
Farnborough Hants 18 F
Farnborough London 19 E1
Farnborough W Berks 17 C1
Farnborough Warks 27 D1
Farnborough Green Hants 18 F
Farncombe Sur 18 G
Farndish Bedford 28 B
Farndon Ches W 43 G
Farndon Notts 45 G1
Farnell Angus 77 B
Farnham Dorset 9 C
Farnham Essex 29 F1
Farnham N Yorks 51 C
Farnham Suff 31 B1
Farnham Sur 18 G
Farnham Common Bucks 18 C
Farnham Green Essex 29 F11
Farnham Royal Bucks 18 C
Farnhill N Yorks 50 E
Farningham Kent 20 C
Farnley N Yorks 51 E
Farnley W Yorks 51 F
Farnley Tyas W Yorks 44 A
Farnsfield Notts 45 G10
Farnworth Gtr Man 43 B10
Farnworth Halton 43 D8
Farr Highld 81 C10
Farr Highld 87 H9
Farr Highld 93 C10
Farr House Highld 87 H9
Farringdon Devon 7 G9
Farrington Gurney Bath 16 F3
Farsley W Yorks 51 F8
Farthinghoe Northants 28 E2
Farthingloe Kent 21 G9
Farthingstone Northants 28 C3
Fartown W Yorks 51 H7
Farway Devon 7 G10
Fasag Highld 85 C13
Fascadale Highld 79 D8
Faslane Port Argyll 73 E11
Fasnacloich Argyll 74 C3
Fasnakyle Ho Highld 80 A5
Fassfern Highld 80 F2
Fatfield T&W 58 A4
Fattahead Aberds 89 C6
Faugh Cumb 57 A7
Fauldhouse W Loth 69 D8
Faulkbourne Essex 30 G4
Faulkland Som 16 F4

auls Shrops 34 B1
aversham Kent 21 E7
avillar Moray 88 E2
awdington N Yorks 51 B10
awfieldhead Staffs 44 F4
awkham Green Kent 20 E2
awler Oxon 27 G10
awley Bucks 18 C4
awley Hants 10 D3
awley W Berks 17 C10
awley Chapel Hereford 26 F2
axfleet E Yorks 52 G4
aygate W Sus 11 A11
azakerley Mers 43 C6
azeley Staffs 35 E8
earby N Yorks 51 A7
earn Highld 87 D11
earn Lodge Highld 87 C9
earn Station Highld 87 D11
earnan Perth 75 C10
earnbeg Highld 85 C12
earnhead Warr 43 C9
earnmore Highld 85 B12
eatherstone Staffs 34 E5
eatherstone W Yorks 51 G10
eatherwood Northumb 62 C4
eckenham Worcs 27 B7
eering Essex 30 F5
eetham N Yorks 57 G11
eizor N Yorks 50 C3
elbridge Sur 12 C2
elbrigg Norf 39 B8
elcourt Sur 12 B2
elden Herts 19 A7
elin-Crai Powys 24 F5
elindre Carms 23 C8
elindre Carms 23 D10
elindre Carms 24 E3
elindre Carms 24 F4
elindre Ceredig 23 A10
elindre Powys 33 G7
elindre Swansea 14 A2
elindre Farchog Pembs 22 C6
elinfach Ceredig 23 A10
elinfach Powys 25 E7
elinfoel Carms 23 F10
elingwm isaf Carms 23 D10
elingwm uchaf Carms 23 D10
elinwynt Ceredig 23 A7
elixkirk N Yorks 51 A10
elixstowe Suff 31 E9
elixstowe Ferry Suff 31 E10
elkington Northumb 71 F8
elkirk W Yorks 45 A7
ell Side Cumb 56 C5
elling T&W 63 G8
elmersham Bedford 28 C6
elmingham Norf 39 C8
elpham W Sus 11 E8
elsham Suff 30 C6
elsted Essex 30 F3
eltham London 19 D8
elthorpe Norf 39 D7
elton Hereford 26 D2
elton N Som 15 E11
elton Northumb 63 C7
elton Butler Shrops 33 D9
eltwell Norf 38 F3
en Ditton Cambs 29 B11
en Drayton Cambs 29 B10
en End W Mid 35 H8
en Side Lincs 47 G7
enay Bridge W Yorks 51 H7
ence Lancs 50 F4
ence Houses T&W 58 A4
engate Norf 39 C7
engate Pboro 37 F8
enham Northumb 71 F9
enhouses Lincs 37 A8
eniscliffe Blackburn 50 G2
eniscowles Blackburn 50 G2
eniton Devon 7 G10
enlake Bedford 29 D7
enny Bentley Derbys 44 G5
enny Bridges Devon 7 G10
enny Compton Warks 27 C11
enny Drayton Leics 35 F9
enny Stratford M Keynes 28 E5
enrother Northumb 63 D7
enstanton Cambs 29 B10
enton Cambs 37 H9
enton Lincs 46 E2
enton Lincs 46 G2
enton Stoke 34 A4
enton Barns E Loth 70 B4
enton Town Northumb 71 G8
enwick E Ayrs 67 B7
enwick Northumb 62 F6
enwick Northumb 71 F9
enwick S Yorks 52 H1
eochaig Argyll 65 G8
eock Corn 3 F7
eolin Ferry Argyll 72 G3
erindonald Highld 85 H11
eriniquarrie Highld 84 C6
erlochan Argyll 74 C2
ern Angus 77 A7
erndale Rhondda 14 B6
erndown Dorset 9 D9
erness Highld 87 G12
erney Green Cumb 56 G6
ernham Oxon 17 B9
ernhill Heath Worcs 26 C5
ernhurst W Sus 11 B7
ernie Fife 76 F6
erniegair S Lanark 68 E6
ernilea Highld 85 E8
ernilee Derbys 44 E4
errensby N Yorks 51 C9
erring W Sus 11 D9
erry Hill Cambs 37 G9
erry Point Highld 87 C10
errybridge W Yorks 51 G10
erryden Angus 77 B10
erryhill Aberdeen 83 C11
erryhill Durham 58 C3
erryhill Station Durham 58 C4
erryside Carms 23 E8
ersfield Norf 39 G6
ersit Highld 80 F5
eshiebridge Highld 81 C10
etcham Sur 19 F8
etterangus Aberds 89 C9
ettercairn Aberds 83 F8
ettes Highld 87 F8
ewcott Oxon 28 F2
ewston N Yorks 51 D7
Ffair-Rhos Ceredig 24 B4
Ffairfach Carms 24 F3
Ffaldybrenin Carms 24 D3
Ffarmers Carms 24 D3
Ffawyddog Powys 25 G9
Fforest Carms 23 F10
Fforest-fâch Swansea 14 B2
Ffos-y-ffin Ceredig 24 B1
Ffostrasol Ceredig 23 B8
Ffridd-Uchaf Gwyn 41 E7
Ffrith Wrex 42 G5
Ffrwd Gwyn 40 E6
Ffynnon ddrain Carms 23 D9
Ffynnon-oer Ceredig 23 A10
Ffynnongroyw Flint 42 D4
Fidden Argyll 78 J6
Fiddes Aberds 83 E10
Fiddington Glos 26 E6
Fiddington Som 7 B11
Fiddleford Dorset 9 C7
Fiddlers Hamlet Essex 19 A11
Field Staffs 34 B6
Field Broughton Cumb 49 A3
Field Dalling Norf 38 B6
Field Head Leics 35 E10
Fifehead Magdalen Dorset 9 B6
Fifehead Neville Dorset 9 C6
Fifield Oxon 27 G9
Fifield Wilts 17 F8
Fifield Windsor 18 D6
Fifield Bavant Wilts 9 B9
Figheldean Wilts 17 G8
Filands Wilts 16 C6
Filby Norf 39 D10
Filey N Yorks 53 A7
Filgrave M Keynes 28 D5
Filkins Oxon 17 A9
Filleigh Devon 6 D5
Filleigh Devon 7 E6
Fillingham Lincs 46 D3
Fillongley Warks 35 G8
Filton S Glos 16 D3
Fimber E Yorks 52 C4
Finavon Angus 77 B7
Finchairn Argyll 73 C8
Fincham Norf 38 E2
Finchampstead Wokingham 18 E4
Finchdean Hants 10 C6
Finchingfield Essex 30 E3
Finchley London 19 B9
Findern Derbys 35 B9
Findhorn Moray 87 E13
Findhorn Bridge Highld 81 A10
Findo Gask Perth 76 E3
Findochty Moray 88 B4
Findon Aberds 83 D11
Findon W Sus 11 D10
Findon Mains Highld 87 E9
Findrack Ho. Aberds 83 C8
Finedon Northants 28 A6
Fingal Street Suff 31 B9
Fingask Aberds 83 A9
Fingerpost Worcs 26 A4
Fingest Bucks 18 B4
Finghall N Yorks 58 H2
Fingland Cumb 61 H8
Fingland Dumfries 60 B3
Finglesham Kent 21 F10
Fingringhoe Essex 31 F7
Finlarig Stirling 75 D8
Finmere Oxon 28 E3
Finnart Perth 75 B8
Finningham Suff 31 B7
Finningley S Yorks 45 C10
Finnygaud Aberds 88 C5
Finsbury London 19 C10
Finstall Worcs 26 B6
Finsthwaite Cumb 56 H5
Finstock Oxon 27 G10
Finstown Orkney 95 G4
Fintry Aberds 89 C7
Fintry Dundee 77 D7
Fintry Stirling 68 B5
Finzean Aberds 83 D8
Fionnphort Argyll 78 J6
Fionnsbhagh W Isles 90 J5
Fir Tree Durham 58 C2
Firbeck S Yorks 45 D9
Firby N Yorks 52 C3
Firby N Yorks 58 H3
Firgrove Gtr Man 44 A3
Firsby Lincs 47 F8
Firsdown Wilts 9 A11
First Coast Highld 86 B2
Fishbourne IoW 10 E4
Fishbourne W Sus 11 D7
Fishburn Durham 58 C4
Fishcross Clack 75 H11
Fisher Place Cumb 56 E5
Fisherford Aberds 89 E6
Fisher's Pond Hants 10 B3
Fisherstreet W Sus 11 A8
Fisherton Highld 87 F10
Fisherton S Ayrs 66 E5
Fishguard = Abergwaun Pembs 22 C4
Fishlake S Yorks 45 A10
Fishleigh Barton Devon 6 D4
Fishponds Bristol 16 D3
Fishpool Glos 26 F3
Fishtoft Lincs 37 A9
Fishtoft Drove Lincs 47 H7
Fishtown of Usan Angus 77 B10
Fishwick Borders 71 E8
Fiskavaig Highld 85 E8
Fiskerton Lincs 46 E4
Fiskerton Notts 45 G11
Fitling E Yorks 53 F8
Fittleton Wilts 17 G8
Fittleworth W Sus 11 C9
Fitton End Cambs 37 D10
Fitz Shrops 33 D10
Fitzhead Som 7 D10
Fitzwilliam W Yorks 51 H10
Fiunary Highld 79 G9
Five Acres Glos 26 G2
Five Ashes E Sus 12 D4
Five Oak Green Kent 20 G3
Five Oaks Jersey 11
Five Oaks W Sus 11 B9
Five Roads Carms 23 F9
Fivecrosses Ches W 43 E8
Fivehead Som 8 B2
Flack's Green Essex 30 G4
Flackwell Heath Bucks 18 C5
Fladbury Worcs 26 D6
Fladdabister Shetland 96 K6
Flagg Derbys 44 F5
Flamborough E Yorks 53 B8
Flamstead Herts 29 G7
Flamstead End Herts 19 A10
Flansham W Sus 11 D8
Flanshaw W Yorks 51 G9
Flasby N Yorks 50 D5
Flash Staffs 44 F4
Flashader Highld 85 C8
Flask Inn N Yorks 59 F10
Flaunden Herts 19 A7
Flawborough Notts 36 A3
Flawith N Yorks 51 C10
Flax Bourton N Som 15 E11
Flaxby N Yorks 51 D9
Flaxholme Derbys 35 A9
Flaxley Glos 26 G3
Flaxpool Som 7 C10
Flaxton N Yorks 52 C2
Fleckney Leics 36 F2
Flecknoe Warks 28 B2
Fledborough Notts 46 E2
Fleet Hants 10 D6
Fleet Hants 18 F5
Fleet Lincs 37 C9
Fleet Hargate Lincs 37 C9
Fleetham Northumb 71 H10
Fleetlands Hants 10 D4
Fleetville Herts 29 H8
Fleetwood Lancs 49 E3
Flemingston V Glam 14 D6
Flemington S Lanark 68 E5
Flempton Suff 30 B5
Fleoideabhagh W Isles 90 J5
Fletchertown Cumb 56 B4
Fletching E Sus 12 D3
Flexbury Corn 6 F1
Flexford Sur 18 G6
Flimby Cumb 56 C2
Flimwell E Sus 12 C6
Flint = Y Fflint Flint 42 E5
Flint Mountain Flint 42 E5
Flintham Notts 45 H11
Flinton E Yorks 53 F8
Flintsham Hereford 25 C10
Flitcham Norf 38 C3
Flitton C Beds 29 E7
Flitwick C Beds 29 E7
Flixborough N Lincs 52 H4
Flixborough Stather N Lincs 46 A2
Flixton Gtr Man 43 C10
Flixton N Yorks 52 B6
Flixton Suff 39 G9
Flockton W Yorks 44 A6
Flodaigh W Isles 84 C3
Flodden Northumb 71 G8
Flodigarry Highld 85 A9
Flood's Ferry Cambs 37 F9
Flookburgh Cumb 49 B3
Florden Norf 39 F7
Flore Northants 28 B3
Flotterton Northumb 62 C5
Flowton Suff 31 D7
Flush House W Yorks 44 B5
Flushing Aberds 89 D10
Flushing Corn 3 F7
Flyford Flavell Worcs 26 C6
Foals Green Suff 31 A9
Fobbing Thurrock 20 C4
Fochabers Moray 88 C3
Fochriw Caerph 25 H8
Fockerby N Lincs 52 H4
Fodderletter Moray 82 A3
Fodderty Highld 87 F8
Foel Powys 32 D5
Foel-gastell Carms 23 E10
Foffarty Angus 77 C7
Foggathorpe E Yorks 52 F3
Fogo Borders 70 F6
Fogorig Borders 70 F6
Foindle Highld 92 E4
Folda Angus 76 A4
Fole Staffs 34 B6
Foleshill W Mid 35 G9
Folke Dorset 8 C5
Folkestone Kent 21 H9
Folkingham Lincs 37 B6
Folkington E Sus 12 F4
Folksworth Cambs 37 G7
Folkton N Yorks 53 B6
Folla Rule Aberds 89 E7
Follifoot N Yorks 51 D9
Folly Gate Devon 6 G4
Fonthill Bishop Wilts 9 A8
Fonthill Gifford Wilts 9 A8
Fontmell Magna Dorset 9 C7
Fontwell W Sus 11 D8
Foolow Derbys 44 E5
Foots Cray London 19 D11
Forbestown Aberds 82 B5
Force Mills Cumb 56 G5
Forcett N Yorks 58 E2
Ford Argyll 73 C7
Ford Bucks 28 H4
Ford Devon 6 D3
Ford Glos 27 F7
Ford Northumb 71 G8
Ford Shrops 33 D10
Ford Staffs 44 G4
Ford W Sus 11 D8
Ford Wilts 16 D5
Ford End Essex 30 G3
Ford Street Som 7 E10
Fordcombe Kent 12 B4
Fordell Fife 69 B10
Forden Powys 33 E8
Forder Green Devon 5 E8
Fordham Cambs 30 A3
Fordham Essex 30 F6
Fordham Norf 38 F2
Fordhouses W Mid 34 E5
Fordingbridge Hants 9 C10
Fordon E Yorks 52 B6
Fordoun Aberds 83 F9
Ford's Green Suff 31 B7
Fordstreet Essex 30 F6
Fordwells Oxon 27 G10
Fordwich Kent 21 F8
Fordyce Aberds 88 B5
Forebridge Staffs 34 C5
Forest Durham 57 C10
Forest Becks Lancs 50 D3
Forest Gate London 19 C11
Forest Green Sur 19 G8
Forest Hall Cumb 57 F7
Forest Head Cumb 61 H11
Forest Hill Oxon 28 H2
Forest Lane Head N Yorks 51 D9
Forest Lodge Argyll 74 C5
Forest Lodge Highld 82 A2
Forest Lodge Perth 81 F11
Forest Mill Clack 69 A8
Forest Row E Sus 12 C3
Forest Town Notts 45 F9
Forestburn Gate Northumb 62 D6
Foresterseat Moray 88 C1
Forestside W Sus 11 C6
Forfar Angus 77 B7
Forgandenny Perth 76 F3
Forge Powys 32 F3
Forge Side Torf 25 H9
Forgewood N Lanark 68 E6
Forgie Moray 88 C3
Forglen Ho. Aberds 89 C6
Formby Mers 42 B6
Forncett End Norf 39 F7
Forncett St Mary Norf 39 F7
Forncett St Peter Norf 39 F7
Forneth Perth 76 C3
Fornham All Saints Suff 30 B5
Fornham St Martin Suff 30 B5
Forres Moray 87 F13
Forrest Lodge Dumfries 67 H8
Forrestfield N Lanark 69 D7
Forsbrook Staffs 34 A5
Forse Highld 94 G4
Forse Ho. Highld 94 G4
Forsinain Highld 93 E12
Forsinard Highld 93 E11
Forsinard Station Highld 93 E11
Forston Dorset 8 E5
Fort Augustus Highld 80 C5
Fort George Guern 11
Fort George Highld 87 F10
Fort William Highld 80 F3
Forteviot Perth 76 F3
Forth S Lanark 69 E8
Forth Road Bridge Edin 69 C10
Forthampton Glos 26 E5
Fortingall Perth 75 C10
Forton Hants 17 G11
Forton Lancs 49 D4
Forton Shrops 33 D10
Forton Som 8 D2
Forton Staffs 34 C3
Forton Heath Shrops 33 D10
Fortrie Aberds 89 D6
Fortrose Highld 87 F10
Fortuneswell Dorset 8 G5
Forty Green Bucks 18 B6
Forty Hill London 19 B10
Forward Green Suff 31 C7
Fosbury Wilts 17 F10
Fosdyke Lincs 37 B9
Foss Perth 75 B10
Foss Cross Glos 27 H7
Fossebridge Glos 27 G7
Foster Street Essex 29 H11
Fosterhouses S Yorks 45 A10
Foston Derbys 35 B7
Foston Lincs 36 A4
Foston N Yorks 52 C2
Foston on the Wolds E Yorks 53 D7
Fotherby Lincs 47 C7
Fotheringhay Northants 37 F6
Foubister Orkney 95 H6
Foul Mile E Sus 12 E5
Foulby W Yorks 51 H9
Foulden Borders 71 E8
Foulden Norf 38 F3
Foulis Castle Highld 87 E8
Foulridge Lancs 50 E4
Foulsham Norf 38 C6
Fountainhall Borders 70 F3
Four Ashes Staffs 34 G4
Four Ashes Suff 31 A7
Four Crosses Powys 33 D8
Four Crosses Powys 33 E6
Four Crosses Wrex 42 G5
Four Elms Kent 19 G11
Four Forks Som 7 C11
Four Gotes Cambs 37 D10
Four Lane Ends Ches W 43 F8
Four Lanes Corn 2 F5
Four Marks Hants 10 A5
Four Mile Bridge Anglesey 40 C4
Four Oaks E Sus 13 D7
Four Oaks W Mid 35 F7
Four Oaks W Mid 35 G8
Four Roads Carms 23 F9
Four Roads IoM 48 F2
Four Throws Kent 13 D6
Fourlane Ends Derbys 45 G7
Fourlanes End Ches E 44 G2
Fourpenny Highld 87 B11
Fourstones Northumb 62 G4
Fovant Wilts 9 B9
Foveran Aberds 89 F9
Fowey Corn 4 F2
Fowley Common Warr 43 C9
Fowlis Angus 76 D6
Fowlis Wester Perth 76 E2
Fowlmere Cambs 29 D11
Fownhope Hereford 26 E2
Fox Corner Sur 18 F6
Fox Lane Hants 18 F5
Fox Street Essex 31 F7
Foxbar Renfs 68 D3
Foxcombe Hill Oxon 17 A11
Foxdale IoM 48 E2
Foxearth Essex 30 D5
Foxfield Cumb 56 H4
Foxham Wilts 16 D6
Foxhole Corn 3 D8
Foxhole Swansea 14 B2
Foxholes N Yorks 52 B6
Foxhunt Green E Sus 12 E4
Foxley Norf 38 C6
Foxley Wilts 16 C5
Foxt Staffs 44 H4
Foxton Cambs 29 D11
Foxton Durham 58 D4
Foxton Leics 36 F3
Foxup N Yorks 50 B4
Foxwist Green Ches W 43 F9
Foxwood Shrops 34 H2
Foy Hereford 26 F2
Foyers Highld 81 A6
Fraddam Corn 2 F4
Fraddon Corn 3 D8
Fradley Staffs 35 D7
Fradswell Staffs 34 B5
Fraisthorpe E Yorks 53 C7
Framfield E Sus 12 D3
Framingham Earl Norf 39 E8
Framingham Pigot Norf 39 E8
Framlingham Suff 31 B9
Frampton Dorset 8 E4
Frampton Lincs 37 B9
Frampton Cotterell S Glos 16 C3
Frampton Mansell Glos 16 A6
Frampton on Severn Glos 26 H4
Frampton West End Lincs 37 A8
Framsden Suff 31 C8
Framwellgate Moor Durham 58 B3
Franche Worcs 34 H4
Frankby Mers 42 D5
Frankley Worcs 34 G5
Frank's Bridge Powys 25 C8
Frankton Warks 27 A11
Frant E Sus 12 C4
Fraserburgh Aberds 89 B9
Frating Green Essex 31 F7
Fratton Ptsmth 10 E5
Freathy Corn 4 F4
Freckenham Suff 30 A3
Freckleton Lancs 49 G4
Freeby Leics 36 C4
Freehay Staffs 34 A6
Freeland Oxon 27 G11
Freester Shetland 96 H6
Freethorpe Norf 39 E10
Freiston Lincs 37 A9
Fremington Devon 6 C4
Fremington N Yorks 58 G1
Frenchay S Glos 16 D3
Frenchbeer Devon 5 C7
Frenich Stirling 75 G7
Frensham Sur 18 G5
Fresgoe Highld 93 C12
Freshfield Mers 42 B5
Freshford Bath 16 E4
Freshwater IoW 10 F2
Freshwater Bay IoW 10 F2
Freshwater East Pembs 22 G5
Fressingfield Suff 39 H8
Freston Suff 31 E8
Freswick Highld 94 D5
Fretherne Glos 26 H4
Frettenham Norf 39 D8
Freuchie Fife 76 G5
Freuchies Angus 76 A5
Freystrop Pembs 22 E4
Friar's Gate E Sus 12 C3
Friarton Perth 76 E4
Friday Bridge Cambs 37 E10
Friday Street E Sus 12 F5
Fridaythorpe E Yorks 52 D4
Friern Barnet London 19 B9
Friesland Argyll 78 F4
Friesthorpe Lincs 46 D4
Frieston Lincs 46 H3
Frieth Bucks 18 B4
Frilford Oxon 17 B11
Frilsham W Berks 18 D2
Frimley Sur 18 F5
Frimley Green Sur 18 F5
Frindsbury Medway 20 D4
Fring Norf 38 B3
Fringford Oxon 28 F3
Frinsted Kent 20 F5
Frinton-on-Sea Essex 31 F9
Friockheim Angus 77 C8
Friog Gwyn 32 D2
Frisby on the Wreake Leics 36 D2
Friskney Lincs 47 G8
Friskney Eaudike Lincs 47 G8
Friskney Tofts Lincs 47 G8
Friston E Sus 12 G4
Friston Suff 31 B11
Fritchley Derbys 45 G7
Frith Bank Lincs 47 H7
Frith Common Worcs 26 B3
Fritham Hants 9 C11
Frithelstock Devon 6 E3
Frithelstock Stone Devon 6 E3
Frithville Lincs 47 G7
Frittenden Kent 13 B7
Frittiscombe Devon 5 G9
Fritton Norf 39 E10
Fritton Norf 39 F8
Fritwell Oxon 28 F2
Frizinghall W Yorks 51 F7
Frizington Cumb 56 E2
Frocester Glos 16 A4
Frodesley Shrops 33 E11
Frodingham N Lincs 46 A2
Frodsham Ches W 43 E8
Frogden Borders 70 H6
Froggatt Derbys 44 E6
Froghall Staffs 44 H4
Frogmore Devon 5 G8
Frogmore Hants 18 F5
Frognall Lincs 37 D7
Frogshall Norf 39 B8
Frolesworth Leics 35 F11
Frome Som 16 G4
Frome St Quintin Dorset 8 D4
Fromes Hill Hereford 26 D3
Fron Denb 42 F3
Fron Gwyn 40 G5
Fron Gwyn 41 E7
Fron Powys 25 B7
Fron Powys 33 E8
Fron Powys 33 F7
Froncysyllte Wrex 33 A8
Frongoch Gwyn 32 B5
Frostenden Suff 39 G10
Frosterley Durham 58 C1
Frotoft Orkney 95 F5
Froxfield Wilts 17 E9
Froxfield Green Hants 10 B6
Froyle Hants 18 G4
Fryerning Essex 20 A3
Fryton N Yorks 52 B2
Fulbeck Lincs 46 G3
Fulbourn Cambs 30 C2
Fulbrook Oxon 27 G9
Fulford Som 7 D11
Fulford Staffs 34 B5
Fulford York 52 E2
Fulham London 19 D9
Fulking W Sus 11 C11
Full Sutton E Yorks 52 D3
Fullarton Glasgow 68 D5
Fullarton N Ayrs 66 C6
Fuller Street Essex 30 G4
Fuller's Moor Ches W 43 G7
Fullerton Hants 17 H10
Fulletby Lincs 46 E6
Fullwood E Ayrs 67 A7
Fulmer Bucks 18 C6
Fulmodestone Norf 38 B5
Fulnetby Lincs 46 E4
Fulstow Lincs 47 C7
Fulwell T&W 63 H9
Fulwood Lancs 49 F5
Fulwood S Yorks 45 D7
Fundenhall Norf 39 F7
Fundenhall Street Norf 39 F7
Funtington W Sus 11 D6
Funtley Hants 10 D4
Funtullich Perth 75 E10
Funzie Shetland 96 D8
Furley Devon 8 D1
Furnace Argyll 73 C9
Furnace Carms 23 F10
Furnace End Warks 35 F8
Furneaux Pelham Herts 29 F11
Furness Vale Derbys 44 D4
Furze Platt Windsor 18 C5
Furzehill Devon 7 B6
Fyfett Som 7 E11
Fyfield Essex 30 H2
Fyfield Glos 17 A9
Fyfield Hants 17 G9
Fyfield Oxon 17 B11
Fyfield Wilts 17 E8
Fylingthorpe N Yorks 59 F10
Fyvie Aberds 89 E7

G

Gabhsann bho Dheas W Isles 91 B9
Gabhsann bho Thuath W Isles 91 B9
Gablon Highld 87 B10
Gabroc Hill E Ayrs 67 A7
Gaddesby Leics 36 D2
Gadebridge Herts 29 H7
Gaer Powys 25 F8
Gaerllwyd Mon 15 B10
Gaerwen Anglesey 40 C6
Gagingwell Oxon 27 F11
Gaick Lodge Highld 81 E9
Gailey Staffs 34 D5
Gainford Durham 58 E2
Gainsborough Lincs 46 C2
Gainsborough Suff 31 D8
Gainsford End Essex 30 E4
Gairloch Highld 85 A13
Gairlochy Highld 80 E3
Gairney Bank Perth 76 H4
Gairnshiel Lodge Aberds 82 C4
Gaisgill Cumb 57 F8
Gaitsgill Cumb 56 B5
Galashiels Borders 70 G3
Galgate Lancs 49 D4
Galhampton Som 8 B5
Gallaberry Dumfries 60 E5
Gallachoille Argyll 72 E6
Gallanach Argyll 78 E5
Gallanach Argyll 79 J11
Gallantry Bank Ches E 43 G8
Gallatown Fife 69 A11
Galley Common Warks 35 F9
Galley Hill Cambs 29 B10
Galleyend Essex 20 A4
Galleywood Essex 20 A4
Gallin Perth 75 C8
Gallowfauld Angus 77 C7
Gallows Green Staffs 35 A6
Galltair Highld 85 F13
Galmisdale Highld 78 C7
Galmpton Devon 5 G7
Galmpton Torbay 5 F9
Galphay N Yorks 51 B8
Galston E Ayrs 67 C8
Galtrigill Highld 84 C6
Gamblesby Cumb 57 C8
Gamesley Derbys 44 C4
Gamlingay Cambs 29 C9
Gammersgill N Yorks 51 A6
Gamston Notts 45 E11
Ganarew Hereford 26 G2
Ganavan Argyll 79 H11
Gang Corn 4 E4
Ganllwyd Gwyn 32 C3
Gannochy Angus 83 F7
Gannochy Perth 76 E4
Gansclet Highld 94 F5
Ganstead E Yorks 53 F7
Ganthorpe N Yorks 52 B2
Ganton N Yorks 52 B5
Garbat Highld 86 E7
Garbhallt Argyll 73 D9
Garboldisham Norf 38 G6
Garden City Flint 42 F6
Garden Village W Yorks 51 F10
Garden Village Wrex 42 G6
Gardenstown Aberds 89 B7
Garderhouse Shetland 96 J5
Gardham E Yorks 52 E5
Gardin Shetland 96 G6
Gare Hill Som 16 G4
Garelochhead Argyll 73 D11
Garford Oxon 17 B11
Garforth W Yorks 51 F10
Gargrave N Yorks 50 D5
Gargunnock Stirling 68 A6
Garlic Street Norf 39 G8
Garlieston Dumfries 55 E7
Garlinge Green Kent 21 F8
Garlogie Aberds 83 C9
Garmond Aberds 89 C8
Garmony Argyll 79 G9
Garmouth Moray 88 B3
Garn-yr-erw Torf 25 G9
Garnant Carms 24 G3
Garndiffaith Torf 15 A8
Garndolbenmaen Gwyn 40 F6
Garnedd Conwy 41 E9
Garnett Bridge Cumb 57 G7
Garnfadryn Gwyn 40 G4
Garnkirk N Lanark 68 D5
Garnlydan Bl Gwent 25 G8
Garnswllt Swansea 24 H3
Garrabost W Isles 91 D10
Garraron Argyll 73 C7
Garras Corn 2 G6
Garreg Gwyn 41 F8
Garrick Perth 75 F11
Garrigill Cumb 57 B9
Garriston N Yorks 58 G2
Garroch Dumfries 67 H8
Garrogie Lodge Highld 81 B7
Garros Highld 85 B9
Garrow Perth 75 C11
Garryhorn Dumfries 67 G8
Garsdale Cumb 57 H9
Garsdale Head Cumb 57 G9
Garsdon Wilts 16 C6
Garshall Green Staffs 34 B5
Garsington Oxon 18 A2
Garstang Lancs 49 E4
Garston Mers 43 D7
Garswood Mers 43 C8
Gartcosh N Lanark 68 D5
Garth Bridgend 14 B4
Garth Gwyn 41 C7
Garth Powys 24 D6
Garth Shetland 96 H4
Garth Wrex 33 A8
Garth Row Cumb 57 G7
Garthamlock Glasgow 68 D5
Garthbrengy Powys 25 E7
Garthdee Aberdeen 83 C11
Gartheli Ceredig 23 A10
Garthmyl Powys 33 F7
Garthorpe Leics 36 C4
Garthorpe N Lincs 52 H4
Gartly Aberds 88 E5
Gartmore Stirling 75 H8
Gartnagrenach Argyll 72 H6
Gartness N Lanark 68 D6
Gartness Stirling 68 B4
Gartocharn W Dunb 68 B3
Garton E Yorks 53 F8
Garton-on-the-Wolds E Yorks 52 D5
Gartsherrie N Lanark 68 D6
Gartymore Highld 93 H13
Garvald E Loth 70 C4
Garvamore Highld 81 D7
Garvard Argyll 72 D2
Garvault Hotel Highld 93 F10
Garve Highld 86 E6
Garvestone Norf 38 E6
Garvock Aberds 83 F9
Garvock Invclyd 73 F11
Garway Hereford 25 F11
Garway Hill Hereford 25 F11
Gaskan Highld 79 D10
Gastard Wilts 16 E5
Gasthorpe Norf 38 G5
Gatcombe IoW 10 F3
Gate Burton Lincs 46 D2
Gate Helmsley N Yorks 52 D2
Gateacre Mers 43 D7
Gatebeck Cumb 57 H7
Gateford Notts 45 D9
Gateforth N Yorks 52 G1
Gatehead E Ayrs 67 C6
Gatehouse Northumb 62 E3
Gatehouse of Fleet Dumfries 55 D9
Gatelawbridge Dumfries 60 D5
Gateley Norf 38 C5
Gatenby N Yorks 58 H4
Gateshead T&W 63 G8
Gatesheath Ches W 43 F7
Gateside Aberds 83 B8
Gateside Angus 77 C7
Gateside E Renf 68 E3
Gateside Fife 76 G4
Gateside N Ayrs 67 A6
Gathurst Gtr Man 43 B8
Gatley Gtr Man 44 D2
Gattonside Borders 70 G4
Gatwick Airport W Sus 12 B1
Gaufron Powys 24 B6
Gaulby Leics 36 E2
Gauldry Fife 76 E6
Gaunt's Common Dorset 9 D9
Gautby Lincs 46 E5
Gavinton Borders 70 E6
Gawber S Yorks 45 B7
Gawcott Bucks 28 E3
Gawsworth Ches E 44 F2
Gawthorpe W Yorks 51 G8
Gawthrop Cumb 57 H8
Gawthwaite Cumb 49 A2
Gay Street W Sus 11 B9
Gaydon Warks 27 C10
Gayfield Orkney 95 C5
Gayhurst M Keynes 28 D5
Gayle N Yorks 57 H10
Gayles N Yorks 58 F2
Gayton Mers 42 D5
Gayton Norf 38 D3
Gayton Northants 28 C4
Gayton Staffs 34 C5
Gayton le Marsh Lincs 47 D8
Gayton le Wold Lincs 46 D6
Gayton Thorpe Norf 38 D3
Gaywood Norf 38 C2
Gazeley Suff 30 B4
Geanies House Highld 87 D11
Gearraidh Bhailteas W Isles 84 F2
Gearraidh Bhaird W Isles 91 E8
Gearraidh na h-Aibhne W Isles 90 D7
Gearraidh na Monadh W Isles 84 G2
Geary Highld 84 B7
Geddes House Highld 87 F11
Gedding Suff 30 C6
Geddington Northants 36 G4
Gedintailor Highld 85 E10
Gedling Notts 36 A2
Gedney Lincs 37 C10
Gedney Broadgate Lincs 37 C10
Gedney Drove End Lincs 37 C10
Gedney Dyke Lincs 37 C10
Gedney Hill Lincs 37 D9
Gee Cross Gtr Man 44 C3
Geilston Argyll 68 C2
Geirinis W Isles 84 D2
Geise Highld 94 D3
Geisiadar W Isles 90 D6
Geldeston Norf 39 F9
Gell Conwy 41 D10
Gelli Pembs 22 E5
Gelli Rhondda 14 B5
Gellideg M Tydf 25 H7
Gellifor Denb 42 F4
Gelligaer Caerph 15 B7
Gellilydan Gwyn 41 G8
Gellinudd Neath 14 A3
Gellyburn Perth 76 D3
Gellywen Carms 23 D7
Gelston Dumfries 55 D10
Gelston Lincs 36 A5
Gembling E Yorks 53 D7
Gentleshaw Staffs 35 D6
Geocrab W Isles 90 H6
George Green Bucks 19 C7
George Nympton Devon 6 D6
Georgefield Dumfries 61 D8
Georgeham Devon 6 C3
Georgetown Bl Gwent 25 H8
Gerlan Gwyn 41 D8
Germansweek Devon 6 G3
Germoe Corn 2 G4
Gerrans Corn 3 F7
Gerrards Cross Bucks 19 C7
Gestingthorpe Essex 30 E5
Geuffordd Powys 33 D8
Gib Hill Ches W 43 E9
Gibbet Hill Warks 35 G11
Gibbshill Dumfries 60 F3
Gidea Park London 20 C2
Gidleigh Devon 5 C7
Giffnock E Renf 68 E4
Gifford E Loth 70 D4
Giffordland N Ayrs 66 B5
Giffordtown Fife 76 F5
Giggleswick N Yorks 50 C4
Gilberdyke E Yorks 52 G4
Gilchriston E Loth 70 D3
Gilcrux Cumb 56 C3
Gildersome W Yorks 51 G8
Gildingwells S Yorks 45 D9
Gileston V Glam 14 E6
Gilfach Caerph 15 B7
Gilfach Goch Rhondda 14 C5
Gilfachrheda Ceredig 23 A9
Gillamoor N Yorks 59 H7
Gillar's Green Mers 43 C7
Gillen Highld 84 C7
Gilling East N Yorks 52 B2
Gilling West N Yorks 58 F2
Gillingham Dorset 9 B7
Gillingham Medway 20 E4
Gillingham Norf 39 F10
Gillock Highld 94 E4
Gillow Heath Staffs 44 G2
Gills Highld 94 C5
Gill's Green Kent 13 C6
Gilmanscleuch Borders 61 A9
Gilmerton Edin 69 D11
Gilmerton Perth 75 E11
Gilmonby Durham 57 E11
Gilmorton Leics 36 G1
Gilmourton S Lanark 68 F5
Gilsland Northumb 62 G2
Gilsland Spa Cumb 62 G2
Gilston Borders 70 E3
Gilston Herts 29 G11
Gilwern Mon 25 G9
Gimingham Norf 39 B8
Giosla W Isles 90 E6
Gipping Suff 31 B7
Gipsey Bridge Lincs 46 H6
Girdle Toll N Ayrs 66 B6
Girlsta Shetland 96 H6
Girsby N Yorks 58 F4
Girtford C Beds 29 C8
Girthon Dumfries 55 D9
Girton Cambs 29 B11
Girton Notts 46 F2
Girvan S Ayrs 66 G4
Gisburn Lancs 50 E4
Gisleham Suff 39 G11
Gislingham Suff 31 A7
Gissing Norf 39 G7
Gittisham Devon 7 G10
Gladestry Powys 25 C9
Gladsmuir E Loth 70 C3
Glais Swansea 14 A3
Glaisdale N Yorks 59 F8
Glame Highld 85 D10
Glamis Angus 76 C6
Glan Adda Gwyn 41 C7
Glan Conwy Conwy 41 C10
Glan Conwy Conwy 41 E10
Glan-Duar Carms 23 B10
Glan-Dwyfach Gwyn 40 F6
Glan Gors Anglesey 40 C6
Glan-rhyd Gwyn 40 E6
Glan-traeth Anglesey 40 C4
Glan-y-don Flint 42 E4
Glan-y-nant Powys 32 G5
Glan-y-wern Gwyn 41 G8
Glan-yr-afon Anglesey 41 B8
Glan-yr-afon Gwyn 32 A5
Glan-yr-afon Gwyn 32 A6
Glanaman Carms 24 G3
Glandford Norf 38 A6
Glandwr Pembs 22 D6
Glandy Cross Carms 22 D6
Glandyfi Ceredig 32 F2
Glangrwyney Powys 25 G9
Glanmule Powys 33 F7
Glanrafon Ceredig 32 G2
Glanrhyd Gwyn 40 G4
Glanrhyd Pembs 22 B6
Glanton Northumb 62 B6
Glanton Pike Northumb 62 B6
Glanvilles Wootton Dorset 8 D5
Glapthorn Northants 36 F6
Glapwell Derbys 45 F8
Glas-allt Shiel Aberds 82 E4
Glasbury Powys 25 E8
Glaschoil Highld 87 H13
Glascoed Denb 42 E2
Glascoed Mon 15 A9
Glascoed Powys 33 D7
Glascorrie Aberds 82 D5
Glascote Staffs 35 E8
Glascwm Powys 25 C8
Glasdrum Argyll 74 C3
Glasfryn Conwy 42 G2
Glasgow Glasgow 68 D4
Glashvin Highld 85 B9
Glasinfryn Gwyn 41 D7
Glasnacardoch Highld 79 B9
Glasnakille Highld 85 G10
Glasphein Highld 84 D6
Glaspwll Powys 32 F3
Glassburn Highld 86 H6
Glasserton Dumfries 55 F7
Glassford S Lanark 68 F6
Glasshouse Hill Glos 26 F4
Glasshouses N Yorks 51 C7
Glasslie Fife 76 G5
Glasson Cumb 61 G8
Glasson Lancs 49 D4
Glassonby Cumb 57 C7
Glasterlaw Angus 77 B8
Glaston Rutland 36 E4
Glastonbury Som 15 H11
Glatton Cambs 37 G7
Glazebrook Warr 43 C9
Glazebury Warr 43 C9
Glazeley Shrops 34 G3
Gleadless S Yorks 45 D7
Gleadsmoss Ches E 44 F2
Gleann Tholàstaidh W Isles 91 C10
Gleaston Cumb 49 B2
Gleiniant Powys 32 F5
Glemsford Suff 30 D5
Glen Dumfries 55 D8
Glen Dumfries 60 F4
Glen Auldyn IoM 48 C4
Glen Bernisdale Highld 85 D9
Glen Ho Borders 69 G11
Glen Mona IoM 48 D4
Glen Nevis House Highld 80 F3
Glen Parva Leics 36 F1
Glen Sluain Argyll 73 D9
Glen Tanar House Aberds 82 D6
Glen Trool Lodge Dumfries 55 A7
Glen Village Falk 69 C7
Glen Vine IoM 48 E3
Glenamachrie Argyll 74 E2
Glenbarr Argyll 65 E7
Glenbeg Highld 79 E8
Glenbeg Highld 82 A2
Glenbervie Aberds 83 E9
Glenboig N Lanark 68 D6
Glenborrodale Highld 79 E9
Glenbranter Argyll 73 D10
Glenbreck Borders 60 A6
Glenbrein Lodge Highld 81 B6
Glenbrittle House Highld 85 F9
Glenbuchat Lodge Aberds 82 B5
Glenbuck E Ayrs 68 H6
Glenburn Renfs 68 D3
Glencalvie Lodge Highld 86 C7
Glencanisp Lodge Highld 92 G4
Glencaple Dumfries 60 G5
Glencarron Lodge Highld 86 F3
Glencarse Perth 76 E4
Glencassley Castle Highld 92 J7
Glenceitlein Highld 74 C4
Glencoe Highld 74 B3
Glencraig Fife 76 H4
Glencripesdale Highld 79 F9
Glencrosh Dumfries 60 E3
Glendavan Ho. Aberds 82 C6
Glendevon Perth 76 G2
Glendoe Lodge Highld 80 C6
Glendoebeg Highld 80 C6
Glendoick Perth 76 E5
Glendoll Lodge Angus 82 F4
Glendoune S Ayrs 66 G4
Glenduckie Fife 76 F5
Glendye Lodge Aberds 83 E8
Gleneagles Hotel Perth 76 F2
Gleneagles House Perth 76 G2
Glenegedale Argyll 64 C4
Glenelg Highld 85 G13
Glenernie Moray 87 G13
Glenfarg Perth 76 F4
Glenfarquhar Lodge Aberds 83 E9
Glenferness House Highld 87 G12
Glenfeshie Lodge Highld 81 D10
Glenfield Leics 35 E11
Glenfinnan Highld 79 C11
Glenfoot Perth 76 F4
Glenfyne Lodge Argyll 74 F5
Glengap Dumfries 55 D9
Glengarnock N Ayrs 66 A6
Glengorm Castle Argyll 78 F7
Glengrasco Highld 85 D9
Glenhead Farm Angus 76 A5
Glenhoul Dumfries 67 H9
Glenhurich Highld 79 E11
Glenkerry Borders 61 B8
Glenkiln Dumfries 60 F4
Glenkindie Aberds 82 B6
Glenlatterach Moray 88 C1
Glenlee Dumfries 55 A9
Glenlichorn Perth 75 F10
Glenlivet Moray 82 A3
Glenlochsie Perth 82 F2
Glenloig N Ayrs 66 C2
Glenluce Dumfries 54 D5
Glenmallan Argyll 74 H5
Glenmarksie Highld 86 F6
Glenmassan Argyll 73 E10
Glenmavis N Lanark 68 D6
Glenmaye IoM 48 E2
Glenmidge Dumfries 60 E4
Glenmore Argyll 73 B7
Glenmore Highld 85 D9
Glenmore Lodge Highld 82 C1
Glenmoy Angus 77 A7
Glenogil Angus 77 A7
Glenprosen Lodge Angus 82 G4
Glenprosen Village Angus 82 G5
Glenquiech Angus 77 A7
Glenreasdell Mains Argyll 73 H7
Glenree N Ayrs 66 D2
Glenridding Cumb 56 E5
Glenrossal Highld 92 J7
Glenrothes Fife 76 G5
Glensanda Highld 79 G11
Glensaugh Aberds 83 F8
Glenshero Lodge Highld 81 D7
Glenstockadale Dumfries 54 C3
Glenstriven Argyll 73 F9
Glentaggart S Lanark 69 H7
Glentham Lincs 46 C4
Glentirranmuir Stirling 68 A5
Glenton Aberds 83 A8
Glentress Borders 69 G11
Glentromie Lodge Highld 81 D9
Glentrool Village Dumfries 54 B6
Glentruan IoM 48 B4
Glentruim House Highld 81 D8
Glentworth Lincs 46 D3
Glenuig Highld 79 D9
Glenurquhart Highld 87 E10
Glespin S Lanark 69 H7
Gletness Shetland 96 H6
Glewstone Hereford 26 F2
Glinton Pboro 37 E7
Glooston Leics 36 F3
Glororum Northumb 71 G10
Glossop Derbys 44 C4
Gloster Hill Northumb 63 C8
Gloucester Glos 26 G5
Gloup Shetland 96 C7
Glusburn N Yorks 50 E6
Glutt Lodge Highld 93 F12
Glutton Bridge Staffs 44 F4
Glympton Oxon 27 F11
Glyn-Ceiriog Wrex 33 B8
Glyn-cywarch Gwyn 41 G8
Glyn Ebwy = Ebbw Vale Bl Gwent 25 H8
Glyn-neath = Glynedd Neath 24 H5
Glynarthen Ceredig 23 B8
Glynbrochan Powys 32 G5
Glyncoch Rhondda 14 B6
Glyncorrwg Neath 14 B4
Glynde E Sus 12 F3

Glyndebourne E Sus 12 E3
Glyndyfrdwy Denb 33 A7
Glynedd = Glyn-neath Neath 24 H5
Glynogwr Bridgend 14 C5
Glyntaff Rhondda 14 C6
Glyntawe Powys 24 G5
Gnosall Staffs 34 C4
Gnosall Heath Staffs 34 C4
Goadby Leics 36 F3
Goadby Marwood Leics 36 C3
Goat Lees Kent 21 G7
Goatacre Wilts 17 D7
Goathill Dorset 8 C5
Goathland N Yorks 59 F9
Goathurst Som 8 A1
Gobernuisgach Lodge Highld 92 E7
Gobhaig W Isles 90 G5
Gobowen Shrops 33 B9
Godalming Sur 18 G6
Godley Gtr Man 44 C3
Godmanchester Cambs 29 A9
Godmanstone Dorset 8 E5
Godmersham Kent 21 F7
Godney Som 15 G10
Godolphin Cross Corn 2 F5
Godre'r-graig Neath 24 H4
Godshill Hants 9 C10
Godshill IoW 10 F4
Godstone Sur 19 F10
Godwinscroft Hants 9 E10
Goetre Mon 25 H10
Goferydd Anglesey 40 B4
Goff's Oak Herts 19 A10
Gogar Edin 69 C10
Goginan Ceredig 32 G2
Golan Gwyn 41 F7
Golant Corn 4 F2
Golberdon Corn 4 D4
Golborne Gtr Man 43 C9
Golcar W Yorks 51 H7
Gold Hill Norf 37 F11
Goldcliff Newport 15 C9
Golden Cross E Sus 12 E4
Golden Green Kent 20 G3
Golden Grove Carms 23 E10
Golden Hill Hants 10 E1
Golden Pot Hants 18 G4
Golden Valley Glos 26 F6
Goldenhill Stoke 44 G2
Golders Green London 19 C9
Goldhanger Essex 30 H6
Golding Shrops 33 E11
Goldington Bedford 29 C7
Goldsborough N Yorks 51 D9
Goldsborough N Yorks 59 E9
Goldsithney Corn 2 F4
Goldsworthy Devon 6 D2
Goldthorpe S Yorks 45 B8
Gollanfield Highld 87 F11
Golspie Highld 93 J11
Golval Highld 93 C11
Gomeldon Wilts 17 H8
Gomersal W Yorks 51 G8
Gomshall Sur 19 G7
Gonalston Notts 45 H10
Gonfirth Shetland 96 G5
Good Easter Essex 30 G3
Gooderstone Norf 38 E3
Goodleigh Devon 6 C5
Goodmanham E Yorks 52 E4
Goodnestone Kent 21 E7
Goodnestone Kent 21 F9
Goodrich Hereford 26 G2
Goodrington Torbay 5 F9
Goodshaw Lancs 50 G4
Goodwick = Wdig Pembs 22 C4
Goodworth Clatford Hants 17 G10
Goole E Yorks 52 G3
Goonbell Corn 2 E6
Goonhavern Corn 3 D6
Goose Eye W Yorks 50 E6
Goose Green Gtr Man 43 B8
Goose Green Norf 39 G7
Goose Green W Sus 11 C10
Gooseham Corn 6 E1
Goosey Oxon 17 B10
Goosnargh Lancs 50 F1
Goostrey Ches E 43 E10
Gorcott Hill Warks 27 B7
Gord Shetland 96 L6
Gordon Borders 70 F5
Gordonbush Highld 93 J11
Gordonsburgh Moray 88 B4
Gordonstoun Moray 88 B1
Gordonstown Aberds 88 C5
Gordonstown Aberds 89 E7
Gore Kent 21 F10
Gore Cross Wilts 17 F7
Gore Pit Essex 30 G5
Gorebridge Midloth 70 D2
Gorefield Cambs 37 D10
Gorey Jersey 11
Gorgie Edin 69 C11
Goring Oxon 18 C3
Goring-by-Sea W Sus 11 D10
Goring Heath Oxon 18 D3
Gorleston-on-Sea Norf 39 E11
Gornalwood W Mid 34 F5
Gorrachie Aberds 89 C7
Gorran Churchtown Corn 3 E8
Gorran Haven Corn 3 E9
Gorrenberry Borders 61 D10
Gors Ceredig 32 H2
Gorse Hill Swindon 17 C8
Gorsedd Flint 42 E4
Gorseinon Swansea 23 G10
Gorseness Orkney 95 G5
Gorsgoch Ceredig 23 A9
Gorslas Carms 23 E10
Gorsley Glos 26 F3
Gorstan Highld 86 E6
Gorstanvorran Highld 79 D11
Gorsteyhill Staffs 43 G10
Gorsty Hill Staffs 35 C7
Gortantaoid Argyll 64 A4
Gorton Gtr Man 44 C2
Gosbeck Suff 31 C8
Gosberton Lincs 37 B8
Gosberton Clough Lincs 37 C7
Gosfield Essex 30 F4
Gosford Hereford 26 B2
Gosforth Cumb 56 F2
Gosforth T&W 63 G8
Gosmore Herts 29 F8
Gosport Hants 10 E5
Gossabrough Shetland 96 E7
Gossington Glos 16 A4
Goswick Northumb 71 F9
Gotham Notts 35 B11
Gotherington Glos 26 F6
Gott Shetland 96 J6
Goudhurst Kent 12 C6
Goulceby Lincs 46 E6
Gourdas Aberds 89 D7
Gourdon Aberds 83 F10
Gourock Invclyd 73 F11
Govan Glasgow 68 D4
Govanhill Glasgow 68 D4
Goveton Devon 5 G8
Govilon Mon 25 G9
Gowanhill Aberds 89 B10
Gowdall E Yorks 52 G2
Gowerton Swansea 23 G10
Gowkhall Fife 69 B9
Gowthorpe E Yorks 52 D3
Goxhill E Yorks 53 E7
Goxhill N Lincs 53 G7
Goxhill Haven N Lincs 53 G7
Goybre Neath 14 C3
Grabhair W Isles 91 F8
Graby Lincs 37 C6
Grade Corn 2 H6
Graffham W Sus 11 C8
Grafham Cambs 29 B8
Grafham Sur 19 G7
Grafton Hereford 25 E11
Grafton N Yorks 51 C10
Grafton Oxon 17 A9
Grafton Shrops 33 D10
Grafton Worcs 26 B2
Grafton Flyford Worcs 26 C6
Grafton Regis Northants 28 D4
Grafton Underwood Northants 36 G5
Grafty Green Kent 20 G5
Graianrhyd Denb 42 G5
Graig Conwy 41 C10
Graig Denb 42 E3
Graig-fechan Denb 42 G4
Grain Medway 20 D5
Grainsby Lincs 46 C6
Grainthorpe Lincs 47 C7
Grampound Corn 3 E8
Grampound Road Corn 3 D8
Gramsdal W Isles 84 C3
Granborough Bucks 28 F4
Granby Notts 36 B3
Grandborough Warks 27 B11
Grandtully Perth 76 B2
Grange Cumb 56 E4
Grange E Ayrs 67 C7
Grange Medway 20 E4
Grange Mers 42 D5
Grange Perth 76 E5
Grange Crossroads Moray 88 C4
Grange Hall Moray 87 E13
Grange Hill Essex 19 B11
Grange Moor W Yorks 51 H8
Grange of Lindores Fife 76 F5
Grange-over-Sands Cumb 49 B4
Grange Villa Durham 58 A3
Grangemill Derbys 44 G6
Grangemouth Falk 69 B8
Grangepans Falk 69 B9
Grangetown Cardiff 15 D7
Grangetown Redcar 59 D6
Granish Highld 81 B11
Gransmoor E Yorks 53 D7
Granston Pembs 22 C3
Grantchester Cambs 29 C11
Grantham Lincs 36 B5
Grantley N Yorks 51 C8
Grantlodge Aberds 83 B9
Granton Dumfries 60 C6
Granton Edin 69 C11
Grantown-on-Spey Highld 82 A2
Grantshouse Borders 71 D7
Grappenhall Warr 43 D9
Grasby Lincs 46 B4
Grasmere Cumb 56 F5
Grasscroft Gtr Man 44 B3
Grassendale Mers 43 D6
Grassholme Durham 57 D11
Grassington N Yorks 50 C6
Grassmoor Derbys 45 F8
Grassthorpe Notts 45 F11
Grateley Hants 17 G9
Gratwich Staffs 34 B6
Graveley Cambs 29 B9
Graveley Herts 29 F9
Gravelly Hill W Mid 35 F7
Gravels Shrops 33 E9
Graven Shetland 96 F6
Graveney Kent 21 E7
Gravesend Herts 29 F11
Gravesend Kent 20 D3
Grayingham Lincs 46 C3
Grayrigg Cumb 57 G7
Grays Thurrock 20 D3
Grayshott Hants 18 H5
Grayswood Sur 11 A8
Graythorp Hrtlpl 58 D6
Grazeley Wokingham 18 E3
Greasbrough S Yorks 45 C8
Greasby Mers 42 D5
Great Abington Cambs 30 D2
Great Addington Northants 28 A6
Great Alne Warks 27 C8
Great Altcar Lancs 42 B6
Great Amwell Herts 29 G10
Great Asby Cumb 57 E8
Great Ashfield Suff 30 B6
Great Ayton N Yorks 59 E6
Great Baddow Essex 20 A4
Great Bardfield Essex 30 E3
Great Barford Bedford 29 C8
Great Barr W Mid 34 F6
Great Barrington Glos 27 G9
Great Barrow Ches W 43 F7
Great Barton Suff 30 B5
Great Barugh N Yorks 52 B3
Great Bavington Northumb 62 E5
Great Bealings Suff 31 D9
Great Bedwyn Wilts 17 E9
Great Bentley Essex 31 F8
Great Billing Northants 28 B5
Great Bircham Norf 38 B3
Great Blakenham Suff 31 C8
Great Blencow Cumb 56 C6
Great Bolas Telford 34 C2
Great Bookham Sur 19 F8
Great Bourton Oxon 27 D11
Great Bowden Leics 36 G3
Great Bradley Suff 30 C3
Great Braxted Essex 30 G5
Great Bricett Suff 31 C7
Great Brickhill Bucks 28 E6
Great Bridge W Mid 34 F5
Great Bridgeford Staffs 34 C4
Great Brington Northants 28 B3
Great Bromley Essex 31 F7
Great Broughton Cumb 56 C2
Great Broughton N Yorks 59 F6
Great Budworth Ches W 43 E9
Great Burdon Darl 58 E4
Great Burgh Sur 19 F9
Great Burstead Essex 20 B3
Great Busby N Yorks 58 F6
Great Canfield Essex 30 G2
Great Carlton Lincs 47 D8
Great Casterton Rutland 36 E6
Great Chart Kent 13 B8
Great Chatwell Staffs 34 D3
Great Chesterford Essex 30 D2
Great Cheverell Wilts 16 F6
Great Chishill Cambs 29 E11
Great Clacton Essex 31 G8
Great Cliff W Yorks 51 H9
Great Clifton Cumb 56 D2
Great Coates NE Lincs 46 B6
Great Comberton Worcs 26 D6
Great Corby Cumb 56 A6
Great Cornard Suff 30 D5
Great Cowden E Yorks 53 E8
Great Coxwell Oxon 17 B9
Great Crakehall N Yorks 58 G3
Great Cransley Northants 36 H4
Great Cressingham Norf 38 E4
Great Crosby Mers 42 C6
Great Cubley Derbys 35 B7
Great Dalby Leics 36 D3
Great Denham Bedford 29 D7
Great Doddington Northants 28 B5
Great Dunham Norf 38 D4
Great Dunmow Essex 30 F3
Great Durnford Wilts 17 H8
Great Easton Essex 30 F3
Great Easton Leics 36 F4
Great Eccleston Lancs 49 E4
Great Edstone N Yorks 52 A3
Great Ellingham Norf 38 F6
Great Elm Som 16 G4
Great Eversden Cambs 29 C10
Great Fencote N Yorks 58 G3
Great Finborough Suff 31 C7
Great Fransham Norf 38 D4
Great Gaddesden Herts 29 G7
Great Gidding Cambs 37 G7
Great Givendale E Yorks 52 D4
Great Glemham Suff 31 B10
Great Glen Leics 36 F2
Great Gonerby Lincs 36 B4
Great Gransden Cambs 29 C9
Great Green Norf 39 G8
Great Green Suff 30 C6
Great Habton N Yorks 52 B3
Great Hale Lincs 37 A7
Great Hallingbury Essex 30 G2
Great Hampden Bucks 18 A5
Great Harrowden Northants 28 A5
Great Harwood Lancs 50 F3
Great Haseley Oxon 18 A3
Great Hatfield E Yorks 53 E7
Great Haywood Staffs 34 C6
Great Heath W Mid 35 G9
Great Heck N Yorks 52 G1
Great Henny Essex 30 E5
Great Hinton Wilts 16 F6
Great Hockham Norf 38 F5
Great Holland Essex 31 G9
Great Horkesley Essex 30 E6
Great Hormead Herts 29 F10
Great Horton W Yorks 51 F7
Great Horwood Bucks 28 E4
Great Houghton Northants 28 C4
Great Houghton S Yorks 45 B8
Great Hucklow Derbys 44 E5
Great Kelk E Yorks 53 D7
Great Kimble Bucks 28 H5
Great Kingshill Bucks 18 B5
Great Langton N Yorks 58 G3
Great Leighs Essex 30 G4
Great Lever Gtr Man 43 B10
Great Limber Lincs 46 B5
Great Linford M Keynes 28 D5
Great Livermere Suff 30 A5
Great Longstone Derbys 44 E6
Great Lumley Durham 58 B3
Great Lyth Shrops 33 E10
Great Malvern Worcs 26 D4
Great Maplestead Essex 30 E5
Great Marton Blackpool 49 F3
Great Massingham Norf 38 C3
Great Melton Norf 39 E7
Great Milton Oxon 18 A3
Great Missenden Bucks 18 A5
Great Mitton Lancs 50 F3
Great Mongeham Kent 21 F10
Great Moulton Norf 39 F7
Great Munden Herts 29 F10
Great Musgrave Cumb 57 E9
Great Ness Shrops 33 D9
Great Notley Essex 30 F4
Great Oakley Essex 31 F8
Great Oakley Northants 36 G4
Great Offley Herts 29 F8
Great Ormside Cumb 57 E9
Great Orton Cumb 56 A5
Great Ouseburn N Yorks 51 C10
Great Oxendon Northants 36 G3
Great Oxney Green Essex 30 H3
Great Palgrave Norf 38 D4
Great Parndon Essex 29 H11
Great Paxton Cambs 29 B9
Great Plumpton Lancs 49 F3
Great Plumstead Norf 39 D9
Great Ponton Lincs 36 B5
Great Preston W Yorks 51 G10
Great Raveley Cambs 37 G8
Great Rissington Glos 27 G8
Great Rollright Oxon 27 E10
Great Ryburgh Norf 38 C5
Great Ryle Northumb 62 B6
Great Ryton Shrops 33 E10
Great Saling Essex 30 F4
Great Salkeld Cumb 57 C7
Great Sampford Essex 30 E3
Great Sankey Warr 43 D8
Great Saxham Suff 30 B4
Great Shefford W Berks 17 D10
Great Shelford Cambs 29 C11
Great Smeaton N Yorks 58 F4
Great Snoring Norf 38 B5
Great Somerford Wilts 16 C6
Great Stainton Darl 58 D4
Great Stambridge Essex 20 B5
Great Staughton Cambs 29 B8
Great Steeping Lincs 47 F8
Great Stonar Kent 21 F10
Great Strickland Cumb 57 D7
Great Stukeley Cambs 29 A9
Great Sturton Lincs 46 E6
Great Sutton Ches W 43 E6
Great Sutton Shrops 33 G11
Great Swinburne Northumb 62 F5
Great Tew Oxon 27 F10
Great Tey Essex 30 F5
Great Thurlkeby N Yorks 51 B10
Great Thurlow Suff 30 C3
Great Torrington Devon 6 E3
Great Tosson Northumb 62 C6
Great Totham Essex 30 G5
Great Totham Essex 30 G5
Great Tows Lincs 46 C6
Great Urswick Cumb 49 B2
Great Wakering Essex 20 C6
Great Waldingfield Suff 30 D6
Great Walsingham Norf 38 B5
Great Waltham Essex 30 G3
Great Warley Essex 20 B2
Great Washbourne Glos 26 E6
Great Weldon Northants 36 G5
Great Welnetham Suff 30 C5
Great Wenham Suff 31 E7
Great Whittington Northumb 62 F6
Great Wigborough Essex 30 G6
Great Wilbraham Cambs 30 C2
Great Wishford Wilts 17 H7
Great Witcombe Glos 26 G6
Great Witley Worcs 26 B4
Great Wolford Warks 27 E9
Great Wratting Suff 30 D3
Great Wymondley Herts 29 F9
Great Wyrley Staffs 34 E5
Great Wytheford Shrops 34 D1
Great Yarmouth Norf 39 E11
Great Yeldham Essex 30 E4
Greater Doward Hereford 26 G2
Greatford Lincs 37 D6
Greatgate Staffs 35 A6
Greatham Hants 11 A6
Greatham Hrtlpl 58 D5
Greatham W Sus 11 C9
Greatstone on Sea Kent 13 D9
Greatworth Northants 28 D2
Greave Lancs 50 G4
Greeba IoM 48 D3
Green Denb 42 F3
Green End Bedford 29 C8
Green Hammerton N Yorks 51 D10
Green Lane Powys 33 F7
Green Ore Som 16 F2
Green St Green London 19 E11
Green Street Herts 19 B8
Greenbank Shetland 96 C7
Greenburn W Loth 69 D8
Greendikes Northumb 71 H9
Greenfield C Beds 29 E7
Greenfield Flint 42 E4
Greenfield Gtr Man 44 B3
Greenfield Highld 80 C4
Greenfield Oxon 18 B4
Greenford London 19 C8
Greengairs N Lanark 68 C6
Greenham W Berks 17 E11
Greenhaugh Northumb 62 E3
Greenhead Northumb 62 G2
Greenhill Falk 69 C7
Greenhill Kent 21 E8
Greenhill Leics 35 D10
Greenhill London 19 C8
Greenhills N Ayrs 67 A6
Greenhithe Kent 20 D2
Greenholm E Ayrs 67 C8
Greenholme Cumb 57 F7
Greenhouse Borders 61 A11
Greenhow Hill N Yorks 51 C7
Greenigoe Orkney 95 H5
Greenland Highld 94 D4
Greenlands Bucks 18 C4
Greenlaw Aberds 89 C6
Greenlaw Borders 70 F6
Greenlea Dumfries 60 F6
Greenloaning Perth 75 G11
Greenmount Gtr Man 43 A10
Greenmow Shetland 96 L6
Greenock Invclyd 73 F11
Greenock West Invclyd 73 F11
Greenodd Cumb 49 A3
Greenrow Cumb 56 A3
Greens Norton Northants 28 D3
Greenside T&W 63 G7
Greensidehill Northumb 62 B5
Greenstead Green Essex 30 F5
Greensted Essex 20 A2
Greenwich London 19 D10
Greet Glos 27 E7
Greete Shrops 26 A2
Greetham Lincs 47 E7
Greetham Rutland 36 D5
Greetland W Yorks 51 G6
Gregg Hall Cumb 56 G6
Gregson Lane Lancs 50 G1
Greinetobht W Isles 84 A3
Greinton Som 15 H10
Gremista Shetland 96 J6
Grenaby IoM 48 E2
Grendon Northants 28 B5
Grendon Warks 35 E8
Grendon Common Warks 35 F8
Grendon Green Hereford 26 C2
Grendon Underwood Bucks 28 F3
Grenofen Devon 4 D5
Grenoside S Yorks 45 C7
Greosabhagh W Isles 90 H6
Gresford Wrex 42 G6
Gresham Norf 39 B7
Greshornish Highld 85 C8
Gressenhall Norf 38 D5
Gressingham Lancs 50 C1
Gresty Green Ches E 43 G10
Greta Bridge Durham 58 E1
Gretna Dumfries 61 G9
Gretna Green Dumfries 61 G9
Gretton Glos 27 E7
Gretton Northants 36 F4
Gretton Shrops 33 F11
Grewelthorpe N Yorks 51 B8
Grey Green N Lincs 45 B11
Greygarth N Yorks 51 B7
Greynor Carms 23 F10
Greysouthen Cumb 56 D2
Greystoke Cumb 56 C6
Greystone Angus 77 C8
Greystone Dumfries 60 F5
Greywell Hants 18 F4
Griais W Isles 91 C9
Grianan W Isles 91 D9
Gribthorpe E Yorks 52 F3
Gridley Corner Devon 6 G2
Griff Warks 35 G9
Griffithstown Torf 15 B8
Grimbister Orkney 95 G4
Grimblethorpe Lincs 46 D6
Grimeford Village Lancs 43 A9
Grimethorpe S Yorks 45 B8
Griminis W Isles 84 C2
Grimister Shetland 96 D6
Grimley Worcs 26 B5
Grimness Orkney 95 J5
Grimoldby Lincs 47 D7
Grimpo Shrops 33 C9
Grimsargh Lancs 50 F1
Grimsbury Oxon 27 D11
Grimsby NE Lincs 46 A6
Grimscote Northants 28 C3
Grimscott Corn 6 F1
Grimsthorpe Lincs 36 C6
Grimston E Yorks 53 F8
Grimston Leics 36 C2
Grimston Norf 38 C3
Grimston York 52 D2
Grimstone Dorset 8 E4
Grinacombe Moor Devon 6 G3
Grindale E Yorks 53 B7
Grindigar Orkney 95 H6
Grindiscol Shetland 96 K6
Grindle Shrops 34 E3
Grindleford Derbys 44 E6
Grindleton Lancs 50 E3
Grindley Staffs 34 C6
Grindley Brook Shrops 33 A11
Grindlow Derbys 44 E5
Grindon Northumb 71 F8
Grindon Staffs 44 G4
Grindonmoor Gate Staffs 44 G4
Gringley on the Hill Notts 45 C11
Grinsdale Cumb 61 H9
Grinshill Shrops 33 C11
Grinton N Yorks 58 G1
Griomsidar W Isles 91 E8
Grishipoll Argyll 78 F4
Grisling Common E Sus 12 D3
Gristhorpe N Yorks 53 A6
Griston Norf 38 F5
Gritley Orkney 95 H6
Grittenham Wilts 17 C7
Grittleton Wilts 16 C5
Grizebeck Cumb 49 A2
Grizedale Cumb 56 G5
Grobister Orkney 95 F7
Groby Leics 35 E11
Groes Conwy 42 F3
Groes Neath 14 C3
Groes-faen Rhondda 14 C6
Groes-lwyd Powys 33 D8
Groesffordd Marli Denb 42 E3
Groeslon Gwyn 40 E6
Groeslon Gwyn 41 D7
Grogport Argyll 65 D9
Gromford Suff 31 C10
Gronant Flint 42 D3
Groombridge E Sus 12 C4
Grosmont Mon 25 F11
Grosmont N Yorks 59 F9
Groton Suff 30 D6
Grougfoot Falk 69 C9
Grouville Jersey 11
Grove Dorset 8 G6
Grove Kent 21 E9
Grove Notts 45 E11
Grove Oxon 17 B11
Grove Park London 19 D11
Grove Vale W Mid 34 F6
Grovesend Swansea 23 F10
Grudie Highld 86 E6
Gruids Highld 93 J8
Gruinard House Highld 86 B2
Grula Highld 85 F8
Gruline Argyll 79 G8
Grunasound Shetland 96 K5
Grundisburgh Suff 31 C9
Grunsagill Lancs 50 D3
Gruting Shetland 96 J4
Grutness Shetland 96 N6
Gualachulain Highld 74 C4
Gualin Ho. Highld 92 D6
Guardbridge Fife 77 F7
Guarlford Worcs 26 D5
Guay Perth 76 C3
Guestling Green E Sus 13 E7
Guestling Thorn E Sus 13 E7
Guestwick Norf 39 C6
Guestwick Green Norf 39 C6
Guide Blackburn 50 G3
Guide Post Northumb 63 E8
Guilden Morden Cambs 29 D9
Guilden Sutton Ches W 43 F7
Guildford Sur 18 G6
Guildtown Perth 76 D4
Guilsborough Northants 28 A3
Guilsfield Powys 33 D8
Guilton Kent 21 F9
Guineaford Devon 6 C4
Guisborough Redcar 59 E7
Guiseley W Yorks 51 E7
Guist Norf 38 C5
Guith Orkney 95 E6
Guiting Power Glos 27 F7
Gulberwick Shetland 96 K6
Gullane E Loth 70 B3
Gulval Corn 2 F3
Gulworthy Devon 4 D5
Gumfreston Pembs 22 F6
Gumley Leics 36 F2
Gummow's Shop Corn 3 D7
Gun Hill E Sus 12 E4
Gunby E Yorks 52 F3
Gunby Lincs 36 C5
Gundleton Hants 10 A5
Gunn Devon 6 C5
Gunnerside N Yorks 57 G11
Gunnerton Northumb 62 F5
Gunness N Lincs 46 A2
Gunnislake Corn 4 D5
Gunnista Shetland 96 J7
Gunthorpe Norf 38 B6
Gunthorpe Notts 36 A2
Gunthorpe Pboro 37 E7
Gunville IoW 10 F3
Gunwalloe Corn 2 G5
Gurnard IoW 10 E3
Gurnett Ches E 44 E3
Gurney Slade Som 16 G3
Gurnos Powys 24 H4
Gussage All Saints Dorset 9 C9
Gussage St Michael Dorset 9 C8
Guston Kent 21 G10
Gutcher Shetland 96 D7
Guthrie Angus 77 B8
Guyhirn Cambs 37 E9
Guyhirn Gull Cambs 37 E9
Guy's Head Lincs 37 C10
Guy's Marsh Dorset 9 B7
Guyzance Northumb 63 C8
Gwaenysgor Flint 42 D3
Gwalchmai Anglesey 40 C5
Gwaun-Cae-Gurwen Neath 24 G4
Gwaun-Leision Neath 24 G4
Gwbert Ceredig 22 B6
Gweek Corn 2 G6
Gwehelog Mon 15 A9
Gwenddwr Powys 25 D7
Gwennap Corn 2 F6
Gwenter Corn 2 H6
Gwernaffield Flint 42 F5
Gwernesney Mon 15 A10
Gwernogle Carms 23 C10
Gwernymynydd Flint 42 F5
Gwersyllt Wrex 42 G6
Gwespyr Flint 42 D4
Gwithian Corn 2 E4
Gwredog Anglesey 40 B6
Gwyddelwern Denb 42 H3
Gwyddgrug Carms 23 C9
Gwydyr Uchaf Conwy 41 D9
Gwynfryn Wrex 42 G5
Gwystre Powys 25 B7
Gwytherin Conwy 41 D10
Gyfelia Wrex 42 H6
Gyffin Conwy 41 C9
Gyre Orkney 95 H4
Gyrn-goch Gwyn 40 F6

H

Habberley Shrops 33 E9
Habergham Lancs 50 F4
Habrough NE Lincs 46 A5
Haceby Lincs 36 B6
Hacheston Suff 31 C10
Hackbridge London 19 E9
Hackenthorpe S Yorks 45 D8
Hackford Norf 39 E6
Hackforth N Yorks 58 G3
Hackland Orkney 95 F4
Hackleton Northants 28 C5
Hackness N Yorks 59 G10
Hackness Orkney 95 J4
Hackney London 19 C10
Hackthorn Lincs 46 D3
Hackthorpe Cumb 57 D7
Haconby Lincs 37 C7
Hacton London 20 C2
Hadden Borders 70 G6
Haddenham Bucks 28 H4
Haddenham Cambs 37 H10
Haddington E Loth 70 C4
Haddington Lincs 46 F3
Haddiscoe Norf 39 F10
Haddon Cambs 37 F7
Haddon Ches E 44 F3
Hade Edge W Yorks 44 B5
Hademore Staffs 35 E7
Hadfield Derbys 44 C4
Hadham Cross Herts 29 G11
Hadham Ford Herts 29 F11
Hadleigh Essex 20 C5
Hadleigh Suff 31 D7
Hadley Telford 34 D2
Hadley End Staffs 35 C7
Hadlow Kent 20 G3
Hadlow Down E Sus 12 D4
Hadnall Shrops 33 D11
Hadstock Essex 30 D2
Hady Derbys 45 E7
Hadzor Worcs 26 B6
Haffenden Quarter Kent 13 B7
Hafod-Dinbych Conwy 41 E10
Hafod-lom Conwy 41 C10
Haggate Lancs 50 F4
Haggbeck Cumb 61 F10
Haggerston Northumb 71 F9
Haggrister Shetland 96 F5
Hagley Hereford 26 D2
Hagley Worcs 34 G5
Hagworthingham Lincs 47 F7
Haigh Gtr Man 43 B9
Haigh S Yorks 44 A6
Haigh Moor W Yorks 51 G8
Haighton Green Lancs 50 F1
Hail Weston Cambs 29 B8
Haile Cumb 56 F2
Hailes Glos 27 E7
Hailey Herts 29 G10
Hailey Oxon 27 G10
Hailsham E Sus 12 F4
Haimer Highld 94 D3
Hainault London 19 B11
Hainford Norf 39 D8
Hainton Lincs 46 D5
Hairmyres S Lanark 68 E5
Haisthorpe E Yorks 53 C7
Hakin Pembs 22 F3
Halam Notts 45 G10
Halbeath Fife 69 B10
Halberton Devon 7 E9
Halcro Highld 94 D4
Hale Gtr Man 43 D10
Hale Halton 43 D7
Hale Hants 9 C10
Hale Bank Halton 43 D7
Hale Street Kent 20 G3
Halebarns Gtr Man 43 D10
Hales Norf 39 F9
Hales Staffs 34 B3
Hales Place Kent 21 F8
Halesfield Telford 34 E3
Halesgate Lincs 37 C9
Halesowen W Mid 34 G5
Halesworth Suff 39 H9
Halewood Mers 43 D7
Halford Shrops 33 G10
Halford Warks 27 D9
Halfpenny Furze Carms 23 E7
Halfpenny Green Staffs 34 F4
Halfway Carms 24 E3
Halfway Carms 24 E5
Halfway W Berks 17 E11
Halfway Bridge W Sus 11 B8
Halfway House Shrops 33 D9
Halfway Houses Kent 20 D6
Halifax W Yorks 51 G6
Halket E Ayrs 67 A7
Halkirk Highld 94 E3
Halkyn Flint 42 E5
Hall Dunnerdale Cumb 56 G4
Hall Green W Mid 35 G7
Hall Green W Yorks 51 H9
Hall Grove Herts 29 G9
Hall of Tankerness Orkney 95 H6
Hall of the Forest Shrops 33 G8
Halland E Sus 12 E3
Hallaton Leics 36 F3
Hallatrow Bath 16 F3
Hallbankgate Cumb 61 H11
Hallen S Glos 15 C11
Halliburton Borders 70 F5
Hallin Highld 84 C7
Halling Medway 20 E4
Hallington Lincs 47 D7
Hallington Northumb 62 F5
Halliwell Gtr Man 43 A10
Halloughton Notts 45 G10
Hallow Worcs 26 C5
Hallrule Borders 61 B11
Halls E Loth 70 C5
Hall's Green Herts 29 F9
Hallsands Devon 5 H9
Hallthwaites Cumb 56 H3
Hallworthy Corn 4 C2
Hallyburton House Perth 76 D5
Hallyne Borders 69 F10
Halmer End Staffs 43 H10
Halmore Glos 16 A3
Halmyre Mains Borders 69 F10
Halnaker W Sus 11 D8
Halsall Lancs 42 A6
Halse Northants 28 D2
Halse Som 7 D10
Halsetown Corn 2 F4
Halsham E Yorks 53 G8
Halsinger Devon 6 C4
Halstead Essex 30 E5
Halstead Kent 19 E11
Halstead Leics 36 E3
Halstock Dorset 8 D4
Haltham Lincs 46 F6
Haltoft End Lincs 47 H7
Halton Bucks 28 G5
Halton Halton 43 D8
Halton Lancs 49 C5
Halton Northumb 62 G5
Halton W Yorks 51 F9
Halton Wrex 33 B9
Halton East N Yorks 50 D6
Halton Gill N Yorks 50 B4
Halton Holegate Lincs 47 F8
Halton Lea Gate Northumb 62 H2
Halton West N Yorks 50 D4
Haltwhistle Northumb 62 G3
Halvergate Norf 39 E10
Halwell Devon 5 F8
Halwill Devon 6 G3
Halwill Junction Devon 6 F3
Ham Devon 7 F11
Ham Glos 16 B3
Ham Highld 94 C4
Ham Kent 21 F10
Ham London 19 D8
Ham Shetland 96 K1
Ham Wilts 17 E10
Ham Common Dorset 9 B7
Ham Green Hereford 26 D4
Ham Green Kent 13 D7
Ham Green Kent 20 E5
Ham Green N Som 15 D11
Ham Green Worcs 27 B7
Ham Street Som 8 A4
Hamble-le-Rice Hants 10 D3
Hambleden Bucks 18 C4
Hambledon Hants 10 C5
Hambledon Sur 18 H6
Hambleton Lancs 49 E3
Hambleton N Yorks 52 F1
Hambridge Som 8 B2
Hambrook S Glos 16 D3
Hambrook W Sus 11 D6
Hameringham Lincs 47 F7
Hamerton Cambs 37 H7
Hametoun Shetland 96 K1
Hamilton S Lanark 68 E6
Hammer W Sus 11 A7
Hammerpot W Sus 11 D9
Hammersmith London 19 D9
Hammerwich Staffs 35 E6
Hammerwood E Sus 12 C3
Hammond Street Herts 19 A10
Hammoon Dorset 9 C7
Hamnavoe Shetland 96 E4
Hamnavoe Shetland 96 E6
Hamnavoe Shetland 96 F6
Hamnavoe Shetland 96 K5
Hampden Park E Sus 12 F5
Hamperden End Essex 30 E2
Hampnett Glos 27 G7
Hampole S Yorks 45 A9
Hampreston Dorset 9 E9
Hampstead London 19 C9
Hampstead Norreys W Berks 18 D2
Hampsthwaite N Yorks 51 D8
Hampton London 19 E8
Hampton Shrops 34 G3
Hampton Worcs 27 D7
Hampton Bishop Hereford 26 E2
Hampton Heath Ches W 43 H7
Hampton in Arden W Mid 35 G8
Hampton Loade Shrops 34 G3
Hampton Lovett Worcs 26 B5
Hampton Lucy Warks 27 C9
Hampton on the Hill Warks 27 B9
Hampton Poyle Oxon 28 G2
Hamrow Norf 38 C5
Hamsey E Sus 12 E3
Hamsey Green London 19 F10
Hamstall Ridware Staffs 35 D7
Hamstead IoW 10 E3
Hamstead W Mid 34 F6
Hamstead Marshall W Berks 17 E11
Hamsterley Durham 58 C2
Hamsterley Durham 63 H7
Hamstreet Kent 13 C9
Hamworthy Poole 9 E8
Hanbury Staffs 35 C7
Hanbury Worcs 26 B6
Hanbury Woodend Staffs 35 C7
Hanby Lincs 36 B6
Hanchurch Staffs 34 A4
Handbridge Ches W 43 F7
Handcross W Sus 12 D1
Handforth Ches E 44 D2
Handley Ches W 43 G7
Handsacre Staffs 35 D6
Handsworth S Yorks 45 D8
Handsworth W Mid 34 F6
Handy Cross Devon 6 D3
Hanford Stoke 34 A4
Hanging Langford Wilts 17 H7
Hangleton W Sus 11 D9
Hanham S Glos 16 D3
Hankelow Ches E 43 H9
Hankerton Wilts 16 B6
Hankham E Sus 12 F5
Hanley Stoke 44 H2
Hanley Castle Worcs 26 D5
Hanley Child Worcs 26 B3
Hanley Swan Worcs 26 D5
Hanley William Worcs 26 B3
Hanlith N Yorks 50 C5
Hanmer Wrex 33 B10
Hannah Lincs 47 E9
Hannington Hants 18 F2
Hannington Northants 28 A5
Hannington Swindon 17 B8
Hannington Wick Swindon 17 B8
Hansel Village S Ayrs 67 C6
Hanslope M Keynes 28 D5
Hanthorpe Lincs 37 C6
Hanwell London 19 C8
Hanwell Oxon 27 D11
Hanwood Shrops 33 E10
Hanworth London 19 D8
Hanworth Norf 39 B7
Happendon S Lanark 69 G7
Happisburgh Norf 39 B9
Happisburgh Common Norf 39 C9
Hapsford Ches W 43 E7
Hapton Lancs 50 F
Hapton Norf 39 F
Harberton Devon 5 F
Harbertonford Devon 5 F
Harbledown Kent 21 F
Harborne W Mid 34 G
Harborough Magna Warks 35 H1
Harbottle Northumb 62 C
Harbury Warks 27 C1
Harby Leics 36 B
Harby Notts 46 E
Harcombe Devon 7 G1
Harden W Mid 34 E
Harden W Yorks 51 F
Hardenhuish Wilts 16 D
Hardgate Aberds 83 C
Hardham W Sus 11 C
Hardingham Norf 38 E
Hardingstone Northants 28 C
Hardington Som 16 F
Hardington Mandeville Som 8 C
Hardington Marsh Som 8 D
Hardley Hants 10 D
Hardley Street Norf 39 E
Hardmead M Keynes 28 D
Hardrow N Yorks 57 G
Hardstoft Derbys 45 F
Hardway Hants 10 D
Hardway Som 8 A
Hardwick Bucks 28 G
Hardwick Cambs 29 C
Hardwick Norf 38 C
Hardwick Norf 39 G
Hardwick Northants 28 B
Hardwick Notts 45 E
Hardwick Oxon 27 H
Hardwick Oxon 28 F
Hardwick W Mid 35 F
Hardwicke Glos 26 F
Hardwicke Glos 26 G
Hardwicke Hereford 25 D
Hardy's Green Essex 30 F
Hare Green Essex 31 F
Hare Hatch Wokingham 18 D
Hare Street Herts 29 F
Hareby Lincs 47 F
Hareden Lancs 50 D
Harefield London 19 B
Harehills W Yorks 51 F
Harehope Northumb 62 A
Harescеugh Cumb 57 B
Harescombe Glos 26 G
Haresfield Glos 26 G
Hareshaw N Lanark 69 D
Hareshaw Head Northumb 62 E
Harewood W Yorks 51 E
Harewood End Hereford 26 F
Harford Carms 24 D
Harford Devon 5 F
Hargate Norf 39 F
Hargatewall Derbys 44 E
Hargrave Ches W 43 F
Hargrave Northants 29 A
Hargrave Suff 30 C
Harker Cumb 61 G
Harkland Shetland 96 E
Harkstead Suff 31 E
Harlaston Staffs 35 D
Harlaw Ho. Aberds 83 A
Harlaxton Lincs 36 B
Harle Syke Lancs 50 F
Harlech Gwyn 41 G
Harlequin Notts 36 B
Harlescott Shrops 33 D
Harlesden London 19 C
Harleston Devon 5 G
Harleston Norf 39 G
Harleston Suff 31 C
Harlestone Northants 28 B
Harley S Yorks 45 C
Harley Shrops 34 E
Harleyholm S Lanark 69 G
Harlington C Beds 29 E
Harlington London 19 D
Harlington S Yorks 45 B
Harlosh Highld 85 D
Harlow Essex 29 G
Harlow Hill N Yorks 51 D
Harlow Hill Northumb 62 G
Harlthorpe E Yorks 52 F
Harlton Cambs 29 C
Harman's Cross Dorset 9 F
Harmby N Yorks 58 H
Harmer Green Herts 29 G
Harmer Hill Shrops 33 C
Harmondsworth London 19 D
Harmston Lincs 46 F
Harnham Northumb 62 F
Harnhill Glos 17 A
Harold Hill London 20 B
Harold Wood London 20 B
Haroldston West Pembs 22 E
Haroldswick Shetland 96 B
Harome N Yorks 52 A
Harpenden Herts 29 G
Harpford Devon 7 G
Harpham E Yorks 53 C
Harpley Norf 38 C
Harpley Worcs 26 B
Harpole Northants 28 B
Harpsdale Highld 94 E
Harpsden Oxon 18 C
Harpswell Lincs 46 D
Harpur Hill Derbys 44 E
Harpurhey Gtr Man 44 B
Harraby Cumb 56 A
Harrapool Highld 85 F
Harrier Shetland 96
Harrietfield Perth 76 E
Harrietsham Kent 20 F
Harrington Cumb 56 D
Harrington Lincs 47 E
Harrington Northants 36 G
Harringworth Northants 36
Harris Highld 78 B
Harrogate N Yorks 51 D
Harrold Bedford 28 C
Harrow London 19 C
Harrow on the Hill London 19 C
Harrow Street Suff 30 E
Harrow Weald London 19 B
Harrowbarrow Corn 4 E
Harrowden Bedford 29 D
Harrowgate Hill Darl 58 E
Harston Cambs 29 C
Harston Leics 36 B
Harswell E Yorks 52 E

Horton Wilts 17 E7
Horton Windsor 19 D7
Horton-cum-Studley Oxon 28 G2
Horton Green Ches W 43 H7
Horton Heath Hants 10 C3
Horton in Ribblesdale N Yorks 50 B4
Horton Kirby Kent 20 E2
Hortonlane Shrops 33 D10
Horwich Gtr Man 43 A9
Horwich End Derbys 44 D4
Horwood Devon 6 D4
Hose Leics 36 C3
Hoselaw Borders 71 G7
Hoses Cumb 56 G4
Hosh Perth 75 E11
Hosta W Isles 84 A2
Hoswick Shetland 96 L6
Hotham E Yorks 52 F4
Hothfield Kent 20 G6
Hoton Leics 36 C1
Houbie Shetland 96 D8
Houdston S Ayrs 66 G4
Hough Ches E 43 G10
Hough Ches E 44 E2
Hough Green Halton 43 D7
Hough-on-the-Hill Lincs 46 H3
Hougham Lincs 36 A4
Houghton Cambs 29 A9
Houghton Cumb 61 H10
Houghton Hants 10 A2
Houghton Pembs 22 F4
Houghton W Sus 11 C9
Houghton Conquest C Beds 29 D7
Houghton Green E Sus 13 D8
Houghton Green Warr 43 C9
Houghton-le-Side Darl 58 D3
Houghton-Le-Spring T&W 58 B4
Houghton on the Hill Leics 36 E2
Houghton Regis C Beds 29 F7
Houghton St Giles Norf 38 B5
Houlland Shetland 96 F7
Houlland Shetland 96 H5
Houlsyke N Yorks 59 F8
Hound Hants 10 D3
Hound Green Hants 18 F4
Houndslow Borders 70 F5
Houndwood Borders 71 D7
Hounslow London 19 D8
Hounslow Green Essex 30 G3
Housay Shetland 96 F8
House of Daviot Highld 87 G10
House of Glenmuick Aberds 82 D5
Housetter Shetland 96 E5
Houss Shetland 96 K5
Houston Renfs 68 D3
Houstry Highld 94 G3
Houton Orkney 95 H4
Hove Brighton 12 F1
Hoveringham Notts 45 H10
Hoveton Norf 39 D9
Hovingham N Yorks 52 B2
How Cumb 61 H11
How Caple Hereford 26 E3
How End C Beds 29 D7
How Green Kent 19 G11
Howbrook S Yorks 45 C7
Howden Borders 62 A2
Howden E Yorks 52 G3
Howden-le-Wear Durham 58 C2
Howe Highld 94 D5
Howe N Yorks 51 A9
Howe Norf 39 E8
Howe Bridge Gtr Man 43 B9
Howe Green Essex 20 A4
Howe of Teuchar Aberds 89 D7
Howe Street Essex 30 E3
Howe Street Essex 30 G3
Howell Lincs 46 H5
Howey Powys 25 C7
Howgate Midloth 69 E11
Howick Northumb 63 B8
Howle Durham 58 D1
Howle Telford 34 C2
Howlett End Essex 30 E2
Howley Som 8 D1
Hownam Borders 62 B3
Hownam Mains Borders 62 A3
Howpasley Borders 61 C9
Howsham N Lincs 46 B4
Howsham N Yorks 52 C3
Howslack Dumfries 60 C6
Howtel Northumb 71 G7
Howton Hereford 25 F11
Howtown Cumb 56 E6
Howwood Renfs 68 D2
Hoxne Suff 39 H7
Hoy Orkney 95 H3
Hoylake Mers 42 D5
Hoyland S Yorks 45 B7
Hoylandswaine S Yorks 44 B6
Hubberholme N Yorks 50 B5
Hubbert's Bridge Lincs 37 A8
Huby N Yorks 51 E8
Huby N Yorks 52 C1
Hucclecote Glos 26 G5
Hucking Kent 20 F5
Hucknall Notts 45 H9
Huddersfield W Yorks 51 H7
Huddington Worcs 26 C6
Hudswell N Yorks 58 F2
Huggate E Yorks 52 D4
Hugglescote Leics 35 D10
Hugh Town Scilly 2 C3
Hughenden Valley Bucks 18 B5
Hughley Shrops 34 F1
Huish Devon 6 E4
Huish Wilts 17 E8
Huish Champflower Som 7 D9
Huish Episcopi Som 8 B3
Huisinis W Isles 90 F4
Hulcott Bucks 28 G5
Hulland Derbys 44 H6
Hulland Ward Derbys 44 H6
Hullavington Wilts 16 C5
Hullbridge Essex 20 B5
Hulme Gtr Man 44 C2
Hulme End Staffs 44 G5
Hulme Walfield Ches E 44 F2
Hulver Street Suff 39 G10
Hulverstone IoW 10 F2
Humber Hereford 26 C2
Humber Bridge N Lincs 52 G6
Humberston NE Lincs 47 B7
Humbie E Loth 70 D3
Humbleton E Yorks 53 F8
Humbleton Northumb 71 H8
Humby Lincs 36 B6
Hume Borders 70 F6
Humshaugh Northumb 62 F5
Huna Highld 94 C5
Huncoat Lancs 50 F3
Huncote Leics 35 F11
Hundalee Borders 62 B2
Hunderthwaite Durham 57 D11
Hundle Houses Lincs 46 G6
Hundleby Lincs 47 F7
Hundleton Pembs 22 F4
Hundon Suff 30 D4
Hundred Acres Hants 10 C4
Hundred End Lancs 49 G4
Hundred House Powys 25 C8
Hungarton Leics 36 E2
Hungerford Hants 9 C10
Hungerford W Berks 17 E10
Hungerford Newtown W Berks 17 D10
Hungerton Lincs 36 C4
Hungladder Highld 85 A8
Hunmanby N Yorks 53 B6
Hunmanby Moor N Yorks 53 B7
Hunningham Warks 27 B10
Hunny Hill IoW 10 F3
Hunsdon Herts 29 G11
Hunsingore N Yorks 51 D10
Hunslet W Yorks 51 F9
Hunsonby Cumb 57 C7
Hunspow Highld 94 C4
Hunstanton Norf 38 A2
Hunstanworth Durham 57 B11
Hunsterson Ches E 43 H9
Hunston Suff 30 B6
Hunston W Sus 11 D7
Hunstrete Bath 16 E3
Hunt End Worcs 27 B7
Hunter's Quay Argyll 73 F10
Hunthill Lodge Angus 82 F6
Hunting-tower Perth 76 E3
Huntingdon Cambs 29 A9
Huntingfield Suff 31 A10
Huntingford Dorset 9 A7
Huntington E Loth 70 C3
Huntington Hereford 25 C9
Huntington Staffs 34 D5
Huntington York 52 D2
Huntley Glos 26 G4
Huntly Aberds 88 E5
Huntlywood Borders 70 F5
Hunton Kent 20 G4
Hunton N Yorks 58 G2
Hunt's Corner Norf 39 G6
Hunt's Cross Mers 43 D7
Huntsham Devon 7 D9
Huntspill Som 15 G9
Huntworth Som 8 A2
Hunwick Durham 58 C2
Hunworth Norf 39 B6
Hurdsfield Ches E 44 E3
Hurley Warks 35 F8
Hurley Windsor 18 C5
Hurlford E Ayrs 67 C7
Hurliness Orkney 95 K3
Hurn Dorset 9 E10
Hurn's End Lincs 47 H8
Hursley Hants 10 B3
Hurst N Yorks 58 F1
Hurst Som 8 C3
Hurst Wokingham 18 D4
Hurst Green E Sus 12 D6
Hurst Green Lancs 50 F2
Hurst Wickham W Sus 12 E1
Hurstbourne Priors Hants 17 G11
Hurstbourne Tarrant Hants 17 F10
Hurstpierpoint W Sus 12 E1
Hurstwood Lancs 50 F4
Hurtmore Sur 18 G6
Hurworth Place Darl 58 F3
Hury Durham 57 E11
Husabost Highld 84 C7
Husbands Bosworth Leics 36 G2
Husborne Crawley C Beds 28 E6
Husthwaite N Yorks 51 B11
Hutchwns Bridgend 14 D4
Huthwaite Notts 45 G8
Huttoft Lincs 47 E9
Hutton Borders 71 E8
Hutton Cumb 56 D6
Hutton E Yorks 52 D6
Hutton Essex 20 B3
Hutton Lancs 49 G4
Hutton N Som 15 F9
Hutton Buscel N Yorks 52 A5
Hutton Conyers N Yorks 51 B9
Hutton Cranswick E Yorks 52 D6
Hutton End Cumb 56 C6
Hutton Gate Redcar 59 E6
Hutton Henry Durham 58 C5
Hutton-le-Hole N Yorks 59 G8
Hutton Magna Durham 58 E2
Hutton Roof Cumb 50 B1
Hutton Roof Cumb 56 C5
Hutton Rudby N Yorks 58 F5
Hutton Sessay N Yorks 51 B10
Hutton Village Redcar 59 E6
Hutton Wandesley N Yorks 51 D11
Huxley Ches W 43 F8
Huxter Shetland 96 G7
Huxter Shetland 96 H5
Huxton Borders 71 D7
Huyton Mers 43 C7
Hwlffordd = Haverfordwest Pembs 22 E4
Hycemoor Cumb 56 H2
Hyde Glos 16 A5
Hyde Gtr Man 44 C3
Hyde Hants 9 C10
Hyde Heath Bucks 18 A6
Hyde Park S Yorks 45 B9
Hydestile Sur 18 G6
Hylton Castle T&W 63 H9
Hyndford Bridge S Lanark 69 F8
Hynish Argyll 78 H2
Hyssington Powys 33 F9
Hythe Hants 10 D3
Hythe Kent 21 H8
Hythe End Windsor 19 D7
Hythie Aberds 89 C10

I

Ibberton Dorset 9 D6
Ible Derbys 44 G6
Ibsley Hants 9 D10
Ibstock Leics 35 D10
Ibstone Bucks 18 B4
Ibthorpe Hants 17 F10
Ibworth Hants 18 F2
Ichrachan Argyll 74 D3
Ickburgh Norf 38 F4
Ickenham London 19 C7
Ickford Bucks 28 H3
Ickham Kent 21 F9
Ickleford Herts 29 E8
Icklesham E Sus 13 E7
Ickleton Cambs 29 D11
Icklingham Suff 30 A4
Ickwell Green C Beds 29 D8
Icomb Glos 27 F9
Idbury Oxon 27 G9
Iddesleigh Devon 6 F4
Ide Devon 7 G7
Ide Hill Kent 19 F11
Ideford Devon 5 D9
Iden E Sus 13 D8
Iden Green Kent 12 C6
Iden Green Kent 13 C7
Idle W Yorks 51 F7
Idlicote Warks 27 D9
Idmiston Wilts 17 H8
Idole Carms 23 E9
Idridgehay Derbys 44 H6
Idrigill Highld 85 B8
Idstone Oxon 17 C9
Idvies Angus 77 C8
Iffley Oxon 18 A2
Ifield W Sus 19 H9
Ifold W Sus 11 A9
Iford E Sus 12 F3
Ifton Heath Shrops 33 B9
Ightfield Shrops 34 B1
Ightham Kent 20 F2
Iken Suff 31 C11
Ilam Staffs 44 G5
Ilchester Som 8 B4
Ilderton Northumb 62 A6
Ilford London 19 C11
Ilfracombe Devon 6 B4
Ilkeston Derbys 35 A10
Ilketshall St Andrew Suff 39 G9
Ilketshall St Lawrence Suff 39 G9
Ilketshall St Margaret Suff 39 G9
Ilkley W Yorks 51 E7
Illey W Mid 34 G5
Illingworth W Yorks 51 G6
Illogan Corn 2 E5
Illston on the Hill Leics 36 F3
Ilmer Bucks 28 H4
Ilmington Warks 27 D9
Ilminster Som 8 C2
Ilsington Devon 5 D8
Ilston Swansea 23 G10
Ilton N Yorks 51 B7
Ilton Som 8 C2
Imachar N Ayrs 66 B1
Imeraval Argyll 64 D4
Immingham NE Lincs 46 A5
Impington Cambs 29 B11
Ince Ches W 43 E7
Ince Blundell Mers 42 B6
Ince in Makerfield Gtr Man 43 B8
Inch of Arnhall Aberds 83 F8
Inchbare Angus 83 G8
Inchberry Moray 88 C3
Inchbraoch Angus 77 B10
Incheril Highld 86 E3
Inchgrundle Angus 82 F6
Inchina Highld 86 B2
Inchinnan Renfs 68 D3
Inchkinloch Highld 93 E8
Inchlaggan Highld 80 C3
Inchlumpie Highld 87 D8
Inchmore Highld 86 G6
Inchnacardoch Hotel Highld 80 B5
Inchnadamph Highld 92 G5
Inchree Highld 74 A3
Inchture Perth 76 E6
Inchyra Perth 76 E4
Indian Queens Corn 3 D8
Inerval Argyll 64 D4
Ingatestone Essex 20 B3
Ingbirchworth S Yorks 44 B6
Ingestre Staffs 34 C5
Ingham Lincs 46 D3
Ingham Norf 39 C9
Ingham Suff 30 A5
Ingham Corner Norf 39 C9
Ingleborough Norf 37 D10
Ingleby Derbys 35 C9
Ingleby Lincs 46 E2
Ingleby Arncliffe N Yorks 58 F5
Ingleby Barwick Stockton 58 E5
Ingleby Greenhow N Yorks 59 F6
Inglemire Hull 53 F6
Inglesbatch Bath 16 E4
Inglesham Swindon 17 B9
Ingleton Durham 58 D2
Ingleton N Yorks 50 B2
Inglewhite Lancs 49 E5
Ingliston Edin 69 C10
Ingoe Northumb 62 F6
Ingol Lancs 49 F5
Ingoldisthorpe Norf 38 B2
Ingoldmells Lincs 47 F9
Ingoldsby Lincs 36 B6
Ingon Warks 27 C9
Ingram Northumb 62 B6
Ingrow W Yorks 51 F6
Ings Cumb 56 G6
Ingst S Glos 16 C2
Ingworth Norf 39 C7
Inham's End Cambs 37 F8
Inkberrow Worcs 27 C7
Inkpen W Berks 17 E10
Inkstack Highld 94 C4
Inn Cumb 56 F6
Innellan Argyll 73 F10
Innerleithen Borders 70 G2
Innerleven Fife 76 G6
Innermessan Dumfries 54 C3
Innerwick E Loth 70 C6
Innerwick Perth 75 C8
Innis Chonain Argyll 74 E4
Insch Aberds 83 A8
Insh Highld 81 C10
Inshore Highld 92 C6
Inskip Lancs 49 F4
Instoneville S Yorks 45 A9
Instow Devon 6 C3
Intake S Yorks 45 B9
Inver Aberds 82 D4
Inver Highld 87 C11
Inver Perth 76 C3
Inver Mallie Highld 80 E3
Inverailort Highld 79 C10
Inveraldie Angus 77 D7
Inveralligin Highld 85 C13
Inverallochy Aberds 89 B10
Inveran Highld 87 B8
Inveraray Argyll 73 C9
Inverarish Highld 85 E10
Inverarity Angus 77 C7
Inverarnan Stirling 74 F6
Inverasdale Highld 91 J13
Inverbeg Argyll 74 H6
Inverbervie Aberds 83 F10
Inverboyndie Aberds 89 B6
Inverbroom Highld 86 C4
Invercassley Highld 92 J7
Invercauld House Aberds 82 D3
Inverchaolain Argyll 73 F9
Invercharnan Highld 74 C4
Inverchoran Highld 86 F5
Invercreran Argyll 74 C3
Inverdruie Highld 81 B11
Inverebrie Aberds 89 E9
Invereck Argyll 73 E10
Inverernan Ho. Aberds 82 B5
Invereshie House Highld 81 C10
Inveresk E Loth 70 C2
Inverey Aberds 82 E2
Inverfarigaig Highld 81 A7
Invergarry Highld 80 C5
Invergelder Aberds 82 D4
Invergeldie Perth 75 E10
Invergordon Highld 87 E10
Invergowrie Perth 76 D6
Inverguseran Highld 85 H12
Inverhadden Perth 75 B9
Inverharroch Moray 88 E3
Inverherive Stirling 74 E6
Inverie Highld 79 B10
Inverinan Argyll 73 B8
Inverinate Highld 85 F14
Inverkeilor Angus 77 C9
Inverkeithing Fife 69 B10
Inverkeithny Aberds 89 D6
Inverkip Invclyd 73 F11
Inverkirkaig Highld 92 H3
Inverlael Highld 86 C4
Inverlochlarig Stirling 75 F7
Inverlochy Argyll 74 E4
Inverlochy Highld 80 F3
Inverlussa Argyll 72 E5
Invermark Lodge Angus 82 E6
Invermoidart Highld 79 D9
Invermoriston Highld 80 B6
Invernaver Highld 93 C10
Inverneill Argyll 73 E7
Inverness Highld 87 G9
Invernettie Aberds 89 D11
Invernoaden Argyll 73 D10
Inveroran Hotel Argyll 74 C5
Inverpolly Lodge Highld 92 H3
Inverquharity Angus 77 B7
Inverquhomery Aberds 89 D10
Inverroy Highld 80 E4
Inversanda Highld 74 B2
Invershiel Highld 80 B1
Invershin Highld 87 B8
Inversnaid Hotel Stirling 74 G6
Inverugie Aberds 89 D11
Inveruglas Argyll 74 G6
Inveruglass Highld 81 C10
Inverurie Aberds 83 A9
Invervar Perth 75 C9
Inverythan Aberds 89 D7
Inwardleigh Devon 6 G4
Inworth Essex 30 G5
Iochdar W Isles 84 D2
Iping W Sus 11 B7
Ipplepen Devon 5 E9
Ipsden Oxon 18 C3
Ipsley Worcs 27 B7
Ipstones Staffs 44 G4
Ipswich Suff 31 D8
Irby Mers 42 D5
Irby in the Marsh Lincs 47 F8
Irby upon Humber NE Lincs 46 B5
Irchester Northants 28 B6
Ireby Cumb 56 C4
Ireby Lancs 50 B2
Ireland Orkney 95 H4
Ireland Shetland 96 L5
Ireland's Cross Shrops 34 A3
Ireleth Cumb 49 B2
Ireshopeburn Durham 57 C10
Irlam Gtr Man 43 C10
Irnham Lincs 36 C6
Iron Acton S Glos 16 C3
Iron Cross Warks 27 C7
Ironbridge Telford 34 E2
Irongray Dumfries 60 F5
Ironmacannie Dumfries 55 B9
Ironside Aberds 89 C8
Ironville Derbys 45 G8
Irstead Norf 39 C9
Irthington Cumb 61 G10
Irthlingborough Northants 28 A6
Irton N Yorks 52 A6
Irvine N Ayrs 66 C6
Isauld Highld 93 C12
Isbister Orkney 95 F3
Isbister Orkney 95 G4
Isbister Shetland 96 D5
Isbister Shetland 96 G7
Isfield E Sus 12 E3
Isham Northants 28 A5
Isle Abbotts Som 8 B2
Isle Brewers Som 8 B2
Isle of Whithorn Dumfries 55 F7
Isleham Cambs 30 A3
Isleornsay Highld 85 G12
Islesburgh Shetland 96 G5
Islesteps Dumfries 60 F5
Isleworth London 19 D8
Isley Walton Leics 35 C10
Islibhig W Isles 90 E4
Islington London 19 C10
Islip Northants 28 A6
Islip Oxon 28 G2
Istead Rise Kent 20 E3
Isycoed Wrex 43 G7
Itchen Soton 10 C3
Itchen Abbas Hants 10 A4
Itchen Stoke Hants 10 A4
Itchingfield W Sus 11 B10
Itchington S Glos 16 C3
Itteringham Norf 39 B7
Itton Devon 6 G5
Itton Common Mon 15 B10
Ivegill Cumb 56 B6
Iver Bucks 19 C7
Iver Heath Bucks 19 C7
Iveston Durham 58 A2
Ivinghoe Bucks 28 G6
Ivinghoe Aston Bucks 28 G6
Ivington Hereford 25 C11
Ivington Green Hereford 25 C11
Ivy Chimneys Essex 19 A11
Ivy Cross Dorset 9 B7
Ivy Hatch Kent 20 F2
Ivybridge Devon 5 F7
Ivychurch Kent 13 D9
Iwade Kent 20 E6
Iwerne Courtney or Shroton Dorset 9 C7
Iwerne Minster Dorset 9 C7
Ixworth Suff 30 A6
Ixworth Thorpe Suff 30 A6

J

Jack Hill N Yorks 51 D8
Jack in the Green Devon 7 G9
Jacksdale Notts 45 G8
Jackstown Aberds 89 E7
Jacobstow Corn 4 B2
Jacobstowe Devon 6 F4
Jameston Pembs 22 G5
Jamestown Dumfries 61 D9
Jamestown Highld 86 F7
Jamestown W Dunb 68 B2
Jarrow T&W 63 G9
Jarvis Brook E Sus 12 D4
Jasper's Green Essex 30 F4
Java Argyll 79 H10
Jawcraig Falk 69 C7
Jaywick Essex 31 G8
Jealott's Hill Brack 18 D5
Jedburgh Borders 62 A2
Jeffreyston Pembs 22 F5
Jellyhill E Dunb 68 C5
Jemimaville Highld 87 E10
Jersey Farm Herts 29 H8
Jesmond T&W 63 G8
Jevington E Sus 12 F4
Jockey End Herts 29 G7
John o' Groats Highld 94 C5
Johnby Cumb 56 C6
John's Cross E Sus 12 D6
Johnshaven Aberds 83 G9
Johnston Pembs 22 E4
Johnstone Renfs 68 D3
Johnstonebridge Dumfries 60 D6
Johnstown Carms 23 E9
Johnstown Wrex 42 H6
Joppa Edin 70 C2
Joppa S Ayrs 67 E7
Jordans Bucks 18 B6
Jordanthorpe S Yorks 45 D7
Jump S Yorks 45 B7
Jumpers Green Dorset 9 E10
Juniper Green Edin 69 D10
Jurby East IoM 48 C3
Jurby West IoM 48 C3

K

Kaber Cumb 57 E9
Kaimend S Lanark 69 F8
Kaimes Edin 69 D11
Kalemouth Borders 70 H6
Kames Argyll 73 B7
Kames Argyll 73 F8
Kames E Ayrs 68 H5
Kea Corn 3 E7
Keadby N Lincs 46 A2
Keal Cotes Lincs 47 F7
Kearsley Gtr Man 43 B10
Kearstwick Cumb 50 A2
Kearton N Yorks 57 G11
Kearvaig Highld 92 B5
Keasden N Yorks 50 C3
Keckwick Halton 43 D8
Keddington Lincs 47 D7
Kedington Suff 30 D4
Kedleston Derbys 35 A9
Keelby Lincs 46 A5
Keele Staffs 44 H2
Keeley Green Bedford 29 D7
Keeston Pembs 22 E4
Keevil Wilts 16 F6
Kegworth Leics 35 C10
Kehelland Corn 2 E5
Keig Aberds 83 B8
Keighley W Yorks 51 E6
Keil Highld 74 B2
Keilarsbrae Clack 69 A7
Keilhill Aberds 89 C7
Keillmore Argyll 72 E5
Keillor Perth 76 C5
Keillour Perth 76 E2
Keills Argyll 64 B5
Keils Argyll 72 G4
Keinton Mandeville Som 8 A4
Keir Mill Dumfries 60 D4
Keisby Lincs 36 C6
Keiss Highld 94 D5
Keith Moray 88 C4
Keith Inch Aberds 89 D11
Keithock Angus 77 A9
Kelbrook Lancs 50 E5
Kelby Lincs 36 A6
Keld Cumb 57 E7
Keld N Yorks 57 F10
Keldholme N Yorks 59 H8
Kelfield N Lincs 46 B2
Kelfield N Yorks 52 F1
Kelham Notts 45 G11
Kellan Argyll 79 G8
Kellas Angus 77 D7
Kellas Moray 88 C1
Kellaton Devon 5 H9
Kelleth Cumb 57 F8
Kelleythorpe E Yorks 52 D5
Kelling Norf 39 A6
Kellingley N Yorks 51 G11
Kellington N Yorks 52 G1
Kelloe Durham 58 C4
Kelloholm Dumfries 60 B3
Kelly Devon 4 C4
Kelly Bray Corn 4 D4
Kelmarsh Northants 36 H3
Kelmscot Oxon 17 B9
Kelsale Suff 31 B10
Kelsall Ches W 43 F8
Kelsall Hill Ches W 43 F8
Kelshall Herts 29 E10
Kelsick Cumb 56 A3
Kelso Borders 70 G6
Kelstedge Derbys 45 F7
Kelstern Lincs 46 C6
Kelston Bath 16 E4
Keltneyburn Perth 75 C10
Kelton Dumfries 60 F5
Kelty Fife 69 A10
Kelvedon Essex 30 G5
Kelvedon Hatch Essex 20 B2
Kelvin S Lanark 68 E5
Kelvinside Glasgow 68 D4
Kelynack Corn 2 F2
Kemback Fife 77 F7
Kemberton Shrops 34 E3
Kemble Glos 16 B6
Kemerton Worcs 26 E6
Kemeys Commander Mon 15 A9
Kemnay Aberds 83 B9
Kemp Town Brighton 12 F2
Kempley Glos 26 F3
Kemps Green Warks 27 A8
Kempsey Worcs 26 D5
Kempsford Glos 17 B8
Kempshott Hants 18 F3
Kempston Bedford 29 D7
Kempston Hardwick Bedford 29 D7
Kempton Shrops 33 G9
Kemsing Kent 20 F2
Kemsley Kent 20 E6
Kenardington Kent 13 C8
Kenchester Hereford 25 D11
Kencot Oxon 17 A9
Kendal Cumb 57 G7
Kendoon Dumfries 67 H9
Kendray S Yorks 45 B7
Kenfig Bridgend 14 C4
Kenfig Hill Bridgend 14 C4
Kenilworth Warks 27 A9
Kenknock Stirling 75 D7
Kenley London 19 F10
Kenley Shrops 34 E1
Kenmore Highld 85 C12
Kenmore Perth 75 C10
Kenn Devon 5 C10
Kenn N Som 15 E10
Kennacley W Isles 90 H6
Kennacraig Argyll 73 G7
Kennerleigh Devon 7 F7
Kennet Clack 69 A8
Kennethmont Aberds 83 A7
Kennett Cambs 30 B3
Kennford Devon 5 C10
Kenninghall Norf 38 G6
Kenninghall Heath Norf 38 G6
Kennington Kent 13 B9
Kennington Oxon 18 A2
Kennoway Fife 76 G6
Kenny Hill Suff 38 H2
Kennythorpe N Yorks 52 C3
Kenovay Argyll 78 G2
Kensaleyre Highld 85 C9
Kensington London 19 D9
Kensworth C Beds 29 G7
Kensworth Common C Beds 29 G7
Kent Street E Sus 13 E6
Kent Street Kent 20 F3
Kent Street W Sus 11 B11
Kentallen Highld 74 B3
Kentchurch Hereford 25 F11
Kentford Suff 30 B4
Kentisbeare Devon 7 F9
Kentisbury Devon 6 B5
Kentisbury Ford Devon 6 B5
Kentmere Cumb 56 F6
Kenton Devon 5 C10
Kenton Suff 31 B8
Kenton T&W 63 G8
Kenton Bankfoot T&W 63 G8
Kentra Highld 79 E9
Kents Bank Cumb 49 B3
Kent's Green Glos 26 F4
Kent's Oak Hants 10 B2
Kenwick Shrops 33 B10
Kenwyn Corn 3 E7
Keoldale Highld 92 C6
Keppanach Highld 74 A3
Keppoch Highld 85 F14
Keprigan Argyll 65 G7
Kepwick N Yorks 58 G5
Kerchesters Borders 70 G6
Keresley W Mid 35 G9
Kernborough Devon 5 G8
Kerne Bridge Hereford 26 G2
Kerris Corn 2 G3
Kerry Powys 33 G7
Kerrycroy Argyll 73 G10
Kerry's Gate Hereford 25 E10
Kerrysdale Highld 85 A13
Kersall Notts 45 F11
Kersey Suff 31 D7
Kershopefoot Cumb 61 E10
Kersoe Worcs 26 E6
Kerswell Devon 7 F9
Kerswell Green Worcs 26 D5
Kesgrave Suff 31 D9
Kessingland Suff 39 G11
Kessingland Beach Suff 39 G11
Kessington E Dunb 68 C4
Kestle Corn 3 E8
Kestle Mill Corn 3 D7
Keston London 19 E11
Keswick Cumb 56 D4
Keswick Norf 39 B9
Keswick Norf 39 E8
Ketley Telford 34 D2
Ketley Bank Telford 34 D2
Ketsby Lincs 47 E7
Kettering Northants 36 H4
Ketteringham Norf 39 E7
Kettins Perth 76 D5
Kettlebaston Suff 30 C6
Kettlebridge Fife 76 G6
Kettleburgh Suff 31 B9
Kettlehill Fife 76 G6
Kettleholm Dumfries 61 F7
Kettleness N Yorks 59 E9
Kettleshume Ches E 44 E3
Kettlesing Bottom N Yorks 51 D8
Kettlesing Head N Yorks 51 D8
Kettlestone Norf 38 B5
Kettlethorpe Lincs 46 E2
Kettletoft Orkney 95 E7
Kettlewell N Yorks 50 B5
Ketton Rutland 36 E5
Kew London 19 D8
Kew Br. London 19 D8
Kewstoke N Som 15 E9
Kexbrough S Yorks 45 B7
Kexby Lincs 46 D2
Kexby York 52 D3
Key Green Ches E 44 F2
Keyham Leics 36 E2
Keyhaven Hants 10 E2
Keyingham E Yorks 53 G8
Keymer W Sus 12 E2
Keynsham Bath 16 E3
Keysoe Bedford 29 B7
Keysoe Row Bedford 29 B7
Keyston Cambs 36 H6
Keyworth Notts 36 B2
Kibblesworth T&W 63 H8
Kibworth Beauchamp Leics 36 F2
Kibworth Harcourt Leics 36 F2
Kidbrooke London 19 D11
Kiddemore Green Staffs 34 E4
Kidderminster Worcs 34 H4
Kiddington Oxon 27 F11
Kidlington Oxon 27 G11
Kidmore End Oxon 18 D3
Kidsgrove Staffs 44 G2
Kidstones N Yorks 50 A5
Kidwelly = Cydweli Carms 23 F9
Kiel Crofts Argyll 74 D2
Kielder Northumb 62 D2
Kierfiold Ho Orkney 95 G3
Kilbagie Fife 69 B8
Kilbarchan Renfs 68 D3
Kilbeg Highld 85 H11
Kilberry Argyll 72 G6
Kilbirnie N Ayrs 66 A6
Kilbride Argyll 74 E2
Kilbride Argyll 79 J11
Kilbride Highld 85 F10
Kilburn Angus 82 G5
Kilburn Derbys 45 H7
Kilburn London 19 C9
Kilburn N Yorks 51 B11
Kilby Leics 36 F2
Kilchamaig Argyll 73 G7
Kilchattan Argyll 72 D2
Kilchattan Bay Argyll 66 A4
Kilchenzie Argyll 65 F7
Kilcheran Argyll 79 H11
Kilchiaran Argyll 64 B3
Kilchoan Argyll 72 B6
Kilchoan Highld 78 E7
Kilchoman Argyll 64 B3
Kilchrenan Argyll 74 E3
Kilconquhar Fife 77 G7
Kilcot Glos 26 F3
Kilcoy Highld 87 F8
Kilcreggan Argyll 73 E11
Kildale N Yorks 59 F7
Kildalloig Argyll 65 G8
Kildary Highld 87 D10
Kildermorie Lodge Highld 87 D8
Kildonan N Ayrs 66 D3
Kildonan Lodge Highld 93 G12
Kildonnan Highld 78 C7
Kildrummy Aberds 82 B6
Kildwick N Yorks 50 E6
Kilfinan Argyll 73 F8
Kilfinnan Highld 80 D4
Kilgetty Pembs 22 F6
Kilgwrrwg Common Mon 15 B10
Kilham E Yorks 53 C6
Kilham Northumb 71 G7
Kilkenneth Argyll 78 G2
Kilkerran Argyll 65 G8
Kilkhampton Corn 6 E1
Killamarsh Derbys 45 D8
Killay Swansea 14 B2
Killbeg Argyll 79 G9
Killean Argyll 65 D7
Killearn Stirling 68 B4
Killen Highld 87 F9
Killerby Darl 58 E2
Killichonan Perth 75 B8
Killiechonate Highld 80 E4
Killiechronan Argyll 79 G8
Killiecrankie Perth 76 A2
Killiemor Argyll 78 H7
Killiemore House Argyll 78 J7
Killilan Highld 86 H2
Killimster Highld 94 E5
Killin Stirling 75 D8
Killin Lodge Highld 81 C7
Killinallan Argyll 64 A4
Killinghall N Yorks 51 D8
Killington Cumb 57 H8
Killingworth T&W 63 F8
Killmahumaig Argyll 72 D6
Killochyett Borders 70 F3
Killocraw Argyll 65 E7
Killundine Highld 79 G8
Kilmacolm Invclyd 68 D2
Kilmaha Argyll 73 C8
Kilmahog Stirling 75 G9
Kilmalieu Highld 79 F11
Kilmaluag Highld 85 A9
Kilmany Fife 76 E6
Kilmarie Highld 85 G10
Kilmarnock E Ayrs 67 C7
Kilmaron Castle Fife 76 F6
Kilmartin Argyll 73 D7
Kilmaurs E Ayrs 67 B7
Kilmelford Argyll 73 B7
Kilmeny Argyll 64 B4
Kilmersdon Som 16 F3
Kilmeston Hants 10 B4
Kilmichael Argyll 65 F7
Kilmichael Glassary Argyll 73 D7
Kilmichael of Inverlussa Argyll 72 E6
Kilmington Devon 8 E1
Kilmington Wilts 16 H4
Kilmonivaig Highld 80 E3
Kilmorack Highld 86 G7
Kilmore Argyll 79 J11
Kilmore Highld 85 H11
Kilmory Argyll 72 F6
Kilmory Highld 79 D8
Kilmory Highld 85 H8
Kilmory N Ayrs 66 D2
Kilmuir Highld 84 D7
Kilmuir Highld 85 A8
Kilmuir Highld 87 D10
Kilmuir Highld 87 G9
Kilmun Argyll 73 B8
Kilmun Argyll 73 E10
Kiln Pit Hill Northumb 58 A1
Kilncadzow S Lanark 69 F7
Kilndown Kent 12 C6
Kilnhurst S Yorks 45 C8
Kilninian Argyll 78 G6
Kilninver Argyll 79 J11
Kilnsea E Yorks 53 H10
Kilnsey N Yorks 50 C5
Kilnwick E Yorks 52 E5
Kilnwick Percy E Yorks 52 D4
Kiloran Argyll 72 D2
Kilpatrick N Ayrs 66 D2
Kilpeck Hereford 25 E11
Kilphedir Highld 93 H12
Kilpin E Yorks 52 G3
Kilpin Pike E Yorks 52 G3
Kilrenny Fife 77 G8
Kilsby Northants 28 A2
Kilspindie Perth 76 E5
Kilsyth N Lanark 68 C6
Kiltarlity Highld 87 G8
Kilton Notts 45 E9
Kilton Som 7 B10
Kilton Thorpe Redcar 59 E7
Kilvaxter Highld 85 B8
Kilve Som 7 B10
Kilvington Notts 36 A3
Kilwinning N Ayrs 66 B6
Kimber worth S Yorks 45 C8
Kimberley Norf 39 E6
Kimberley Notts 35 A11
Kimble Wick Bucks 28 H5
Kimblesworth Durham 58 B3
Kimbolton Cambs 29 B7
Kimbolton Hereford 26 B2
Kimcote Leics 36 G1
Kimmeridge Dorset 9 G8
Kimmerston Northumb 71 G8
Kimpton Hants 17 G9
Kimpton Herts 29 G8
Kinbrace Highld 93 F11
Kinbuck Stirling 75 G10
Kincaple Fife 77 F7
Kincardine Fife 69 B8
Kincardine Highld 87 C9
Kincardine Bridge Falk 69 B8
Kincardine O'Neil Aberds 83 D7
Kinclaven Perth 76 D4
Kincorth Aberdeen 83 C11
Kincorth Ho. Moray 87 E13
Kincraig Highld 81 C10
Kincraigie Perth 76 C2
Kindallachan Perth 76 C2
Kineton Glos 27 F7
Kineton Warks 27 C10
Kinfauns Perth 76 E4
King Edward Aberds 89 C7
King Sterndale Derbys 44 E4
Kingairloch Highld 79 F11
Kingarth Argyll 73 H9
Kingcoed Mon 25 H11
Kingerby Lincs 46 C4
Kingham Oxon 27 F9
Kingholm Quay Dumfries 60 F5
Kinghorn Fife 69 B11
Kingie Highld 80 C3
Kinglassie Fife 76 H5
Kingoodie Perth 76 E6
King's Acre Hereford 25 D11
King's Bromley Staffs 35 D7
King's Caple Hereford 26 F2
King's Cliffe Northants 36 F6
King's Coughton Warks 27 C7
King's Heath W Mid 35 G6
Kings Hedges Cambs 29 B11
King's Hill Kent 20 F3
Kings Langley Herts 19 A7
King's Lynn Norf 38 C2
King's Meaburn Cumb 57 D8
King's Mills Wrex 42 H6
Kings Muir Borders 69 G11
King's Newnham Warks 35 H10
King's Newton Derbys 35 C9
King's Norton Leics 36 E2
King's Norton W Mid 35 H6
King's Nympton Devon 6 E5
King's Pyon Hereford 25 C11
King's Ripton Cambs 37 H8
King's Somborne Hants 10 A2
King's Stag Dorset 8 C6
King's Stanley Glos 16 A5
King's Sutton Northants 27 E11
King's Thorn Hereford 26 E2
King's Walden Herts 29 F8
Kings Worthy Hants 10 A3
Kingsand Corn 4 F5
Kingsbarns Fife 77 F8
Kingsbridge Devon 5 G8
Kingsbridge Som 7 C8
Kingsburgh Highld 85 C8
Kingsbury London 19 C9
Kingsbury Warks 35 F8
Kingsbury Episcopi Som 8 B3
Kingsclere Hants 18 F2
Kingscote Glos 16 B5
Kingscott Devon 6 E4
Kingscross N Ayrs 66 D3
Kingsdon Som 8 B4
Kingsdown Kent 21 G10
Kingseat Fife 69 A10
Kingsey Bucks 28 H4
Kingsfold W Sus 19 H8
Kingsford E Ayrs 67 B7
Kingsford Worcs 34 G4
Kingsforth N Lincs 52 H6
Kingsgate Kent 21 D10
Kingsheanton Devon 6 C4
Kingshouse Hotel Highld 74 B5
Kingside Hill Cumb 56 A3
Kingskerswell Devon 5 E9
Kingskettle Fife 76 G6
Kingsland Anglesey 40 B4
Kingsland Hereford 25 B11
Kingsley Ches W 43 E8
Kingsley Hants 18 H4
Kingsley Staffs 44 H4
Kingsley Green W Sus 11 A7
Kingsley Holt Staffs 44 H4
Kingsley Park Northants 28 B4
Kingsmuir Angus 77 C7
Kingsmuir Fife 77 G8
Kingsnorth Kent 13 C9
Kingstanding W Mid 35 F6
Kingsteignton Devon 5 D9
Kingsthorpe Northants 28 B4
Kingston Cambs 29 C10
Kingston Devon 5 G7
Kingston Dorset 9 D6
Kingston Dorset 9 G8
Kingston E Loth 70 B4
Kingston Hants 9 D10
Kingston IoW 10 F3
Kingston Kent 21 F8
Kingston Moray 88 B3
Kingston Bagpuize Oxon 17 B11
Kingston Blount Oxon 18 B4
Kingston by Sea W Sus 11 D11
Kingston Deverill Wilts 16 H5
Kingston Gorse W Sus 11 D9
Kingston Lisle Oxon 17 C10
Kingston Maurward Dorset 8 E6
Kingston near Lewes E Sus 12 F2
Kingston on Soar Notts 35 C11
Kingston Russell Dorset 8 E4
Kingston St Mary Som 7 D11
Kingston Seymour N Som 15 E10
Kingston Upon Hull Hull 53 G6
Kingston upon Thames London 19 E8
Kingston Vale London 19 D9
Kingstone Hereford 25 E11
Kingstone Som 8 C2
Kingstone Staffs 35 C6
Kingstown Cumb 61 H9
Kingswear Devon 5 F9
Kingswells Aberdeen 83 C10
Kingswinford W Mid 34 G4
Kingswood Bucks 28 G3
Kingswood Glos 16 B4
Kingswood Hereford 25 C9
Kingswood Kent 20 F5
Kingswood Powys 33 E8
Kingswood S Glos 16 D3
Kingswood Sur 19 F9
Kingswood Warks 27 A8
Kingthorpe Lincs 46 E5
Kington Hereford 25 C9
Kington Worcs 26 C6
Kington Langley Wilts 16 D6
Kington Magna Dorset 9 B6
Kington St Michael Wilts 16 D6
Kingussie Highld 81 C9
Kingweston Som 8 A4
Kininvie Ho. Moray 88 D3
Kinkell Bridge Perth 76 F2
Kinknockie Aberds 89 D10
Kinlet Shrops 34 G3
Kinloch Fife 76 F5
Kinloch Highld 78 B6
Kinloch Highld 85 G11
Kinloch Highld 92 F6
Kinloch Perth 76 C5
Kinloch Perth 76 C4
Kinloch Hourn Highld 80 C1
Kinloch Laggan Highld 81 E7
Kinloch Lodge Highld 93 D8
Kinloch Rannoch Perth 75 B9
Kinlochan Highld 79 E11
Kinlochard Stirling 75 G7
Kinlochbeoraid Highld 79 C11
Kinlochbervie Highld 92 D5
Kinlocheil Highld 80 F1
Kinlochewe Highld 86 E3
Kinlochleven Highld 74 A4
Kinlochmoidart Highld 79 D10
Kinlochmorar Highld 79 B11
Kinlochmore Highld 74 A4
Kinlochspelve Argyll 79 J9
Kinloid Highld 79 C9
Kinloss Moray 87 E13
Kinmel Bay Conwy 42 D2
Kinmuck Aberds 83 B10
Kinmundy Aberds 83 B10
Kinnadie Aberds 89 D9
Kinnaird Perth 76 E5
Kinnaird Castle Angus 77 B9
Kinneff Aberds 83 F10
Kinnelhead Dumfries 60 C6
Kinnell Angus 77 B9
Kinnerley Shrops 33 C9
Kinnersley Hereford 25 D10
Kinnersley Worcs 26 D5
Kinnerton Powys 25 B9
Kinnesswood Perth 76 G4
Kinninvie Durham 58 D1
Kinnordy Angus 76 B6
Kinoulton Notts 36 B2
Kinross Perth 76 G4
Kinrossie Perth 76 D4
Kinsbourne Green Herts 29 G8
Kinsey Heath Ches E 34 A2
Kinsham Hereford 25 B10
Kinsham Worcs 26 E6
Kinsley W Yorks 45 A8
Kinson Bmouth 9 E9
Kintbury W Berks 17 E10
Kintessack Moray 87 E12
Kintillo Perth 76 F4
Kintocher Aberds 83 C7
Kinton Hereford 25 A11
Kinton Shrops 33 D9
Kintore Aberds 83 B9
Kintour Argyll 64 C5
Kintra Argyll 64 D4
Kintra Argyll 78 J6
Kintraw Argyll 73 C7
Kinuachdrachd Argyll 72 D6
Kinveachy Highld 81 B11
Kinver Staffs 34 G4
Kippax W Yorks 51 F10
Kippen Stirling 68 A5
Kippford or Scaur Dumfries 55 D11
Kirbister Orkney 95 F7
Kirbister Orkney 95 H4
Kirbuster Orkney 95 F3
Kirby Bedon Norf 39 E8
Kirby Bellars Leics 36 D3
Kirby Cane Norf 39 F9
Kirby Cross Essex 31 F9
Kirby Grindalythe N Yorks 52 C5
Kirby Hill N Yorks 51 C9
Kirby Hill N Yorks 58 F2
Kirby Knowle N Yorks 58 H5
Kirby-le-Soken Essex 31 F9
Kirby Misperton N Yorks 52 B3
Kirby Muxloe Leics 35 E11
Kirby Row Norf 39 F9
Kirby Sigston N Yorks 58 G5

Lutterworth Leics 35 G11
Lutton Devon 5 F6
Lutton Lincs 37 C10
Lutton Northants 37 G7
Lutworthy Devon 7 E6
Luxborough Som 7 C8
Luxulyan Corn 4 F1
Lybster Highld 94 G4
Lydbury North Shrops 33 G9
Lydcott Devon 6 C5
Lydd Kent 13 D9
Lydd on Sea Kent 13 D9
Lydden Kent 21 G9
Lyddington Rutland 36 F4
Lyde Green Hants 18 F4
Lydeard St Lawrence Som 7 C10
Lydford Devon 4 C6
Lydford-on-Fosse Som 8 A4
Lydgate W Yorks 50 G5
Lydham Shrops 33 F9
Lydiard Green Wilts 17 C7
Lydiard Millicent Wilts 17 C7
Lydiate Mers 42 B6
Lydlinch Dorset 8 C6
Lydney Glos 16 A3
Lydstep Pembs 22 G5
Lye W Mid 34 G5
Lye Green Bucks 18 A6
Lye Green E Sus 12 C4
Lyford Oxon 17 B10
Lymbridge Green Kent 13 B10
Lyme Regis Dorset 8 E2
Lyminge Kent 21 G8
Lymington Hants 10 E2
Lyminster W Sus 11 D9
Lymm Warr 43 D9
Lymore Hants 10 E1
Lympne Kent 13 C10
Lympsham Som 15 F9
Lympstone Devon 5 C10
Lynchat Highld 81 C9
Lyndale Ho. Highld 85 C8
Lyndhurst Hants 10 D2
Lyndon Rutland 36 E5
Lyne Sur 19 E7
Lyne Down Hereford 26 E3
Lyne of Gorthleck Highld 81 A7
Lyne of Skene Aberds 83 B9
Lyneal Shrops 33 B10
Lyneham Oxon 27 F9
Lyneham Wilts 17 D7
Lynemore Highld 82 A2
Lynemouth Northumb 63 D8
Lyness Orkney 95 J4
Lyng Norf 39 D6
Lyng Som 8 B2
Lynmouth Devon 7 B6
Lynsted Kent 20 E6
Lynton Devon 6 B6
Lyon's Gate Dorset 8 D5
Lyonshall Hereford 25 C10
Lytchett Matravers Dorset 9 E8
Lytchett Minster Dorset 9 E8
Lyth Highld 94 D4
Lytham Lancs 49 G3
Lytham St Anne's Lancs 49 G3
Lythe N Yorks 59 E9
Lythes Orkney 95 K5

M

Mabe Burnthouse Corn 3 F6
Mabie Dumfries 60 F5
Mablethorpe Lincs 47 D9
Macclesfield Ches E 44 E3
Macclesfield Forest Ches E 44 E3
Macduff Aberds 89 B7
Mace Green Suff 31 D8
Macharioch Argyll 65 H8
Machen Caerph 15 C8
Machrihanish Argyll 65 F7
Machynlleth Powys 32 E3
Machynys Carms 23 G10
Mackerel's Common W Sus 11 B9
Mackworth Derbys 35 B9
Macmerry E Loth 70 C3
Madderty Perth 76 E2
Maddiston Falk 69 C8
Madehurst W Sus 11 C8
Madeley Staffs 34 A3
Madeley Telford 34 E2
Madeley Heath Staffs 43 H10
Madeley Park Staffs 34 A3
Madingley Cambs 29 B10
Madley Hereford 25 E11
Madresfield Worcs 26 D5
Madron Corn 2 F3
Maen-y-groes Ceredig 23 A8
Maenaddwyn Anglesey 40 B6
Maenclochog Pembs 22 D5
Maendy V Glam 14 D6
Maentwrog Gwyn 41 F8
Maer Staffs 34 B3
Maerdy Conwy 32 A6
Maerdy Rhondda 14 B5
Maes-Treylow Powys 25 B9
Maesbrook Shrops 33 C8
Maesbury Shrops 33 C9
Maesbury Marsh Shrops 33 C9
Maesgwyn-Isaf Powys 33 D7
Maesgwynne Carms 23 D7
Maeshafn Denb 42 F5
Maesllyn Ceredig 23 B8
Maesmynis Powys 25 D7
Maesteg Bridgend 14 B4
Maestir Ceredig 23 B10
Maesy cwmmer Caerph 15 B7
Maesybont Carms 23 E10
Maesycrugiau Carms 23 B9
Maesymeillion Ceredig 23 B9
Magdalen Laver Essex 30 H2
Maggieknockater Moray 88 D3
Magham Down E Sus 12 E5
Maghull Mers 43 B6
Magor Mon 15 C10
Magpie Green Suff 39 H6
Maiden Bradley Wilts 16 H5
Maiden Law Durham 58 B2
Maiden Newton Dorset 8 E4
Maiden Wells Pembs 22 G4
Maidencombe Torbay 5 E10
Maidenhall Suff 31 D8
Maidenhead Windsor 18 C5
Maidens S Ayrs 66 F5
Maiden's Green Brack 18 D5
Maidensgrave Suff 31 D9
Maidenwell Corn 4 D2
Maidenwell Lincs 47 E7
Maidford Northants 28 C3
Maids Moreton Bucks 28 E4
Maidstone Kent 20 F4
Maidwell Northants 36 H3
Mail Shetland 96 L6
Main Powys 33 D7
Maindee Newport 15 C9
Mains of Airies Dumfries 54 C2
Mains of Allardice Aberds 83 F10
Mains of Annochie Aberds 89 D9
Mains of Ardestie Angus 77 D8
Mains of Balhall Angus 77 A8
Mains of Ballindarg Angus 77 B7
Mains of Balnakettle Aberds 83 F8
Mains of Birness Aberds 89 E9
Mains of Burgie Moray 87 F13
Mains of Clunas Highld 87 G11
Mains of Crichie Aberds 89 D9
Mains of Dalvey Highld 87 H14
Mains of Dellavaird Aberds 83 E9
Mains of Drum Aberds 83 D10
Mains of Edingight Moray 88 C5
Mains of Fedderate Aberds 89 D8
Mains of Inkhorn Aberds 89 E9
Mains of Mayen Moray 88 D5
Mains of Melgund Angus 77 B8
Mains of Thornton Aberds 83 F8
Mains of Watten Highld 94 E4
Mainsforth Durham 58 C4
Mainsriddle Dumfries 60 H5
Mainstone Shrops 33 G8
Maisemore Glos 26 F5
Malacleit W Isles 84 A2
Malborough Devon 5 H8
Malcoff Derbys 44 D4
Maldon Essex 30 H5
Malham N Yorks 50 C5
Maligar Highld 85 B9
Mallaig Highld 79 B9
Malleny Mills Edin 69 D10
Malling Stirling 75 G8
Malltraeth Anglesey 40 D6
Mallwyd Gwyn 32 D4
Malmesbury Wilts 16 C6
Malmsmead Devon 7 B6
Malpas Ches W 43 H7
Malpas Corn 3 E7
Malpas Newport 15 B9
Malswick Glos 26 F4
Maltby S Yorks 45 C9
Maltby Stockton 58 E5
Maltby le Marsh Lincs 47 D8
Malting Green Essex 30 F6
Maltman's Hill Kent 13 B8
Malton N Yorks 52 B3
Malvern Link Worcs 26 D4
Malvern Wells Worcs 26 D4
Mamble Worcs 26 A3
Man-moel Caerph 15 A7
Manaccan Corn 3 G6
Manafon Powys 33 E7
Manais W Isles 90 J6
Manar Ho. Aberds 83 A9
Manaton Devon 5 C8
Manby Lincs 47 D7
Mancetter Warks 35 F9
Manchester Gtr Man 44 C2
Manchester Airport Gtr Man 44 D2
Mancot Flint 42 F6
Mandally Highld 80 C4
Manea Cambs 37 G10
Manfield N Yorks 58 E3
Mangaster Shetland 96 F5
Mangotsfield S Glos 16 D3
Mangurstadh W Isles 90 D5
Mankinholes W Yorks 50 G5
Manley Ches W 43 E8
Mannal Argyll 78 G2
Mannerston W Loth 69 C9
Manningford Bohune Wilts 17 F8
Manningford Bruce Wilts 17 F8
Manningham W Yorks 51 F7
Mannings Heath W Sus 11 B11
Mannington Dorset 9 D9
Manningtree Essex 31 E7
Mannofield Aberdeen 83 C11
Manor London 19 C11
Manor Estate S Yorks 45 D7
Manorbier Pembs 22 G5
Manordeilo Carms 24 F3
Manorhill Borders 70 G5
Manorowen Pembs 22 C4
Mansel Lacy Hereford 25 D11
Manselfield Swansea 23 H10
Mansell Gamage Hereford 25 D10
Mansergh Cumb 50 A2
Mansfield E Ayrs 67 E9
Mansfield Notts 45 F9
Mansfield Woodhouse Notts 45 F9
Mansriggs Cumb 49 A2
Manston Dorset 9 C7
Manston Kent 21 E10
Manston W Yorks 51 F9
Manswood Dorset 9 D8
Manthorpe Lincs 36 B5
Manthorpe Lincs 37 D6
Manton N Lincs 46 B3
Manton Notts 45 E9
Manton Rutland 36 E4
Manton Wilts 17 E8
Manuden Essex 29 F11
Maperton Som 8 B5
Maple Cross Herts 19 B7
Maplebeck Notts 45 F11
Mapledurham Oxon 18 D3
Mapledurwell Hants 18 F3
Maplehurst W Sus 11 B10
Maplescombe Kent 20 E2
Mapleton Derbys 44 H5
Mapperley Derbys 35 A10
Mapperley Park Nottingham 36 A1
Mapperton Dorset 8 E4
Mappleborough Green Warks 27 B7
Mappleton E Yorks 53 E8
Mappowder Dorset 8 D6
Mar Lodge Aberds 82 D2
Maraig W Isles 90 G6
Marazanvose Corn 3 D7
Marazion Corn 2 F4
Marbhig W Isles 91 F9
Marbury Ches E 43 H8
March Cambs 37 F10
March S Lanark 60 B5
Marcham Oxon 17 B11
Marchamley Shrops 34 C1
Marchington Staffs 35 B7
Marchington Woodlands Staffs 35 C7
Marchroes Gwyn 40 H5
Marchwiel Wrex 42 H6
Marchwood Hants 10 C2
Marcross V Glam 14 E5
Marden Hereford 26 D2
Marden Kent 12 B6
Marden T&W 63 F9
Marden Wilts 17 F7
Marden Beech Kent 12 B6
Marden Thorn Kent 13 B6
Mardy Mon 25 G10
Marefield Leics 36 E3
Mareham le Fen Lincs 46 F6
Mareham on the Hill Lincs 46 F6
Marehay Derbys 45 H7
Marehill W Sus 11 C9
Maresfield E Sus 12 D3
Marfleet Hull 53 G7
Marford Wrex 42 G6
Margam Neath 14 C3
Margaret Marsh Dorset 9 C7
Margaret Roding Essex 30 G2
Margaretting Essex 20 A3
Margate Kent 21 D10
Margnaheglish N Ayrs 66 C3
Margrove Park Redcar 59 E7
Marham Norf 38 D3
Marhamchurch Corn 4 A3
Marholm Pboro 37 E7
Mariandyrys Anglesey 41 B8
Marianglas Anglesey 41 B7
Mariansleigh Devon 7 D6
Marionburgh Aberds 83 C9
Marishader Highld 85 B9
Marjoriebanks Dumfries 60 E6
Mark Dumfries 54 D4
Mark S Ayrs 54 B3
Mark Som 15 G9
Mark Causeway Som 15 G9
Mark Cross E Sus 12 C4
Mark Cross E Sus 12 E3
Markbeech Kent 12 B3
Markby Lincs 47 E8
Market Bosworth Leics 35 E10
Market Deeping Lincs 37 E7
Market Drayton Shrops 34 B2
Market Harborough Leics 36 G3
Market Lavington Wilts 17 F7
Market Overton Rutland 36 D4
Market Rasen Lincs 46 D5
Market Stainton Lincs 46 E6
Market Warsop Notts 45 F9
Market Weighton E Yorks 52 E4
Market Weston Suff 38 H5
Markethill Perth 76 D5
Markfield Leics 35 D10
Markham Caerph 15 A7
Markham Moor Notts 45 E11
Markinch Fife 76 G5
Markington N Yorks 51 C8
Marks Tey Essex 30 F6
Marksbury Bath 16 E3
Markyate Herts 29 G7
Marland Gtr Man 44 A2
Marlborough Wilts 17 E8
Marlbrook Hereford 26 C2
Marlbrook Worcs 26 A6
Marlcliff Warks 27 C7
Marldon Devon 5 E9
Marlesford Suff 31 C10
Marley Green Ches E 43 H8
Marley Hill T&W 63 H8
Marley Mount Hants 10 E1
Marlingford Norf 39 E7
Marloes Pembs 22 F2
Marlow Bucks 18 C5
Marlow Hereford 33 H10
Marlow Bottom Bucks 18 C5
Marlpit Hill Kent 19 G11
Marlpool Derbys 45 H8
Marnhull Dorset 9 C6
Marnoch Aberds 88 C5
Marnock N Lanark 68 D6
Marple Gtr Man 44 D3
Marple Bridge Gtr Man 44 D3
Marr S Yorks 45 B9
Marrel Highld 93 H13
Marrick N Yorks 58 G1
Marrister Shetland 96 G7
Marros Carms 23 F7
Marsden T&W 63 G9
Marsden W Yorks 44 A4
Marsett N Yorks 57 H11
Marsh Devon 8 C1
Marsh W Yorks 50 F6
Marsh Baldon Oxon 18 B2
Marsh Gibbon Bucks 28 F3
Marsh Green Devon 7 G9
Marsh Green Kent 12 B3
Marsh Green Staffs 44 G2
Marsh Lane Derbys 45 E8
Marsh Street Som 7 B8
Marshall's Heath Herts 29 G8
Marshalsea Dorset 8 D2
Marshalswick Herts 29 H8
Marsham Norf 39 C7
Marshaw Lancs 50 D1
Marshborough Kent 21 F10
Marshbrook Shrops 33 G10
Marshchapel Lincs 47 C7
Marshfield Newport 15 C8
Marshfield S Glos 16 D4
Marshgate Corn 4 B2
Marshland St James Norf 37 E11
Marshside Mers 49 H3
Marshwood Dorset 8 E2
Marske N Yorks 58 F2
Marske-by-the-Sea Redcar 59 D7
Marston Ches W 43 E9
Marston Hereford 25 C10
Marston Lincs 36 A4
Marston Oxon 28 H2
Marston Staffs 34 C5
Marston Staffs 34 D4
Marston Warks 35 F8
Marston Wilts 16 F6
Marston Doles Warks 27 C11
Marston Green W Mid 35 G7
Marston Magna Som 8 B4
Marston Meysey Wilts 17 B8
Marston Montgomery Derbys 35 B7
Marston Moretaine C Beds 28 D6
Marston on Dove Derbys 35 C8
Marston St Lawrence Northants 28 D2
Marston Stannett Hereford 26 C2
Marston Trussell Northants 36 G2
Marstow Hereford 26 G2
Marsworth Bucks 28 G6
Marten Wilts 17 F9
Marthall Ches E 44 E2
Martham Norf 39 D10
Martin Hants 9 C9
Martin Kent 21 G10
Martin Lincs 46 F5
Martin Lincs 46 G5
Martin Dales Lincs 46 F5
Martin Drove End Hants 9 B9
Martin Hussingtree Worcs 26 B5
Martin Mill Kent 21 G10
Martinhoe Devon 6 B5
Martinhoe Cross Devon 6 B5
Martinscroft Warr 43 D9
Martinstown Dorset 8 F5
Martlesham Suff 31 D9
Martlesham Heath Suff 31 D9
Martletwy Pembs 22 E5
Martley Worcs 26 C4
Martock Som 8 C3
Marton Ches E 44 F2
Marton E Yorks 53 F7
Marton Lincs 46 D2
Marton Mbro 58 E6
Marton N Yorks 51 C10
Marton N Yorks 52 A3
Marton Shrops 33 C10
Marton Shrops 33 E8
Marton Warks 27 B11
Marton-le-Moor N Yorks 51 B9
Martyr Worthy Hants 10 A4
Martyr's Green Sur 19 F7
Marwick Orkney 95 F3
Marwood Devon 6 C4
Mary Tavy Devon 4 D6
Marybank Highld 86 F7
Maryburgh Highld 87 F8
Maryhill Glasgow 68 D4
Marykirk Aberds 83 G8
Marylebone Gtr Man 43 B8
Marypark Moray 88 E1
Maryport Cumb 56 C2
Maryport Dumfries 54 F4
Maryton Angus 77 B9
Marywell Aberds 83 D7
Marywell Aberds 83 D11
Marywell Angus 77 C9
Masham N Yorks 51 A8
Mashbury Essex 30 G3
Masongill N Yorks 50 B2
Masonhill S Ayrs 67 D6
Mastin Moor Derbys 45 E8
Mastrick Aberdeen 83 C10
Matching Essex 30 G2
Matching Green Essex 30 G2
Matching Tye Essex 30 G2
Matfen Northumb 62 F6
Matfield Kent 12 B5
Mathern Mon 15 B11
Mathon Hereford 26 D4
Mathry Pembs 22 C3
Matlaske Norf 39 B7
Matlock Derbys 44 F6
Matlock Bath Derbys 44 G6
Matson Glos 26 G5
Matterdale End Cumb 56 D5
Mattersey Notts 45 D10
Mattersey Thorpe Notts 45 D10
Mattingley Hants 18 F4
Mattishall Norf 39 D6
Mattishall Burgh Norf 39 D6
Mauchline E Ayrs 67 D7
Maud Aberds 89 D9
Maugersbury Glos 27 F9
Maughold IoM 48 C4
Mauld Highld 86 H7
Maulden C Beds 29 E7
Maulds Meaburn Cumb 57 E8
Maunby N Yorks 58 H4
Maund Bryan Hereford 26 C2
Maundown Som 7 D9
Mautby Norf 39 D10
Mavis Enderby Lincs 47 F7
Maw Green Ches E 43 G10
Mawbray Cumb 56 B2
Mawdesley Lancs 43 A7
Mawdlam Bridgend 14 C4
Mawgan Corn 2 G6
Mawla Corn 2 E6
Mawnan Corn 3 G6
Mawnan Smith Corn 3 G6
Mawsley Northants 36 H4
Maxey Pboro 37 E7
Maxstoke Warks 35 G8
Maxton Borders 70 G5
Maxton Kent 21 G10
Maxwellheugh Borders 70 G6
Maxwelltown Dumfries 60 F5
Maxworthy Corn 6 G1
May Bank Staffs 44 H2
Mayals Swansea 14 B2
Maybole S Ayrs 66 F6
Mayfield E Sus 12 D4
Mayfield Midloth 70 D2
Mayfield Staffs 44 H5
Mayfield W Loth 69 D8
Mayford Sur 18 F6
Mayland Essex 20 A6
Maynard's Green E Sus 12 E4
Maypole Mon 25 G11
Maypole Scilly 2 C3
Maypole Green Essex 30 F6
Maypole Green Norf 39 F10
Maypole Green Suff 31 B9
Maywick Shetland 96 L5
Meadle Bucks 28 H5
Meadowtown Shrops 33 E9
Meaford Staffs 34 B4
Meal Bank Cumb 57 G7
Mealabost W Isles 91 D9
Mealabost Bhuirgh W Isles 91 B9
Mealsgate Cumb 56 B4
Meanwood W Yorks 51 F8
Mearbeck N Yorks 50 C4
Meare Som 15 G10
Meare Green Som 8 B2
Mears Ashby Northants 28 B5
Measham Leics 35 D9
Meath Green Sur 12 B1
Meathop Cumb 49 A4
Meaux E Yorks 53 F6
Meavy Devon 4 E6
Medbourne Leics 36 F3
Medburn Northumb 63 F7
Meddon Devon 6 E1
Meden Vale Notts 45 F9
Medlam Lincs 47 G7
Medmenham Bucks 18 C5
Medomsley Durham 58 A2
Medstead Hants 18 H3
Meer End W Mid 27 A9
Meerbrook Staffs 44 F3
Meers Bridge Lincs 47 D8
Meesden Herts 29 E11
Meeth Devon 6 F4
Meggethead Borders 61 A7
Meidrim Carms 23 D7
Meifod Denb 42 G3
Meifod Powys 33 D7
Meigle N Ayrs 73 G10
Meigle Perth 76 C5
Meikle Earnock S Lanark 68 E6
Meikle Ferry Highld 87 C10
Meikle Forter Angus 76 A4
Meikle Gluich Highld 87 C9
Meikle Pinkerton E Loth 70 C6
Meikle Strath Aberds 83 F8
Meikle Tarty Aberds 89 F9
Meikle Wartle Aberds 89 E7
Meikleour Perth 76 D4
Meinciau Carms 23 E9
Meir Stoke 34 A5
Meir Heath Staffs 34 A5
Melbourn Cambs 29 D10
Melbourne Derbys 35 C9
Melbourne E Yorks 52 E3
Melbourne S Lanark 69 F9
Melbury Abbas Dorset 9 B7
Melbury Bubb Dorset 8 D4
Melbury Osmond Dorset 8 D4
Melbury Sampford Dorset 8 D4
Melby Shetland 96 H3
Melchbourne Bedford 29 B7
Melcombe Bingham Dorset 9 D6
Melcombe Regis Dorset 8 F5
Meldon Devon 6 G4
Meldon Northumb 63 E7
Meldreth Cambs 29 D10
Meldrum Ho. Aberds 89 F8
Melfort Argyll 73 B7
Melgarve Highld 81 D6
Meliden Denb 42 D3
Melin-y-coed Conwy 41 D10
Melin-y-ddôl Powys 33 E6
Melin-y-grug Powys 33 E6
Melin-y-Wig Denb 42 H3
Melinbyrhedyn Powys 32 F4
Melincourt Neath 14 A4
Melkinthorpe Cumb 57 D7
Melkridge Northumb 62 G3
Melksham Wilts 16 E6
Melldalloch Argyll 73 F8
Melling Lancs 50 B1
Melling Mers 43 B6
Melling Mount Mers 43 B7
Mellis Suff 31 A8
Mellon Charles Highld 91 H13
Mellon Udrigle Highld 91 H13
Mellor Gtr Man 44 D3
Mellor Lancs 50 F2
Mellor Brook Lancs 50 F2
Mells Som 16 G4
Melmerby Cumb 57 C8
Melmerby N Yorks 51 B9
Melmerby N Yorks 58 H1
Melplash Dorset 8 E3
Melrose Borders 70 G4
Melsetter Orkney 95 K3
Melsonby N Yorks 58 F2
Meltham W Yorks 44 A5
Melton Suff 31 C9
Melton Constable Norf 38 B6
Melton Mowbray Leics 36 D3
Melton Ross N Lincs 46 A4
Meltonby E Yorks 52 D3
Melvaig Highld 91 J12
Melverley Shrops 33 D9
Melverley Green Shrops 33 D9
Melvich Highld 93 C11
Membury Devon 8 D1
Memsie Aberds 89 B9
Memus Angus 77 B7
Menabilly Corn 4 F1
Menai Bridge = Porthaethwy Anglesey 41 C7
Mendham Suff 39 G8
Mendlesham Suff 31 B8
Mendlesham Green Suff 31 B7
Menheniot Corn 4 E3
Mennock Dumfries 60 C4
Menston W Yorks 51 E7
Menstrie Clack 75 H11
Menthorpe N Yorks 52 F2
Mentmore Bucks 28 G6
Meoble Highld 79 C10
Meole Brace Shrops 33 D10
Meols Mers 42 C5
Meonstoke Hants 10 C5
Meopham Kent 20 E3
Meopham Station Kent 20 E3
Mepal Cambs 37 G10
Meppershall C Beds 29 E8
Merbach Hereford 25 D10
Mere Ches E 43 D10
Mere Wilts 9 A7
Mere Brow Lancs 49 H4
Mere Green W Mid 35 F7
Mereclough Lancs 50 F4
Mereside Blackpool 49 F3
Mereworth Kent 20 F3
Mergie Aberds 83 E9
Meriden W Mid 35 G8
Merkadale Highld 85 E8
Merkland Dumfries 60 F3
Merkland S Ayrs 66 G5
Merkland Lodge Highld 92 G7
Merley Poole 9 E9
Merlin's Bridge Pembs 22 E4
Merrington Shrops 33 C10
Merrion Pembs 22 G4
Merriott Som 8 C3
Merrivale Devon 4 D6
Merrow Sur 19 F7
Merrymeet Corn 4 E3
Mersham Kent 13 C9
Merstham Sur 19 F9
Merston W Sus 11 D7
Merstone IoW 10 F4
Merther Corn 3 E7
Merthyr Carms 23 D8
Merthyr Cynog Powys 24 E6
Merthyr-Dyfan V Glam 15 E7
Merthyr Mawr Bridgend 14 D4
Merthyr Tudful = Merthyr Tydfil M Tydf 25 H7
Merthyr Tydfil = Merthyr Tudful M Tydf 25 H7
Merthyr Vale M Tydf 14 B6
Merton Devon 6 E4
Merton London 19 D9
Merton Norf 38 F5
Merton Oxon 28 G2
Mervinslaw Borders 62 B2
Meshaw Devon 7 E6
Messing Essex 30 G5
Messingham N Lincs 46 B2
Metfield Suff 39 G8
Metheringham Lincs 46 F4
Methil Fife 76 H6
Methlem Gwyn 40 G3
Methley W Yorks 51 G9
Methlick Aberds 89 E8
Methven Perth 76 E3
Methwold Norf 38 F3
Methwold Hythe Norf 38 F3
Mettingham Suff 39 G9
Mevagissey Corn 3 E9
Mewith Head N Yorks 50 C3
Mexborough S Yorks 45 B8
Mey Highld 94 C4
Meysey Hampton Glos 17 B8
Miabhag W Isles 90 G5
Miabhag W Isles 90 H6
Miabhig W Isles 90 D5
Michaelchurch Hereford 26 F2
Michaelchurch Escley Hereford 25 E10
Michaelchurch on Arrow Powys 25 C9
Michaelston-le-Pit V Glam 15 D7
Michaelston-y-Fedw Newport 15 C8
Michaelstow Corn 4 D1
Michealston-super-Ely Cardiff 15 D7
Micheldever Hants 18 H2
Michelmersh Hants 10 B2
Mickfield Suff 31 B8
Mickle Trafford Ches W 43 F7
Micklebring S Yorks 45 C9
Mickleby N Yorks 59 E9
Mickleham Sur 19 F8
Mickleover Derby 35 B9
Micklethwaite W Yorks 51 E7
Mickleton Durham 57 D11
Mickleton Glos 27 D8
Mickletown W Yorks 51 G9
Mickley N Yorks 51 B8
Mickley Square Northumb 62 G6
Mid Ardlaw Aberds 89 B9
Mid Auchinlech Invclyd 68 C2
Mid Beltie Aberds 83 C8
Mid Calder W Loth 69 D9
Mid Cloch Forbie Aberds 89 C7
Mid Clyth Highld 94 G4
Mid Lavant W Sus 11 D7
Mid Main Highld 86 H7
Mid Urchany Highld 87 G11
Mid Walls Shetland 96 H4
Mid Yell Shetland 96 D7
Midbea Orkney 95 D5
Middle Assendon Oxon 18 C4
Middle Aston Oxon 27 F11
Middle Barton Oxon 27 F11
Middle Cairncake Aberds 89 D8
Middle Claydon Bucks 28 F4
Middle Drums Angus 77 B8
Middle Handley Derbys 45 E8
Middle Littleton Worcs 27 D7
Middle Maes-coed Hereford 25 E10
Middle Mill Pembs 22 D3
Middle Rasen Lincs 46 D4
Middle Rigg Perth 76 G3
Middle Tysoe Warks 27 D10
Middle Wallop Hants 17 H9
Middle Winterslow Wilts 9 A11
Middle Woodford Wilts 17 H8
Middlebie Dumfries 61 F8
Middleforth Green Lancs 49 G5
Middleham N Yorks 58 H2
Middlehope Shrops 33 G10
Middlemarsh Dorset 8 D5
Middlemuir Aberds 89 F9
Middlesbrough Mbro 58 D5
Middleshaw Cumb 57 H7
Middleshaw Dumfries 61 F7
Middlesmoor N Yorks 51 B6
Middlestone Durham 58 C3
Middlestone Moor Durham 58 C3
Middlestown W Yorks 51 H8
Middlethird Borders 70 F5
Middleton Aberds 83 B10
Middleton Argyll 78 G2
Middleton Cumb 57 H8
Middleton Derbys 44 F5
Middleton Derbys 44 G6
Middleton Essex 30 E5
Middleton Gtr Man 44 B2
Middleton Hants 17 G11
Middleton Hereford 26 B2
Middleton Lancs 49 D4
Middleton Midloth 70 E2
Middleton N Yorks 51 E7
Middleton N Yorks 59 H8
Middleton Norf 38 D2
Middleton Northants 36 G4
Middleton Northumb 62 E6
Middleton Northumb 71 G10
Middleton Perth 76 G4
Middleton Perth 76 C4
Middleton Shrops 33 C9
Middleton Shrops 33 F8
Middleton Shrops 33 H11
Middleton Suff 31 B11
Middleton Swansea 23 H9
Middleton W Yorks 51 G8
Middleton Warks 35 F7
Middleton Cheney Northants 27 D11
Middleton Green Staffs 34 B5
Middleton Hall Northumb 71 H8
Middleton-in-Teesdale Durham 57 D11
Middleton Moor Suff 31 B11
Middleton-on-Leven N Yorks 58 F5
Middleton-on-Sea W Sus 11 D8
Middleton on the Hill Hereford 26 B2
Middleton-on-the-Wolds E Yorks 52 E5
Middleton One Row Darl 58 E4
Middleton Priors Shrops 34 F2
Middleton Quernham N Yorks 51 B9
Middleton St George Darl 58 E4
Middleton Scriven Shrops 34 G2
Middleton Stoney Oxon 28 F2
Middleton Tyas N Yorks 58 F3
Middletown Cumb 56 F1
Middletown Powys 33 D9
Middlewich Ches E 43 F9
Middlewood Green Suff 31 B7
Middlezoy Som 8 A2
Middridge Durham 58 D3
Midfield Highld 93 C8
Midge Hall Lancs 49 G5
Midgeholme Cumb 62 H2
Midgham W Berks 18 E2
Midgley W Yorks 44 A6
Midgley W Yorks 50 G6
Midhopestones S Yorks 44 C6
Midhurst W Sus 11 B7
Midlem Borders 70 H4
Midmar Aberds 83 C8
Midsomer Norton Bath 16 F3
Midton Invclyd 73 F11
Midtown Highld 91 J13
Midtown Highld 93 C8
Midtown of Buchromb Moray 88 D3
Midville Lincs 47 G7
Midway Ches E 44 D3
Migdale Highld 87 B9
Migvie Aberds 82 C6
Milarrochy Stirling 68 A3
Milborne Port Som 8 C5
Milborne St Andrew Dorset 9 E7
Milborne Wick Som 8 B5
Milbourne Northumb 63 F7
Milburn Cumb 57 D8
Milbury Heath S Glos 16 B3
Milcombe Oxon 27 E11
Milden Suff 30 D6
Mildenhall Suff 30 A4
Mildenhall Wilts 17 E9
Mile Cross Norf 39 D8
Mile Elm Wilts 16 E6
Mile End Essex 30 F6
Mile End Glos 26 G2
Mile Oak Brighton 11 D11
Milebrook Powys 25 A10
Milebush Kent 20 G4
Mileham Norf 38 D5
Milesmark Fife 69 B9
Milfield Northumb 71 G8
Milford Derbys 45 H7
Milford Devon 6 D1
Milford Powys 33 F6
Milford Staffs 34 C5
Milford Sur 18 G6
Milford Wilts 9 B10
Milford Haven = Aberdaugleddau Pembs 22 F4
Milford on Sea Hants 10 E1
Milkwall Glos 26 H2
Milkwell Wilts 9 B8
Mill Bank W Yorks 50 G6
Mill Common Suff 39 G10
Mill End Bucks 18 C4
Mill End Herts 29 E10
Mill Green Essex 20 A3
Mill Green Norf 39 G7
Mill Green Suff 30 D6
Mill Hill London 19 B9
Mill Lane Hants 18 F4
Mill of Kingoodie Aberds 89 F8
Mill of Muiresk Aberds 89 D6
Mill of Sterin Aberds 82 D5
Mill of Uras Aberds 83 E10
Mill Place N Lincs 46 B3
Mill Side Cumb 49 A4
Mill Street Norf 39 D6
Milland W Sus 11 B7
Millarston Renfs 68 D3
Millbank Aberds 89 D11
Millbank Highld 94 D3
Millbeck Cumb 56 D4
Millbounds Orkney 95 E6
Millbreck Aberds 89 D10
Millbridge Sur 18 G5
Millbrook C Beds 29 E7
Millbrook Corn 4 F5
Millbrook Soton 10 C2
Millburn S Ayrs 67 D7
Millcombe Devon 5 G9
Millcorner E Sus 13 D7
Milldale Staffs 44 G5
Millden Lodge Angus 83 F7
Milldens Angus 77 B8
Millerhill Midloth 70 D2
Miller's Dale Derbys 44 E5
Miller's Green Derbys 44 G6
Millgreen Shrops 34 C2
Millhalf Hereford 25 D9
Millhayes Devon 7 F11
Millhead Lancs 49 B4
Millheugh S Lanark 68 E6
Millholme Cumb 57 G7
Millhouse Argyll 73 F8
Millhouse Cumb 56 C5
Millhouse Green S Yorks 44 B6
Millhousebridge Dumfries 61 E7
Millhouses S Yorks 45 D7
Millikenpark Renfs 68 D3
Millin Cross Pembs 22 E4
Millington E Yorks 52 D4
Millmeece Staffs 34 B4
Millom Cumb 49 A1
Millook Corn 4 B2
Millpool Corn 4 D2
Millport N Ayrs 66 A4
Millquarter Dumfries 55 A9
Millthorpe Lincs 37 B7
Millthrop Cumb 57 G8
Milltimber Aberdeen 83 C10
Milltown Corn 4 F2
Milltown Derbys 45 F7
Milltown Devon 6 C4
Milltown Dumfries 61 F9
Milltown of Aberdalgie Perth 76 E3
Milltown of Auchindoun Moray 88 D3
Milltown of Craigston Aberds 89 C7
Milltown of Edinvillie Moray 88 D2
Milltown of Kildrummy Aberds 82 B6
Milltown of Rothiemay Moray 88 D5
Milltown of Towie Aberds 82 B6
Milnathort Perth 76 G4
Milner's Heath Ches W 43 F7
Milngavie E Dunb 68 C4
Milnrow Gtr Man 44 A3
Milnshaw Lancs 50 G3
Milnthorpe Cumb 49 A4
Milo Carms 23 E10
Milson Shrops 26 A3
Milstead Kent 20 F6
Milston Wilts 17 G8
Milton Angus 76 C6
Milton Cambs 29 B11
Milton Cumb 61 G11
Milton Derbys 35 C9
Milton Dumfries 54 D5
Milton Dumfries 60 E4
Milton Dumfries 60 F4
Milton Highld 86 F6
Milton Highld 86 H7
Milton Highld 87 D10
Milton Highld 87 G8
Milton Highld 94 E5
Milton Moray 88 B5
Milton N Som 15 E9
Milton Notts 45 E11
Milton Oxon 17 B11
Milton Oxon 27 E11
Milton Pembs 22 F5
Milton Perth 76 F2
Milton Ptsmth 10 E5
Milton Stirling 75 G8
Milton Stoke 44 G3
Milton W Dunb 68 C3
Milton Abbas Dorset 9 D7
Milton Abbot Devon 4 D5
Milton Bridge Midloth 69 D11
Milton Bryan C Beds 28 E6
Milton Clevedon Som 16 H3
Milton Coldwells Aberds 89 E9
Milton Combe Devon 4 E5
Milton Damerel Devon 6 E2
Milton End Glos 17 A8
Milton Ernest Bedford 29 C7
Milton Green Ches W 43 G7
Milton Hill Oxon 17 B11
Milton Keynes M Keynes 28 E5
Milton Keynes Village M Keynes 28 E5
Milton Lilbourne Wilts 17 E8
Milton Malsor Northants 28 C4
Milton Morenish Perth 75 D9
Milton of Auchinhove Aberds 83 C7
Milton of Balgonie Fife 76 G6
Milton of Buchanan Stirling 68 A3
Milton of Campfield Aberds 83 C8
Milton of Campsie E Dunb 68 C5
Milton of Corsindae Aberds 83 C8
Milton of Cushnie Aberds 83 B7
Milton of Dalcapon Perth 76 B2
Milton of Edradour Perth 76 B2
Milton of Gollanfield Highld 87 F10
Milton of Lesmore Aberds 82 A6
Milton of Logie Aberds 82 C6
Milton of Murtle Aberdeen 83 C10
Milton of Noth Aberds 83 A7
Milton of Tullich Aberds 82 D5
Milton on Stour Dorset 9 B6
Milton Regis Kent 20 E6
Milton under Wychwood Oxon 27 G9
Miltonduff Moray 88 B1
Miltonhill Moray 87 E13
Miltonise Dumfries 54 B4
Milverton Som 7 D10
Milverton Warks 27 B10
Milwich Staffs 34 B5
Minard Argyll 73 D8
Minchinhampton Glos 16 A5
Mindrum Northumb 71 G7
Minehead Som 7 B8
Minera Wrex 42 G5
Minety Wilts 17 B7
Minffordd Gwyn 32 D3
Minffordd Gwyn 41 C7
Minffordd Gwyn 41 G7
Miningsby Lincs 47 F7
Minions Corn 4 D3
Minishant S Ayrs 66 E6
Minllyn Gwyn 32 D4
Minnes Aberds 89 F9
Minngearraidh W Isles 84 F2
Minnigaff Dumfries 55 C7
Minnonie Aberds 89 B7
Minskip N Yorks 51 C9
Minstead Hants 10 C1
Minsted W Sus 11 B7
Minster Kent 20 D6
Minster Kent 21 E10
Minster Lovell Oxon 27 G10
Minsterley Shrops 33 E9
Minsterworth Glos 26 G4
Minterne Magna Dorset 8 D5
Minting Lincs 46 E5
Mintlaw Aberds 89 D10
Minto Borders 61 A11
Minton Shrops 33 F10
Minwear Pembs 22 E5
Minworth W Mid 35 F7
Mirbister Orkney 95 F4
Mirehouse Cumb 56 E1
Mireland Highld 94 D5
Mirfield W Yorks 51 H8
Miserden Glos 26 H6
Miskin Rhondda 14 C6
Misson Notts 45 C10
Misterton Leics 36 G1
Misterton Notts 45 C11
Misterton Som 8 D3
Mistley Essex 31 E8
Mitcham London 19 E9
Mitchel Troy Mon 25 G11
Mitcheldean Glos 26 G3
Mitchell Corn 3 D7
Mitcheltroy Common Mon 25 H11
Mitford Northumb 63 E7
Mithian Corn 2 D6
Mitton Staffs 34 D4
Mixbury Oxon 28 E3
Moat Cumb 61 F10
Moats Tye Suff 31 C7
Mobberley Ches E 43 E10
Mobberley Staffs 34 A6
Moccas Hereford 25 D10
Mochdre Conwy 41 C10
Mochdre Powys 33 G6
Mochrum Dumfries 54 E6
Mockbeggar Hants 9 D10
Mockerkin Cumb 56 D2
Modbury Devon 5 F7
Moddershall Staffs 34 B5
Moelfre Anglesey 41 B7
Moelfre Powys 33 C7
Moffat Dumfries 60 C6
Moggerhanger C Beds 29 D8
Moira Leics 35 D9
Mol-chlach Highld 85 G9
Molash Kent 21 F7
Mold = Yr Wyddgrug Flint 42 F5
Moldgreen W Yorks 51 H7
Molehill Green Essex 30 F2
Molescroft E Yorks 52 E6
Molesden Northumb 63 E7
Molesworth Cambs 37 H6
Moll Highld 85 E10
Molland Devon 7 D7
Mollington Ches W 43 E6
Mollington Oxon 27 D11
Mollinsburn N Lanark 68 C6
Monachty Ceredig 24 B2
Monachylemore Stirling 75 F7
Monar Lodge Highld 86 G5
Monaughty Powys 25 B9
Monboddo House Aberds 83 F9
Mondynes Aberds 83 F9
Monevechadan Argyll 74 G4
Monewden Suff 31 C9
Moneydie Perth 76 E3
Moniaive Dumfries 60 D3
Monifieth Angus 77 D7
Monikie Angus 77 D7
Monimail Fife 76 F5
Monington Pembs 22 B6
Monk Bretton S Yorks 45 B7
Monk Fryston N Yorks 51 G11
Monk Sherborne Hants 18 F3
Monk Soham Suff 31 B9
Monk Street Essex 30 F3
Monken Hadley London 19 B9
Monkhopton Shrops 34 F2
Monkland Hereford 25 C11
Monkleigh Devon 6 D3
Monknash V Glam 14 D5
Monkokehampton Devon 6 F4
Monks Eleigh Suff 30 D6
Monk's Gate W Sus 11 B11
Monks Heath Ches E 44 E2
Monks Kirby Warks 35 G10
Monks Risborough Bucks 18 A5
Monkseaton T&W 63 F9
Monkshill Aberds 89 D7
Monksilver Som 7 C9
Monkspath W Mid 35 H7
Monkswood Mon 15 A9
Monkton Devon 7 F10
Monkton Kent 21 E9
Monkton Pembs 22 F4
Monkton S Ayrs 67 D6
Monkton Combe Bath 16 E4
Monkton Deverill Wilts 16 H5
Monkton Farleigh Wilts 16 E5
Monkton Heathfield Som 8 B1
Monkton Up Wimborne Dorset 9 C9
Monkwearmouth T&W 63 H9
Monkwood Hants 10 A5
Monmouth = Trefynwy Mon 26 G2

128 Mon–Nor

Monmouth Cap Mon 25 F10
Monnington on Wye Hereford 25 D10
Monreith Dumfries 54 E6
Monreith Mains Dumfries 54 E6
Mont Saint Guern 11
Montacute Som 8 C3
Montcoffer Ho. Aberds 89 B6
Montford Argyll 73 G10
Montford Shrops 33 D10
Montford Bridge Shrops 33 D10
Montgarrie Aberds 83 B7
Montgomery = Trefaldwyn Powys 33 F8
Montrave Fife 76 G6
Montrose Angus 77 B10
Montsale Essex 21 B7
Monxton Hants 17 G10
Monyash Derbys 44 F5
Monymusk Aberds 83 B8
Monzie Perth 75 E11
Monzie Castle Perth 75 E11
Moodiesburn N Lanark 68 C5
Moonzie Fife 76 F6
Moor Allerton W Yorks 51 F8
Moor Crichel Dorset 9 D8
Moor End E Yorks 52 F4
Moor End York 52 D2
Moor Monkton N Yorks 51 D11
Moor of Granary Moray 87 F13
Moor of Ravenstone Dumfries 54 E6
Moor Row Cumb 56 E2
Moor Street Kent 20 E5
Moorby Lincs 46 F6
Moordown Bmouth 9 E9
Moore Halton 43 D8
Moorend Glos 16 A4
Moorends S Yorks 52 H2
Moorgate S Yorks 45 C8
Moorgreen Notts 45 H8
Moorhall Derbys 45 E7
Moorhampton Hereford 25 D10
Moorhead W Yorks 51 F7
Moorhouse Cumb 61 H9
Moorhouse Notts 45 F11
Moorlinch Som 15 H9
Moorsholm Redcar 59 E7
Moorside Gtr Man 44 B3
Moorthorpe W Yorks 45 A8
Moortown Hants 9 D10
Moortown IoW 10 F3
Moortown Lincs 46 C4
Morangie Highld 87 C10
Morar Highld 79 B9
Morborne Cambs 37 F7
Morchard Bishop Devon 7 F6
Morcombelake Dorset 8 E3
Morcott Rutland 36 E5
Morda Shrops 33 C8
Morden Dorset 9 E8
Morden London 19 E9
Mordiford Hereford 26 E2
Mordon Durham 58 D4
More Shrops 33 F9
Morebath Devon 7 D8
Morebattle Borders 62 A3
Morecambe Lancs 49 C4
Morefield Highld 86 B4
Moreleigh Devon 5 F8
Morenish Perth 75 D8
Moresby Cumb 56 D1
Moresby Parks Cumb 56 E1
Morestead Hants 10 B4
Moreton Dorset 9 F7
Moreton Essex 30 H2
Moreton Mers 42 C5
Moreton Oxon 18 A3
Moreton Staffs 34 D3
Moreton Corbet Shrops 34 C1
Moreton-in-Marsh Glos 27 E9
Moreton Jeffries Hereford 26 D3
Moreton Morrell Warks 27 C10
Moreton on Lugg Hereford 26 D2
Moreton Pinkney Northants 28 D2
Moreton Say Shrops 34 B2
Moreton Valence Glos 26 H4
Moretonhampstead Devon 5 C8
Morfa Carms 23 E10
Morfa Carms 23 G10
Morfa Bach Carms 23 E8
Morfa Bychan Gwyn 41 G7
Morfa Dinlle Gwyn 40 E6
Morfa Glas Neath 24 H5
Morfa Nefyn Gwyn 40 F4
Morfydd Denb 42 H4
Morgan's Vale Wilts 9 B10
Moriah Ceredig 32 H2
Morland Cumb 57 D7
Morley Derbys 35 A9
Morley Durham 58 D2
Morley W Yorks 51 G8
Morley Green Ches E 44 D2
Morley St Botolph Norf 39 F6
Morningside Edin 69 C11
Morningside N Lanark 69 E7
Morningthorpe Norf 39 F8
Morpeth Northumb 63 E8
Morphie Aberds 77 A10
Morrey Staffs 35 D7
Morris Green Essex 30 E4
Morriston Swansea 14 B2
Morston Norf 38 A6
Mortehoe Devon 6 B3
Mortimer W Berks 18 E3
Mortimer West End Hants 18 E3
Mortimer's Cross Hereford 25 B11
Mortlake London 19 D9
Morton Cumb 56 A5
Morton Derbys 45 F8
Morton Lincs 37 C6
Morton Lincs 46 C2
Morton Lincs 46 F2
Morton Norf 39 D7
Morton Notts 45 G11
Morton S Glos 16 B3
Morton Shrops 33 C8
Morton Bagot Warks 27 B8
Morton-on-Swale N Yorks 58 G4
Morvah Corn 2 F3
Morval Corn 4 F3
Morvich Highld 80 A1
Morvich Highld 93 J10
Morville Shrops 34 F2
Morville Heath Shrops 34 F2
Morwenstow Corn 6 E1
Mosborough S Yorks 45 D8
Moscow E Ayrs 67 B7
Mosedale Cumb 56 C5
Moseley W Mid 34 F5
Moseley W Mid 35 G6
Moseley Worcs 26 C5
Moss Argyll 78 G2
Moss Highld 79 E9
Moss S Yorks 45 A9
Moss Wrex 42 G6
Moss Bank Mers 43 C8
Moss Edge Lancs 49 E4
Moss End Brack 18 D5
Moss of Barmuckity Moray 88 B2
Moss Pit Staffs 34 C5
Moss-side Highld 87 F11
Moss Side Lancs 49 F3
Mossat Aberds 82 B6
Mossbank Shetland 96 F6
Mossbay Cumb 56 D1
Mossblown S Ayrs 67 D7
Mossbrow Gtr Man 43 D10
Mossburnford Borders 62 B2
Mossdale Dumfries 55 B9
Mossend N Lanark 68 D6
Mosser Cumb 56 D3
Mossfield Highld 87 D9
Mossgiel E Ayrs 67 D7
Mosside Angus 77 B7
Mossley Ches E 44 F2
Mossley Gtr Man 44 B3
Mossley Hill Mers 43 D6
Mosstodloch Moray 88 C3
Mosston Angus 77 C8
Mossy Lea Lancs 43 A8
Mosterton Dorset 8 D3
Moston Gtr Man 44 B2
Moston Shrops 34 C1
Moston Green Ches E 43 F10
Mostyn Flint 42 D4
Mostyn Quay Flint 42 D4
Motcombe Dorset 9 B7
Mothecombe Devon 5 G7
Motherby Cumb 56 D6
Motherwell N Lanark 68 E6
Mottingham London 19 D11
Mottisfont Hants 10 B2
Mottistone IoW 10 F3
Mottram in Longdendale Gtr Man 44 C3
Mottram St Andrew Ches E 44 E2
Mouilpied Guern 11
Mouldsworth Ches W 43 E8
Moulin Perth 76 B2
Moulsecoomb Brighton 12 F2
Moulsford Oxon 18 C2
Moulsoe M Keynes 28 D6
Moulton Ches W 43 F9
Moulton Lincs 37 C9
Moulton N Yorks 58 F3
Moulton Northants 28 B4
Moulton Suff 30 B3
Moulton V Glam 14 D6
Moulton Chapel Lincs 37 D8
Moulton Eaugate Lincs 37 D9
Moulton St Mary Norf 39 E9
Moulton Seas End Lincs 37 C9
Mounie Castle Aberds 83 A9
Mount Corn 3 D6
Mount Corn 4 E2
Mount Highld 87 G12
Mount Bures Essex 30 E6
Mount Canisp Highld 87 D10
Mount Hawke Corn 2 E6
Mount Pleasant Ches E 44 G2
Mount Pleasant Derbys 35 D8
Mount Pleasant Derbys 45 H7
Mount Pleasant Flint 42 E5
Mount Pleasant Hants 10 E1
Mount Pleasant W Yorks 51 G8
Mount Sorrel Wilts 9 B9
Mount Tabor W Yorks 51 G6
Mountain W Yorks 51 F6
Mountain Ash = Aberpennar Rhondda 14 B6
Mountain Cross Borders 69 F10
Mountain Water Pembs 22 D4
Mountbenger Borders 70 H2
Mountfield E Sus 12 D6
Mountgerald Highld 87 E8
Mountjoy Corn 3 C7
Mountnessing Essex 20 B3
Mounton Mon 15 B11
Mountsorrel Leics 36 D1
Mousehole Corn 2 G3
Mousen Northumb 71 G10
Mouswald Dumfries 60 F6
Mow Cop Ches E 44 G2
Mowhaugh Borders 62 A4
Mowsley Leics 36 G2
Moxley W Mid 34 F5
Moy Highld 80 E6
Moy Highld 87 H10
Moy Hall Highld 87 H10
Moy Ho. Moray 87 E13
Moy Lodge Highld 80 E6
Moyles Court Hants 9 D10
Moylgrove Pembs 22 B6
Muasdale Argyll 65 D7
Much Birch Hereford 26 E2
Much Cowarne Hereford 26 D3
Much Dewchurch Hereford 25 E11
Much Hadham Herts 29 G11
Much Hoole Lancs 49 G4
Much Marcle Hereford 26 E3
Much Wenlock Shrops 34 E2
Muchalls Aberds 83 D11
Muchelney Som 8 B3
Muchlarnick Corn 4 F3
Muchrachd Highld 86 H5
Muckernich Highld 87 F8
Mucking Thurrock 20 C3
Muckleford Dorset 8 E5
Mucklestone Staffs 34 B3
Muckleton Shrops 34 C1
Muckletown Aberds 83 A7
Muckley Corner Staffs 35 E6
Muckton Lincs 47 D7
Mudale Highld 93 F8
Muddiford Devon 6 C4
Mudeford Dorset 9 E10
Mudford Som 8 C4
Mudgley Som 15 G10
Mugdock Stirling 68 C4
Mugeary Highld 85 E9
Mugginton Derbys 35 A8
Muggleswick Durham 58 B1
Muie Highld 93 J9
Muir Aberds 82 E2
Muir of Fairburn Highld 86 F7
Muir of Fowlis Aberds 83 B7
Muir of Ord Highld 87 F8
Muir of Pert Angus 77 D7
Muirden Aberds 89 C7
Muirdrum Angus 77 D8
Muirhead Angus 76 D6
Muirhead Fife 76 G5
Muirhead N Lanark 68 D5
Muirhead S Ayrs 66 C6
Muirhouselaw Borders 70 H5
Muirhouses Falk 69 B9
Muirkirk E Ayrs 68 H5
Muirmill Stirling 68 B6
Muirshearlich Highld 80 E3
Muirskie Aberds 83 D10
Muirtack Aberds 89 E9
Muirton Highld 87 E10
Muirton Perth 76 E4
Muirton Perth 76 F2
Muirton Mains Highld 86 F7
Muirton of Ardblair Perth 76 C4
Muirton of Ballochy Angus 77 A9
Muiryfold Aberds 89 C7
Muker N Yorks 57 G11
Mulbarton Norf 39 E7
Mulben Moray 88 C3
Mulindry Argyll 64 C4
Mullardoch House Highld 86 H5
Mullion Corn 2 H5
Mullion Cove Corn 2 H5
Mumby Lincs 47 E9
Munderfield Row Hereford 26 C3
Munderfield Stocks Hereford 26 C3
Mundesley Norf 39 B9
Mundford Norf 38 F4
Mundham Norf 39 F9
Mundon Essex 20 A5
Mundurno Aberdeen 83 B11
Munerigie Highld 80 C4
Muness Shetland 96 C8
Mungasdale Highld 86 B2
Mungrisdale Cumb 56 C5
Munlochy Highld 87 F9
Munsley Hereford 26 D3
Munslow Shrops 33 G11
Murchington Devon 5 C7
Murcott Oxon 28 G2
Murkle Highld 94 D3
Murlaggan Highld 80 D2
Murlaggan Highld 80 E5
Murra Orkney 95 H3
Murrayfield Edin 69 C11
Murrow Cambs 37 E9
Mursley Bucks 28 F5
Murthill Angus 77 B7
Murthly Perth 76 D3
Murton Cumb 57 D9
Murton Durham 58 B4
Murton Northumb 71 F8
Murton York 52 D2
Musbury Devon 8 E1
Muscoates N Yorks 52 A2
Musdale Argyll 74 E2
Musselburgh E Loth 70 C2
Muston Leics 36 B4
Muston N Yorks 53 B6
Mustow Green Worcs 26 A5
Mutehill Dumfries 55 E9
Mutford Suff 39 G10
Muthill Perth 75 F11
Mutterton Devon 7 F9
Muxton Telford 34 D3
Mybster Highld 94 E3
Myddfai Carms 24 F4
Myddle Shrops 33 C10
Mydroilyn Ceredig 23 A9
Myerscough Lancs 49 F4
Mylor Bridge Corn 3 F7
Mynachlog-ddu Pembs 22 C6
Myndtown Shrops 33 G9
Mynydd Bach Ceredig 32 H3
Mynydd-bach Mon 15 B10
Mynydd Bodafon Anglesey 40 B6
Mynydd-isa Flint 42 F5
Mynyddygarreg Carms 23 F9
Mynytho Gwyn 40 G5
Myrebird Aberds 83 D9
Myrelandhorn Highld 94 E4
Myreside Perth 76 E5
Myrtle Hill Carms 24 E4
Mytchett Sur 18 F5
Mytholm W Yorks 50 G5
Mytholmroyd W Yorks 50 G6
Myton-on-Swale N Yorks 51 C10
Mytton Shrops 33 D10

N

Na Gearrannan W Isles 90 C6
Naast Highld 91 J13
Naburn York 52 E1
Nackington Kent 21 F8
Nacton Suff 31 D9
Nafferton E Yorks 53 D6
Nailbridge Glos 26 G3
Nailsbourne Som 7 D11
Nailsea N Som 15 D10
Nailstone Leics 35 E10
Nailsworth Glos 16 B5
Nairn Highld 87 F11
Nalderswood Sur 19 G9
Nancegollan Corn 2 F5
Nancledra Corn 2 F3
Nanhoron Gwyn 40 G4
Nannau Gwyn 32 C3
Nannerch Flint 42 F4
Nanpantan Leics 35 D11
Nanpean Corn 3 D8
Nanstallon Corn 3 C9
Nant-ddu Powys 25 G7
Nant-glas Powys 24 B6
Nant Peris Gwyn 41 E8
Nant Uchaf Denb 42 G3
Nant-y-Bai Carms 24 D4
Nant-y-cafn Neath 24 H5
Nant-y-derry Mon 25 H10
Nant-y-ffin Carms 23 C10
Nant-y-moel Bridgend 14 B5
Nant-y-pandy Conwy 41 C8
Nanternis Ceredig 23 A8
Nantgaredig Carms 23 D9
Nantgarw Rhondda 15 C7
Nantglyn Denb 42 F3
Nantgwyn Powys 32 H5
Nantlle Gwyn 41 E7
Nantmawr Shrops 33 C8
Nantmel Powys 25 B7
Nantmor Gwyn 41 F8
Nantwich Ches E 43 G9
Nantycaws Carms 23 E9
Nantyffyllon Bridgend 14 B4
Nantyglo Bl Gwent 25 G8
Naphill Bucks 18 B5
Nappa N Yorks 50 D4
Napton on the Hill Warks 27 B11
Narberth = Arberth Pembs 22 E6
Narborough Leics 35 F11
Narborough Norf 38 D3
Nasareth Gwyn 40 E6
Naseby Northants 36 H2
Nash Bucks 28 E4
Nash Hereford 25 B10
Nash Newport 15 C9
Nash Shrops 26 A3
Nash Lee Bucks 28 H5
Nassington Northants 37 F6
Nasty Herts 29 F10
Nateby Cumb 57 F9
Nateby Lancs 49 E4
Natland Cumb 57 H7
Naughton Suff 31 D7
Naunton Glos 27 F8
Naunton Worcs 26 E5
Naunton Beauchamp Worcs 26 C6
Navenby Lincs 46 G3
Navestock Heath Essex 20 B2
Navestock Side Essex 20 B2
Navidale Highld 93 H13
Nawton N Yorks 52 A2
Nayland Suff 30 E6
Nazeing Essex 29 H11
Neacroft Hants 9 E10
Neal's Green Warks 35 G9
Neap Shetland 96 H7
Near Sawrey Cumb 56 G5
Neasham Darl 58 E4
Neath = Castell-Nedd Neath 14 B3
Neath Abbey Neath 14 B3
Neatishead Norf 39 C9
Nebo Anglesey 40 A6
Nebo Ceredig 24 B2
Nebo Conwy 41 E10
Nebo Gwyn 40 E6
Necton Norf 38 E4
Nedd Highld 92 F4
Nedderton Northumb 63 E8
Nedging Tye Suff 31 D7
Needham Norf 39 G8
Needham Market Suff 31 C7
Needingworth Cambs 29 A10
Needwood Staffs 35 C7
Neen Savage Shrops 34 H2
Neen Sollars Shrops 26 A3
Neenton Shrops 34 G2
Nefyn Gwyn 40 F5
Neilston E Renf 68 E3
Neinthirion Powys 32 E5
Neithrop Oxon 27 D11
Nelly Andrews Green Powys 33 E8
Nelson Caerph 15 B7
Nelson Lancs 50 F4
Nelson Village Northumb 63 F8
Nemphlar S Lanark 69 F7
Nempnett Thrubwell N Som 15 E11
Nene Terrace Lincs 37 E8
Nenthall Cumb 57 B9
Nenthead Cumb 57 B9
Nenthorn Borders 70 G5
Nerabus Argyll 64 C3
Nercwys Flint 42 F5
Nerston S Lanark 68 E5
Nesbit Northumb 71 G8
Ness Ches W 42 E6
Nesscliffe Shrops 33 D9
Neston Ches W 42 E5
Neston Wilts 16 E5
Nether Alderley Ches E 44 E2
Nether Blainslie Borders 70 F4
Nether Booth Derbys 44 D5
Nether Broughton Leics 36 C2
Nether Burrow Lancs 50 B2
Nether Cerne Dorset 8 E5
Nether Compton Dorset 8 C4
Nether Crimond Aberds 89 F8
Nether Dalgliesh Borders 61 C8
Nether Dallachy Moray 88 B3
Nether Exe Devon 7 F8
Nether Glasslaw Aberds 89 C8
Nether Handwick Angus 76 C6
Nether Haugh S Yorks 45 C8
Nether Heage Derbys 45 G7
Nether Heyford Northants 28 C3
Nether Hindhope Borders 62 B3
Nether Howecleuch S Lanark 60 B6
Nether Kellet Lancs 49 C5
Nether Kinmundy Aberds 89 D10
Nether Langwith Notts 45 E9
Nether Leask Aberds 89 E10
Nether Lenshie Aberds 89 D6
Nether Monynut Borders 70 D6
Nether Padley Derbys 44 E6
Nether Park Aberds 89 C10
Nether Poppleton York 52 D1
Nether Silton N Yorks 58 G5
Nether Stowey Som 7 C10
Nether Urquhart Fife 76 G4
Nether Wallop Hants 17 H10
Nether Wasdale Cumb 56 F3
Nether Whitacre Warks 35 F8
Nether Worton Oxon 27 E11
Netheravon Wilts 17 G8
Netherbrae Aberds 89 C7
Netherbrough Orkney 95 G4
Netherburn S Lanark 69 F7
Netherbury Dorset 8 E3
Netherby Cumb 61 F9
Netherby N Yorks 51 E9
Nethercote Warks 28 B2
Nethercott Devon 6 C3
Netherend Glos 16 A2
Netherfield E Sus 12 E6
Netherhampton Wilts 9 B10
Netherlaw Dumfries 55 E10
Netherley Aberds 83 D10
Netherley Mers 43 D7
Nethermill Dumfries 60 E6
Nethermuir Aberds 89 D9
Netherplace E Renf 68 E4
Netherseal Derbys 35 D8
Netherthird E Ayrs 67 E8
Netherthong W Yorks 44 B5
Netherthorpe S Yorks 45 D9
Netherton Angus 77 B8
Netherton Devon 5 D9
Netherton Hants 17 F10
Netherton Mers 42 B6
Netherton Northumb 62 C5
Netherton Oxon 17 B11
Netherton Perth 76 B4
Netherton Stirling 68 C4
Netherton W Mid 34 G5
Netherton W Yorks 44 A5
Netherton W Yorks 51 H8
Netherton Worcs 26 D6
Nethertown Cumb 56 F1
Nethertown Highld 94 C5
Netherwitton Northumb 63 D7
Netherwood E Ayrs 68 H5
Nethy Bridge Highld 82 A2
Netley Hants 10 D3
Netley Marsh Hants 10 C2
Netteswell Essex 29 G11
Nettlebed Oxon 18 C4
Nettlebridge Som 16 G3
Nettlecombe Dorset 8 E4
Nettleden Herts 29 G7
Nettleham Lincs 46 E4
Nettlestead Kent 20 F3
Nettlestead Green Kent 20 F3
Nettlestone IoW 10 E5
Nettlesworth Durham 58 B3
Nettleton Lincs 46 B5
Nettleton Wilts 16 D5
Neuadd Carms 24 F3
Nevendon Essex 20 B4
Nevern Pembs 22 B5
New Abbey Dumfries 60 G5
New Aberdour Aberds 89 B8
New Addington London 19 E10
New Alresford Hants 10 A4
New Alyth Perth 76 C5
New Arley Warks 35 G8
New Ash Green Kent 20 E3
New Barn Kent 20 E3
New Barnetby N Lincs 46 A4
New Barton Northants 28 B5
New Bewick Northumb 62 A6
New-bigging Angus 76 C5
New Bilton Warks 35 H10
New Bolingbroke Lincs 47 G7
New Boultham Lincs 46 E3
New Bradwell M Keynes 28 D5
New Brancepeth Durham 58 B3
New Bridge Wrex 33 A8
New Brighton Flint 42 F5
New Brighton Mers 42 C6
New Brinsley Notts 45 G8
New Broughton Wrex 42 G6
New Buckenham Norf 39 F6
New Byth Aberds 89 C8
New Catton Norf 39 D8
New Cheriton Hants 10 B4
New Costessey Norf 39 D7
New Cowper Cumb 56 B3
New Cross Ceredig 32 H2
New Cross London 19 D10
New Cumnock E Ayrs 67 E9
New Deer Aberds 89 D8
New Delaval Northumb 63 F8
New Duston Northants 28 B4
New Earswick York 52 D2
New Edlington S Yorks 45 C9
New Elgin Moray 88 B2
New Ellerby E Yorks 53 F7
New Eltham London 19 D11
New End Worcs 27 C7
New Farnley W Yorks 51 F8
New Ferry Mers 42 D6
New Fryston W Yorks 51 G10
New Galloway Dumfries 55 B9
New Gilston Fife 77 G7
New Grimsby Scilly 2 C2
New Hainford Norf 39 D8
New Hartley Northumb 63 F9
New Haw Sur 19 E7
New Hedges Pembs 22 F6
New Herrington T&W 58 A4
New Hinksey Oxon 18 A2
New Holkham Norf 38 B4
New Holland N Lincs 53 G6
New Houghton Derbys 45 F8
New Houghton Norf 38 C3
New Houses N Yorks 50 B4
New Humberstone Leicester 36 E2
New Hutton Cumb 57 G7
New Hythe Kent 20 F4
New Inn Carms 23 C9
New Inn Mon 15 A10
New Inn Pembs 22 C5
New Inn Torf 15 B9
New Invention Shrops 33 H8
New Invention W Mid 34 E5
New Kelso Highld 86 G2
New Kingston Notts 35 C11
New Lanark S Lanark 69 F7
New Lane Lancs 43 A7
New Lane End Warr 43 C9
New Leake Lincs 47 G8
New Leeds Aberds 89 C9
New Longton Lancs 49 G5
New Luce Dumfries 54 C4
New Malden London 19 E9
New Marske Redcar 59 D7
New Marton Shrops 33 B9
New Micklefield W Yorks 51 F10
New Mill Aberds 83 E9
New Mill Herts 28 G6
New Mill W Yorks 44 B5
New Mill Wilts 17 E8
New Mills Ches E 43 D10
New Mills Corn 3 D7
New Mills Derbys 44 D3
New Mills Powys 33 E6
New Milton Hants 9 E11
New Moat Pembs 22 D5
New Ollerton Notts 45 F10
New Oscott W Mid 35 F6
New Park N Yorks 51 D8
New Pitsligo Aberds 89 C8
New Polzeath Corn 3 B8
New Quay = Ceinewydd Ceredig 23 A8
New Rackheath Norf 39 D8
New Radnor Powys 25 B9
New Rent Cumb 56 C6
New Ridley Northumb 62 H6
New Road Side N Yorks 50 E5
New Romney Kent 13 D9
New Rossington S Yorks 45 C10
New Row Ceredig 24 A4
New Row Lancs 50 F2
New Row N Yorks 59 E7
New Sarum Wilts 9 A10
New Silksworth T&W 58 A4
New Stevenston N Lanark 68 E6
New Street Staffs 44 G4
New Street Lane Shrops 34 B2
New Swanage Dorset 9 F9
New Totley S Yorks 45 E7
New Town E Loth 70 C3
New Tredegar = Tredegar Newydd Caerph 15 A7
New Trows S Lanark 69 G7
New Ulva Argyll 72 E6
New Walsoken Cambs 37 E10
New Waltham NE Lincs 46 B6
New Whittington Derbys 45 E7
New Wimpole Cambs 29 D10
New Winton E Loth 70 C3
New Yatt Oxon 27 G10
New York Lincs 46 G6
New York N Yorks 51 C7
Newall W Yorks 51 E7
Newark Orkney 95 D8
Newark Pboro 37 E8
Newark-on-Trent Notts 45 G11
Newarthill N Lanark 68 E6
Newbarns Cumb 49 B2
Newbattle Midloth 70 D2
Newbiggin Cumb 49 C2
Newbiggin Cumb 56 D6
Newbiggin Cumb 56 G2
Newbiggin Cumb 57 B7
Newbiggin Cumb 57 D8
Newbiggin Durham 57 D11
Newbiggin N Yorks 57 G11
Newbiggin N Yorks 57 H11
Newbiggin-by-the-Sea Northumb 63 E9
Newbiggin-on-Lune Cumb 57 F9
Newbigging Angus 77 D7
Newbigging Angus 77 D7
Newbigging S Lanark 69 F9
Newbold Derbys 45 E7
Newbold Leics 35 D10
Newbold on Avon Warks 35 H10
Newbold on Stour Warks 27 D9
Newbold Pacey Warks 27 C9
Newbold Verdon Leics 35 E10
Newborough Anglesey 40 D6
Newborough Pboro 37 E8
Newborough Staffs 35 C7
Newbottle Northants 28 E2
Newbottle T&W 58 A4
Newbourne Suff 31 D9
Newbridge Caerph 15 B8
Newbridge Ceredig 23 A10
Newbridge Corn 2 F3
Newbridge Corn 4 E4
Newbridge Dumfries 60 F5
Newbridge Edin 69 C10
Newbridge Hants 10 C1
Newbridge IoW 10 F3
Newbridge Pembs 22 C4
Newbridge Green Worcs 26 E5
Newbridge-on-Usk Mon 15 B9
Newbridge on Wye Powys 25 C7
Newbrough Northumb 62 G4
Newbuildings Devon 7 F6
Newburgh Aberds 89 C9
Newburgh Aberds 89 F9
Newburgh Borders 61 B9
Newburgh Fife 76 F5
Newburgh Lancs 43 A7
Newburn T&W 63 G7
Newbury W Berks 17 E11
Newbury Park London 19 C11
Newby Cumb 57 D7
Newby Lancs 50 E4
Newby N Yorks 50 B3
Newby N Yorks 58 E6
Newby N Yorks 59 E11
Newby Bridge Cumb 56 H5
Newby East Cumb 61 H10
Newby West Cumb 56 A5
Newby Wiske N Yorks 58 H4
Newcastle Mon 25 G11
Newcastle Shrops 33 G8
Newcastle Emlyn = Castell Newydd Emlyn Carms 23 B8
Newcastle-under-Lyme Staffs 44 H2
Newcastle Upon Tyne T&W 63 G8
Newcastleton or Copshaw Holm Borders 61 E10
Newchapel Pembs 23 C7
Newchapel Powys 32 G5
Newchapel Staffs 44 G2
Newchapel Sur 12 B2
Newchurch Carms 23 D8
Newchurch IoW 10 F4
Newchurch Kent 13 C9
Newchurch Lancs 50 F4
Newchurch Mon 15 B10
Newchurch Powys 25 C9
Newchurch Staffs 35 C7
Newcott Devon 7 F11
Newcraighall Edin 70 C2
Newdigate Sur 19 G8
Newell Green Brack 18 D5
Newenden Kent 13 D7
Newent Glos 26 F4
Newerne Glos 16 A3
Newfield Durham 58 C3
Newfield Highld 87 D10
Newford Scilly 2 C3
Newfound Hants 18 F2
Newgale Pembs 22 D3
Newgate Norf 39 A6
Newgate Street Herts 19 A10
Newhall Ches E 43 H9
Newhall Derbys 35 C8
Newhall House Highld 87 E9
Newhall Point Highld 87 E10
Newham Northumb 71 H10
Newham Hall Northumb 71 H10
Newhaven Derbys 44 G5
Newhaven E Sus 12 F3
Newhaven Edin 69 C11
Newhey Gtr Man 44 A3
Newholm N Yorks 59 E9
Newhouse N Lanark 68 D6
Newick E Sus 12 D3
Newingreen Kent 13 C10
Newington Kent 20 E5
Newington Kent 21 E10
Newington Kent 21 H8
Newington Notts 45 C10
Newington Oxon 18 B3
Newington Shrops 33 G10
Newland Glos 26 H2
Newland Hull 53 F6
Newland N Yorks 52 G2
Newland Worcs 26 D4
Newlandrig Midloth 70 D2
Newlands Borders 61 D11
Newlands Highld 87 G10
Newlands Moray 88 C3
Newlands Northumb 62 H6
Newland's Corner Sur 19 G7
Newlands of Geise Highld 94 D2
Newlands of Tynet Moray 88 B3
Newlands Park Anglesey 40 B4
Newlandsmuir S Lanark 68 E5
Newlot Orkney 95 G6
Newlyn Corn 2 G3
Newmachar Aberds 83 B10
Newmains N Lanark 69 E7
Newmarket Suff 30 B3
Newmarket W Isles 91 D9
Newmill Borders 61 B10
Newmill Corn 2 F3
Newmill Moray 88 C4
Newmill of Inshewan Angus 77 A7
Newmills of Boyne Aberds 88 C5
Newmiln Perth 76 D4
Newmilns E Ayrs 67 C8
Newnham Cambs 29 C11
Newnham Glos 26 G3
Newnham Hants 18 F4
Newnham Herts 29 E9
Newnham Kent 20 F6
Newnham Northants 28 C2
Newnham Bridge Worcs 26 B3
Newpark Fife 77 F7
Newport Devon 6 C4
Newport E Yorks 52 F4
Newport Essex 30 E2
Newport Highld 94 H3
Newport IoW 10 F4
Newport = Casnewydd Newport 15 C9
Newport Norf 39 D11
Newport = Trefdraeth Pembs 22 C5
Newport Telford 34 D3
Newport-on-Tay Fife 77 E7
Newport Pagnell M Keynes 28 D5
Newpound Common W Sus 11 B9
Newquay Corn 3 C7
Newsbank Ches E 44 F2
Newseat Aberds 89 D10
Newseat Aberds 89 E7
Newsham N Yorks 51 A9
Newsham N Yorks 58 E2
Newsham Northumb 63 F9
Newsholme E Yorks 52 G3
Newsholme Lancs 50 D4
Newsome W Yorks 44 A5
Newstead Borders 70 G4
Newstead Northumb 71 H10
Newstead Notts 45 G9
Newthorpe N Yorks 51 F10
Newton Argyll 73 D9
Newton Borders 62 A2
Newton Bridgend 14 D4
Newton Cambs 29 D11
Newton Cambs 37 D10
Newton Cardiff 15 D8
Newton Ches W 43 E8
Newton Ches W 43 F7
Newton Ches W 43 G8
Newton Cumb 49 B2
Newton Derbys 45 G8
Newton Dorset 9 C6
Newton Dumfries 61 D7
Newton Dumfries 61 F8
Newton Gtr Man 44 C3
Newton Hereford 25 E10
Newton Hereford 26 C2
Newton Highld 87 E10
Newton Highld 87 G10
Newton Highld 94 F5
Newton Lancs 49 F4
Newton Lancs 50 B1
Newton Lancs 50 D2
Newton Lincs 36 B6
Newton Moray 88 B1
Newton Norf 38 D4
Newton Northants 36 G4
Newton Northumb 62 G6
Newton Notts 36 A2
Newton Perth 75 D11
Newton S Lanark 68 D5
Newton S Lanark 69 G8
Newton S Yorks 45 B9
Newton Staffs 34 C6
Newton Suff 30 D6
Newton Swansea 14 C2
Newton W Loth 69 C9
Newton Warks 35 H11
Newton Wilts 9 B11
Newton Abbot Devon 5 D9
Newton Arlosh Cumb 61 H7
Newton Aycliffe Durham 58 D3
Newton Bewley Hrtlpl 58 D5
Newton Blossomville M Keynes 28 C6
Newton Bromswold Northants 28 B6
Newton Burgoland Leics 35 E9
Newton by Toft Lincs 46 D4
Newton Ferrers Devon 4 G6
Newton Flotman Norf 39 F8
Newton Hall Northumb 62 G6
Newton Harcourt Leics 36 F2
Newton Heath Gtr Man 44 B2
Newton Ho. Aberds 83 A8
Newton Kyme N Yorks 51 E10
Newton-le-Willows Mers 43 C8
Newton-le-Willows N Yorks 58 H3
Newton Longville Bucks 28 E5
Newton Mearns E Renf 68 E4
Newton Morrell N Yorks 58 F3
Newton Mulgrave N Yorks 59 E8
Newton of Ardtoe Highld 79 D9
Newton of Balcanquhal Perth 76 F4
Newton of Falkland Fife 76 G5
Newton on Ayr S Ayrs 66 D6
Newton on Ouse N Yorks 51 D11
Newton-on-Rawcliffe N Yorks 59 G9
Newton-on-the-Moor Northumb 63 C7
Newton on Trent Lincs 46 E2
Newton Park Argyll 73 G10
Newton Poppleford Devon 7 H9
Newton Purcell Oxon 28 E3
Newton Regis Warks 35 E8
Newton Reigny Cumb 57 C6
Newton St Cyres Devon 7 G7
Newton St Faith Norf 39 D8
Newton St Loe Bath 16 E4
Newton St Petrock Devon 6 E3
Newton Solney Derbys 35 C8
Newton Stacey Hants 17 G11
Newton Stewart Dumfries 55 C7
Newton Tony Wilts 17 G9
Newton Tracey Devon 6 D4
Newton under Roseberry Redcar 59 E6
Newton upon Derwent E Yorks 52 E3
Newton Valence Hants 10 A6
Newtonairds Dumfries 60 E4
Newtongrange Midloth 70 D2
Newtonhill Aberds 83 D11
Newtonhill Highld 87 G8
Newtonmill Angus 77 A9
Newtonmore Highld 81 D9
Newtown Argyll 73 C9
Newtown Ches W 43 E8
Newtown Corn 2 G6
Newtown Cumb 61 G11
Newtown Cumb 61 H9
Newtown Derbys 44 D3
Newtown Devon 7 D6
Newtown Glos 16 A3
Newtown Glos 26 E6
Newtown Hants 10 B2
Newtown Hants 10 C4
Newtown Hants 10 C5
Newtown Hants 10 D3
Newtown Hants 10 D5
Newtown Hants 17 E11
Newtown Hereford 26 D3
Newtown Highld 80 C5
Newtown IoM 48 E3
Newtown IoW 10 E3
Newtown Northumb 62 C6
Newtown Northumb 71 G8
Newtown Northumb 71 H9
Newtown Poole 9 E9
Newtown = Y Drenewydd Powys 33 F7
Newtown Shrops 33 B10
Newtown Staffs 44 F4
Newtown Staffs 44 F3
Newtown Wilts 9 B8
Newtown Linford Leics 35 E11
Newtown St Boswells Borders 70 G4
Newtown Unthank Leics 35 E10
Newtyle Angus 76 C5
Neyland Pembs 22 F4
Niarbyl IoM 48 E2
Nibley S Glos 16 C3
Nibley Green Glos 16 B4
Nibon Shetland 96 F5
Nicholashayne Devon 7 E10
Nicholaston Swansea 23 H1
Nidd N Yorks 51 C
Nigg Aberdeen 83 C1
Nigg Highld 87 D1
Nigg Ferry Highld 87 E1
Nightcott Som 7 D
Nilig Denb 42 G
Nine Ashes Essex 20 A
Nine Mile Burn Midloth 69 E1
Nine Wells Pembs 22 D
Ninebanks Northumb 57 A
Ninfield E Sus 12 E
Ningwood IoW 10 F
Nisbet Borders 70 H
Nisthouse Orkney 95 G
Nisthouse Shetland 96 G
Niton IoW 10 G
Nitshill Glasgow 68 D
No Man's Heath Ches W 43 H
No Man's Heath Warks 35 E
Noak Hill London 20 B
Noblethorpe S Yorks 44 B
Nobottle Northants 28 B
Nocton Lincs 46 F
Noke Oxon 28 G
Nolton Pembs 22 E
Nolton Haven Pembs 22 E
Nomansland Devon 7 E
Nomansland Wilts 10 C
Noneley Shrops 33 C1
Nonikiln Highld 87 D
Nonington Kent 21 F
Noonsbrough Shetland 96 H
Norbreck Blackpool 49 E
Norbridge Hereford 26 D
Norbury Ches E 43 H
Norbury Derbys 35 A
Norbury Shrops 33 F
Norbury Staffs 34 C
Nordelph Norf 38 E
Norden Gtr Man 44 A
Norden Heath Dorset 9 F
Nordley Shrops 34 F
Norham Northumb 71 F
Norley Ches W 43 E
Norleywood Hants 10 E
Norman Cross Cambs 37 F
Normanby N Lincs 52 H4
Normanby N Yorks 52 A3
Normanby Redcar 59 E6
Normanby-by-Spital Lincs 46 D4
Normanby by Stow Lincs 46 D2
Normanby le Wold Lincs 46 C5
Normandy Sur 18 F6
Norman's Bay E Sus 12 F5
Norman's Green Devon 7 F9
Normanstone Suff 39 F11
Normanton Derby 35 B9
Normanton Leics 36 A4
Normanton Lincs 46 H3
Normanton Notts 45 G11
Normanton Rutland 36 E5
Normanton W Yorks 51 G9
Normanton le Heath Leics 35 D9
Normanton on Soar Notts 35 C11
Normanton-on-the-Wolds Notts 36 B2
Normanton on Trent Notts 45 F11
Normoss Lancs 49 F3
Norney Sur 18 G6
Norrington Common Wilts 16 E5
Norris Green Mers 43 C6
Norris Hill Leics 35 D9
North Anston S Yorks 45 D9
North Aston Oxon 27 F11
North Baddesley Hants 10 C2
North Ballachulish Highld 74 A3
North Barrow Som 8 B5
North Barsham Norf 38 B5
North Benfleet Essex 20 C4
North Bersted W Sus 11 D8
North Berwick E Loth 70 B4
North Boarhunt Hants 10 C5
North Bovey Devon 5 C8
North Bradley Wilts 16 F5
North Brentor Devon 4 C5
North Brewham Som 16 H4
North Buckland Devon 6 B3
North Burlingham Norf 39 D9
North Cadbury Som 8 B5
North Cairn Dumfries 54 B2
North Carlton Lincs 46 E3
North Carrine Argyll 65 H7
North Cave E Yorks 52 F4
North Cerney Glos 27 H7
North Charford Wilts 9 C10
North Charlton Northumb 63 A7
North Cheriton Som 8 B5
North Cliff E Yorks 53 E8
North Cliffe E Yorks 52 F4
North Clifton Notts 46 E2
North Cockerington Lincs 47 C7
North Coker Som 8 C4
North Collafirth Shetland 96 E5
North Common E Sus 12 D2
North Connel Argyll 74 D2
North Cornelly Bridgend 14 C4
North Cotes Lincs 47 B7
North Cove Suff 39 G10
North Cowton N Yorks 58 F3
North Crawley M Keynes 28 D6
North Cray London 19 D11
North Creake Norf 38 B4
North Curry Som 8 B2
North Dalton E Yorks 52 D5
North Dawn Orkney 95 H5
North Deighton N Yorks 51 D9
North Duffield N Yorks 52 F2
North Elkington Lincs 46 C6
North Elmham Norf 38 C5

Nor–Pen 129

North Elmshall W Yorks 45 A8
North End Bucks 28 F5
North End E Yorks 53 F8
North End Essex 30 G3
North End Hants 17 E11
North End Lincs 37 A8
North End N Som 15 E10
North End Ptsmth 10 D5
North End Som 8 B1
North End W Sus 11 D10
North Erradale Highld 91 J12
North Fambridge Essex 20 B5
North Fearns Highld 85 E10
North Featherstone W Yorks 51 G10
North Ferriby E Yorks 52 G5
North Frodingham E Yorks 53 D7
North Gluss Shetland 96 F5
North Gorley Hants 9 C10
North Green Norf 39 G8
North Green Suff 31 B10
North Greetwell Lincs 46 E4
North Grimston N Yorks 52 C4
North Halley Orkney 95 H6
North Halling Medway 20 E4
North Hayling Hants 10 D6
North Hazelrigg Northumb 71 G9
North Heasley Devon 7 C6
North Heath W Sus 11 B9
North Hill Cambs 37 H10
North Hill Corn 4 D3
North Hinksey Oxon 27 H11
North Holmwood Sur 19 G8
North Howden E Yorks 52 F3
North Huish Devon 5 F8
North Hykeham Lincs 46 F3
North Johnston Pembs 22 E4
North Kelsey Lincs 46 B4
North Kelsey Moor Lincs 46 B4
North Kessock Highld 87 G9
North Killingholme N Lincs 53 H7
North Kilvington N Yorks 58 H5
North Kilworth Leics 36 G2
North Kirkton Aberds 89 C11
North Kiscadale N Ayrs 66 D3
North Kyme Lincs 46 G5
North Lancing W Sus 11 D10
North Lee Bucks 28 H5
North Leigh Oxon 27 G10
North Leverton with Habblesthorpe Notts 45 D11
North Littleton Worcs 27 D7
North Lopham Norf 38 G6
North Luffenham Rutland 36 E5
North Marden W Sus 11 C7
North Marston Bucks 28 F4
North Middleton Midloth 70 E2
North Middleton Northumb 62 A6
North Molton Devon 7 D6
North Moreton Oxon 18 C2
North Mundham W Sus 11 D7
North Muskham Notts 45 G11
North Newbald E Yorks 52 F5
North Newington Oxon 27 E11
North Newnton Wilts 17 F8
North Newton Som 8 A1
North Nibley Glos 16 B4
North Oakley Hants 18 F2
North Ockendon London 20 C2
North Ormesby Mbro 58 D6
North Ormsby Lincs 46 C6
North Otterington N Yorks 58 H4
North Owersby Lincs 46 C4
North Perrott Som 8 D3
North Petherton Som 8 A1
North Petherwin Corn 4 C3
North Pickenham Norf 38 E4
North Piddle Worcs 26 C6
North Poorton Dorset 8 E4
North Port Argyll 74 E3
North Queensferry Fife 69 B10
North Radworthy Devon 7 C6
North Rauceby Lincs 46 H4
North Reston Lincs 47 D7
North Rigton N Yorks 51 E8
North Rode Ches E 44 F2
North Roe Shetland 96 E5
North Runcton Norf 38 D2
North Sandwick Shetland 96 D7
North Scale Cumb 49 C1
North Scarle Lincs 46 F2
North Seaton Northumb 63 E8
North Shian Argyll 74 C2
North Shields T&W 63 G9
North Shoebury Southend 20 C6
North Shore Blackpool 49 F3
North Side Cumb 56 D2
North Side Pboro 37 F8
North Skelton Redcar 59 E7
North Somercotes Lincs 47 C8
North Stainley N Yorks 51 B8
North Stainmore Cumb 57 E10
North Stifford Thurrock 20 C3
North Stoke Bath 16 E4
North Stoke Oxon 18 C3
North Stoke W Sus 11 C9
North Street Hants 10 A5
North Street Kent 21 F7
North Street Medway 20 D5
North Street W Berks 18 D3
North Sunderland Northumb 71 G11
North Tamerton Corn 6 G2
North Tawton Devon 6 F5
North Thoresby Lincs 46 C6
North Tidworth Wilts 17 G9
North Togston Northumb 63 C8
North Tuddenham Norf 38 D6
North Walbottle T&W 63 G7
North Walsham Norf 39 B8
North Waltham Hants 18 G2
North Warnborough Hants 18 F4
North Water Bridge Angus 83 G8
North Watten Highld 94 E4
North Weald Bassett Essex 19 A11
North Wheatley Notts 45 D11
North Whilborough Devon 5 E9
North Wick Bath 16 E2
North Willingham Lincs 46 D5
North Wingfield Derbys 45 F8
North Witham Lincs 36 C5
North Woolwich London 19 D11
North Wootton Dorset 8 C5
North Wootton Norf 38 C2
North Wootton Som 16 G2
North Wraxall Wilts 16 D5
North Wroughton Swindon 17 C8
Northacre Norf 38 F5
Northallerton N Yorks 58 G4
Northam Devon 6 D3
Northam Soton 10 C3
Northampton Northants 28 B4
Northaw Herts 19 A9
Northbeck Lincs 37 A6
Northborough Pboro 37 E7
Northbourne Kent 21 F10
Northbridge Street E Sus 12 D6
Northchapel W Sus 11 B8
Northchurch Herts 28 H6
Northcott Devon 6 G2
Northdown Kent 21 D10
Northdyke Orkney 95 F3
Northend Bath 16 E4
Northend Bucks 18 B4
Northend Warks 27 C10
Northenden Gtr Man 44 C2
Northfield Aberdeen 83 C11
Northfield Borders 71 D8
Northfield E Yorks 52 G6
Northfield W Mid 34 H6
Northfields Lincs 36 E6
Northfleet Kent 20 D3
Northgate Lincs 37 C7
Northhouse Borders 61 C10
Northiam E Sus 13 D7
Northill C Beds 29 D8
Northington Hants 18 H2
Northlands Lincs 47 G7
Northlea Durham 58 A5
Northleach Glos 27 G8
Northleigh Devon 7 G10
Northlew Devon 6 G4
Northmoor Oxon 17 A11
Northmoor Green or Moorland Som 8 A2
Northmuir Angus 76 B6
Northney Hants 10 D6
Northolt London 19 C8
Northop Flint 42 F5
Northop Hall Flint 42 F5
Northorpe Lincs 37 B8
Northorpe Lincs 37 D6
Northorpe Lincs 46 C2
Northover Som 8 A3
Northover Som 15 H10
Northowram W Yorks 51 G7
Northport Dorset 9 F8
Northpunds Shetland 96 L6
Northrepps Norf 39 B8
Northtown Orkney 95 J5
Northway Glos 26 E6
Northwich Ches W 43 E9
Northwick S Glos 16 C2
Northwold Norf 38 F3
Northwood Derbys 44 F6
Northwood IoW 10 E3
Northwood Kent 21 E10
Northwood London 19 B7
Northwood Shrops 33 B10
Northwood Green Glos 26 G4
Norton E Sus 12 F3
Norton Glos 26 F5
Norton Halton 43 D8
Norton Herts 29 E9
Norton IoW 10 F2
Norton Mon 25 G11
Norton Northants 28 B3
Norton Notts 45 E9
Norton Powys 25 B10
Norton S Yorks 51 H11
Norton Shrops 33 G10
Norton Shrops 34 E1
Norton Shrops 34 E3
Norton Stockton 58 D5
Norton Suff 30 B6
Norton W Sus 11 D8
Norton W Sus 11 E7
Norton Wilts 16 C5
Norton Worcs 26 C5
Norton Worcs 27 D7
Norton Bavant Wilts 16 G6
Norton Bridge Staffs 34 B4
Norton Canes Staffs 34 E6
Norton Canon Hereford 25 D10
Norton Corner Norf 39 C6
Norton Disney Lincs 46 G2
Norton East Staffs 34 E6
Norton Ferris Wilts 16 H4
Norton Fitzwarren Som 7 D10
Norton Green IoW 10 F2
Norton Hawkfield Bath 16 E2
Norton Heath Essex 20 A3
Norton in Hales Shrops 34 B3
Norton-in-the-Moors Stoke 44 G2
Norton-Juxta-Twycross Leics 35 E9
Norton-le-Clay N Yorks 51 B10
Norton Lindsey Warks 27 B9
Norton Malreward Bath 16 E3
Norton Mandeville Essex 20 A2
Norton-on-Derwent N Yorks 52 B3
Norton St Philip Som 16 F4
Norton sub Hamdon Som 8 C3
Norton Woodseats S Yorks 45 D7
Norwell Notts 45 F11
Norwell Woodhouse Notts 45 F11
Norwich Norf 39 E8
Norwick Shetland 96 B8
Norwood Derbys 45 D8
Norwood Hill Sur 19 G9
Norwoodside Cambs 37 F10
Noseley Leics 36 F3
Noss Shetland 96 M5
Noss Mayo Devon 4 G6
Nosterfield N Yorks 51 A8
Nostie Highld 85 F13
Notgrove Glos 27 F8
Nottage Bridgend 14 D4
Nottingham Nottingham 36 B1
Nottington Dorset 8 F5
Notton W Yorks 45 A7
Notton Wilts 16 E6
Nounsley Essex 30 G4
Noutard's Green Worcs 26 B4
Novar House Highld 87 E9
Nox Shrops 33 D10
Nuffield Oxon 18 C3
Nun Hills Lancs 50 G4
Nun Monkton N Yorks 51 D11
Nunburnholme E Yorks 52 E4
Nuncargate Notts 45 G9
Nuneaton Warks 35 F9
Nuneham Courtenay Oxon 18 B2
Nunney Som 16 G4
Nunnington N Yorks 52 B2
Nunnykirk Northumb 62 D6
Nunsthorpe NE Lincs 46 B6
Nunthorpe Mbro 59 E6
Nunthorpe York 52 D2
Nunton Wilts 9 B10
Nunwick N Yorks 51 B9
Nupend Glos 26 H4
Nursling Hants 10 C2
Nursted Hants 11 B6
Nutbourne W Sus 11 C9
Nutbourne W Sus 11 D6
Nutfield Sur 19 F10
Nuthall Notts 35 A11
Nuthampstead Herts 29 E11
Nuthurst W Sus 11 B10
Nutley E Sus 12 D3
Nutley Hants 18 G3
Nutwell S Yorks 45 B10
Nybster Highld 94 D5
Nyetimber W Sus 11 E7
Nyewood W Sus 11 B7
Nymet Rowland Devon 7 F6
Nymet Tracey Devon 7 F6
Nympsfield Glos 16 A5
Nynehead Som 7 D10
Nyton W Sus 11 D8

O

Oad Street Kent 20 E5
Oadby Leics 36 E2
Oak Cross Devon 6 G4
Oakamoor Staffs 35 A6
Oakbank W Loth 69 D9
Oakdale Caerph 15 B7
Oake Som 7 D10
Oaken Staffs 34 E4
Oakenclough Lancs 49 E5
Oakengates Telford 34 D3
Oakenholt Flint 42 E5
Oakenshaw Durham 58 C3
Oakenshaw W Yorks 51 G7
Oakerthorpe Derbys 45 G7
Oakes W Yorks 51 H7
Oakfield Torf 15 B9
Oakford Ceredig 23 A9
Oakford Devon 7 D8
Oakfordbridge Devon 7 D8
Oakgrove Ches E 44 F3
Oakham Rutland 36 E4
Oakhanger Hants 18 H4
Oakhill Som 16 G3
Oakhurst Kent 20 F2
Oakington Cambs 29 B11
Oaklands Herts 29 G9
Oaklands Powys 25 C7
Oakle Street Glos 26 G4
Oakley Bedford 29 C7
Oakley Bucks 28 G3
Oakley Fife 69 B9
Oakley Hants 18 F2
Oakley Oxon 18 A4
Oakley Poole 9 E9
Oakley Suff 39 H7
Oakley Green Windsor 18 D6
Oakley Park Powys 32 G5
Oakmere Ches W 43 F8
Oakridge Glos 16 A6
Oakridge Hants 18 F3
Oaks Shrops 33 E10
Oaks Green Derbys 35 B7
Oaksey Wilts 16 B6
Oakthorpe Leics 35 D9
Oakwoodhill Sur 19 H8
Oakworth W Yorks 51 F6
Oape Highld 92 J7
Oare Kent 21 E7
Oare Som 7 B7
Oare W Berks 18 D2
Oare Wilts 17 E8
Oasby Lincs 36 B6
Oathlaw Angus 77 B7
Oatlands N Yorks 51 D9
Oban Argyll 79 J11
Oban Highld 79 C11
Oborne Dorset 8 C5
Obthorpe Lincs 37 D6
Occlestone Green Ches W 43 F9
Occold Suff 31 A8
Ochiltree E Ayrs 67 D8
Ochtermuthill Perth 75 F11
Ochtertyre Perth 75 E11
Ockbrook Derbys 35 B10
Ockham Sur 19 F7
Ockle Highld 79 D8
Ockley Sur 19 H8
Ocle Pychard Hereford 26 D2
Octon E Yorks 52 C6
Octon Cross Roads E Yorks 52 C6
Odcombe Som 8 C4
Odd Down Bath 16 E4
Oddendale Cumb 57 E7
Odder Lincs 46 E3
Oddingley Worcs 26 C6
Oddington Glos 27 F9
Oddington Oxon 28 G2
Odell Bedford 28 C6
Odie Orkney 95 F7
Odiham Hants 18 F4
Odstock Wilts 9 B10
Odstone Leics 35 E9
Offchurch Warks 27 B10
Offenham Worcs 27 D7
Offham E Sus 12 E2
Offham Kent 20 F3
Offham W Sus 11 D9
Offord Cluny Cambs 29 B9
Offord Darcy Cambs 29 B9
Offton Suff 31 D7
Offwell Devon 7 G10
Ogbourne Maizey Wilts 17 D8
Ogbourne St Andrew Wilts 17 D8
Ogbourne St George Wilts 17 D9
Ogil Angus 77 A7
Ogle Northumb 63 F7
Ogmore V Glam 14 D4
Ogmore-by-Sea V Glam 14 D4
Ogmore Vale Bridgend 14 B5
Okeford Fitzpaine Dorset 9 C7
Okehampton Devon 6 G4
Okehampton Camp Devon 6 G4
Okraquoy Shetland 96 K6
Old Northants 28 A4
Old Aberdeen Aberdeen 83 C11
Old Alresford Hants 10 A4
Old Arley Warks 35 F8
Old Basford Nottingham 35 A11
Old Basing Hants 18 F3
Old Bewick Northumb 62 A6
Old Bolingbroke Lincs 47 F7
Old Bramhope W Yorks 51 E8
Old Brampton Derbys 45 E7
Old Bridge of Tilt Perth 81 G10
Old Bridge of Urr Dumfries 55 C10
Old Buckenham Norf 39 F6
Old Burghclere Hants 17 F11
Old Byland N Yorks 59 H6
Old Cassop Durham 58 C4
Old Castleton Borders 61 D11
Old Catton Norf 39 D8
Old Clee NE Lincs 46 B6
Old Cleeve Som 7 B9
Old Clipstone Notts 45 F10
Old Colwyn Conwy 41 C10
Old Coulsdon London 19 F10
Old Crombie Aberds 88 C5
Old Dailly S Ayrs 66 G5
Old Dalby Leics 36 C2
Old Deer Aberds 89 D9
Old Denaby S Yorks 45 C8
Old Edlington S Yorks 45 C9
Old Eldon Durham 58 D3
Old Ellerby E Yorks 53 F7
Old Felixstowe Suff 31 E10
Old Fletton Pboro 37 F7
Old Glossop Derbys 44 C4
Old Goole E Yorks 52 G3
Old Hall Powys 32 G5
Old Heath Essex 31 F7
Old Heathfield E Sus 12 D4
Old Hill W Mid 34 G5
Old Hunstanton Norf 38 A2
Old Hurst Cambs 37 H8
Old Hutton Cumb 57 H7
Old Kea Corn 3 E7
Old Kilpatrick W Dunb 68 C3
Old Kinnernie Aberds 83 C9
Old Knebworth Herts 29 F9
Old Langho Lancs 50 F3
Old Laxey IoM 48 D4
Old Leake Lincs 47 G8
Old Malton N Yorks 52 B3
Old Micklefield W Yorks 51 F10
Old Milton Hants 9 E11
Old Milverton Warks 27 B9
Old Monkland N Lanark 68 D6
Old Netley Hants 10 D3
Old Philpstoun W Loth 69 C9
Old Quarrington Durham 58 C4
Old Radnor Powys 25 C9
Old Rattray Aberds 89 C10
Old Rayne Aberds 83 A8
Old Romney Kent 13 D9
Old Sodbury S Glos 16 C4
Old Somerby Lincs 36 B5
Old Stratford Northants 28 D4
Old Thirsk N Yorks 51 A10
Old Town Cumb 50 A1
Old Town Cumb 57 B6
Old Town Northumb 62 D4
Old Town Scilly 2 C3
Old Trafford Gtr Man 44 C2
Old Tupton Derbys 45 F7
Old Warden C Beds 29 D8
Old Weston Cambs 37 H6
Old Whittington Derbys 45 E7
Old Wick Highld 94 E5
Old Windsor Windsor 18 D6
Old Wives Lees Kent 21 F7
Old Woking Sur 19 F7
Old Woodhall Lincs 46 F6
Oldany Highld 92 F4
Oldberrow Warks 27 B8
Oldborough Devon 7 F6
Oldbury Shrops 34 F3
Oldbury W Mid 34 G5
Oldbury Warks 35 F9
Oldbury-on-Severn S Glos 16 B3
Oldbury on the Hill Glos 16 C5
Oldcastle Bridgend 14 D5
Oldcastle Mon 25 F10
Oldcotes Notts 45 D9
Oldfallow Staffs 34 D5
Oldfield Worcs 26 B5
Oldford Som 16 F4
Oldham Gtr Man 44 B3
Oldhamstocks E Loth 70 C6
Oldland S Glos 16 D3
Oldmeldrum Aberds 89 F8
Oldshore Beg Highld 92 D4
Oldshoremore Highld 92 D5
Oldstead N Yorks 51 A11
Oldtown Aberds 83 A7
Oldtown of Ord Aberds 88 C6
Oldway Swansea 23 H10
Oldways End Devon 7 D7
Oldwhat Aberds 89 C8
Olgrinmore Highld 94 E2
Oliver's Battery Hants 10 B3
Ollaberry Shetland 96 E5
Ollerton Ches E 43 E10
Ollerton Notts 45 F10
Ollerton Shrops 34 C2
Olmarch Ceredig 24 C3
Olney M Keynes 28 C5
Olrig Ho. Highld 94 D3
Olton W Mid 35 G7
Olveston S Glos 16 C3
Olwen Ceredig 23 B10
Ombersley Worcs 26 B5
Ompton Notts 45 F10
Onchan IoM 48 E3
Onecote Staffs 44 G4
Onen Mon 25 G11
Ongar Hill Norf 38 C1
Ongar Street Hereford 25 B10
Onibury Shrops 33 H10
Onich Highld 74 A3
Onllwyn Neath 24 G5
Onneley Staffs 34 A3
Onslow Village Sur 18 G6
Onthank E Ayrs 67 B7
Openwoodgate Derbys 45 H7
Opinan Highld 85 A12
Opinan Highld 91 H13
Orange Lane Borders 70 F6
Orange Row Norf 37 C11
Orasaigh W Isles 91 F8
Orbliston Moray 88 C3
Orbost Highld 84 D7
Orby Lincs 47 F8
Orchard Hill Devon 6 D3
Orchard Portman Som 8 B1
Orcheston Wilts 17 G7
Orcop Hereford 25 F11
Orcop Hill Hereford 25 F11
Ord Highld 85 G11
Ordhead Aberds 83 B8
Ordie Aberds 82 C6
Ordiequish Moray 88 C3
Ordsall Notts 45 D10
Ore E Sus 13 E7
Oreton Shrops 34 G2
Orford Suff 31 D11
Orford Warr 43 C9
Orgreave Staffs 35 D7
Orlestone Kent 13 C8
Orleton Hereford 25 B11
Orleton Worcs 26 B3
Orlingbury Northants 28 A5
Ormesby Redcar 59 E6
Ormesby St Margaret Norf 39 D10
Ormesby St Michael Norf 39 D10
Ormiclate Castle W Isles 84 E2
Ormiscaig Highld 91 H13
Ormiston E Loth 70 D3
Ormsaigbeg Highld 78 E7
Ormsaigmore Highld 78 E7
Ormsary Argyll 72 F6
Ormsgill Cumb 49 B1
Ormskirk Lancs 43 B7
Orpington London 19 E11
Orrell Gtr Man 43 B8
Orrell Mers 42 C6
Orrisdale IoM 48 C3
Orroland Dumfries 55 E10
Orsett Thurrock 20 C3
Orslow Staffs 34 D4
Orston Notts 36 A3
Orthwaite Cumb 56 C4
Ortner Lancs 49 D5
Orton Cumb 57 F8
Orton Northants 36 H4
Orton Longueville Pboro 37 F7
Orton-on-the-Hill Leics 35 E9
Orton Waterville Pboro 37 F7
Orwell Cambs 29 C10
Osbaldeston Lancs 50 F2
Osbaldwick York 52 D2
Osbaston Shrops 33 C9
Osbournby Lincs 37 B6
Oscroft Ches W 43 F8
Ose Highld 85 D8
Osgathorpe Leics 35 D10
Osgodby Lincs 46 C4
Osgodby N Yorks 52 F2
Osgodby N Yorks 53 A6
Oskaig Highld 85 E10
Oskamull Argyll 78 G7
Osmaston Derby 35 B9
Osmaston Derbys 35 A8
Osmington Dorset 8 F6
Osmington Mills Dorset 8 F6
Osmotherley N Yorks 58 G5
Ospisdale Highld 87 C10
Ospringe Kent 21 E7
Ossett W Yorks 51 G8
Ossington Notts 45 F11
Ostend Essex 20 B6
Oswaldkirk N Yorks 52 B2
Oswaldtwistle Lancs 50 G3
Oswestry Shrops 33 C8
Otford Kent 20 F2
Otham Kent 20 F4
Othery Som 8 A2
Otley Suff 31 C9
Otley W Yorks 51 E8
Otter Ferry Argyll 73 E8
Otterbourne Hants 10 B3
Otterburn N Yorks 50 D4
Otterburn Northumb 62 D4
Otterburn Camp Northumb 62 D4
Otterham Corn 4 B2
Otterhampton Som 15 G8
Ottershaw Sur 19 E7
Otterswick Shetland 96 E7
Otterton Devon 7 H9
Ottery St Mary Devon 7 G10
Ottinge Kent 21 G8
Ottringham E Yorks 53 G8
Oughterby Cumb 61 H8
Oughtershaw N Yorks 50 A4
Oughterside Cumb 56 B3
Oughtibridge S Yorks 45 C7
Oughtrington Warr 43 D9
Oulston N Yorks 51 B11
Oulton Cumb 56 A4
Oulton Norf 39 C7
Oulton Staffs 34 B5
Oulton Suff 39 F11
Oulton W Yorks 51 G9
Oulton Broad Suff 39 F11
Oulton Street Norf 39 C7
Oundle Northants 36 G6
Ousby Cumb 57 C8
Ousdale Highld 94 H2
Ousden Suff 30 C4
Ousefleet E Yorks 52 G4
Ouston Durham 58 A3
Ouston Northumb 62 F6
Out Newton E Yorks 53 G9
Out Rawcliffe Lancs 49 E4
Outertown Orkney 95 G3
Outgate Cumb 56 G5
Outhgill Cumb 57 F9
Outlane W Yorks 51 H6
Outwell Norf 37 E11
Outwick Hants 9 C10
Outwood Sur 19 G10
Outwood W Yorks 51 G9
Outwoods Staffs 34 D3
Ovenden W Yorks 51 G6
Ovenscloss Borders 70 G3
Over Cambs 29 A10
Over Ches W 43 F9
Over S Glos 16 C2
Over Compton Dorset 8 C4
Over Green W Mid 35 F7
Over Haddon Derbys 44 F6
Over Hulton Gtr Man 43 B9
Over Kellet Lancs 49 B5
Over Kiddington Oxon 27 F11
Over Knutsford Ches E 43 E10
Over Monnow Mon 26 G2
Over Norton Oxon 27 F10
Over Peover Ches E 43 E10
Over Silton N Yorks 58 G5
Over Stowey Som 7 C10
Over Stratton Som 8 C3
Over Tabley Ches E 43 D10
Over Wallop Hants 17 H9
Over Whitacre Warks 35 F8
Over Worton Oxon 27 F11
Overbister Orkney 95 D7
Overbury Worcs 26 E6
Overcombe Dorset 8 F5
Overgreen Derbys 45 E7
Overleigh Som 15 H10
Overley Green Warks 27 C7
Overpool Ches W 43 E6
Overscaig Hotel Highld 92 G7
Overseal Derbys 35 D8
Oversland Kent 21 F7
Overstone Northants 28 B5
Overstrand Norf 39 A8
Overthorpe Northants 27 D11
Overton Aberdeen 83 B10
Overton Ches W 43 E8
Overton Dumfries 60 G5
Overton Hants 18 G2
Overton Lancs 49 D4
Overton N Yorks 52 D1
Overton Shrops 26 A2
Overton Swansea 23 H9
Overton W Yorks 51 H8
Overton = Owrtyn Wrex 33 A9
Overton Bridge Wrex 33 A9
Overtown N Lanark 69 E7
Oving Bucks 28 F4
Oving W Sus 11 D8
Ovingdean Brighton 12 F2
Ovingham Northumb 62 G6
Ovington Durham 58 E2
Ovington Essex 30 D4
Ovington Hants 10 A4
Ovington Norf 38 E5
Ovington Northumb 62 G6
Ower Hants 10 C2
Owermoigne Dorset 9 F6
Owlbury Shrops 33 F9
Owler Bar Derbys 44 E6
Owlerton S Yorks 45 D7
Owl's Green Suff 31 B9
Owlswick Bucks 28 H4
Owmby Lincs 46 B4
Owmby-by-Spital Lincs 46 D4
Owrtyn = Overton Wrex 33 A9
Owslebury Hants 10 B4
Owston Leics 36 E3
Owston S Yorks 45 A9
Owston Ferry N Lincs 46 B2
Owstwick E Yorks 53 F8
Owthorne E Yorks 53 G9
Owthorpe Notts 36 B2
Oxborough Norf 38 E3
Oxcombe Lincs 47 E7
Oxen Park Cumb 56 H5
Oxenholme Cumb 57 H7
Oxenhope W Yorks 50 F6
Oxenton Glos 26 E6
Oxenwood Wilts 17 F10
Oxford Oxon 28 H2
Oxhey Herts 19 B8
Oxhill Warks 27 D10
Oxley W Mid 34 E5
Oxley Green Essex 30 G6
Oxley's Green E Sus 12 D5
Oxnam Borders 62 B3
Oxshott Sur 19 E8
Oxspring S Yorks 44 B6
Oxted Sur 19 F10
Oxton Borders 70 E3
Oxton Notts 45 G10
Oxwich Swansea 23 H9
Oxwich Green Swansea 23 H9
Oxwick Norf 38 C5
Oykel Bridge Highld 92 J6
Oyne Aberds 83 A8

P

Pabail Iarach W Isles 91 D10
Pabail Uarach W Isles 91 D10
Pace Gate N Yorks 51 D7
Packington Leics 35 D9
Padanaram Angus 77 B7
Padbury Bucks 28 E4
Paddington London 19 C9
Paddlesworth Kent 21 H8
Paddock Wood Kent 12 B5
Paddockhaugh Moray 88 C2
Paddockhole Dumfries 61 E8
Padfield Derbys 44 C4
Padiham Lancs 50 F3
Padog Conwy 41 E10
Padside N Yorks 51 D7
Padstow Corn 3 B8
Padworth W Berks 18 E3
Page Bank Durham 58 C3
Pagham W Sus 11 E7
Paglesham Churchend Essex 20 B6
Paglesham Eastend Essex 20 B6
Paibeil W Isles 84 B2
Paible W Isles 90 H5
Paignton Torbay 5 E9
Pailton Warks 35 G10
Painscastle Powys 25 D8
Painshawfield Northumb 62 G6
Painsthorpe E Yorks 52 D4
Painswick Glos 26 H5
Pairc Shiaboist W Isles 90 C7
Paisley Renfs 68 D3
Pakefield Suff 39 F11
Pakenham Suff 30 B6
Pale Gwyn 32 B5
Palestine Hants 17 G9
Paley Street Windsor 18 D5
Palfrey W Mid 34 F6
Palgowan Dumfries 54 A6
Palgrave Suff 39 H7
Pallion T&W 63 H9
Palmarsh Kent 13 C10
Palnackie Dumfries 55 D11
Palnure Dumfries 55 C7
Palterton Derbys 45 F8
Pamber End Hants 18 F3
Pamber Green Hants 18 F3
Pamber Heath Hants 18 E3
Pamphill Dorset 9 D8
Pampisford Cambs 29 D11
Pan Orkney 95 J4
Panbride Angus 77 D8
Pancrasweek Devon 6 F1
Pandy Gwyn 32 E2
Pandy Mon 25 F10
Pandy Powys 32 E5
Pandy Wrex 33 B7
Pandy Tudur Conwy 41 D10
Panfield Essex 30 F4
Pangbourne W Berks 18 D3
Pannal N Yorks 51 D9
Panshanger Herts 29 G9
Pant Shrops 33 C8
Pant-glas Powys 32 F3
Pant-glas Carms 23 D10
Pant-glas Gwyn 40 F6
Pant-glas Shrops 33 B8
Pant-lasau Swansea 14 B2
Pant Mawr Powys 32 G4
Pant-teg Carms 23 D9
Pant-y-Caws Carms 22 D6
Pant-y-dwr Powys 32 H5
Pant-y-ffridd Powys 33 E7
Pant-y-Wacco Flint 42 E4
Pant-yr-awel Bridgend 14 C5
Pantgwyn Carms 23 D10
Pantgwyn Ceredig 23 B7
Panton Lincs 46 E5
Pantperthog Gwyn 32 E3
Pantyffynnon Carms 24 G3
Pantymwyn Flint 42 F4
Panxworth Norf 39 D9
Papcastle Cumb 56 C3
Papigoe Highld 94 E5
Papil Shetland 96 K5
Papley Orkney 95 J5
Papple E Loth 70 C4
Papplewick Notts 45 G9
Papworth Everard Cambs 29 B9
Papworth St Agnes Cambs 29 B9
Par Corn 4 F1
Parbold Lancs 43 A7
Parbrook Som 16 H2
Parbrook W Sus 11 B9
Parc Gwyn 41 G10
Parc-Seymour Newport 15 B10
Parc-y-rhôs Carms 23 B10
Parcllyn Ceredig 23 A7
Pardshaw Cumb 56 D2
Parham Suff 31 B10
Park Dumfries 60 D5
Park Corner Oxon 18 C3
Park Corner Windsor 18 C5
Park End Mbro 58 E6
Park End Northumb 62 F4
Park Gate Hants 10 D4
Park Hill N Yorks 51 C9
Park Hill Notts 45 G10
Park Street W Sus 11 A10
Parkend Glos 26 H3
Parkeston Essex 31 E9
Parkgate Ches W 42 E5
Parkgate Dumfries 60 E6
Parkgate Kent 13 C7
Parkgate Sur 19 G9
Parkham Devon 6 D2
Parkham Ash Devon 6 D2
Parkhill Ho. Aberds 83 B10
Parkhouse Mon 15 A10
Parkhouse Green Derbys 45 F8
Parkhurst IoW 10 E3
Parkmill Swansea 23 H10
Parkneuk Aberds 83 F9
Parkstone Poole 9 E9
Parley Cross Dorset 9 E9
Parracombe Devon 6 B5
Parrog Pembs 22 C5
Parsley Hay Derbys 44 F5
Parson Cross S Yorks 45 C7
Parson Drove Cambs 37 E9
Parsonage Green Essex 30 H4
Parsonby Cumb 56 C3
Parson's Heath Essex 31 F7
Partick Glasgow 68 D4
Partington Gtr Man 43 C10
Partney Lincs 47 F8
Parton Cumb 56 D1
Parton Dumfries 55 B9
Parton Glos 26 F5
Partridge Green W Sus 11 C10
Parwich Derbys 44 G5
Passenham Northants 28 E4
Paston Norf 39 B9
Patchacott Devon 6 G3
Patcham Brighton 12 F2
Patching W Sus 11 D9
Patchole Devon 6 B5
Pateley Bridge N Yorks 51 C7
Paternoster Heath Essex 30 G6
Path of Condie Perth 76 F3
Pathe Som 8 A2
Pathhead Aberds 77 A10
Pathhead E Ayrs 67 E9
Pathhead Fife 69 A11
Pathhead Midloth 70 D2
Pathstruie Perth 76 F3
Patna E Ayrs 67 E7
Patney Wilts 17 F7
Patrick IoM 48 D2
Patrick Brompton N Yorks 58 G3
Patrington E Yorks 53 G9
Patrixbourne Kent 21 F8
Patterdale Cumb 56 E5
Pattingham Staffs 34 F4
Pattishall Northants 28 C3
Pattiswick Green Essex 30 F5
Patton Bridge Cumb 57 G7
Paul Corn 2 G3
Paulerspury Northants 28 D4
Paull E Yorks 53 G7
Paulton Bath 16 F3
Pavenham Bedford 28 C6
Pawlett Som 15 G9
Pawston Northumb 71 G7
Paxford Glos 27 E8
Paxton Borders 71 E8
Payhembury Devon 7 F9
Paythorne Lancs 50 D4
Peacehaven E Sus 12 F3
Peak Dale Derbys 44 E4
Peak Forest Derbys 44 E5
Peakirk Pboro 37 E7
Pearsie Angus 76 B6
Pease Pottage W Sus 12 C1
Peasedown St John Bath 16 F4
Peasemore W Berks 17 D11
Peasenhall Suff 31 B10
Peaslake Sur 19 G7
Peasley Cross Mers 43 C8
Peasmarsh E Sus 13 D7
Peaston E Loth 70 D3
Peastonbank E Loth 70 D3
Peat Inn Fife 77 G7
Peathill Aberds 89 B9
Peatling Magna Leics 36 F1
Peatling Parva Leics 36 G1
Peaton Shrops 33 G11
Peats Corner Suff 31 B8
Pebmarsh Essex 30 E5
Pebworth Worcs 27 D8
Pecket Well W Yorks 50 G5
Peckforton Ches E 43 G8
Peckham London 19 D10
Peckleton Leics 35 E10
Pedlinge Kent 13 C10
Pedmore W Mid 34 G5
Pedwell Som 15 H10
Peebles Borders 69 F11
Peel IoM 48 D2
Peel Common Hants 10 D4
Peel Park S Lanark 68 E5
Peening Quarter Kent 13 D7
Pegsdon C Beds 29 E8
Pegswood Northumb 63 E8
Pegwell Kent 21 E10
Peinchorran Highld 85 E10
Peinlich Highld 85 C9
Pelaw T&W 63 G8
Pelcomb Bridge Pembs 22 E4
Pelcomb Cross Pembs 22 E4
Peldon Essex 30 G6
Pellon W Yorks 51 G6
Pelsall W Mid 34 E6
Pelton Durham 58 A3
Pelutho Cumb 56 B3
Pelynt Corn 4 F3
Pemberton Gtr Man 43 B8
Pembrey Carms 23 F9
Pembridge Hereford 25 C10
Pembroke = Penfro Pembs 22 F4
Pembroke Dock = Doc Penfro Pembs 22 F4
Pembury Kent 12 B5
Pen-bont Rhydybeddau Ceredig 32 G2
Pen-clawdd Swansea 23 G10
Pen-ffordd Pembs 22 D5
Pen-groes-oped Mon 25 H10
Pen-llyn Anglesey 40 B5
Pen-lon Anglesey 40 D6
Pen-sarn Gwyn 32 C1
Pen-sarn Gwyn 40 F6
Pen-twyn Mon 26 H2
Pen-y-banc Carms 24 F3
Pen-y-bont Carms 23 D8
Pen-y-bont Gwyn 32 C2
Pen-y-bont Gwyn 32 E3
Pen-y-bont Powys 33 C8
Pen-y-bont ar Ogwr = Bridgend Bridgend 14 D5
Pen-y-bryn Gwyn 32 D2
Pen-y-bryn Pembs 22 B6
Pen-y-cae Powys 24 G5
Pen-y-cae-mawr Mon 15 B10
Pen-y-cefn Flint 42 E4
Pen-y-clawdd Mon 25 H11
Pen-y-coedcae Rhondda 14 C6
Pen-y-fai Bridgend 14 C4
Pen-y-garn Carms 23 C10
Pen-y-garn Ceredig 32 G2
Pen-y-garnedd Anglesey 41 C7
Pen-y-gop Conwy 32 A5
Pen-y-graig Gwyn 40 G3
Pen-y-groes Carms 23 E10
Pen-y-groeslon Gwyn 40 G4
Pen-y-Gwryd Hotel Gwyn 41 E8
Pen-y-stryt Denb 42 G4
Pen-yr-heol Mon 25 G11
Pen-yr-Heolgerrig M Tydf 25 H7
Penallt Mon 26 G2
Penally Pembs 22 G6
Penalt Hereford 26 F2
Penare Corn 3 E8
Penarlâg = Hawarden Flint 42 F6
Penarth V Glam 15 D7
Penbryn Ceredig 23 A7
Pencader Carms 23 C9
Pencaenewydd Gwyn 40 F6
Pencaitland E Loth 70 D3
Pencarnisiog Anglesey 40 C5
Pencarreg Carms 23 B10
Pencelli Powys 25 F7
Pencoed Bridgend 14 C5
Pencombe Hereford 26 C2
Pencoyd Hereford 26 F2
Pencraig Hereford 26 F2
Pencraig Powys 32 C6
Pendeen Corn 2 F2
Penderyn Rhondda 24 H6
Pendine Carms 23 F7
Pendlebury Gtr Man 43 B10
Pendleton Lancs 43 F3
Pendock Worcs 26 E4
Pendoggett Corn 3 B9
Pendomer Som 8 C4
Pendoylan V Glam 14 D6
Pendre Bridgend 14 C5
Penegoes Powys 32 E3
Penfro = Pembroke Pembs 22 F4
Pengam Caerph 15 B7
Penge London 19 D10
Pengenffordd Powys 25 E8
Pengorffwysfa Anglesey 40 A6
Pengover Green Corn 4 E3
Penhale Corn 2 H5
Penhale Corn 3 D8
Penhalvaen Corn 2 F6
Penhill Swindon 17 C8
Penhow Newport 15 B10
Penhurst E Sus 12 E5
Peniarth Gwyn 32 E2
Penicuik Midloth 69 D11
Peniel Carms 23 D9
Peniel Denb 42 F3
Penifiler Highld 85 D9
Peninver Argyll 65 F8
Penisarwaun Gwyn 41 D7
Penistone S Yorks 44 B6
Penjerrick Corn 3 F6
Penketh Warr 43 D8
Penkill S Ayrs 66 G5
Penkridge Staffs 34 D5
Penley Wrex 33 B10
Penllergaer Swansea 14 B2
Penllyn V Glam 14 D5
Penmachno Conwy 41 E9
Penmaen Swansea 23 H10
Penmaenan Conwy 41 C9
Penmaenmawr Conwy 41 C9
Penmaenpool Gwyn 32 D2
Penmark V Glam 14 E6
Penmarth Corn 2 F6
Penmon Anglesey 41 B8
Penmore Mill Argyll 78 F7
Penmorfa Ceredig 23 A8
Penmorfa Gwyn 41 F7
Penmynydd Anglesey 41 C7
Penn Bucks 18 B6
Penn W Mid 34 F4
Penn Street Bucks 18 B6
Pennal Gwyn 32 E3
Pennan Aberds 89 B8
Pennant Ceredig 24 B2
Pennant Denb 32 B6
Pennant Denb 42 G3
Pennant Powys 32 F4
Pennant Melangell Powys 32 C6
Pennar Pembs 22 F4
Pennard Swansea 23 H10
Pennerley Shrops 33 F9
Pennington Cumb 49 B2
Pennington Gtr Man 43 C9
Pennington Hants 10 E2
Penny Bridge Cumb 49 A3
Pennycross Argyll 79 J8
Pennygate Norf 39 C9
Pennygown Argyll 79 G8
Pennymoor Devon 7 E7
Pennywell T&W 63 H9
Penparc Ceredig 23 B7
Penparc Pembs 22 C3
Penparcau Ceredig 32 G1
Penperlleni Mon 15 A9
Penpillick Corn 4 F1
Penpol Corn 3 F7
Penpoll Corn 4 F2
Penpont Dumfries 60 D4
Penpont Powys 24 F6
Penrhôs Mon 25 G11
Penrherber Carms 23 C7
Penrhiw goch Carms 23 E10
Penrhiw-llan Ceredig 23 B8
Penrhiw-pâl Ceredig 23 B8
Penrhiwceiber Rhondda 14 B6
Penrhos Gwyn 40 G5
Penrhos Powys 24 G4
Penrhosfeilw Anglesey 40 B4
Penrhyn Bay Conwy 41 B10
Penrhyn-coch Ceredig 32 G2
Penrhyndeudraeth Gwyn 41 G8
Penrhynside Conwy 41 B10
Penrice Swansea 23 H9
Penrith Cumb 57 C7
Penrose Corn 3 B7
Penruddock Cumb 56 D6
Penryn Corn 3 F6
Pensarn Carms 23 E9
Pensarn Conwy 42 E2
Pensax Worcs 26 B4
Pensby Mers 42 D5
Penselwood Som 9 A6
Pensford Bath 16 E3
Penshaw T&W 58 A4
Penshurst Kent 12 B4
Pensilva Corn 4 E3
Penston E Loth 70 C3
Pentewan Corn 3 E9
Pentir Gwyn 41 D7
Pentire Corn 3 C6
Pentlow Essex 30 D5
Pentney Norf 38 D3
Penton Mewsey Hants 17 G10
Pentraeth Anglesey 41 C7
Pentre Carms 23 E10
Pentre Powys 33 F8
Pentre Powys 33 G6
Pentre Rhondda 14 B5
Pentre Shrops 33 D9
Pentre Wrex 33 A8
Pentre Wrex 33 B7
Pentre-bâch Ceredig 23 B10
Pentre-bach Powys 24 E6
Pentre Berw Anglesey 40 C6
Pentre-bont Conwy 41 E9
Pentre-celyn Denb 42 G4
Pentre-Celyn Powys 32 E4
Pentre-chwyth Swansea 14 B2
Pentre-cwrt Carms 23 C8
Pentre Dolau-Honddu Powys 24 D6
Pentre-dwr Swansea 14 B2
Pentre-galar Pembs 22 C6
Pentre-Gwenlais Carms 24 G3
Pentre Gwynfryn Gwyn 32 C1
Pentre Halkyn Flint 42 E5
Pentre-Isaf Conwy 41 D10
Pentre Llanrhaeadr Denb 42 F3
Pentre-llwyn-llŵyd Powys 24 C6
Pentre-llyn Ceredig 24 A3

Pentre-llyn cymmer Conwy 42 G2
Pentre Meyrick V Glam 14 D5
Pentre-poeth Newport 15 C8
Pentre-rhew Ceredig 24 C3
Pentre-tafarn-y-fedw Conwy 41 D10
Pentre-ty-gwyn Carms 24 E5
Pentrebach M Tydf 14 A6
Pentrebach Swansea 24 H3
Pentrebeirdd Powys 33 D7
Pentrecagal Carms 23 B8
Pentredwr Denb 42 H4
Pentrefelin Carms 23 D10
Pentrefelin Ceredig 24 D3
Pentrefelin Conwy 41 C10
Pentrefelin Gwyn 41 G7
Pentrefoelas Conwy 41 E10
Pentregat Ceredig 23 A8
Pentreheyling Shrops 33 F8
Pentre'r Felin Conwy 41 D10
Pentre'r-felin Powys 24 E6
Pentrich Derbys 45 G7
Pentridge Dorset 9 C9
Pentyrch Cardiff 15 C7
Penuchadre V Glam 14 D4
Penuwch Ceredig 24 B2
Penwithick Corn 3 D9
Penwyllt Powys 24 G5
Penybanc Carms 24 G3
Penybont Powys 25 B8
Penybontfawr Powys 33 C6
Penycae Wrex 42 H5
Penycwm Pembs 22 D3
Penyffordd Flint 42 F6
Penyffridd Gwyn 41 E7
Penygarnedd Powys 33 C7
Penygraig Rhondda 14 B5
Penygroes Gwyn 40 E6
Penygroes Pembs 22 C6
Penyrheol Caerph 15 C7
Penysarn Anglesey 40 A6
Penywaun Rhondda 14 A5
Penzance Corn 2 F3
Peopleton Worcs 26 C6
Peover Heath Ches E 43 E10
Peper Harow Sur 18 G6
Perceton N Ayrs 67 B6
Percie Aberds 83 D7
Percyhorner Aberds 89 B9
Periton Som 7 B8
Perivale London 19 C8
Perkinsville Durham 58 A3
Perlethorpe Notts 45 E10
Perranarworthal Corn 3 F6
Perranporth Corn 3 D6
Perranuthnoe Corn 2 G4
Perranzabuloe Corn 3 D6
Perry Barr W Mid 35 F6
Perry Green Herts 29 G11
Perry Green Wilts 16 C6
Perry Street Kent 20 D3
Perryfoot Derbys 44 D5
Pershall Staffs 34 B4
Pershore Worcs 26 D6
Pert Angus 83 G8
Pertenhall Bedford 29 B7
Perth Perth 76 E4
Perthy Shrops 33 B9
Perton Staffs 34 F4
Pertwood Wilts 16 H5
Peter Tavy Devon 4 D6
Peterborough Pboro 37 F7
Peterburn Highld 91 J12
Peterchurch Hereford 25 E10
Peterculter Aberdeen 83 C10
Peterhead Aberds 89 D11
Peterlee Durham 58 B5
Peter's Green Herts 29 G8
Peters Marland Devon 6 E3
Petersfield Hants 10 B6
Peterston super-Ely V Glam 14 D6
Peterstone Wentlooge Newport 15 C8
Peterstow Hereford 26 F2
Petertown Orkney 95 H4
Petham Kent 21 F8
Petrockstow Devon 6 F4
Pett E Sus 13 E7
Pettaugh Suff 31 C8
Petteridge Kent 12 B5
Pettinain S Lanark 69 F8
Pettistree Suff 31 C9
Petton Devon 7 D9
Petton Shrops 33 C10
Petts Wood London 19 E11
Petty Aberds 89 E7
Pettycur Fife 69 B11
Pettymuick Aberds 89 F9
Petworth W Sus 11 B8
Pevensey E Sus 12 F5
Pevensey Bay E Sus 12 F5
Pewsey Wilts 17 E8
Philham Devon 6 D1
Philiphaugh Borders 70 H3
Phillack Corn 2 F4
Philleigh Corn 3 F7
Philpstoun W Loth 69 C9
Phocle Green Hereford 26 F3
Phoenix Green Hants 18 F4
Pica Cumb 56 D2
Piccotts End Herts 29 H7
Pickering N Yorks 52 A3
Picket Piece Hants 17 G10
Picket Post Hants 9 D10
Pickhill N Yorks 51 A9
Picklescott Shrops 33 F10
Pickletillem Fife 77 E7
Pickmere Ches E 43 E9
Pickney Som 7 D10
Pickstock Telford 34 C3
Pickwell Devon 6 B3
Pickwell Leics 36 D3
Pickworth Lincs 36 B6
Pickworth Rutland 36 D5
Picton Ches W 43 E7
Picton Flint 42 D4
Picton N Yorks 58 F5
Piddinghoe E Sus 12 F3
Piddington Northants 28 C5
Piddington Oxon 28 G3
Piddlehinton Dorset 8 E6
Piddletrenthide Dorset 8 E6
Pidley Cambs 37 H9
Piercebridge Darl 58 E3
Pierowall Orkney 95 D5
Pigdon Northumb 63 E7
Pikehall Derbys 44 G5
Pilgrims Hatch Essex 20 B2
Pilham Lincs 46 C2
Pill N Som 15 D11
Pillaton Corn 4 E4
Pillerton Hersey Warks 27 D10
Pillerton Priors Warks 27 D9
Pilleth Powys 25 B9
Pilley Hants 10 E2
Pilley S Yorks 45 B7
Pilling Lancs 49 E4
Pilling Lane Lancs 49 E3
Pillowell Glos 26 H3
Pillwell Dorset 9 C6
Pilning S Glos 16 C2
Pilsbury Derbys 44 F5
Pilsdon Dorset 8 E3
Pilsgate Pboro 37 E6
Pilsley Derbys 44 E6
Pilsley Derbys 45 F8
Pilton Devon 6 C4
Pilton Northants 36 G6
Pilton Rutland 36 E5
Pilton Som 16 G2
Pilton Green Swansea 23 H9
Pimperne Dorset 9 D8
Pin Mill Suff 31 E9
Pinchbeck Lincs 37 C8
Pinchbeck Bars Lincs 37 C7
Pinchbeck West Lincs 37 C8
Pincheon Green S Yorks 52 H2
Pinehurst Swindon 17 C8
Pinfold Lancs 43 A6
Pinged Carms 23 F9
Pinhoe Devon 7 G8
Pinkneys Green Windsor 18 C5
Pinley W Mid 35 H9
Pinminnoch S Ayrs 66 G4
Pinmore S Ayrs 66 G5
Pinmore Mains S Ayrs 66 G5
Pinner London 19 C8
Pinvin Worcs 26 D6
Pinwherry S Ayrs 66 H4
Pinxton Derbys 45 G8
Pipe and Lyde Hereford 26 D2
Pipe Gate Shrops 34 A3
Piperhill Highld 87 F11
Piper's Pool Corn 4 C3
Pipewell Northants 36 G4
Pippacott Devon 6 C4
Pipton Powys 25 E8
Pirbright Sur 18 F6
Pirnmill N Ayrs 66 B1
Pirton Herts 29 E8
Pirton Worcs 26 D5
Pisgah Ceredig 32 H2
Pisgah Stirling 75 G10
Pishill Oxon 18 C4
Pistyll Gwyn 40 F5
Pitagowan Perth 81 G10
Pitblae Aberds 89 B9
Pitcairngreen Perth 76 E3
Pitcalnie Highld 87 D11
Pitcaple Aberds 83 A9
Pitch Green Bucks 18 A4
Pitch Place Sur 18 F6
Pitchcombe Glos 26 H5
Pitchcott Bucks 28 F4
Pitchford Shrops 33 E11
Pitcombe Som 8 A5
Pitcorthie Fife 77 G8
Pitcox E Loth 70 C5
Pitcur Perth 76 D5
Pitfichie Aberds 83 B8
Pitforthie Aberds 83 F10
Pitgrudy Highld 87 B10
Pitkennedy Angus 77 B8
Pitkevy Fife 76 G5
Pitkierie Fife 77 G8
Pitlessie Fife 76 G6
Pitlochry Perth 76 B2
Pitmachie Aberds 83 A8
Pitmain Highld 81 C9
Pitmedden Aberds 89 F8
Pitminster Som 7 E11
Pitmuies Angus 77 C8
Pitmunie Aberds 83 B8
Pitney Som 8 B3
Pitscottie Fife 77 F7
Pitsea Essex 20 C4
Pitsford Northants 28 B4
Pitsmoor S Yorks 45 D7
Pitstone Bucks 28 G6
Pitstone Green Bucks 28 G6
Pittendreich Moray 88 B1
Pittentrail Highld 93 J10
Pittenweem Fife 77 G8
Pittington Durham 58 B4
Pittodrie Aberds 83 A8
Pitton Wilts 9 A11
Pittswood Kent 20 G3
Pittulie Aberds 89 B9
Pity Me Durham 58 B3
Pityme Corn 3 B8
Pityoulish Highld 81 B11
Pixey Green Suff 39 H8
Pixham Sur 19 F8
Pixley Hereford 26 E3
Place Newton N Yorks 52 B4
Plaidy Aberds 89 C7
Plains N Lanark 68 D6
Plaish Shrops 33 F11
Plaistow W Sus 11 A9
Plaitford Wilts 10 C1
Plank Lane Gtr Man 43 C9
Plas-canol Gwyn 32 D1
Plas Gogerddan Ceredig 32 G2
Plas Llwyngwern Powys 32 E3
Plas Nantyr Wrex 33 B7
Plas-yn-Cefn Denb 42 E3
Plastow Green Hants 18 E2
Platt Kent 20 F3
Platt Bridge Gtr Man 43 B9
Platts Common S Yorks 45 B7
Plawsworth Durham 58 B3
Plaxtol Kent 20 F3
Play Hatch Oxon 18 D4
Playden E Sus 13 D8
Playford Suff 31 D9
Playing Place Corn 3 E7
Playley Green Glos 26 E4
Plealey Shrops 33 E10
Plean Stirling 69 B7
Pleasington Blackburn 50 G2
Pleasley Derbys 45 F9
Pleckgate Blackburn 50 F2
Plenmeller Northumb 62 G3
Pleshey Essex 30 G3
Plockton Highld 85 E13
Plocrapol W Isles 90 H6
Ploughfield Hereford 25 D10
Plowden Shrops 33 G9
Ploxgreen Shrops 33 E9
Pluckley Kent 20 G6
Pluckley Thorne Kent 13 B8
Plumbland Cumb 56 C3
Plumley Ches E 43 E10
Plumpton Cumb 57 C6
Plumpton E Sus 12 E2
Plumpton Green E Sus 12 E2
Plumpton Head Cumb 57 C7
Plumstead London 19 D11
Plumstead Norf 39 B7
Plumtree Notts 36 B2
Plungar Leics 36 B3
Plush Dorset 8 D6
Plwmp Ceredig 23 A8
Plymouth Plym 4 F5
Plympton Plym 4 F6
Plymstock Plym 4 F6
Plymtree Devon 7 F9
Pockley N Yorks 59 H7
Pocklington E Yorks 52 E4
Pode Hole Lincs 37 C8
Podimore Som 8 B4
Podington Bedford 28 B6
Podmore Staffs 34 B3
Point Clear Essex 31 G7
Pointon Lincs 37 B7
Pokesdown Bmouth 9 E10
Pol a Charra W Isles 84 G2
Polbae Dumfries 54 B5
Polbain Highld 92 H2
Polbathic Corn 4 F4
Polbeth W Loth 69 D9
Polchar Highld 81 C10
Pole Elm Worcs 26 D5
Polebrook Northants 37 G6
Polegate E Sus 12 F4
Poles Highld 87 B10
Polesworth Warks 35 E8
Polgigga Corn 2 G2
Polglass Highld 92 J3
Polgooth Corn 3 D8
Poling W Sus 11 D9
Polkerris Corn 4 F1
Polla Highld 92 D6
Pollington E Yorks 52 H2
Polloch Highld 79 E10
Pollok Glasgow 68 D4
Pollokshields Glasgow 68 D4
Polmassick Corn 3 E8
Polmont Falk 69 C8
Polnessan E Ayrs 67 E7
Polnish Highld 79 C10
Polperro Corn 4 F3
Polruan Corn 4 F2
Polsham Som 15 G11
Polstead Suff 30 E6
Poltalloch Argyll 73 D7
Poltimore Devon 7 G8
Polton Midloth 69 D11
Polwarth Borders 70 E6
Polyphant Corn 4 C3
Polzeath Corn 3 B8
Ponders End London 19 B10
Pondersbridge Cambs 37 F8
Pondtail Hants 18 F5
Ponsanooth Corn 3 F6
Ponsworthy Devon 5 D8
Pont Aber Carms 24 F4
Pont Aber-Geirw Gwyn 32 C3
Pont-ar-gothi Carms 23 D10
Pont ar Hydfer Powys 24 F5
Pont-ar-llechau Carms 24 F4
Pont Cwm Pydew Denb 32 B6
Pont Cyfyng Conwy 41 E9
Pont Cysyllte Wrex 33 A8
Pont Dolydd Prysor Gwyn 41 G9
Pont-faen Powys 24 E6
Pont Fronwydd Gwyn 32 C4
Pont-gareg Pembs 22 B6
Pont-Henri Carms 23 F9
Pont-Llogel Powys 32 D6
Pont Pen-y-benglog Gwyn 41 D8
Pont Rhyd-goch Conwy 41 D8
Pont-Rhyd-sarn Gwyn 32 C4
Pont Rhyd-y-cyff Bridgend 14 C4
Pont-rhyd-y-groes Ceredig 24 A4
Pont-rug Gwyn 41 D7
Pont Senni = Sennybridge Powys 24 F6
Pont-siân Ceredig 23 B9
Pont-y-gwaith Rhondda 14 B6
Pont-y-Pŵl = Pontypool Torf 15 A8
Pont-y-pant Conwy 41 E9
Pont y Pennant Gwyn 32 C5
Pont yr Afon-Gam Gwyn 41 F9
Pont-yr-hafod Pembs 22 D4
Pontamman Carms 24 G3
Pontantwn Carms 23 E9
Pontardawe Neath 14 A3
Pontarddulais Swansea 23 F10
Pontarsais Carms 23 D9
Pontblyddyn Flint 42 F5
Pontbren Araeth Carms 24 F3
Pontbren Llwyd Rhondda 24 H6
Pontefract W Yorks 51 G10
Ponteland Northumb 63 F7
Ponterwyd Ceredig 32 G3
Pontesbury Shrops 33 E9
Pontfadog Wrex 33 B8
Pontfaen Pembs 22 C5
Pontgarreg Ceredig 23 A8
Ponthir Torf 15 B9
Ponthirwaun Ceredig 23 B7
Pontllanfraith Caerph 15 B7
Pontlliw Swansea 14 A2
Pontllyfni Gwyn 40 E6
Pontlottyn Caerph 25 H8
Pontneddfechan Powys 24 H6
Pontnewydd Torf 15 B8
Pontrhydfendigaid Ceredig 24 B4
Pontrhydyfen Neath 14 B3
Pontrilas Hereford 25 F10
Pontrobert Powys 33 D7
Ponts Green E Sus 12 E5
Pontshill Hereford 26 F3
Pontsticill M Tydf 25 G7
Pontwgan Conwy 41 C9
Pontyates Carms 23 F9
Pontyberem Carms 23 E10
Pontyclun Rhondda 14 C6
Pontycymer Bridgend 14 B5
Pontyglasier Pembs 22 C6
Pontypool = Pont-y-Pŵl Torf 15 A8
Pontypridd Rhondda 14 C6
Pontywaun Caerph 15 B8
Pooksgreen Hants 10 C2
Pool Corn 2 E5
Pool W Yorks 51 E8
Pool o' Muckhart Clack 76 G3
Pool Quay Powys 33 D8
Poole Poole 9 E9
Poole Keynes Glos 16 B6
Poolend Staffs 44 G3
Poolewe Highld 91 J13
Pooley Bridge Cumb 56 D6
Poolfold Staffs 44 G2
Poolhill Glos 26 F4
Poolsbrook Derbys 45 E8
Pootings Kent 19 G11
Pope Hill Pembs 22 E4
Popeswood Brack 18 E5
Popham Hants 18 G2
Poplar London 19 C10
Popley Hants 18 F3
Porchester Nottingham 36 A1
Porchfield IoW 10 E3
Porin Highld 86 F6
Poringland Norf 39 E8
Porkellis Corn 2 F5
Porlock Som 7 B7
Porlock Weir Som 7 B7
Port Ann Argyll 73 E8
Port Appin Argyll 74 C2
Port Arthur Shetland 96 K5
Port Askaig Argyll 64 B5
Port Bannatyne Argyll 73 G9
Port Carlisle Cumb 61 G8
Port Charlotte Argyll 64 C3
Port Clarence Stockton 58 D5
Port Driseach Argyll 73 F8
Port e Vullen IoM 48 C4
Port Ellen Argyll 64 D4
Port Elphinstone Aberds 83 B9
Port Erin IoM 48 F1
Port Erroll Aberds 89 E10
Port-Eynon Swansea 23 H9
Port Gaverne Corn 3 A9
Port Glasgow Invclyd 68 C2
Port Henderson Highld 85 A12
Port Isaac Corn 3 A8
Port Lamont Argyll 73 F9
Port Lion Pembs 22 F4
Port Logan Dumfries 54 E3
Port Mholair W Isles 91 D10
Port Mor Highld 78 D7
Port Mulgrave N Yorks 59 E8
Port Nan Giùran W Isles 91 D10
Port nan Long W Isles 84 A3
Port Nis W Isles 91 A10
Port of Menteith Stirling 75 G8
Port Quin Corn 3 A8
Port Ramsay Argyll 79 G11
Port St Mary IoM 48 F2
Port Sunlight Mers 42 D6
Port Talbot Neath 14 B3
Port Tennant Swansea 14 B2
Port Wemyss Argyll 64 C2
Port William Dumfries 54 E6
Portachoillan Argyll 72 H6
Portavadie Argyll 73 G8
Portbury N Som 15 D11
Portchester Hants 10 D5
Portclair Highld 80 B6
Portencalzie Dumfries 54 B3
Portencross N Ayrs 66 B4
Portesham Dorset 8 F5
Portessie Moray 88 B4
Portfield Gate Pembs 22 E4
Portgate Devon 4 C5
Portgordon Moray 88 B3
Portgower Highld 93 H13
Porth Corn 3 C7
Porth Rhondda 14 B6
Porth Navas Corn 3 G6
Porth Tywyn = Burry Port Carms 23 F9
Porth-y-waen Shrops 33 C8
Porthaethwy = Menai Bridge Anglesey 41 C7
Porthallow Corn 3 G6
Porthallow Corn 4 F3
Porthcawl Bridgend 14 D4
Porthcothan Corn 3 B7
Porthcurno Corn 2 G2
Porthgain Pembs 22 C3
Porthill Shrops 33 D10
Porthkerry V Glam 14 E6
Porthleven Corn 2 G5
Porthllechog Anglesey 40 A6
Porthmadog Gwyn 41 G7
Porthmeor Corn 2 F3
Portholland Corn 3 E8
Porthoustock Corn 3 G7
Porthpean Corn 3 D9
Porthtowan Corn 2 E5
Porthyrhyd Carms 23 E10
Porthyrhyd Carms 24 E4
Portincaple Argyll 73 D11
Portington E Yorks 52 F3
Portinnisherrich Argyll 73 B8
Portinscale Cumb 56 D4
Portishead N Som 15 D10
Portkil Argyll 73 E11
Portknockie Moray 88 B4
Portlethen Aberds 83 D11
Portling Dumfries 55 D11
Portloe Corn 3 F8
Portmahomack Highld 87 C12
Portmeirion Gwyn 41 G7
Portmellon Corn 3 E9
Portmore Hants 10 E2
Portnacroish Argyll 74 C2
Portnahaven Argyll 64 C2
Portnalong Highld 85 E8
Portnaluchaig Highld 79 C9
Portnancon Highld 92 C7
Portnellan Stirling 75 E7
Portobello Edin 70 C2
Porton Wilts 17 H8
Portpatrick Dumfries 54 D3
Portreath Corn 2 E5
Portree Highld 85 D9
Portscatho Corn 3 F7
Portsea Ptsmth 10 D5
Portskerra Highld 93 C11
Portskewett Mon 15 C11
Portslade Brighton 12 F1
Portslade-by-Sea Brighton 12 F1
Portsmouth Ptsmth 10 D5
Portsmouth W Yorks 50 G5
Portsonachan Argyll 74 E3
Portsoy Aberds 88 B5
Portswood Soton 10 C3
Porttanachy Moray 88 B3
Portuairk Highld 78 E7
Portway Hereford 25 E11
Portway Worcs 27 A7
Portwrinkle Corn 4 F4
Poslingford Suff 30 D4
Postbridge Devon 5 D7
Postcombe Oxon 18 B4
Postling Kent 13 C10
Postwick Norf 39 E8
Potholm Dumfries 61 E9
Potsgrove C Beds 28 F6
Pott Row Norf 38 C3
Pott Shrigley Ches E 44 E3
Potten End Herts 29 H7
Potter Brompton N Yorks 52 B5
Potter Heigham Norf 39 D10
Potter Street Essex 29 H11
Potterhanworth Lincs 46 F4
Potterhanworth Booths Lincs 46 F4
Potterne Wilts 16 F6
Potterne Wick Wilts 17 F7
Potternewton W Yorks 51 F9
Potters Bar Herts 19 A9
Potter's Cross Staffs 34 G4
Potterspury Northants 28 D4
Potterton Aberds 83 B11
Potterton W Yorks 51 F10
Potto N Yorks 58 F5
Potton C Beds 29 D9
Poughill Corn 6 F1
Poughill Devon 7 F7
Poulshot Wilts 16 F6
Poulton Glos 17 A8
Poulton Mers 42 C6
Poulton-le-Fylde Lancs 49 F3
Pound Bank Worcs 26 A4
Pound Green E Sus 12 D4
Pound Green IoW 10 F2
Pound Green Worcs 34 H3
Pound Hill W Sus 12 C1
Poundfield E Sus 12 C4
Poundland S Ayrs 66 H4
Poundon Bucks 28 F3
Poundsgate Devon 5 D8
Poundstock Corn 4 B3
Powburn Northumb 62 B6
Powderham Devon 5 C10
Powerstock Dorset 8 E4
Powfoot Dumfries 61 G7
Powick Worcs 26 C5
Powmill Perth 76 H3
Poxwell Dorset 8 F6
Poyle Slough 19 D7
Poynings W Sus 12 E1
Poyntington Dorset 8 C5
Poynton Ches E 44 D3
Poynton Green Telford 34 D1
Poystreet Green Suff 30 C6
Praa Sands Corn 2 G4
Pratt's Bottom London 19 E11
Praze Corn 2 F4
Praze-an-Beeble Corn 2 F5
Predannack Wollas Corn 2 H5
Prees Shrops 34 B1
Prees Green Shrops 34 B1
Prees Heath Shrops 34 B1
Prees Higher Heath Shrops 34 B1
Prees Lower Heath Shrops 34 B1
Preesall Lancs 49 E3
Preesgweene Shrops 33 B8
Prenderguest Borders 71 E8
Prendwick Northumb 62 B6
Prengwyn Ceredig 23 B9
Prenteg Gwyn 41 F7
Prenton Mers 42 D6
Prescot Mers 43 C7
Prescott Shrops 33 C10
Pressen Northumb 71 G7
Prestatyn Denb 42 D3
Prestbury Ches E 44 E3
Prestbury Glos 26 F6
Presteigne = Llanandras Powys 25 B10
Presthope Shrops 34 F1
Prestleigh Som 16 G3
Preston Borders 70 E6
Preston Brighton 12 F2
Preston Devon 5 D9
Preston Dorset 8 F6
Preston E Loth 70 C4
Preston E Yorks 53 F7
Preston Glos 17 A7
Preston Glos 26 E3
Preston Herts 29 F8
Preston Kent 21 E9
Preston Kent 21 E7
Preston Lancs 49 G5
Preston Northumb 71 H11
Preston Rutland 36 E4
Preston Shrops 33 D11
Preston Wilts 17 D7
Preston Wilts 17 D9
Preston Bagot Warks 27 B8
Preston Bissett Bucks 28 F3
Preston Bowyer Som 7 D10
Preston Brockhurst Shrops 33 C11
Preston Brook Halton 43 D8
Preston Candover Hants 18 G3
Preston Capes Northants 28 C2
Preston Crowmarsh Oxon 18 B3
Preston Gubbals Shrops 33 D10
Preston on Stour Warks 27 C9
Preston on the Hill Halton 43 D8
Preston on Wye Hereford 25 D10
Preston Plucknett Som 8 C4
Preston St Mary Suff 30 C6
Preston-under-Scar N Yorks 58 G1
Preston upon the Weald Moors Telford 34 D2
Preston Wynne Hereford 26 D2
Prestonmill Dumfries 60 H5
Prestonpans E Loth 70 C2
Prestwich Gtr Man 44 B2
Prestwick Northumb 63 F7
Prestwick S Ayrs 67 D6
Prestwood Bucks 18 A5
Price Town Bridgend 14 B5
Prickwillow Cambs 38 G1
Priddy Som 15 F11
Priest Hutton Lancs 49 B5
Priest Weston Shrops 33 F8
Priesthaugh Borders 61 C10
Primethorpe Leics 35 F11
Primrose Green Norf 39 D6
Primrose Valley N Yorks 53 B7
Primrosehill Herts 19 A7
Princes Gate Pembs 22 E6
Princes Risborough Bucks 18 A5
Princethorpe Warks 27 A11
Princetown Caerph 25 G8
Princetown Devon 5 D6
Prion Denb 42 F3
Prior Muir Fife 77 F8
Prior Park Northumb 71 E8
Priors Frome Hereford 26 E2
Priors Hardwick Warks 27 C11
Priors Marston Warks 27 C11
Priorslee Telford 34 D3
Priory Wood Hereford 25 D9
Priston Bath 16 E3
Pristow Green Norf 39 G7
Prittlewell Southend 20 C5
Privett Hants 10 B5
Prixford Devon 6 C4
Probus Corn 3 E7
Proncy Highld 87 B10
Prospect Cumb 56 B3
Prudhoe Northumb 62 G6
Ptarmigan Lodge Stirling 74 G6
Pubil Perth 75 C7
Puckeridge Herts 29 F10
Puckington Som 8 C2
Pucklechurch S Glos 16 D3
Pucknall Hants 10 B2
Puckrup Glos 26 E5
Puddinglake Ches W 43 F10
Puddington Ches W 42 E6
Puddington Devon 7 E7
Puddledock Norf 39 F6
Puddletown Dorset 9 E6
Pudleston Hereford 26 C2
Pudsey W Yorks 51 F8
Pulborough W Sus 11 C9
Puleston Telford 34 C3
Pulford Ches W 43 G6
Pulham Dorset 8 D6
Pulham Market Norf 39 G7
Pulham St Mary Norf 39 G8
Pulloxhill C Beds 29 E7
Pumpherston W Loth 69 D9
Pumsaint Carms 24 D3
Puncheston Pembs 22 D5
Puncknowle Dorset 8 F4
Punnett's Town E Sus 12 D5
Purbrook Hants 10 D5
Purewell Dorset 9 E10
Purfleet Thurrock 20 D2
Puriton Som 15 G9
Purleigh Essex 20 A5
Purley London 19 E10
Purley W Berks 18 D3
Purlogue Shrops 33 H8
Purls Bridge Cambs 37 G10
Purse Caundle Dorset 8 C5
Purslow Shrops 33 G9
Purston Jaglin W Yorks 51 H10
Purton Glos 16 A3
Purton Glos 16 A3
Purton Wilts 17 C7
Purton Stoke Wilts 17 B7
Pury End Northants 28 D4
Pusey Oxon 17 B10
Putley Hereford 26 E3
Putney London 19 D9
Putsborough Devon 6 B3
Puttenham Herts 28 G5
Puttenham Sur 18 G6
Puxton N Som 15 E10
Pwll Carms 23 F9
Pwll-glas Denb 42 G4
Pwll-trap Carms 23 E7
Pwll-y-glaw Neath 14 B3
Pwllcrochan Pembs 22 F4
Pwllgloyw Powys 25 E7
Pwllheli Gwyn 40 G5
Pwllmeyric Mon 15 B11
Pye Corner Newport 15 C9
Pye Green Staffs 34 D5
Pyecombe W Sus 12 E1
Pyewipe NE Lincs 46 A6
Pyle = Y Pîl Bridgend 14 C4
Pyle IoW 10 G3
Pylle Som 16 H3
Pymoor Cambs 37 G10
Pyrford Sur 19 F7
Pyrton Oxon 18 B3
Pytchley Northants 28 A5
Pyworthy Devon 6 F2

Q

Quabbs Shrops 33 G8
Quadring Lincs 37 B8
Quainton Bucks 28 G4
Quarley Hants 17 G9
Quarndon Derbys 35 A9
Quarrier's Homes Invclyd 68 D2
Quarrington Lincs 37 A6
Quarrington Hill Durham 58 C4
Quarry Bank W Mid 34 G5
Quarryford E Loth 70 D4
Quarryhill Highld 87 C10
Quarrywood Moray 88 B1
Quarter S Lanark 68 E6
Quatford Shrops 34 F3
Quatt Shrops 34 G3
Quebec Durham 58 B2
Quedgeley Glos 26 G5
Queen Adelaide Cambs 38 G1
Queen Camel Som 8 B4
Queen Charlton Bath 16 E3
Queen Dart Devon 7 E7
Queen Oak Dorset 9 A6
Queen Street Kent 20 G3
Queen Street Wilts 17 C7
Queenborough Kent 20 D6
Queenhill Worcs 26 E5
Queen's Head Shrops 33 C9
Queen's Park Bedford 29 D7
Queen's Park Northants 28 B4
Queensbury W Yorks 51 F7
Queensferry Edin 69 C10
Queensferry Flint 42 F6
Queenstown Blackpool 49 F3
Queenzieburn N Lanark 68 C5
Quemerford Wilts 17 E7
Quendale Shetland 96 M5
Quendon Essex 30 E2
Queniborough Leics 36 D2
Quenington Glos 17 A8
Quernmore Lancs 49 D5
Quethiock Corn 4 E4
Quholm Orkney 95 G3
Quicks Green W Berks 18 D2
Quidenham Norf 38 G6
Quidhampton Hants 18 F2
Quidhampton Wilts 9 A10
Quilquox Aberds 89 E9
Quina Brook Shrops 33 B11
Quindry Orkney 95 J5
Quinton Northants 28 C4
Quinton W Mid 34 G5
Quintrell Downs Corn 3 C7
Quixhill Staffs 35 A7
Quoditch Devon 6 G3
Quoig Perth 75 E11
Quorndon Leics 36 D1
Quothquan S Lanark 69 G8
Quoyloo Orkney 95 F3
Quoyness Orkney 95 H3
Quoys Shetland 96 B8
Quoys Shetland 96 G6

R

Raasay Ho. Highld 85 E10
Rabbit's Cross Kent 20 G4
Raby Mers 42 E6
Rachan Mill Borders 69 G10
Rachub Gwyn 41 D8
Rackenford Devon 7 E7
Rackham W Sus 11 C9
Rackheath Norf 39 D8
Racks Dumfries 60 F6
Rackwick Orkney 95 D5
Rackwick Orkney 95 J3
Radbourne Derbys 35 B8
Radcliffe Gtr Man 43 B10
Radcliffe Northumb 63 C8
Radcliffe on Trent Notts 36 B2
Radclive Bucks 28 E3
Radcot Oxon 17 B9
Raddery Highld 87 F10
Radernie Fife 77 G7
Radford Semele Warks 27 B10
Radipole Dorset 8 F5
Radlett Herts 19 B8
Radley Oxon 18 B2
Radmanthwaite Notts 45 F9
Radmoor Shrops 34 C2
Radmore Green Ches E 43 G8
Radnage Bucks 18 B4
Radstock Bath 16 F3
Radstone Northants 28 D2
Radway Warks 27 D10
Radway Green Ches E 43 G10
Radwell Bedford 29 C7
Radwell Herts 29 E9
Radwinter Essex 30 E3
Radyr Cardiff 15 C7
Rafford Moray 87 F13
Ragdale Leics 36 D2
Raglan Mon 25 H11
Ragnall Notts 46 E2
Rahane Argyll 73 E11
Rainford Mers 43 B7
Rainford Junction Mers 43 B7
Rainham London 20 C2
Rainham Medway 20 E5
Rainhill Mers 43 C7
Rainhill Stoops Mers 43 C8
Rainow Ches E 44 E3
Rainton N Yorks 51 B9
Rainworth Notts 45 G9
Raisbeck Cumb 57 F8
Raise Cumb 57 B9
Rait Perth 76 E5
Raithby Lincs 47 D7
Raithby Lincs 47 F7
Rake W Sus 11 B7
Rakewood Gtr Man 44 A3
Ram Carms 23 B10
Ram Lane Kent 20 G6
Ramasaig Highld 84 D6
Rame Corn 2 F6
Rame Corn 4 G5
Rameldry Mill Bank Fife 76 G6
Ramnageo Shetland 96 C8
Rampisham Dorset 8 D4
Rampside Cumb 49 C2
Rampton Cambs 29 B11
Rampton Notts 45 E11
Ramsbottom Gtr Man 50 H3
Ramsbury Wilts 17 D9
Ramscraigs Highld 94 H3
Ramsdean Hants 10 B6
Ramsdell Hants 18 F2
Ramsden Oxon 27 G10
Ramsden Bellhouse Essex 20 B4
Ramsden Heath Essex 20 B4
Ramsey Cambs 37 G8
Ramsey Essex 31 E9
Ramsey IoM 48 C4
Ramsey Forty Foot Cambs 37 G9
Ramsey Heights Cambs 37 G8
Ramsey Island Essex 30 H6
Ramsey Mereside Cambs 37 G8
Ramsey St Mary's Cambs 37 G8
Ramseycleuch Borders 61 B8
Ramsgate Kent 21 E10
Ramsgill N Yorks 51 B7
Ramshorn Staffs 44 H4
Ramsnest Common Sur 11 A8
Ranais W Isles 91 E9
Ranby Lincs 46 E6
Ranby Notts 45 D10
Rand Lincs 46 E5
Randwick Glos 26 H5
Ranfurly Renfs 68 D2
Rangag Highld 94 F3
Rangemore Staffs 35 C7
Rangeworthy S Glos 16 C3
Rankinston E Ayrs 67 E7
Ranmoor S Yorks 45 D7
Ranmore Common Sur 19 F8
Rannerdale Cumb 56 E3
Rannoch Station Perth 75 B7
Ranochan Highld 79 C11
Ranskill Notts 45 D10
Ranton Staffs 34 C4
Ranworth Norf 39 D9
Raploch Stirling 68 A6
Rapness Orkney 95 D6
Rascal Moor E Yorks 52 F4
Rascarrel Dumfries 55 E10
Rashiereive Aberds 89 F9
Raskelf N Yorks 51 B10
Rassau Bl Gwent 25 G8
Rastrick W Yorks 51 G7
Ratagan Highld 85 G14
Ratby Leics 35 E11
Ratcliffe Culey Leics 35 F9
Ratcliffe on Soar Leics 35 C10
Ratcliffe on the Wreake Leics 36 D2
Rathen Aberds 89 B10
Rathillet Fife 76 E6
Rathmell N Yorks 50 D4
Ratho Edin 69 C10
Ratho Station Edin 69 C10
Rathven Moray 88 B4
Ratley Warks 27 D10
Ratlinghope Shrops 33 F10
Rattar Highld 94 C4
Ratten Row Lancs 49 E4
Rattery Devon 5 E8
Rattlesden Suff 30 C6
Rattray Perth 76 C4
Raughton Head Cumb 56 B5
Raunds Northants 28 A6
Ravenfield S Yorks 45 C8
Ravenglass Cumb 56 G2
Raveningham Norf 39 F9
Ravenscar N Yorks 59 F10
Ravenscraig Invclyd 73 F11
Ravensdale IoM 48 C3
Ravensden Bedford 29 C7
Ravenseat N Yorks 57 F10
Ravenshead Notts 45 G9
Ravensmoor Ches E 43 G9
Ravensthorpe Northants 28 A3
Ravensthorpe W Yorks 51 G8
Ravenstone Leics 35 D10
Ravenstone M Keynes 28 C5
Ravenstonedale Cumb 57 F9
Ravenstown Cumb 49 B3
Ravenstruther S Lanark 69 F8
Ravensworth N Yorks 58 F2
Raw N Yorks 59 F10
Rawcliffe E Yorks 52 G2
Rawcliffe York 52 D1
Rawcliffe Bridge E Yorks 52 G2
Rawdon W Yorks 51 F8
Rawmarsh S Yorks 45 C8
Rawreth Essex 20 B4
Rawridge Devon 7 F11
Rawtenstall Lancs 50 G4
Raxton Aberds 89 E8
Raydon Suff 31 E7
Raylees Northumb 62 D5
Rayleigh Essex 20 B5
Rayne Essex 30 F4
Rayners Lane London 19 C8
Raynes Park London 19 E9
Reach Cambs 30 B2
Read Lancs 50 F3
Reading Reading 18 D4
Reading Street Kent 13 C8
Reagill Cumb 57 E8
Rearquhar Highld 87 B10
Rearsby Leics 36 D2
Reaster Highld 94 D4
Reawick Shetland 96 J5
Reay Highld 93 C12
Rechullin Highld 85 C13
Reculver Kent 21 E9
Red Dial Cumb 56 B4
Red Hill Worcs 26 C5
Red Houses Jersey 11
Red Lodge Suff 30 A3
Red Rail Hereford 26 F2
Red Rock Gtr Man 43 B8
Red Roses Carms 23 E7
Red Row Northumb 63 D8
Red Street Staffs 44 G2
Red Wharf Bay Anglesey 41 B7
Redberth Pembs 22 F5
Redbourn Herts 29 G8
Redbourne N Lincs 46 C3
Redbrook Mon 26 G2
Redbrook Wrex 33 A11
Redburn Highld 87 E8
Redburn Highld 87 G12
Redburn Northumb 62 G3
Redcar Redcar 59 D7
Redcastle Angus 77 B9
Redcastle Highld 87 G8
Redcliff Bay N Som 15 D10
Redding Falk 69 C8
Reddingmuirhead Falk 69 C8
Reddish Gtr Man 44 C2
Redditch Worcs 27 B7
Rede Suff 30 C5
Redenhall Norf 39 G8
Redesdale Camp Northumb 62 D4
Redesmouth Northumb 62 E4
Redford Aberds 83 F9
Redford Angus 77 C8
Redford Durham 58 C1
Redfordgreen Borders 61 B9
Redgorton Perth 76 E3
Redgrave Suff 38 H6
Redhill Aberds 83 C9
Redhill Aberds 89 E6
Redhill N Som 15 E11
Redhill Sur 19 F9
Redhouse Argyll 73 G7
Redhouses Argyll 64 B4
Redisham Suff 39 G10
Redland Bristol 16 D2
Redland Orkney 95 F4
Redlingfield Suff 31 A8
Redlynch Som 8 A6
Redlynch Wilts 9 B11
Redmarley D'Abitot Glos 26 E4
Redmarshall Stockton 58 D4
Redmile Leics 36 B3
Redmire N Yorks 58 G1
Redmoor Corn 4 E1
Rednal Shrops 33 C9
Redpath Borders 70 G4
Redpoint Highld 85 B12
Redruth Corn 2 E
Redvales Gtr Man 44 B
Redwick Newport 15 C1
Redwick S Glos 15 C1
Redworth Darl 58 D
Reed Herts 29 E1
Reedham Norf 39 E1
Reedness E Yorks 52 G
Reeds Beck Lincs 46 F
Reepham Lincs 46 E
Reepham Norf 39 C
Reeth N Yorks 58 G
Regaby IoM 48 C
Regoul Highld 87 F1
Reiff Highld 92 H
Reigate Sur 19 F
Reighton N Yorks 53 B
Reighton Gap N Yorks 53 B
Reinigeadal W Isles 90 G
Reiss Highld 94 E
Rejerrah Corn 3 D
Releath Corn 2 F
Relubbus Corn 2 F
Relugas Moray 87 G1
Remenham Wokingham 18 C
Remenham Hill Wokingham 18 C
Remony Perth 75 C1
Rempstone Notts 36 C
Rendcomb Glos 27 H
Rendham Suff 31 B1
Rendlesham Suff 31 C1
Renfrew Renfs 68 D
Renhold Bedford 29 C
Renishaw Derbys 45 E
Rennington Northumb 63 B
Renton W Dunb 68 C
Renwick Cumb 57 B
Repps Norf 39 D1
Repton Derbys 35 C
Reraig Highld 85 F1
Rescobie Angus 77 B
Resipole Highld 79 E1
Resolis Highld 87 E
Resolven Neath 14 A
Reston Borders 71 D
Reswallie Angus 77 B
Retew Corn 3 D
Retford Notts 45 D1
Rettendon Essex 20 B
Rettendon Place Essex 20 B
Revesby Lincs 46 F
Revesby Bridge Lincs 47 F
Rew Street IoW 10 E
Rewe Devon 7 G
Reydon Suff 39 H1
Reydon Smear Suff 39 H1
Reymerston Norf 38 E
Reynalton Pembs 22 F
Reynoldston Swansea 23 G
Rezare Corn 4 D
Rhôs Carms 23 C
Rhôs Neath 14 A
Rhlŷd-y-foel Conwy 42 E
Rhaeadr Gwy = Rhayader Powys 24 B
Rhandirmwyn Carms 24 D
Rhayader = Rhaeadr Gwy Powys 24 B
Rhedyn Gwyn 40 G
Rhemore Highld 79 F
Rhencullen IoM 48 C
Rhes-y-cae Flint 42 E
Rhewl Denb 42 F
Rhewl Denb 42 H
Rhian Highld 93 H
Rhicarn Highld 92 G
Rhiconich Highld 92 D
Rhicullen Highld 87 D
Rhidorroch Ho. Highld 86 B
Rhifail Highld 93 E1
Rhigos Rhondda 24 H
Rhilochan Highld 93 J1
Rhiroy Highld 86 C
Rhisga = Risca Caerph 15 B
Rhiw Gwyn 40 H
Rhiwabon = Ruabon Wrex 33 A
Rhiwbina Cardiff 15 C
Rhiwbryfdir Gwyn 41 F
Rhiwderin Newport 15 C
Rhiwlas Gwyn 32 B
Rhiwlas Gwyn 41 D
Rhiwlas Powys 33 B
Rhodes Gtr Man 44 B
Rhodes Minnis Kent 21 G
Rhodesia Notts 45 E
Rhodiad Pembs 22 D
Rhondda Rhondda 14 B
Rhonehouse or Kelton Hill Dumfries 55 D1
Rhoose = Y Rhws V Glam 14 E
Rhos-fawr Gwyn 40 G
Rhos-goch Powys 25 D
Rhos-hill Pembs 22 B
Rhos-on-Sea Conwy 41 B1
Rhos-y-brithdir Powys 33 C
Rhos-y-garth Ceredig 24 A
Rhos-y-gwaliau Gwyn 32 B
Rhos-y-llan Gwyn 40 G
Rhos-y-Madoc Wrex 33 A
Rhos-y-meirch Powys 25 B
Rhosaman Carms 24 G
Rhosbeirio Anglesey 40 A
Rhoscefnhir Anglesey 41 C
Rhoscolyn Anglesey 40 C
Rhoscrowther Pembs 22 F
Rhosesmor Flint 42 F
Rhosgadfan Gwyn 41 E
Rhosgoch Anglesey 40 B
Rhoshirwaun Gwyn 40 H
Rhoslan Gwyn 40 F
Rhoslefain Gwyn 32 E
Rhosllanerchrugog Wrex 42 H
Rhosmaen Carms 24 F
Rhosmeirch Anglesey 40 C
Rhosneigr Anglesey 40 C
Rhosnesni Wrex 42 G
Rhosrobin Wrex 42 G
Rhossili Swansea 23 H
Rhosson Pembs 22 D
Rhostryfan Gwyn 40 E
Rhostyllen Wrex 42 H
Rhosybol Anglesey 40 B
Rhu Argyll 73 E1
Rhu Argyll 73 G
Rhuallt Denb 42 E

huddall Heath Ches W 43 F8
huddlan Ceredig 23 B9
huddlan Denb 42 E3
hue Highld 86 B3
hulen Powys 25 D8
hunahaorine Argyll 65 D8
huthun = Ruthin Denb 42 G4
hyd Gwyn 41 F8
hyd Powys 32 E5
hyd-Ddu Gwyn 41 E7
hyd-moel-ddu Powys 33 H6
hyd-Rosser Ceredig 24 B2
hyd-uchaf Gwyn 32 B5
hyd-wen Gwyn 32 D3
hyd-y-clafdy Gwyn 40 G5
hyd-y-fro Neath 24 H4
hyd-y-gwin Swansea 14 A2
hyd-y-meirch Mon 25 H10
hyd-y-meudwy Denb 42 G4
hyd-y-pandy Swansea 14 A2
hyd-y-sarn Gwyn 41 F8
hyd-yr-onen Gwyn 32 E2
hydaman = Ammanford Carms 24 G3
hydargaeau Carms 23 D9
hydcymerau Carms 23 C10
hydd Worcs 26 D5
hydding Neath 14 B3
hydfudr Ceredig 24 B2
hydlewis Ceredig 23 B8
hydlios Gwyn 40 G3
hydlydan Conwy 41 E10
hydness Powys 25 D8
hydowen Ceredig 23 B9
hydspence Hereford 25 D9
hydtalog Flint 42 G5
hydwyn Anglesey 40 B5
hydycroesau Powys 33 B8
hydyfelin Ceredig 32 H1
hydyfelin Rhondda 14 C6
hydymain Gwyn 32 C4
hydymwyn Flint 42 F5
hyl = Y Rhyl Denb 42 D3
hymney = Rhymni Caerph 25 H8
hymni = Rhymney Caerph 25 H8
hynd Fife 77 E7
hynd Perth 76 E4
hynie Aberds 82 A6
hynie Highld 87 D11
ibbesford Worcs 26 A4
ibblehead N Yorks 50 B3
ibbleton Lancs 50 F1
ibchester Lancs 50 F2
ibigill Highld 93 D8
iby Lincs 46 B5
iby Cross Roads Lincs 46 B5
iccall N Yorks 52 F2
iccarton E Ayrs 67 C7
ichards Castle Hereford 25 B11
ichings Park Bucks 19 D7
ichmond London 19 D8
ichmond N Yorks 58 F2
ickarton Aberds 83 E10
ickinghall Suff 38 H6
ickleton T&W 58 A3
ickling Essex 29 E11
ickmansworth Herts 19 B7
iddings Cumb 61 F10
iddings Derbys 45 G8
iddlecombe Devon 6 E5
iddlesden W Yorks 51 E6
iddrie Glasgow 68 D5
idge Dorset 9 F8
idge Hants 10 C2
idge Wilts 9 A8
idge Green Sur 19 G10
idge Lane Warks 35 F8
idgebourne Powys 25 B7
idgehill N Som 15 E11
idgeway Cross Hereford 26 D4
idgewell Essex 30 D4
idgewood E Sus 12 E3
idgmont C Beds 28 E6
iding Mill Northumb 62 G6
idleywood Wrex 43 G7
idlington Norf 39 B9
idlington Rutland 36 E4
idsdale Northumb 62 E5
iechip Perth 76 C3
iemore Perth 76 C3
ienachait Highld 92 F3
ievaulx N Yorks 59 H6
ift House Hrtlpl 58 C5
igg Dumfries 61 G8
iggend N Lanark 68 C6
igsby Lincs 47 E8
igside S Lanark 69 G7
iley Green Lancs 50 G2
ileyhill Staffs 35 D7
illa Mill Corn 4 D3
illington N Yorks 52 B4
imington Lancs 50 E4
impton Som 8 B5
imswell E Yorks 53 G9
inaston Pembs 22 D4
ingasta Shetland 96 M5
ingford Dumfries 55 D9
inginglow S Yorks 44 D6
ingland Norf 39 D7
ingles Cross E Sus 12 D3
ingmer E Sus 12 E3
ingmore Devon 5 G7
ingorm Moray 88 D2
ing's End Cambs 37 E9
ingsfield Suff 39 G10
ingsfield Corner Suff 39 G10
ingshall Herts 28 G6
ingshall Suff 31 C7
ingshall Stocks Suff 31 C7
ingstead Norf 38 A3
ingstead Northants 36 H5
ingwood Hants 9 D10
ingwould Kent 21 G10
inmore Aberds 82 B6
innigill Orkney 95 J4
insey Corn 2 G4
iof W Isles 90 D6
ipe E Sus 12 E4
ipley Derbys 45 G7
ipley Hants 9 E10
ipley N Yorks 51 C8
ipley Sur 19 F7
iplingham E Yorks 52 F5
ipon N Yorks 51 B9
ippingale Lincs 37 C6
ipple Kent 21 G10
ipple Worcs 26 E5
ipponden W Yorks 50 H6
ireavach Highld 86 B3
isabus Argyll 64 D4
Risbury Hereford 26 C2
Risby Suff 30 B4
Risca = Rhisga Caerph 15 B8
Rise E Yorks 53 E7
Riseden E Sus 12 C5
Risegate Lincs 37 C8
Riseholme Lincs 46 E3
Riseley Bedford 29 B7
Riseley Wokingham 18 E4
Rishangles Suff 31 B8
Rishton Lancs 50 F3
Rishworth W Yorks 50 H6
Rising Bridge Lancs 50 G3
Risley Derbys 35 B10
Risley Warr 43 C9
Risplith N Yorks 51 C8
Rispond Highld 92 C7
Rivar Wilts 17 E10
Rivenhall End Essex 30 G5
River Bank Cambs 30 B2
Riverhead Kent 20 F2
Rivington Lancs 43 A9
Roa Island Cumb 49 C2
Roachill Devon 7 D7
Road Green Norf 39 F8
Roade Northants 28 C4
Roadhead Cumb 61 F11
Roadmeetings S Lanark 69 F7
Roadside Highld 94 D3
Roadside of Catterline Aberds 83 F10
Roadside of Kinneff Aberds 83 F10
Roadwater Som 7 C9
Roag Highld 85 D7
Roath Cardiff 15 D7
Roberton Borders 61 B10
Roberton S Lanark 69 H8
Robertsbridge E Sus 12 D6
Roberttown W Yorks 51 G7
Robeston Cross Pembs 22 F3
Robeston Wathen Pembs 22 E5
Robin Hood W Yorks 51 G9
Robin Hood's Bay N Yorks 59 F10
Roborough Devon 4 E6
Roborough Devon 6 E4
Roby Mers 43 C7
Roby Mill Lancs 43 B8
Rocester Staffs 35 B7
Roch Pembs 22 D3
Roch Gate Pembs 22 D3
Rochdale Gtr Man 44 A2
Roche Corn 3 C8
Rochester Medway 20 E4
Rochester Northumb 62 D4
Rochford Essex 20 B5
Rock Corn 3 B8
Rock Northumb 63 A8
Rock W Sus 11 C10
Rock Worcs 26 A4
Rock Ferry Mers 42 D6
Rockbeare Devon 7 G9
Rockbourne Hants 9 C10
Rockcliffe Cumb 61 G9
Rockcliffe Dumfries 55 D11
Rockfield Highld 87 C12
Rockfield Mon 25 G11
Rockford Hants 9 D10
Rockhampton S Glos 16 B3
Rockingham Northants 36 F4
Rockland All Saints Norf 38 F5
Rockland St Mary Norf 39 E9
Rockland St Peter Norf 38 F5
Rockley Wilts 17 D8
Rockwell End Bucks 18 C4
Rockwell Green Som 7 D10
Rodborough Glos 16 A5
Rodbourne Swindon 17 C8
Rodbourne Wilts 16 C6
Rodbourne Cheney Swindon 17 C8
Rodd Hereford 25 B10
Roddam Northumb 62 A6
Rodden Dorset 8 F5
Rode Som 16 F5
Rode Heath Ches E 44 G2
Rodeheath Ches E 44 F2
Roden Telford 34 D1
Rodhuish Som 7 C9
Rodington Telford 34 D1
Rodley Glos 26 G4
Rodley W Yorks 51 F8
Rodmarton Glos 16 B6
Rodmell E Sus 12 F3
Rodmersham Kent 20 E6
Rodney Stoke Som 15 F10
Rodsley Derbys 35 A8
Rodway Som 15 H8
Rodwell Dorset 8 G5
Roe Green Herts 29 E10
Roecliffe N Yorks 51 C9
Roehampton London 19 D9
Roesound Shetland 96 G5
Roffey W Sus 11 A10
Rogart Highld 93 J10
Rogart Station Highld 93 J10
Rogate W Sus 11 B7
Rogerstone Newport 15 C8
Roghadal W Isles 90 J5
Rogiet Mon 15 C10
Rogue's Alley Cambs 37 E9
Roke Oxon 18 B3
Roker T&W 63 H10
Rollesby Norf 39 D10
Rolleston Leics 36 E3
Rolleston Notts 45 G11
Rolleston-on-Dove Staffs 35 C8
Rolston E Yorks 53 E8
Rolvenden Kent 13 C7
Rolvenden Layne Kent 13 C7
Romaldkirk Durham 57 D11
Romanby N Yorks 58 G4
Romannobridge Borders 69 F10
Romansleigh Devon 7 D6
Romford London 20 C2
Romiley Gtr Man 44 C3
Romsey Hants 10 B2
Romsey Town Cambs 29 C11
Romsley Shrops 34 G3
Romsley Worcs 34 H5
Ronague IoM 48 E2
Rookhope Durham 57 B11
Rookley IoW 10 F4
Rooks Bridge Som 15 F9
Roos E Yorks 53 F8
Roosebeck Cumb 49 C2
Rootham's Green Bedford 29 C8
Rootpark S Lanark 69 E8
Ropley Hants 10 A5
Ropley Dean Hants 10 A5
Ropsley Lincs 36 B5
Rora Aberds 89 C10
Rorandle Aberds 83 B8
Rorrington Shrops 33 E9
Roscroggan Corn 2 E5
Rose Corn 3 D6
Rose Ash Devon 7 D6
Rose Green W Sus 11 E8
Rose Grove Lancs 50 F4
Rose Hill E Sus 12 E3
Rose Hill Lancs 50 F4
Rose Hill Suff 31 D8
Roseacre Kent 20 F4
Roseacre Lancs 49 F4
Rosebank S Lanark 69 F7
Rosebrough Northumb 71 H10
Rosebush Pembs 22 D5
Rosecare Corn 4 B2
Rosedale Abbey N Yorks 59 G8
Roseden Northumb 62 A6
Rosefield Highld 87 F11
Rosehall Highld 92 J7
Rosehaugh Mains Highld 87 F9
Rosehearty Aberds 89 B9
Rosehill Shrops 34 B2
Roseisle Moray 88 B1
Roselands E Sus 12 F5
Rosemarket Pembs 22 F4
Rosemarkie Highld 87 F10
Rosemary Lane Devon 7 E10
Rosemount Perth 76 C4
Rosenannon Corn 3 C8
Rosewell Midloth 69 D11
Roseworth Stockton 58 D5
Roseworthy Corn 2 F5
Rosgill Cumb 57 E7
Roshven Highld 79 D10
Roskhill Highld 85 D7
Roskill House Highld 87 F9
Rosley Cumb 56 B5
Roslin Midloth 69 D11
Rosliston Derbys 35 D8
Rosneath Argyll 73 E11
Ross Dumfries 55 E9
Ross Northumb 71 G10
Ross Perth 75 E10
Ross-on-Wye Hereford 26 F3
Rossett Wrex 42 G6
Rossett Green N Yorks 51 D9
Rossie Ochill Perth 76 F3
Rossie Priory Perth 76 D5
Rossington S Yorks 45 C10
Rosskeen Highld 87 E9
Rossland Renfs 68 C3
Roster Highld 94 G4
Rostherne Ches E 43 D10
Rosthwaite Cumb 56 E4
Roston Derbys 35 A7
Rosyth Fife 69 B10
Rothbury Northumb 62 C6
Rotherby Leics 36 D2
Rotherfield E Sus 12 D4
Rotherfield Greys Oxon 18 C4
Rotherfield Peppard Oxon 18 C4
Rotherham S Yorks 45 C8
Rothersthorpe Northants 28 C4
Rotherwick Hants 18 F4
Rothes Moray 88 D2
Rothesay Argyll 73 G9
Rothiebrisbane Aberds 89 E7
Rothienorman Aberds 89 E7
Rothiesholm Orkney 95 F7
Rothley Leics 36 D1
Rothley Northumb 62 E6
Rothley Shield East Northumb 62 D6
Rothmaise Aberds 89 E6
Rothwell Lincs 46 C5
Rothwell Northants 36 G4
Rothwell W Yorks 51 G9
Rothwell Haigh W Yorks 51 G9
Rotsea E Yorks 53 D6
Rottal Angus 82 G5
Rotten End Suff 31 B10
Rottingdean Brighton 12 F2
Rottington Cumb 56 E1
Roud IoW 10 F4
Rough Close Staffs 34 B5
Rough Common Kent 21 F8
Rougham Norf 38 C4
Rougham Suff 30 B6
Rougham Green Suff 30 B6
Roughburn Highld 80 E5
Roughlee Lancs 50 E4
Roughley W Mid 35 F7
Roughsike Cumb 61 F11
Roughton Lincs 46 F6
Roughton Norf 39 B8
Roughton Shrops 34 F3
Roughton Moor Lincs 46 F6
Roundhay W Yorks 51 F9
Roundstonefoot Dumfries 61 C7
Roundstreet Common W Sus 11 B9
Roundway Wilts 17 E7
Rous Lench Worcs 27 C7
Rousdon Devon 8 E1
Routenburn N Ayrs 73 G10
Routh E Yorks 53 E6
Row Corn 4 D1
Row Cumb 56 H6
Row Heath Essex 31 G8
Rowanburn Dumfries 61 F10
Rowardennan Stirling 74 H6
Rowde Wilts 16 E6
Rowen Conwy 41 C9
Rowfoot Northumb 62 G2
Rowhedge Essex 31 F7
Rowhook W Sus 11 A10
Rowington Warks 27 B9
Rowland Derbys 44 E6
Rowlands Castle Hants 10 C6
Rowlands Gill T&W 63 H7
Rowledge Sur 18 G5
Rowlestone Hereford 25 F10
Rowley E Yorks 52 F5
Rowley Shrops 33 E9
Rowley Hill W Yorks 44 A5
Rowley Regis W Mid 34 G5
Rowly Sur 19 G7
Rowney Green Worcs 27 A7
Rownhams Hants 10 C2
Rowrah Cumb 56 E2
Rowsham Bucks 28 G5
Rowsley Derbys 44 F6
Rowstock Oxon 17 C11
Rowston Lincs 46 G4
Rowton Ches W 43 F7
Rowton Shrops 33 D9
Rowton Telford 34 D2
Roxburgh Borders 70 G6
Roxby N Lincs 52 H5
Roxby N Yorks 59 E8
Roxton Bedford 29 C8
Roxwell Essex 30 H3
Royal Leamington Spa Warks 27 B10
Royal Oak Darl 58 D3
Royal Oak Lancs 43 B7
Royal Tunbridge Wells Kent 12 C4
Roybridge Highld 80 E4
Roydhouse W Yorks 44 A6
Roydon Essex 29 H11
Roydon Norf 38 C3
Roydon Norf 39 G6
Roydon Hamlet Essex 29 H11
Royston Herts 29 D10
Royston S Yorks 45 A7
Royton Gtr Man 44 B3
Rozel Jersey 11
Ruabon = Rhiwabon Wrex 33 A9
Ruaig Argyll 78 G3
Ruan Lanihorne Corn 3 E7
Ruan Minor Corn 2 H6
Ruarach Highld 80 A1
Ruardean Glos 26 G3
Ruardean Woodside Glos 26 G3
Rubery Worcs 34 H5
Ruckcroft Cumb 57 B7
Ruckhall Hereford 25 E11
Ruckinge Kent 13 C9
Ruckland Lincs 47 E7
Ruckley Shrops 33 E11
Rudbaxton Pembs 22 D4
Rudby N Yorks 58 F5
Ruddington Notts 36 B1
Rudford Glos 26 F4
Rudge Shrops 34 F4
Rudge Som 16 F5
Rudgeway S Glos 16 C3
Rudgwick W Sus 11 A9
Rudhall Hereford 26 F3
Rudheath Ches W 43 E9
Rudley Green Essex 20 A5
Rudry Caerph 15 C7
Rudston E Yorks 53 C6
Rudyard Staffs 44 G3
Rufford Lancs 49 H4
Rufforth York 51 D11
Rugby Warks 35 H11
Rugeley Staffs 34 D6
Ruglen S Ayrs 66 F5
Ruilick Highld 87 G8
Ruishton Som 8 B1
Ruisigearraidh W Isles 90 J4
Ruislip London 19 C7
Ruislip Common London 19 C7
Rumbling Bridge Perth 76 H3
Rumburgh Suff 39 G9
Rumford Corn 3 B7
Rumney Cardiff 15 D8
Runcorn Halton 43 D8
Runcton W Sus 11 D7
Runcton Holme Norf 38 E2
Rundlestone Devon 5 D6
Runfold Sur 18 G5
Runhall Norf 39 E6
Runham Norf 39 D10
Runham Norf 39 E11
Runnington Som 7 D10
Runsell Green Essex 30 H4
Runswick Bay N Yorks 59 E9
Runwell Essex 20 B4
Ruscombe Wokingham 18 D4
Rush Green London 20 C2
Rush-head Aberds 89 D8
Rushall Hereford 26 E3
Rushall Norf 39 G7
Rushall W Mid 34 E6
Rushall Wilts 17 F8
Rushbrooke Suff 30 B5
Rushbury Shrops 33 F11
Rushden Herts 29 E10
Rushden Northants 28 B6
Rushenden Kent 20 D6
Rushford Norf 38 G5
Rushlake Green E Sus 12 E5
Rushmere Suff 39 G10
Rushmere St Andrew Suff 31 D9
Rushmoor Sur 18 G5
Rushock Worcs 26 A5
Rusholme Gtr Man 44 C2
Rushton Ches W 43 F8
Rushton Northants 36 G4
Rushton Shrops 34 E2
Rushton Spencer Staffs 44 F3
Rushwick Worcs 26 C5
Rushyford Durham 58 D3
Ruskie Stirling 75 G9
Ruskington Lincs 46 G4
Rusland Cumb 56 H5
Rusper W Sus 19 H9
Ruspidge Glos 26 G3
Russell's Water Oxon 18 C4
Russel's Green Suff 31 A9
Rusthall Kent 12 C4
Rustington W Sus 11 D9
Ruston N Yorks 52 A5
Ruston Parva E Yorks 53 C6
Ruswarp N Yorks 59 F9
Rutherford Borders 70 G5
Rutherglen S Lanark 68 D5
Ruthernbridge Corn 3 C9
Ruthin = Rhuthun Denb 42 G4
Ruthrieston Aberdeen 83 C11
Ruthven Aberds 88 D5
Ruthven Angus 76 C5
Ruthven Highld 81 D9
Ruthven Highld 87 H11
Ruthven House Angus 76 C6
Ruthvoes Corn 3 C8
Ruthwell Dumfries 60 G6
Ruyton-XI-Towns Shrops 33 C9
Ryal Northumb 62 F6
Ryal Fold Blackburn 50 G2
Ryall Dorset 8 E3
Ryarsh Kent 20 F3
Rydal Cumb 56 F5
Ryde IoW 10 E4
Rye E Sus 13 D8
Rye Foreign E Sus 13 D7
Rye Harbour E Sus 13 E8
Rye Park Herts 29 G10
Rye Street Worcs 26 E4
Ryecroft Gate Staffs 44 F3
Ryehill E Yorks 53 G8
Ryhall Rutland 36 D6
Ryhill W Yorks 45 A7
Ryhope T&W 58 A5
Rylstone N Yorks 50 D5
Ryme Intrinseca Dorset 8 C4
Ryther N Yorks 52 F1
Ryton Glos 26 E4
Ryton N Yorks 52 B3
Ryton Shrops 34 E3
Ryton T&W 63 G7
Ryton-on-Dunsmore Warks 27 A10

S

Sabden Lancs 50 F3
Sacombe Herts 29 G10
Sacriston Durham 58 B3
Sadberge Darl 58 E4
Saddell Argyll 65 E8
Saddington Leics 36 F2
Saddle Bow Norf 38 D2
Saddlescombe W Sus 12 E1
Sadgill Cumb 57 F6
Saffron Walden Essex 30 E2
Sageston Pembs 22 F5
Saham Hills Norf 38 E5
Saham Toney Norf 38 E5
Saighdinis W Isles 84 B3
Saighton Ches W 43 F7
St Abbs Borders 71 D8
St Abb's Haven Borders 71 D8
St Agnes Corn 2 D6
St Agnes Scilly 2 D2
St Albans Herts 29 H8
St Allen Corn 3 D7
St Andrews Fife 77 F8
St Andrew's Major V Glam 15 D7
St Anne Ald 11
St Annes Lancs 49 G3
St Ann's Dumfries 60 D6
St Ann's Chapel Corn 4 D5
St Ann's Chapel Devon 5 G7
St Anthony-in-Meneage Corn 3 G6
St Anthony's Hill E Sus 12 F5
St Arvans Mon 15 B11
St Asaph = Llanelwy Denb 42 E3
St Athan V Glam 14 E6
St Aubin Jersey 11
St Austell Corn 3 D9
St Bees Cumb 56 E1
St Blazey Corn 4 F1
St. Boswells Borders 70 G4
St Brelade Jersey 11
St Breock Corn 3 B8
St Breward Corn 4 D1
St Briavels Glos 16 A2
St Bride's Pembs 22 E3
St Brides Major V Glam 14 D4
St Bride's Netherwent Mon 15 C10
St Brides super Ely V Glam 14 D6
St Brides Wentlooge Newport 15 C8
St Budeaux Plym 4 F5
St Buryan Corn 2 G3
St Catherine Bath 16 D4
St Catherine's Argyll 73 C10
St Clears = Sanclêr Carms 23 E7
St Cleer Corn 4 E3
St Clement Corn 3 E7
St Clements Jersey 11
St Clether Corn 4 C3
St Colmac Argyll 73 G9
St Columb Major Corn 3 C8
St Columb Minor Corn 3 C7
St Columb Road Corn 3 D8
St Combs Aberds 89 B10
St Cross South Elmham Suff 39 G8
St Cyrus Aberds 77 A10
St David's = Tyddewi Pembs 22 D2
St David's Perth 76 E2
St Day Corn 2 E6
St Dennis Corn 3 D8
St Devereux Hereford 25 E11
St Dogmaels Pembs 22 B6
St Dogwells Pembs 22 D4
St Dominick Corn 4 E5
St Donat's V Glam 14 E5
St Edith's Wilts 16 E6
St Endellion Corn 3 B8
St Enoder Corn 3 D7
St Erme Corn 3 D7
St Erney Corn 4 F4
St Erth Corn 2 F4
St Ervan Corn 3 B7
St Eval Corn 3 C7
St Ewe Corn 3 E8
St Fagans Cardiff 15 D7
St Fergus Aberds 89 C10
St Fillans Perth 75 E9
St Florence Pembs 22 F5
St Genny's Corn 4 B2
St George Conwy 42 E2
St George's V Glam 14 D6
St Germans Corn 4 F4
St Giles Lincs 46 E3
St Giles in the Wood Devon 6 E4
St Giles on the Heath Devon 6 G2
St Harmon Powys 24 A6
St Helen Auckland Durham 58 D2
St Helena Warks 35 E8
St Helen's E Sus 13 E7
St Helens IoW 10 F5
St Helens Mers 43 C8
St Helier Jersey 11
St Helier London 19 E9
St Hilary Corn 2 F4
St Hilary V Glam 14 D6
Saint Hill W Sus 12 C2
St Illtyd Bl Gwent 15 A8
St Ippollytts Herts 29 F8
St Ishmael's Pembs 22 F3
St Issey Corn 3 B8
St Ive Corn 4 E4
St Ives Cambs 29 A10
St Ives Corn 2 E4
St Ives Dorset 9 D10
St James South Elmham Suff 39 G9
St Jidgey Corn 3 C8
St John Corn 4 F5
St John's IoM 48 D2
St John's Jersey 11
St John's Sur 18 F6
St John's Worcs 26 C5
St John's Chapel Durham 57 C10
St John's Fen End Norf 37 D11
St John's Highway Norf 37 D11
St John's Town of Dalry Dumfries 55 A9
St Judes IoM 48 C3
St Just in Roseland Corn 3 F7
St Just Corn 2 F2
St Katherine's Aberds 89 E7
St Keverne Corn 3 G6
St Kew Corn 3 B9
St Kew Highway Corn 3 B9
St Keyne Corn 4 E3
St Lawrence Corn 3 C9
St Lawrence Essex 20 A6
St Lawrence IoW 10 G4
St Leonard's Bucks 28 H6
St Leonards Dorset 9 D10
St Leonards E Sus 13 F6
Saint Leonards S Lanark 68 E5
St Levan Corn 2 G2
St Lythans V Glam 15 D7
St Mabyn Corn 3 B9
St Madoes Perth 76 E4
St Margaret South Elmham Suff 39 G9
St Margaret's Hereford 25 E10
St Margarets Herts 29 G10
St Margaret's at Cliffe Kent 21 G10
St Margaret's Hope Orkney 95 J5
St Mark's IoM 48 E2
St Martin Corn 4 F3
St Martins Corn 2 G6
St Martin's Jersey 11
St Martins Perth 76 D4
St Martin's Shrops 33 B9
St Mary Bourne Hants 17 F11
St Mary Church V Glam 14 D6
St Mary Cray London 19 E11
St Mary Hill V Glam 14 D5
St Mary Hoo Medway 20 D5
St Mary in the Marsh Kent 13 D9
St Mary's Jersey 11
St Mary's Orkney 95 H5
St Mary's Bay Kent 13 D9
St Maughans Mon 25 G11
St Mawes Corn 3 F7
St Mawgan Corn 3 C7
St Mellion Corn 4 E4
St Mellons Cardiff 15 C8
St Merryn Corn 3 B7
St Mewan Corn 3 D8
St Michael Caerhays Corn 3 E8
St Michael Penkevil Corn 3 E7
St Michael South Elmham Suff 39 G9
St Michael's Kent 13 C7
St Michaels Worcs 26 B2
St Michael's on Wyre Lancs 49 E4
St Minver Corn 3 B8
St Monans Fife 77 G8
St Neot Corn 4 E2
St Neots Cambs 29 B8
St Newlyn East Corn 3 D7
St Nicholas Pembs 22 C3
St Nicholas V Glam 14 D6
St Nicholas at Wade Kent 21 E9
St Ninians Stirling 68 A6
St Osyth Essex 31 G8
St Osyth Heath Essex 31 G8
St Ouens Jersey 11
St Owens Cross Hereford 26 F2
St Paul's Cray London 19 E11
St Paul's Walden Herts 29 F8
St Peter Port Guern 11
St Peter's Jersey 11
St Peter's Kent 21 E10
St Petrox Pembs 22 G4
St Pinnock Corn 4 E3
St Quivox S Ayrs 67 D6
St Ruan Corn 2 H6
St Sampson Guern 11
St Stephen Corn 3 D8
St Stephen's Corn 4 C4
St Stephens Corn 4 F5
St Stephens Herts 29 H8
St Teath Corn 4 C1
St Thomas Devon 7 G8
St Tudy Corn 4 D1
St Twynnells Pembs 22 G4
St Veep Corn 4 F2
St Vigeans Angus 77 C9
St Wenn Corn 3 C8
St Weonards Hereford 25 F11
Saintbury Glos 27 E8
Salcombe Devon 5 H8
Salcombe Regis Devon 7 H10
Salcott Essex 30 G6
Sale Gtr Man 43 C10
Sale Green Worcs 26 C6
Saleby Lincs 47 E8
Salehurst E Sus 12 D6
Salem Carms 24 F3
Salem Ceredig 32 G2
Salen Argyll 79 G8
Salen Highld 79 E9
Salesbury Lancs 50 F2
Salford C Beds 28 E6
Salford Gtr Man 44 C2
Salford Oxon 27 F9
Salford Priors Warks 27 C7
Salfords Sur 19 G9
Salhouse Norf 39 D9
Saline Fife 69 A9
Salisbury Wilts 9 B10
Sallachan Highld 74 A2
Sallachy Highld 86 H2
Sallachy Highld 93 J8
Salle Norf 39 C7
Salmonby Lincs 47 E7
Salmond's Muir Angus 77 D8
Salperton Glos 27 F7
Salph End Bedford 29 C7
Salsburgh N Lanark 69 D7
Salt Staffs 34 C5
Salt End E Yorks 53 G7
Saltaire W Yorks 51 F7
Saltash Corn 4 F5
Saltburn Highld 87 E10
Saltburn-by-the-Sea Redcar 59 D7
Saltby Leics 36 C4
Saltcoats Cumb 56 G2
Saltcoats N Ayrs 66 B5
Saltdean Brighton 12 F2
Salter Lancs 50 C2
Salterforth Lancs 50 E4
Salterswall Ches W 43 F9
Saltfleet Lincs 47 C8
Saltfleetby All Saints Lincs 47 C8
Saltfleetby St Clements Lincs 47 C8
Saltfleetby St Peter Lincs 47 D8
Saltford Bath 16 E3
Salthouse Norf 39 A6
Saltmarshe E Yorks 52 G3
Saltney Flint 43 F6
Salton N Yorks 52 B3
Saltwick Northumb 63 F7
Saltwood Kent 21 H8
Salum Argyll 78 G3
Salvington W Sus 11 D10
Salwarpe Worcs 26 B5
Salwayash Dorset 8 E3
Sambourne Warks 27 B7
Sambrook Telford 34 C3
Samhla W Isles 84 B2
Samlesbury Lancs 50 F1
Samlesbury Bottoms Lancs 50 G2
Sampford Arundel Som 7 E10
Sampford Brett Som 7 B9
Sampford Courtenay Devon 6 F5
Sampford Peverell Devon 7 E9
Sampford Spiney Devon 4 D6
Sampool Bridge Cumb 56 H6
Samuelston E Loth 70 C3
Sanachan Highld 85 D13
Sanaigmore Argyll 64 A3
Sanclêr = St Clears Carms 23 E7
Sancreed Corn 2 G3
Sancton E Yorks 52 F5
Sand Highld 86 B2
Sand Shetland 96 J5
Sand Hole E Yorks 52 F4
Sand Hutton N Yorks 52 D2
Sandaig Highld 85 H12
Sandal Magna W Yorks 51 H9
Sandale Cumb 56 B4
Sandbach Ches E 43 F10
Sandbank Argyll 73 E10
Sandbanks Poole 9 F9
Sandend Aberds 88 B5
Sanderstead London 19 E10
Sandfields Glos 26 F6
Sandford Cumb 57 E9
Sandford Devon 7 F7
Sandford Dorset 9 F8
Sandford IoW 10 F4
Sandford N Som 15 F10
Sandford S Lanark 68 F6
Sandford Shrops 34 B1
Sandford on Thames Oxon 18 A2
Sandford Orcas Dorset 8 B5
Sandford St Martin Oxon 27 F11
Sandfordhill Aberds 89 D11
Sandgate Kent 21 H8
Sandgreen Dumfries 55 D8
Sandhaven Aberds 89 B9
Sandhead Dumfries 54 E3
Sandhills Sur 18 H6
Sandhoe Northumb 62 G5
Sandholme E Yorks 52 F4
Sandholme Lincs 37 B9
Sandhurst Brack 18 E5
Sandhurst Glos 26 F5
Sandhurst Kent 13 D6
Sandhurst Cross Kent 13 D6
Sandhutton N Yorks 51 A9
Sandiacre Derbys 35 B10
Sandilands Lincs 47 D9
Sandilands S Lanark 69 G7
Sandiway Ches W 43 E9
Sandleheath Hants 9 C10
Sandling Kent 20 F4
Sandlow Green Ches E 43 F10
Sandness Shetland 96 H3
Sandon Essex 20 A4
Sandon Herts 29 E10
Sandon Staffs 34 B5
Sandown IoW 10 F4
Sandplace Corn 4 F3
Sandridge Herts 29 G8
Sandridge Wilts 16 E6
Sandringham Norf 38 C2
Sandsend N Yorks 59 E9
Sandside Ho. Highld 93 C12
Sandsound Shetland 96 J5
Sandtoft N Lincs 45 B11
Sandway Kent 20 F5
Sandwell W Mid 34 G6
Sandwich Kent 21 F10
Sandwick Cumb 56 E6
Sandwick Orkney 95 K5
Sandwick Shetland 96 L6
Sandwith Cumb 56 E1
Sandy C Beds 29 D8
Sandy Carms 23 F9
Sandy Bank Lincs 46 G6
Sandy Haven Pembs 22 F3
Sandy Lane Wilts 16 E6
Sandy Lane Wrex 33 A9
Sandycroft Flint 42 F6
Sandyford Dumfries 61 D8
Sandyford Stoke 44 G2
Sandygate IoM 48 C3
Sandyhills Dumfries 55 D11
Sandylands Lancs 49 C4
Sandypark Devon 5 C8
Sandysike Cumb 61 G9
Sangobeg Highld 92 C7
Sangomore Highld 92 C7
Sanna Highld 78 E7
Sanndabhaig W Isles 84 D3
Sanndabhaig W Isles 91 D9
Sannox N Ayrs 66 B3
Sanquhar Dumfries 60 C3
Santon N Lincs 46 A3
Santon Bridge Cumb 56 F3
Santon Downham Suff 38 G4
Sapcote Leics 35 F10
Sapey Common Hereford 26 B4
Sapiston Suff 38 H5
Sapley Cambs 29 A9
Sapperton Glos 16 A6
Sapperton Lincs 36 B6
Saracen's Head Lincs 37 C9
Sarclet Highld 94 F5
Sardis Carms 23 F10
Sarn Bridgend 14 C5
Sarn Powys 33 F8
Sarn Bach Gwyn 40 H5
Sarn Meyllteyrn Gwyn 40 G4
Sarnau Carms 23 E8
Sarnau Ceredig 23 A8
Sarnau Gwyn 32 B5
Sarnau Powys 25 E7
Sarnau Powys 33 D8
Sarnesfield Hereford 25 C10
Saron Carms 23 C8
Saron Carms 24 G3
Saron Denb 42 F3
Saron Gwyn 40 E6
Saron Gwyn 41 D7
Sarratt Herts 19 B7
Sarre Kent 21 E9
Sarsden Oxon 27 F9
Sarsgrum Highld 92 C6
Satley Durham 58 B2
Satron N Yorks 57 G11
Satterleigh Devon 6 D5
Satterthwaite Cumb 56 G5
Satwell Oxon 18 C4
Sauchen Aberds 83 B8
Saucher Perth 76 D4
Sauchie Clack 69 A7
Sauchieburn Aberds 83 G8
Saughall Ches W 42 E6
Saughtree Borders 61 D11
Saul Glos 26 H4
Saundby Notts 45 D11
Saundersfoot Pembs 22 F6
Saunderton Bucks 18 A4
Saunton Devon 6 C3
Sausthorpe Lincs 47 F7
Saval Highld 93 J8
Savary Highld 79 G9
Savile Park W Yorks 51 G6
Sawbridge Warks 28 B2
Sawbridgeworth Herts 29 G11
Sawdon N Yorks 59 H10
Sawley Derbys 35 B10
Sawley Lancs 50 E3
Sawley N Yorks 51 C8
Sawston Cambs 29 D11
Sawtry Cambs 37 G7
Saxby Leics 36 D4
Saxby Lincs 46 D4
Saxby All Saints N Lincs 52 H5
Saxelbye Leics 36 C3
Saxham Street Suff 31 B7
Saxilby Lincs 46 E2
Saxlingham Norf 38 B6
Saxlingham Green Norf 39 F8
Saxlingham Nethergate Norf 39 F8
Saxlingham Thorpe Norf 39 F8
Saxmundham Suff 31 B10
Saxon Street Cambs 30 C3
Saxondale Notts 36 B2
Saxtead Suff 31 B9
Saxtead Green Suff 31 B9
Saxthorpe Norf 39 B7
Saxton N Yorks 51 F10
Sayers Common W Sus 12 E1
Scackleton N Yorks 52 B2
Scadabhagh W Isles 90 H6
Scaftworth Notts 45 C10
Scagglethorpe N Yorks 52 B4
Scaitcliffe Lancs 50 G3
Scalasaig Argyll 72 D2
Scalby E Yorks 52 G4
Scalby N Yorks 59 G11
Scaldwell Northants 28 A4
Scale Houses Cumb 57 B7
Scaleby Cumb 61 G10
Scaleby Hill Cumb 61 G10
Scales Cumb 49 B2
Scales Cumb 56 D5
Scales Lancs 49 F4
Scalford Leics 36 C3
Scaling Redcar 59 E8
Scallastle Argyll 79 H9
Scalloway Shetland 96 K6
Scalpay W Isles 90 H7
Scalpay Ho. Highld 85 F11
Scalpsie Argyll 73 H9
Scamadale Highld 79 B10
Scamblesby Lincs 46 E6
Scamodale Highld 79 D11
Scampston N Yorks 52 B4
Scampton Lincs 46 E3
Scapa Orkney 95 H5
Scapegoat Hill W Yorks 51 H6
Scar Orkney 95 D7
Scarborough N Yorks 59 H11
Scarcliffe Derbys 45 F8
Scarcroft W Yorks 51 E9
Scarcroft Hill W Yorks 51 E9
Scardroy Highld 86 F5
Scarff Shetland 96 E4
Scarfskerry Highld 94 C4
Scargill Durham 58 E1
Scarinish Argyll 78 G3
Scarisbrick Lancs 43 A6
Scarning Norf 38 D5
Scarrington Notts 36 A3
Scartho NE Lincs 46 B6
Scarwell Orkney 95 F3
Scatness Shetland 96 M5
Scatraig Highld 87 H10
Scawby N Lincs 46 B3
Scawsby S Yorks 45 B9
Scawton N Yorks 51 A11
Scayne's Hill W Sus 12 D2
Scethrog Powys 25 F8
Scholar Green Ches E 44 G2
Scholes W Yorks 44 B5
Scholes W Yorks 51 F9
Scholes W Yorks 51 G7
School Green Ches W 43 F9
Scleddau Pembs 22 C4
Sco Ruston Norf 39 C8
Scofton Notts 45 D10
Scole Norf 39 H7
Scolpaig W Isles 84 A2
Scone Perth 76 E4
Sconser Highld 85 E10
Scoonie Fife 76 G6
Scoor Argyll 78 K7
Scopwick Lincs 46 G4
Scoraig Highld 86 B3
Scorborough E Yorks 52 E6
Scorrier Corn 2 E6
Scorton Lancs 49 E5
Scorton N Yorks 58 F3
Scotbheinn W Isles 84 C3
Scotby Cumb 61 H10
Scotch Corner N Yorks 58 F3
Scotforth Lancs 49 D4
Scothern Lincs 46 E4
Scotland Gate Northumb 63 E8
Scotlandwell Perth 76 G4
Scots' Gap Northumb 62 E6
Scotsburn Highld 87 D10
Scotscalder Station Highld 94 E2
Scotscraig Fife 77 E7
Scotston Aberds 83 F9
Scotston Perth 76 C2
Scotstoun Glasgow 68 D4
Scotstown Highld 79 E11
Scotswood T&W 63 G7
Scottas Highld 85 H12
Scotter Lincs 46 B2
Scotterthorpe Lincs 46 B2
Scottlethorpe Lincs 37 C6
Scotton Lincs 46 C2
Scotton N Yorks 51 D9
Scotton N Yorks 58 G2
Scottow Norf 39 C8
Scoughall E Loth 70 B5
Scoulag Argyll 73 H10
Scoulton Norf 38 E5
Scourie Highld 92 E4
Scourie More Highld 92 E4
Scousburgh Shetland 96 M5
Scrabster Highld 94 C2
Scrafield Lincs 47 F7
Scrainwood Northumb 62 C5
Scrane End Lincs 37 A9
Scraptoft Leics 36 E2
Scratby Norf 39 D11
Scrayingham N Yorks 52 C3
Scredington Lincs 37 A6
Scremby Lincs 47 F8
Scremerston Northumb 71 F9
Screveton Notts 36 A3
Scrivelsby Lincs 46 F6
Scriven N Yorks 51 D9
Scrooby Notts 45 C10
Scropton Derbys 35 B7
Scrub Hill Lincs 46 G6
Scruton N Yorks 58 G3
Sculcoates Hull 53 F6
Sculthorpe Norf 38 B4
Scunthorpe N Lincs 46 A2
Scurlage Swansea 23 H9
Sea Palling Norf 39 C10
Seaborough Dorset 8 D3
Seacombe Mers 42 C6
Seacroft Lincs 47 F9
Seacroft W Yorks 51 F9
Seadyke Lincs 37 B9
Seafield S Ayrs 66 D6
Seafield W Loth 69 D9
Seaford E Sus 12 G3
Seaforth Mers 42 C6
Seagrave Leics 36 D2
Seaham Durham 58 B5
Seahouses Northumb 71 G11
Seal Kent 20 F2
Sealand Flint 42 F6
Seale Sur 18 G5
Seamer N Yorks 52 A6
Seamer N Yorks 58 E5
Seamill N Ayrs 66 B5
Searby Lincs 46 B4
Seasalter Kent 21 E7
Seascale Cumb 56 F2
Seathorne Lincs 47 F9
Seathwaite Cumb 56 E4
Seathwaite Cumb 56 G4
Seatoller Cumb 56 E4
Seaton Corn 4 F4
Seaton Cumb 56 C2
Seaton Devon 8 F1
Seaton Durham 58 A4
Seaton E Yorks 53 E7
Seaton Northumb 63 F9
Seaton Rutland 36 F5
Seaton Burn T&W 63 F8
Seaton Carew Hrtlpl 58 D6
Seaton Delaval Northumb 63 F9
Seaton Ross E Yorks 52 E3
Seaton Sluice Northumb 63 F9
Seatown Aberds 88 B5
Seatown Dorset 8 E3
Seave Green N Yorks 59 F6
Seaview IoW 10 E5
Seaville Cumb 56 A3
Seavington St Mary Som 8 C3
Seavington St Michael Som 8 C3
Sebergham Cumb 56 B5
Seckington Warks 35 E8
Second Coast Highld 86 B2
Sedbergh Cumb 57 G8
Sedbury Glos 15 B11
Sedbusk N Yorks 57 G10
Sedgeberrow Worcs 27 E7
Sedgebrook Lincs 36 B4
Sedgefield Durham 58 D4
Sedgeford Norf 38 B3
Sedgehill Wilts 9 B7
Sedgley W Mid 34 F5
Sedgwick Cumb 57 H7
Sedlescombe E Sus 13 E6
Sedlescombe Street E Sus 13 E6
Seend Wilts 16 E6
Seend Cleeve Wilts 16 E6
Seer Green Bucks 18 B6
Seething Norf 39 F9
Sefton Mers 42 B6
Seghill Northumb 63 F8
Seifton Shrops 33 G10
Seighford Staffs 34 C4
Seilebost W Isles 90 H5
Seion Gwyn 41 D7
Seisdon Staffs 34 F4
Seisiadar W Isles 91 D10
Selattyn Shrops 33 B8
Selborne Hants 10 A6
Selby N Yorks 52 F2
Selham W Sus 11 B8
Selhurst London 19 E10
Selkirk Borders 70 H3
Sellack Hereford 26 F2
Sellafirth Shetland 96 D7
Sellibister Orkney 95 D8
Sellindge Kent 13 C9
Sellindge Lees Kent 13 C10
Selling Kent 21 F7
Sells Green Wilts 16 E6
Selly Oak W Mid 34 G6
Selmeston E Sus 12 F4
Selsdon London 19 E10
Selsey W Sus 11 E7
Selsfield Common W Sus 12 C2
Selsted Kent 21 G9
Selston Notts 45 G8
Selworthy Som 7 B8
Semblister Shetland 96 H5
Semer Suff 30 D6
Semington Wilts 16 E5
Semley Wilts 9 B7
Send Sur 19 F7
Send Marsh Sur 19 F7
Senghenydd Caerph 15 B7
Sennen Corn 2 G2
Sennen Cove Corn 2 G2
Sennybridge = Pont Senni Powys 24 F6
Serlby Notts 45 D10
Sessay N Yorks 51 B10
Setchey Norf 38 D2

Stanton Harcourt Oxon 27 H11
Stanton Hill Notts 45 F8
Stanton in Peak Derbys 44 F6
Stanton Lacy Shrops 33 H10
Stanton Long Shrops 34 F1
Stanton-on-the-Wolds Notts 36 B2
Stanton Prior Bath 16 E3
Stanton St Bernard Wilts 17 E7
Stanton St John Oxon 28 H2
Stanton St Quintin Wilts 16 D6
Stanton Street Suff 30 B6
Stanton under Bardon Leics 35 D10
Stanton upon Hine Heath Shrops 34 C1
Stanton Wick Bath 16 E3
Stanwardine in the Fields Shrops 33 C10
Stanwardine in the Wood Shrops 33 C10
Stanway Essex 30 F6
Stanway Glos 27 E7
Stanway Green Suff 31 A9
Stanwell Sur 19 D7
Stanwell Moor Sur 19 D7
Stanwick Northants 28 A6
Stanwick-St-John N Yorks 58 E2
Stanwix Cumb 61 H10
Stanydale Shetland 96 H4
Staoinebrig W Isles 84 E2
Stape N Yorks 59 G8
Stapehill Dorset 9 D9
Stapeley Ches E 43 H9
Stapenhill Staffs 35 C8
Staple Kent 21 F9
Staple Som 7 B10
Staple Cross E Sus 13 D6
Staple Fitzpaine Som 8 C1
Staplefield W Sus 12 D1
Stapleford Cambs 29 C11
Stapleford Herts 29 G10
Stapleford Leics 36 D4
Stapleford Lincs 46 G2
Stapleford Notts 35 B10
Stapleford Wilts 17 H7
Stapleford Abbotts Essex 20 B2
Stapleford Tawney Essex 20 B2
Staplegrove Som 7 D11
Staplehay Som 7 D11
Staplehurst Kent 13 B6
Staplers IoW 10 F4
Stapleton Bristol 16 D3
Stapleton Cumb 61 F11
Stapleton Hereford 25 B10
Stapleton Leics 35 F10
Stapleton N Yorks 58 E3
Stapleton Shrops 33 E10
Stapleton Som 8 B3
Stapley Som 7 E10
Staploe Bedford 29 B8
Staplow Hereford 26 D3
Star Fife 76 G6
Star Pembs 23 C7
Star Som 15 F10
Stara Orkney 95 F3
Starbeck N Yorks 51 D9
Starbotton N Yorks 50 B5
Starcross Devon 5 C10
Stareton Warks 27 A10
Starkholmes Derbys 45 G7
Starlings Green Essex 29 E11
Starston Norf 39 G8
Startforth Durham 58 E1
Startley Wilts 16 C6
Stathe Som 8 B2
Stathern Leics 36 B3
Station Town Durham 58 C5
Staughton Green Cambs 29 B8
Staughton Highway Cambs 29 B8
Staunton Glos 26 F4
Staunton Glos 26 G2
Staunton in the Vale Notts 36 A4
Staunton on Arrow Hereford 25 B10
Staunton on Wye Hereford 25 D10
Staveley Cumb 56 G6
Staveley Cumb 56 H5
Staveley Derbys 45 E8
Staveley N Yorks 51 C9
Staverton Devon 5 E8
Staverton Glos 26 F5
Staverton Northants 28 B2
Staverton Wilts 16 E5
Staverton Bridge Glos 26 F5
Stawell Som 15 H9
Staxigoe Highld 94 E5
Staxton N Yorks 52 B6
Staylittle Powys 32 F4
Staynall Lancs 49 E3
Staythorpe Notts 45 G11
Stean N Yorks 51 B6
Stearsby N Yorks 52 B2
Steart Som 15 G8
Stebbing Essex 30 F3
Stebbing Green Essex 30 F3
Stedham W Sus 11 B7
Steele Road Borders 61 D11
Steen's Bridge Hereford 26 C2
Steep Hants 10 B6
Steep Marsh Hants 11 B6
Steeple Dorset 9 F8
Steeple Essex 20 A6
Steeple Ashton Wilts 16 F6
Steeple Aston Oxon 27 F11
Steeple Barton Oxon 27 F11
Steeple Bumpstead Essex 30 D3
Steeple Claydon Bucks 28 F3
Steeple Gidding Cambs 37 G7
Steeple Langford Wilts 17 H7
Steeple Morden Cambs 29 D9
Steeton W Yorks 50 E6
Stein Highld 84 C7
Steinmanhill Aberds 89 D7
Stelling Minnis Kent 21 G8
Stemster Highld 94 D3
Stemster Ho. Highld 94 D3
Stenalees Corn 3 D9
Stenhousemuir Falk 69 B7
Stenigot Lincs 46 D6
Stenness Shetland 96 F4
Stenscholl Highld 85 B9
Stenso Orkney 95 F4
Stenson Derbys 35 C9
Stenton E Loth 70 C5
Stenton Fife 76 H5
Stenwith Lincs 36 B4
Stepaside Pembs 22 F6
Stepping Hill Gtr Man 44 D3
Steppingley C Beds 29 E7
Stepps N Lanark 68 D5
Sterndale Moor Derbys 44 F5
Sternfield Suff 31 B10
Sterridge Devon 6 B4
Stert Wilts 17 F7
Stetchworth Cambs 30 C3
Stevenage Herts 29 F9
Stevenston N Ayrs 66 B5
Steventon Hants 18 G2
Steventon Oxon 17 B11
Stevington Bedford 28 C6
Stewartby Bedford 29 D7
Stewarton Argyll 65 G7
Stewarton E Ayrs 67 B7
Stewkley Bucks 28 F5
Stewton Lincs 47 D7
Steyne Cross IoW 10 F5
Steyning W Sus 11 C10
Steynton Pembs 22 F4
Stibb Corn 6 E1
Stibb Cross Devon 6 E3
Stibb Green Wilts 17 E9
Stibbard Norf 38 C5
Stibbington Cambs 37 F6
Stichill Borders 70 G6
Sticker Corn 3 D8
Stickford Lincs 47 G7
Sticklepath Devon 6 G5
Stickney Lincs 47 G7
Stiffkey Norf 38 A5
Stifford's Bridge Hereford 26 D4
Stillingfleet N Yorks 52 E1
Stillington N Yorks 52 C1
Stillington Stockton 58 D4
Stilton Cambs 37 G7
Stinchcombe Glos 16 B4
Stinsford Dorset 8 E6
Stirchley Telford 34 E3
Stirkoke Ho. Highld 94 E5
Stirling Aberds 89 D11
Stirling Stirling 68 A6
Stisted Essex 30 F4
Stithians Corn 2 F6
Stittenham Highld 87 D9
Stivichall W Mid 35 H9
Stixwould Lincs 46 F5
Stoak Ches W 43 E7
Stobieside S Lanark 68 G5
Stobo Borders 69 G10
Stoborough Dorset 9 F8
Stoborough Green Dorset 9 F8
Stobshiel E Loth 70 D3
Stobswood Northumb 63 D8
Stock Essex 20 B3
Stock Green Worcs 26 C6
Stock Wood Worcs 27 C7
Stockbridge Hants 10 A2
Stockbury Kent 20 E5
Stockcross W Berks 17 E11
Stockdalewath Cumb 56 B5
Stockerston Leics 36 F4
Stockheath Hants 10 D6
Stockiemuir Stirling 68 B4
Stocking Pelham Herts 29 F11
Stockingford Warks 35 F9
Stockland Devon 8 D1
Stockland Bristol Som 15 G8
Stockleigh English Devon 7 F7
Stockleigh Pomeroy Devon 7 F7
Stockley Wilts 17 E7
Stocklinch Som 8 C2
Stockport Gtr Man 44 C2
Stocksbridge S Yorks 44 C6
Stocksfield Northumb 62 G6
Stockton Hereford 26 B2
Stockton Norf 39 F9
Stockton Shrops 33 E8
Stockton Shrops 34 F3
Stockton Warks 27 B11
Stockton Wilts 16 H6
Stockton Heath Warr 43 D9
Stockton-on-Tees Stockton 58 E5
Stockton on Teme Worcs 26 B4
Stockton on the Forest York 52 D2
Stodmarsh Kent 21 E9
Stody Norf 39 B6
Stoer Highld 92 G3
Stoford Som 8 C4
Stoford Wilts 17 H7
Stogumber Som 7 C9
Stogursey Som 7 B11
Stoke Devon 6 D1
Stoke Hants 10 D6
Stoke Hants 17 F11
Stoke Medway 20 D5
Stoke Suff 31 D8
Stoke Abbott Dorset 8 D3
Stoke Albany Northants 36 G4
Stoke Ash Suff 31 A8
Stoke Bardolph Notts 36 A2
Stoke Bliss Worcs 26 B3
Stoke Bruerne Northants 28 D4
Stoke by Clare Suff 30 D4
Stoke-by-Nayland Suff 30 E6
Stoke Canon Devon 7 G8
Stoke Charity Hants 17 H11
Stoke Climsland Corn 4 D4
Stoke D'Abernon Sur 19 F8
Stoke Doyle Northants 36 G6
Stoke Dry Rutland 36 F4
Stoke Farthing Wilts 9 B9
Stoke Ferry Norf 38 F3
Stoke Fleming Devon 5 G9
Stoke Gabriel Devon 5 F9
Stoke Gifford S Glos 16 D3
Stoke Golding Leics 35 F9
Stoke Goldington M Keynes 28 D5
Stoke Green Bucks 18 C6
Stoke Hammond Bucks 28 F5
Stoke Heath Shrops 34 C2
Stoke Holy Cross Norf 39 E8
Stoke Lacy Hereford 26 D3
Stoke Lyne Oxon 28 F2
Stoke Mandeville Bucks 28 G5
Stoke Newington London 19 C10
Stoke on Tern Shrops 34 C2
Stoke-on-Trent Stoke 44 H2
Stoke Orchard Glos 26 F6
Stoke Poges Bucks 18 C6
Stoke Prior Hereford 26 C2
Stoke Prior Worcs 26 B6
Stoke Rivers Devon 6 C5
Stoke Rochford Lincs 36 C5
Stoke Row Oxon 18 C3
Stoke St Gregory Som 8 B2
Stoke St Mary Som 8 B1
Stoke St Michael Som 16 G3
Stoke St Milborough Shrops 34 G1
Stoke sub Hamdon Som 8 C3
Stoke Talmage Oxon 18 B3
Stoke Trister Som 8 B6
Stoke Wake Dorset 9 D6
Stokeford Dorset 9 F7
Stokeham Notts 45 E11
Stokeinteignhead Devon 5 D10
Stokenchurch Bucks 18 B4
Stokenham Devon 5 G9
Stokesay Shrops 33 G10
Stokesby Norf 39 D10
Stokesley N Yorks 59 F6
Stolford Som 7 B11
Ston Easton Som 16 F3
Stondon Massey Essex 20 A2
Stone Bucks 28 G4
Stone Glos 16 B3
Stone Kent 13 D8
Stone Kent 20 D2
Stone S Yorks 45 D9
Stone Staffs 34 B5
Stone Worcs 34 H4
Stone Allerton Som 15 F10
Stone Bridge Corner Pboro 37 E8
Stone Chair W Yorks 51 G7
Stone Cross E Sus 12 F5
Stone Cross Kent 21 F10
Stone-edge Batch N Som 15 D10
Stone House Cumb 57 H9
Stone Street Kent 20 F2
Stone Street Suff 30 E6
Stone Street Suff 39 G9
Stonebroom Derbys 45 G8
Stoneferry Hull 53 F7
Stonefield S Lanark 68 E5
Stonegate E Sus 12 D5
Stonegate N Yorks 59 F8
Stonegrave N Yorks 52 B2
Stonehaugh Northumb 62 F3
Stonehaven Aberds 83 E10
Stonehouse Glos 26 H5
Stonehouse Northumb 62 H2
Stonehouse S Lanark 68 F6
Stoneleigh Warks 27 A10
Stonely Cambs 29 B8
Stoner Hill Hants 10 B6
Stone's Green Essex 31 F8
Stonesby Leics 36 C4
Stonesfield Oxon 27 G10
Stonethwaite Cumb 56 E4
Stoney Cross Hants 10 C1
Stoney Middleton Derbys 44 E6
Stoney Stanton Leics 35 F10
Stoney Stoke Som 8 A6
Stoney Stratton Som 16 H3
Stoney Stretton Shrops 33 E9
Stoneybreck Shetland 96 N8
Stoneyburn W Loth 69 D8
Stoneygate Aberds 89 E10
Stoneygate Leicester 36 E2
Stoneyhills Essex 20 B6
Stoneykirk Dumfries 54 D3
Stoneywood Aberdeen 83 B10
Stoneywood Falk 68 B6
Stonganess Shetland 96 C7
Stonham Aspal Suff 31 C8
Stonnall Staffs 35 E6
Stonor Oxon 18 C4
Stonton Wyville Leics 36 F3
Stony Cross Hereford 26 D4
Stony Stratford M Keynes 28 D4
Stonyfield Highld 87 D9
Stoodleigh Devon 7 E8
Stopes S Yorks 44 D6
Stopham W Sus 11 C9
Stopsley Luton 29 F8
Stores Corner Suff 31 D10
Storeton Mers 42 D6
Stornoway W Isles 91 D9
Storridge Hereford 26 D4
Storrington W Sus 11 C9
Storrs Cumb 56 G5
Storth Cumb 49 A4
Storwood E Yorks 52 E3
Stotfield Moray 88 A2
Stotfold C Beds 29 E9
Stottesdon Shrops 34 G2
Stoughton Leics 36 E2
Stoughton Sur 18 F6
Stoughton W Sus 11 C7
Stoul Highld 79 B10
Stoulton Worcs 26 D6
Stour Provost Dorset 9 B6
Stour Row Dorset 9 B7
Stourbridge W Mid 34 G5
Stourpaine Dorset 9 D7
Stourport on Severn Worcs 26 A5
Stourton Staffs 34 G4
Stourton Warks 27 E9
Stourton Wilts 9 A6
Stourton Caundle Dorset 8 C6
Stove Orkney 95 E7
Stove Shetland 96 L6
Stoven Suff 39 G10
Stow Borders 70 F3
Stow Lincs 37 B6
Stow Lincs 46 D2
Stow Bardolph Norf 38 E2
Stow Bedon Norf 38 F5
Stow cum Quy Cambs 30 B2
Stow Longa Cambs 29 A8
Stow Maries Essex 20 B5
Stow-on-the-Wold Glos 27 F8
Stowbridge Norf 38 E2
Stowe Shrops 25 A10
Stowe-by-Chartley Staffs 34 C6
Stowe Green Glos 26 H2
Stowell Som 8 B5
Stowford Devon 4 C5
Stowlangtoft Suff 30 B6
Stowmarket Suff 31 C7
Stowting Kent 13 B10
Stowupland Suff 31 C7
Straad Argyll 73 G9
Strachan Aberds 83 D8
Stradbroke Suff 31 A9
Stradishall Suff 30 C4
Stradsett Norf 38 E2
Stragglethorpe Lincs 46 G3
Straid S Ayrs 66 G4
Straith Dumfries 60 E4
Straiton Edin 69 D11
Straiton S Ayrs 67 F6
Straloch Aberds 89 F8
Straloch Perth 76 A3
Stramshall Staffs 35 B6
Strang IoM 48 E3
Stranraer Dumfries 54 C3
Stratfield Mortimer W Berks 18 E3
Stratfield Saye Hants 18 E3
Stratfield Turgis Hants 18 F3
Stratford London 19 C10
Stratford St Andrew Suff 31 B10
Stratford St Mary Suff 31 E7
Stratford Sub Castle Wilts 9 A10
Stratford Tony Wilts 9 B9
Stratford-upon-Avon Warks 27 C8
Strath Highld 85 A12
Strath Highld 94 E4
Strathan Highld 80 D1
Strathan Highld 92 G3
Strathan Highld 93 C8
Strathaven S Lanark 68 F6
Strathblane Stirling 68 C4
Strathcanaird Highld 92 J4
Strathcarron Highld 86 G2
Strathcoil Argyll 79 H9
Strathdon Aberds 82 B5
Strathellie Aberds 89 B10
Strathkinness Fife 77 F7
Strathmashie House Highld 81 D7
Strathmiglo Fife 76 F5
Strathmore Lodge Highld 94 F3
Strathpeffer Highld 86 F7
Strathrannoch Highld 86 D6
Strathtay Perth 76 B2
Strathvaich Lodge Highld 86 D6
Strathwhillan N Ayrs 66 C3
Strathy Highld 93 C11
Strathyre Stirling 75 F8
Stratton Corn 6 F1
Stratton Dorset 8 E5
Stratton Glos 17 A7
Stratton Audley Oxon 28 F3
Stratton on the Fosse Som 16 F3
Stratton St Margaret Swindon 17 C8
Stratton St Michael Norf 39 F8
Stratton Strawless Norf 39 C8
Stravithie Fife 77 F8
Streat E Sus 12 E2
Streatham London 19 D10
Streatley C Beds 29 F7
Streatley W Berks 18 C2
Street Lancs 49 D5
Street N Yorks 59 F8
Street Som 15 H10
Street Dinas Shrops 33 B9
Street End Kent 21 F8
Street End W Sus 11 E7
Street Gate T&W 63 H8
Street Lydan Wrex 33 B10
Streethay Staffs 35 D7
Streetlam N Yorks 58 G4
Streetly W Mid 35 F6
Streetly End Cambs 30 D3
Strefford Shrops 33 G10
Strelley Notts 35 A11
Strensall York 52 C2
Stretcholt Som 15 G8
Strete Devon 5 G9
Stretford Gtr Man 44 C2
Strethall Essex 29 E11
Stretham Cambs 30 A2
Strettington W Sus 11 D7
Stretton Ches W 43 G7
Stretton Derbys 45 F7
Stretton Rutland 36 D5
Stretton Staffs 34 D4
Stretton Staffs 35 C8
Stretton Warr 43 D9
Stretton Grandison Hereford 26 D3
Stretton-on-Dunsmore Warks 27 A11
Stretton-on-Fosse Warks 27 E9
Stretton Sugwas Hereford 25 D11
Stretton under Fosse Warks 35 G10
Stretton Westwood Shrops 34 F1
Strichen Aberds 89 C9
Strines Gtr Man 44 D3
Stringston Som 7 B10
Strixton Northants 28 B6
Stroat Glos 16 B2
Stromeferry Highld 85 E13
Stromemore Highld 85 E13
Stromness Orkney 95 H3
Stronaba Highld 80 E4
Stronachlachar Stirling 75 F7
Stronchreggan Highld 80 F2
Stronchrubie Highld 92 H5
Strone Argyll 73 E10
Strone Highld 80 E3
Strone Highld 81 A7
Strone Involyd 73 F11
Stronmilchan Argyll 74 E4
Strontian Highld 79 E11
Strood Medway 20 E4
Strood Green Sur 19 G9
Strood Green W Sus 11 A10
Strood Green W Sus 11 B9
Stroud Glos 26 H5
Stroud Hants 10 B6
Stroud Green Essex 20 B5
Stroxton Lincs 36 B5
Struan Highld 85 E8
Struan Perth 81 G10
Strubby Lincs 47 D8
Strumpshaw Norf 39 E9
Strutherhill S Lanark 68 F6
Struy Highld 86 H6
Stryt-issa Wrex 42 H5
Stuartfield Aberds 89 D9
Stub Place Cumb 56 G2
Stubbington Hants 10 D4
Stubbins Lancs 50 H3
Stubbs Cross Kent 13 C8
Stubbs Green Norf 39 F9
Stubb's Green Norf 39 E8
Stubhampton Dorset 9 C8
Stubton Lincs 46 H2
Stuckgowan Argyll 74 G6
Stuckton Hants 9 C10
Stud Green Windsor 18 D5
Studham C Beds 29 G7
Studland Dorset 9 F9
Studley Warks 27 B7
Studley Wilts 16 D6
Studley Roger N Yorks 51 B8
Stump Cross Essex 30 D2
Stuntney Cambs 38 H1
Sturbridge Staffs 34 B4
Sturmer Essex 30 D3
Sturminster Marshall Dorset 9 D8
Sturminster Newton Dorset 9 C6
Sturry Kent 21 E8
Sturton N Lincs 46 B3
Sturton by Stow Lincs 46 D2
Sturton le Steeple Notts 45 D11
Stuston Suff 39 H7
Stutton N Yorks 51 E10
Stutton Suff 31 E8
Styal Ches E 44 D2
Styrrup Notts 45 C10
Suainebost W Isles 91 A10
Suardail W Isles 91 D9
Succoth Aberds 88 E4
Succoth Argyll 74 G5
Suckley Worcs 26 C4
Suckquoy Orkney 95 K5
Sudborough Northants 36 G5
Sudbourne Suff 31 C11
Sudbrook Lincs 36 A5
Sudbrook Mon 15 C11
Sudbrooke Lincs 46 E4
Sudbury Derbys 35 B7
Sudbury London 19 C8
Sudbury Suff 30 D5
Suddie Highld 87 F9
Sudgrove Glos 26 H6
Suffield N Yorks 59 G10
Suffield Norf 39 B8
Sugnall Staffs 34 B3
Suladale Highld 85 C8
Sulaisiadar W Isles 91 D10
Sulby IoM 48 C3
Sulgrave Northants 28 D2
Sulham W Berks 18 D3
Sulhamstead W Berks 18 E3
Sulland Orkney 95 D6
Sullington W Sus 11 C9
Sullom Shetland 96 F5
Sullom Voe Oil Terminal Shetland 96 F5
Sully V Glam 15 E7
Sumburgh Shetland 96 N6
Summer Bridge N Yorks 51 C8
Summer-house Darl 58 E3
Summercourt Corn 3 D7
Summerfield Norf 38 B3
Summergangs Hull 53 F7
Summerleaze Mon 15 C10
Summersdale W Sus 11 D7
Summerseat Gtr Man 43 A10
Summertown Oxon 28 H2
Summit Gtr Man 44 B3
Sunbury-on-Thames Sur 19 E8
Sundaywell Dumfries 60 E4
Sunderland Argyll 64 B3
Sunderland Cumb 56 C3
Sunderland T&W 63 H9
Sunderland Bridge Durham 58 C3
Sundhope Borders 70 H2
Sundon Park Luton 29 F7
Sundridge Kent 19 F11
Sunipol Argyll 78 F6
Sunk Island E Yorks 53 H8
Sunningdale Windsor 18 E6
Sunninghill Windsor 18 E6
Sunningwell Oxon 17 A11
Sunniside Durham 58 C2
Sunniside T&W 63 H8
Sunnyhurst Blackburn 50 G2
Sunnylaw Stirling 75 H10
Sunnyside W Sus 12 C2
Sunton Wilts 17 F9
Surbiton London 19 E8
Surby IoM 48 E2
Surfleet Lincs 37 C8
Surfleet Seas End Lincs 37 C8
Surlingham Norf 39 E9
Sustead Norf 39 B7
Susworth Lincs 46 B2
Sutcombe Devon 6 E2
Suton Norf 39 F6
Sutors of Cromarty Highld 87 E11
Sutterby Lincs 47 E7
Sutterton Lincs 37 B8
Sutton C Beds 29 D9
Sutton Cambs 37 H10
Sutton Kent 21 G10
Sutton London 19 E9
Sutton Mers 43 C8
Sutton N Yorks 51 G10
Sutton Norf 39 C9
Sutton Notts 36 B3
Sutton Notts 45 D10
Sutton Oxon 27 H11
Sutton Pboro 37 F6
Sutton S Yorks 45 A9
Sutton Shrops 34 B2
Sutton Shrops 34 G3
Sutton Som 8 A5
Sutton Staffs 34 C3
Sutton Suff 31 D10
Sutton Sur 19 G7
Sutton W Sus 11 C8
Sutton at Hone Kent 20 D2
Sutton Bassett Northants 36 F3
Sutton Benger Wilts 16 D6
Sutton Bonington Notts 35 C11
Sutton Bridge Lincs 37 C10
Sutton Cheney Leics 35 E10
Sutton Coldfield W Mid 35 F7
Sutton Courtenay Oxon 18 B2
Sutton Crosses Lincs 37 C10
Sutton Grange N Yorks 51 B8
Sutton Green Sur 19 F7
Sutton Howgrave N Yorks 51 B9
Sutton In Ashfield Notts 45 G8
Sutton-in-Craven N Yorks 50 E6
Sutton in the Elms Leics 35 F11
Sutton Ings Hull 53 F7
Sutton Lane Ends Ches E 44 E3
Sutton Leach Mers 43 C8
Sutton Maddock Shrops 34 E3
Sutton Mallet Som 15 H9
Sutton Mandeville Wilts 9 B8
Sutton Manor Mers 43 C8
Sutton Montis Som 8 B5
Sutton on Hull Hull 53 F7
Sutton on Sea Lincs 47 D9
Sutton-on-the-Forest N Yorks 52 C1
Sutton on the Hill Derbys 35 B8
Sutton on Trent Notts 45 F11
Sutton St Edmund Lincs 37 D9
Sutton St James Lincs 37 D9
Sutton St Nicholas Hereford 26 D2
Sutton Scarsdale Derbys 45 F8
Sutton Scotney Hants 17 H11
Sutton under Brailes Warks 27 E10
Sutton-under-Whitestonecliffe N Yorks 51 A10
Sutton upon Derwent E Yorks 52 E3
Sutton Valence Kent 20 G5
Sutton Veny Wilts 16 G5
Sutton Waldron Dorset 9 C7
Sutton Weaver Ches W 43 E8
Sutton Wick Bath 16 F2
Swaby Lincs 47 E7
Swadlincote Derbys 35 D9
Swaffham Norf 38 E4
Swaffham Bulbeck Cambs 30 B2
Swaffham Prior Cambs 30 B2
Swafield Norf 39 B8
Swainby N Yorks 58 F5
Swainshill Hereford 25 D11
Swainsthorpe Norf 39 E8
Swainswick Bath 16 E4
Swalcliffe Oxon 27 E10
Swalecliffe Kent 21 E8
Swallow Lincs 46 B5
Swallowcliffe Wilts 9 B8
Swallowfield Wokingham 18 E4
Swallownest S Yorks 45 D8
Swallows Cross Essex 20 B3
Swan Green Ches W 43 E10
Swan Green Suff 31 A9
Swanage Dorset 9 G9
Swanbister Orkney 95 H4
Swanbourne Bucks 28 F5
Swanland E Yorks 52 G5
Swanley Kent 20 E2
Swanley Village Kent 20 E2
Swanmore Hants 10 C4
Swannington Leics 35 D10
Swannington Norf 39 D7
Swanscombe Kent 20 D3
Swansea = Abertawe Swansea 14 B2
Swanton Abbott Norf 39 C8
Swanton Morley Norf 38 D6
Swanton Novers Norf 38 B6
Swanton Street Kent 20 F5
Swanwick Derbys 45 G8
Swanwick Hants 10 D4
Swarby Lincs 36 A6
Swardeston Norf 39 E8
Swarister Shetland 96 E7
Swarkestone Derbys 35 C9
Swarland Northumb 63 C7
Swarland Estate Northumb 63 C7
Swarthmoor Cumb 49 B2
Swathwick Derbys 45 F7
Swaton Lincs 37 B7
Swavesey Cambs 29 B10
Sway Hants 10 E1
Swayfield Lincs 36 C5
Swaythling Soton 10 C3
Sweet Green Worcs 26 B3
Sweetham Devon 7 G7
Sweethouse Corn 4 E1
Sweffling Suff 31 B10
Swepstone Leics 35 D9
Swerford Oxon 27 E10
Swettenham Ches E 44 F2
Swetton N Yorks 51 B7
Swffryd Caerph 15 B8
Swiftsden E Sus 12 D6
Swilland Suff 31 C8
Swillington W Yorks 51 F9
Swimbridge Devon 6 D5
Swimbridge Newland Devon 6 C5
Swinbrook Oxon 27 G9
Swinderby Lincs 46 F2
Swindon Glos 26 F6
Swindon Staffs 34 F4
Swindon Swindon 17 C8
Swine E Yorks 53 F7
Swinefleet E Yorks 52 G3
Swineshead Bedford 29 B7
Swineshead Lincs 37 A8
Swineshead Bridge Lincs 37 A8
Swiney Highld 94 G4
Swinford Leics 36 H1
Swinford Oxon 27 H11
Swingate Notts 35 A11
Swingfield Minnis Kent 21 G9
Swingfield Street Kent 21 G9
Swinhoe Northumb 71 H11
Swinhope Lincs 46 C6
Swining Shetland 96 G6
Swinithwaite N Yorks 58 H1
Swinnow Moor W Yorks 51 F8
Swinscoe Staffs 44 H5
Swinside Hall Borders 62 B3
Swinstead Lincs 36 C6
Swinton Borders 71 F7
Swinton Gtr Man 43 B10
Swinton N Yorks 51 B8
Swinton N Yorks 52 B3
Swinton S Yorks 45 C8
Swintonmill Borders 71 F7
Swithland Leics 35 D11
Swordale Highld 87 E8
Swordland Highld 79 B10
Swordly Highld 93 C10
Sworton Heath Ches E 43 D9
Swydd-ffynnon Ceredig 24 B3
Swynnerton Staffs 34 B4
Swyre Dorset 8 F4
Sychtyn Powys 32 E5
Syde Glos 26 G6
Sydenham London 19 D10
Sydenham Oxon 18 A4
Sydenham Damerel Devon 4 D5
Syderstone Norf 38 B4
Sydling St Nicholas Dorset 8 E5
Sydmonton Hants 17 F11
Syerston Notts 45 H11
Syke Gtr Man 50 H4
Sykehouse S Yorks 52 H2
Sykes Lancs 50 D2
Syleham Suff 39 H8
Sylen Carms 23 F10
Symbister Shetland 96 G7
Symington S Ayrs 67 C6
Symington S Lanark 69 G8
Symonds Yat Hereford 26 G2
Symondsbury Dorset 8 E3
Synod Inn Ceredig 23 A9
Syre Highld 93 E9
Syreford Glos 27 F7
Syresham Northants 28 D3
Syston Leics 36 D2
Syston Lincs 36 A5
Sytchampton Worcs 26 B5
Sywell Northants 28 B5

T

Taagan Highld 86 E3
Tabost W Isles 91 F8
Tàbost W Isles 91 A10
Tackley Oxon 27 F11
Tacleit W Isles 90 D6
Tacolneston Norf 39 F7
Tadcaster N Yorks 51 E10
Taddington Derbys 44 E5
Taddiport Devon 6 E3
Tadley Hants 18 E3
Tadlow C Beds 29 D9
Tadmarton Oxon 27 E10
Tadworth Sur 19 F9
Tafarn-y-gelyn Denb 42 F4
Tafarnau-bach Bl Gwent 25 G8
Taff's Well Rhondda 15 C7
Tafolwern Powys 32 E4
Tai Conwy 41 D9
Tai-bach Powys 33 C7
Tai-mawr Conwy 32 A5
Tai-Ucha Denb 42 G3
Taibach Neath 14 C3
Taigh a Ghearraidh W Isles 84 A2
Tain Highld 87 C10
Tain Highld 94 D4
Tainant Wrex 42 H5
Tainlon Gwyn 40 E6
Tai'r-Bull Powys 24 F6
Tairbeart = Tarbert W Isles 90 G6
Tairgwaith Neath 24 G4
Takeley Essex 30 F2
Takeley Street Essex 30 F2
Tal-sarn Ceredig 23 A10
Tal-y-bont Ceredig 32 G2
Tal-y-Bont Conwy 41 D9
Tal-y-bont Gwyn 32 C1
Tal-y-bont Gwyn 41 C8
Tal-y-cafn Conwy 41 C9
Tal-y-llyn Gwyn 32 E3
Tal-y-wern Powys 32 E4
Talachddu Powys 25 E7
Talacre Flint 42 D4
Talardd Gwyn 32 C4
Talaton Devon 7 G9
Talbenny Pembs 22 E3
Talbot Green Rhondda 14 C6
Talbot Village Poole 9 E9
Tale Devon 7 F9
Talerddig Powys 32 E5
Talgarreg Ceredig 23 A9
Talgarth Powys 25 E8
Talisker Highld 85 E8
Talke Staffs 44 G2
Talkin Cumb 61 H11
Talla Linnfoots Borders 61 A7
Talladale Highld 86 D2
Tallarn Green Wrex 33 A10
Tallentire Cumb 56 C3
Talley Carms 24 E3
Tallington Lincs 37 E6
Talmine Highld 93 C8
Talog Carms 23 D8
Talsarn Carms 24 F4
Talsarnau Gwyn 41 G8
Talskiddy Corn 3 C8
Talwrn Anglesey 40 C6
Talwrn Wrex 42 H5
Talybont-on-Usk Powys 25 F8
Talygarn Rhondda 14 C6
Talyllyn Powys 25 F8
Talysarn Gwyn 40 E6
Talywain Torf 15 A8
Tame Bridge N Yorks 58 F6
Tamerton Foliot Plym 4 E5
Tamworth Staffs 35 E8
Tan Hinon Powys 32 G4
Tan-lan Conwy 41 D9
Tan-lan Gwyn 41 F8
Tan-y-bwlch Gwyn 41 F8
Tan-y-fron Conwy 42 F2
Tan-y-graig Anglesey 41 C7
Tan-y-graig Gwyn 40 G5
Tan-y-groes Ceredig 23 B7
Tan-y-pistyll Powys 33 C6
Tan-yr-allt Gwyn 40 E6
Tandem W Yorks 51 H7
Tanden Kent 13 C8
Tandridge Sur 19 F10
Tanerdy Carms 23 D9
Tanfield Durham 63 H7
Tanfield Lea Durham 58 A2
Tangasdal W Isles 84 J1
Tangiers Pembs 22 E4
Tangley Hants 17 F10
Tanglwst Carms 23 C8
Tangmere W Sus 11 D8
Tangwick Shetland 96 F4
Tankersley S Yorks 45 B7
Tankerton Kent 21 E8
Tannach Highld 94 F5
Tannachie Aberds 83 E9
Tannadice Angus 77 B7
Tannington Suff 31 B9
Tansley Derbys 45 G7
Tansley Knoll Derbys 45 F7
Tansor Northants 37 F6
Tantobie Durham 58 A2
Tanton N Yorks 58 E6
Tanworth-in-Arden Warks 27 A8
Tanygrisiau Gwyn 41 F8
Tanyrhydiau Ceredig 24 B4
Taobh a Chaolais W Isles 84 G2
Taobh a' Ghlinne W Isles 91 F8
Taobh a Thuath Loch Aineort W Isles 84 F2
Taobh a Tuath Loch Baghasdail W Isles 84 F2
Taobh Tuath W Isles 90 J4
Taplow Bucks 18 C6
Tapton Derbys 45 E7
Tarbat Ho. Highld 87 D10
Tarbert Argyll 65 C7
Tarbert Argyll 72 E5
Tarbert Argyll 73 G7
Tarbert = Tairbeart W Isles 90 G6
Tarbet Argyll 74 G6
Tarbet Highld 79 B10
Tarbet Highld 92 E4
Tarbock Green Mers 43 D7
Tarbolton S Ayrs 67 D7
Tarbrax S Lanark 69 E9
Tardebigge Worcs 27 B7
Tarfside Angus 82 F6
Tarland Aberds 82 C6
Tarleton Lancs 49 G4
Tarlogie Highld 87 C10
Tarlscough Lancs 43 A7
Tarlton Glos 16 B6
Tarnbrook Lancs 50 D1
Tarporley Ches W 43 F8
Tarr Som 7 C10
Tarrant Crawford Dorset 9 D8
Tarrant Gunville Dorset 9 C8
Tarrant Hinton Dorset 9 C8
Tarrant Keyneston Dorset 9 D8
Tarrant Launceston Dorset 9 D8
Tarrant Monkton Dorset 9 D8
Tarrant Rawston Dorset 9 D8
Tarrant Rushton Dorset 9 D8
Tarrel Highld 87 C11
Tarring Neville E Sus 12 F3
Tarrington Hereford 26 D3
Tarsappie Perth 76 E4
Tarskavaig Highld 85 H10
Tarves Aberds 89 E8
Tarvie Highld 86 F7
Tarvie Perth 76 A3
Tarvin Ches W 43 F7
Tasburgh Norf 39 F8
Tasley Shrops 34 F2
Taston Oxon 27 F10
Tatenhill Staffs 35 C8
Tathall End M Keynes 28 D5
Tatham Lancs 50 C2
Tathwell Lincs 47 D7
Tatling End Bucks 19 C7
Tatsfield Sur 19 F11
Tattenhall Ches W 43 G7
Tattenhoe M Keynes 28 E5
Tatterford Norf 38 C4
Tattersett Norf 38 B4
Tattershall Lincs 46 G6
Tattershall Bridge Lincs 46 G5
Tattershall Thorpe Lincs 46 G6
Tattingstone Suff 31 E8
Tatworth Som 8 D2
Taunton Som 7 D11
Taverham Norf 39 D7
Tavernspite Pembs 22 E6
Tavistock Devon 4 D5
Taw Green Devon 6 G5
Tawstock Devon 6 D4
Taxal Derbys 44 E4
Tay Bridge Dundee 77 E7
Tayinloan Argyll 65 D7
Taymouth Castle Perth 75 C10
Taynish Argyll 72 E6
Taynton Glos 26 F4
Taynton Oxon 27 G9
Taynuilt Argyll 74 D3
Tayport Fife 77 E7
Tayvallich Argyll 72 E6
Tealby Lincs 46 C5
Tealing Angus 77 D7
Teangue Highld 85 H11
Teanna Mhachair W Isles 84 B2
Tebay Cumb 57 F8
Tebworth C Beds 28 F6
Tedburn St Mary Devon 7 G7
Teddington Glos 26 E6
Teddington London 19 D8
Tedstone Delamere Hereford 26 C3
Tedstone Wafre Hereford 26 C3
Teeton Northants 28 A3
Teffont Evias Wilts 9 A8
Teffont Magna Wilts 9 A8
Tegryn Pembs 23 C7
Teigh Rutland 36 D4
Teigncombe Devon 5 C7
Teigngrace Devon 5 D9
Teignmouth Devon 5 D10
Telford Telford 34 E2
Telham E Sus 13 E6
Tellisford Som 16 F5
Telscombe E Sus 12 F3
Telscombe Cliffs E Sus 12 F2
Templand Dumfries 60 E6
Temple Corn 4 D2
Temple Glasgow 68 D4
Temple Midloth 70 E2
Temple Balsall W Mid 35 H8
Temple Bar Carms 23 E10
Temple Bar Ceredig 23 A10
Temple Cloud Bath 16 F3
Temple Combe Som 8 B6
Temple Ewell Kent 21 G9
Temple Grafton Warks 27 C8
Temple Guiting Glos 27 F7
Temple Herdewyke Warks 27 C10
Temple Hirst N Yorks 52 G2
Temple Normanton Derbys 45 F8
Temple Sowerby Cumb 57 D8
Templehall Fife 69 A11
Templeton Devon 7 E7
Templeton Pembs 22 E6
Templeton Bridge Devon 7 E7
Templetown Durham 58 A2
Tempsford C Beds 29 C8
Ten Mile Bank Norf 38 F2
Tenbury Wells Worcs 26 B2
Tenby = Dinbych-y-Pysgod Pembs 22 F6
Tendring Essex 31 F8
Tendring Green Essex 31 F8
Tenston Orkney 95 G3
Tenterden Kent 13 C7
Terling Essex 30 G4
Ternhill Shrops 34 B2
Terregles Banks Dumfries 60 F5
Terrick Bucks 28 H5
Terrington N Yorks 52 B2
Terrington St Clement Norf 37 D11
Terrington St John Norf 37 D11
Teston Kent 20 F4
Testwood Hants 10 C2
Tetbury Glos 16 B5
Tetbury Upton Glos 16 B5
Tetchill Shrops 33 B9
Tetcott Devon 6 G2
Tetford Lincs 47 E7
Tetney Lincs 47 B7
Tetney Lock Lincs 47 B7
Tetsworth Oxon 18 A3
Tettenhall W Mid 34 E4
Teuchan Aberds 89 E10
Teversal Notts 45 F8
Teversham Cambs 29 C11
Teviothead Borders 61 C10
Tewel Aberds 83 E10
Tewin Herts 29 G9
Tewkesbury Glos 26 E5
Teynham Kent 20 E6
Thackthwaite Cumb 56 D3
Thainston Aberds 83 F8
Thakeham W Sus 11 C10
Thame Oxon 28 H4
Thames Ditton Sur 19 E8
Thames Haven Thurrock 20 C4
Thamesmead London 19 C11
Thanington Kent 21 F8
Thankerton S Lanark 69 G8
Tharston Norf 39 F7
Thatcham W Berks 18 E2
Thatto Heath Mers 43 C8
Thaxted Essex 30 E3
The Aird Highld 85 C9
The Arms Norf 38 F4
The Bage Hereford 25 D9
The Balloch Perth 75 F11
The Barony Orkney 95 F3
The Bog Shrops 33 F9
The Bourne Sur 18 G5
The Braes Highld 85 E10
The Broad Hereford 25 B11
The Butts Som 16 G4
The Camp Glos 26 H6
The Camp Herts 29 H8
The Chequer Wrex 33 A10
The City Bucks 18 B4
The Common Wilts 9 A11
The Craigs Highld 86 B7
The Cronk IoM 48 C3
The Dell Suff 39 F10
The Den N Ayrs 66 A6
The Eals Northumb 62 E3
The Eaves Glos 26 H3
The Flatt Cumb 61 F11
The Four Alls Shrops 34 B2
The Garths Shetland 96 B8
The Green Cumb 49 A1
The Green Wilts 9 A7
The Grove Dumfries 60 F5
The Hall Shetland 96 D8
The Haven W Sus 11 A9
The Heath Norf 39 C7
The Heath Suff 31 E8
The Hill Cumb 49 A1
The Howe Cumb 56 H6
The Howe IoM 48 F1
The Hundred Hereford 26 B2
The Lee Bucks 18 A6
The Lhen IoM 48 B3
The Marsh Powys 33 F9
The Marsh Wilts 17 C7
The Middles Durham 58 A3
The Moor Kent 13 D6
The Mumbles = Y Mwmbwls Swansea 14 C2
The Murray S Lanark 68 E5
The Neuk Aberds 83 D9
The Oval Bath 16 E4
The Pole of Itlaw Aberds 89 C6
The Quarry Glos 16 B4
The Rhos Pembs 22 E5
The Rock Telford 34 E2
The Ryde Herts 29 H9
The Sands Sur 18 G5
The Stocks Kent 13 D8
The Throat Wokingham 18 E5
The Vauld Hereford 26 D2
The Wyke Shrops 34 E3
Theakston N Yorks 58 H4
Thealby N Lincs 52 H4
Theale Som 15 G10
Theale W Berks 18 D3
Thearne E Yorks 53 F6
Theberton Suff 31 B11
Theddingworth Leics 36 G2
Theddlethorpe All Saints Lincs 47 D8
Theddlethorpe St Helen Lincs 47 D8
Thelbridge Barton Devon 7 E6
Thelnetham Suff 38 H6
Thelveton Norf 39 G7
Thelwall Warr 43 D9
Themelthorpe Norf 39 C6
Thenford Northants 28 D2
Therfield Herts 29 E10
Thetford Lincs 37 D7
Thetford Norf 38 G4
Theydon Bois Essex 19 B11
Thickwood Wilts 16 D5
Thimbleby Lincs 46 F6
Thimbleby N Yorks 58 G5
Thingwall Mers 42 D5
Thirdpart N Ayrs 66 B4
Thirlby N Yorks 51 A10
Thirlestane Borders 70 F4
Thirn N Yorks 58 H3
Thirsk N Yorks 51 A10
Thirtleby E Yorks 53 F7
Thistleton Lancs 49 F4
Thistleton Rutland 36 D5
Thistley Green Suff 38 H2

Upper Quinton Warks 27 D8
Upper Ratley Hants 10 B2
Upper Rissington Glos 27 G9
Upper Rochford Worcs 26 B3
Upper Sandaig Highld 85 G12
Upper Sanday Orkney 95 H6
Upper Sapey Hereford 26 B3
Upper Saxondale Notts 36 B2
Upper Seagry Wilts 16 C6
Upper Shelton C Beds 28 D6
Upper Sheringham Norf 39 A7
Upper Skelmorlie N Ayrs 73 G11
Upper Slaughter Glos 27 F8
Upper Soudley Glos 26 G3
Upper Stondon C Beds 29 E8
Upper Stowe Northants 28 C3
Upper Stratton Swindon 17 C8
Upper Street Hants 9 C10
Upper Street Norf 39 D9
Upper Street Norf 39 D9
Upper Street Suff 31 E8
Upper Strensham Worcs 26 E6
Upper Sundon C Beds 29 F7
Upper Swell Glos 27 F8
Upper Tean Staffs 34 B6
Upper Tillyrie Perth 76 G4
Upper Tooting London 19 D9
Upper Tote Highld 85 C10
Upper Town N Som 15 E11
Upper Treverward Shrops 33 H8
Upper Tysoe Warks 27 D10
Upper Upham Wilts 17 D9
Upper Wardington Oxon 27 D11
Upper Weald M Keynes 28 E4
Upper Weedon Northants 28 C3
Upper Wield Hants 18 H3
Upper Winchendon Bucks 28 G4
Upper Witton W Mid 35 F6
Upper Woodend Aberds 83 B8
Upper Woodford Wilts 17 H8
Upper Wootton Hants 18 F2
Upper Wyche Hereford 26 D4
Upperby Cumb 56 A6
Uppermill Gtr Man 44 B3
Uppersound Shetland 96 J6
Upperthong W Yorks 44 B5
Upperthorpe N Lincs 45 B11
Upperton W Sus 11 B8
Uppertown Derbys 45 F7
Uppertown Highld 94 C5
Uppertown Orkney 95 J5
Uppingham Rutland 36 F4
Uppington Shrops 34 E2
Upsall N Yorks 58 H5
Upshire Essex 19 A11
Upstreet Kent 21 E9
Upthorpe Suff 30 A6
Upton Cambs 37 H7
Upton Ches W 43 F7
Upton Corn 6 F1
Upton Dorset 8 F6
Upton Dorset 9 E8
Upton Hants 10 C2
Upton Hants 17 F10
Upton Leics 35 F9
Upton Lincs 46 D2
Upton Mers 42 D5
Upton Norf 39 D9
Upton Northants 28 B4
Upton Notts 45 E11
Upton Notts 45 G11
Upton Oxon 18 C2
Upton Pboro 37 E7
Upton Slough 18 D6
Upton Som 7 D8
Upton W Yorks 45 A8
Upton Bishop Hereford 26 F3
Upton Cheyney S Glos 16 E3
Upton Cressett Shrops 34 F2
Upton Cross Corn 4 D3
Upton Grey Hants 18 G3
Upton Hellions Devon 7 F7
Upton Lovell Wilts 16 G6
Upton Magna Shrops 34 D1
Upton Noble Som 16 H4
Upton Pyne Devon 7 G8
Upton St Leonard's Glos 26 G5
Upton Scudamore Wilts 16 G5
Upton Snodsbury Worcs 26 C6
Upton upon Severn Worcs 26 D5
Upton Warren Worcs 26 B6
Upwaltham W Sus 11 C8
Upware Cambs 30 A2
Upwell Norf 37 E10
Upwey Dorset 8 F5
Upwood Cambs 37 G8
Uradale Shetland 96 K6
Urafirth Shetland 96 F5
Urchfont Wilts 17 F7
Urdimarsh Hereford 26 D2
Ure Shetland 96 F4
Ure Bank N Yorks 51 B9
Urgha W Isles 90 H6
Urishay Common Hereford 25 E10
Urlay Nook Stockton 58 E4
Urmston Gtr Man 43 C10
Urpeth Durham 58 A3
Urquhart Highld 87 F8
Urquhart Moray 88 B2
Urra N Yorks 59 F6
Urray Highld 87 F8
Ushaw Moor Durham 58 B3
Usk = Brynbuga Mon 15 A9
Usselby Lincs 46 C4
Usworth T&W 63 H9
Utkinton Ches W 43 F8
Utley W Yorks 50 E6
Uton Devon 7 G7
Utterby Lincs 47 C7
Uttoxeter Staffs 35 B6
Uwchmynydd Gwyn 40 H3
Uxbridge London 19 C7
Uyeasound Shetland 96 C7
Uzmaston Pembs 22 E4

V

Valley Anglesey 40 C4
Valley Truckle Corn 4 C1
Valleyfield Dumfries 55 D9
Valsgarth Shetland 96 B8
Valtos Highld 85 B10
Van Powys 32 G5
Vange Essex 20 C4
Varteg Torf 25 H9
Vatten Highld 85 D7
Vaul Argyll 78 G3
Vaynor M Tydf 25 G7
Veensgarth Shetland 96 J6
Velindre Powys 25 E8
Vellow Som 7 C9
Veness Orkney 95 F6
Venn Green Devon 6 E2
Venn Ottery Devon 7 G9
Vennington Shrops 33 E9
Venny Tedburn Devon 7 G7
Ventnor IoW 10 G4
Vernham Dean Hants 17 F10
Vernham Street Hants 17 F10
Vernolds Common Shrops 33 G10
Verwood Dorset 9 D9
Veryan Corn 3 F8
Vicarage Devon 7 H11
Vickerstown Cumb 49 C1
Victoria Corn 3 C8
Victoria S Yorks 44 B5
Vidlin Shetland 96 G6
Viewpark N Lanark 68 D6
Vigo Village Kent 20 E3
Vinehall Street E Sus 13 D6
Vine's Cross E Sus 12 E4
Viney Hill Glos 26 H3
Virginia Water Sur 18 E6
Virginstow Devon 6 G2
Vobster Som 16 G4
Voe Shetland 96 E5
Voe Shetland 96 G6
Vowchurch Hereford 25 E10
Voxter Shetland 96 F5
Voy Orkney 95 G3

W

Wackerfield Durham 58 D2
Wacton Norf 39 F7
Wadbister Shetland 96 J6
Wadborough Worcs 26 D6
Waddesdon Bucks 28 G4
Waddingham Lincs 46 C3
Waddington Lancs 50 E3
Waddington Lincs 46 F3
Wadebridge Corn 3 B8
Wadeford Som 8 C2
Wadenhoe Northants 36 G6
Wadesmill Herts 29 G10
Wadhurst E Sus 12 C5
Wadshelf Derbys 45 E7
Wadsley S Yorks 45 C7
Wadsley Bridge S Yorks 45 C7
Wadworth S Yorks 45 C9
Waen Denb 42 F4
Waen Denb 42 F2
Waen Fach Powys 33 D8
Waen Goleugoed Denb 42 E3
Wag Highld 93 G13
Wainfleet All Saints Lincs 47 G8
Wainfleet Bank Lincs 47 G8
Wainfleet St Mary Lincs 47 G9
Wainfleet Tofts Lincs 47 G8
Wainhouse Corner Corn 4 B2
Wainscott Medway 20 D4
Wainstalls W Yorks 50 G6
Waitby Cumb 57 F9
Waithe Lincs 46 B6
Wake Lady Green N Yorks 59 G7
Wakefield W Yorks 51 G9
Wakerley Northants 36 F5
Wakes Colne Essex 30 F5
Walberswick Suff 31 A11
Walberton W Sus 11 D8
Walbottle T&W 63 G7
Walcot Lincs 37 B6
Walcot N Lincs 52 G4
Walcot Shrops 33 G9
Walcot Swindon 17 C8
Walcot Telford 34 D1
Walcot Green Norf 39 G7
Walcote Leics 36 G1
Walcote Warks 27 C8
Walcott Lincs 46 G5
Walcott Norf 39 B9
Walden N Yorks 50 A6
Walden Head N Yorks 50 A5
Walden Stubbs N Yorks 52 H1
Waldersey Cambs 37 E10
Walderslade Medway 20 E4
Walderton W Sus 11 C6
Walditch Dorset 8 E3
Waldley Derbys 35 B7
Waldridge Durham 58 A3
Waldringfield Suff 31 D9
Waldringfield Heath Suff 31 D9
Waldron E Sus 12 E4
Wales S Yorks 45 D8
Walesby Lincs 46 C5
Walesby Notts 45 E10
Walford Hereford 25 A10
Walford Hereford 26 F2
Walford Shrops 33 C10
Walford Heath Shrops 33 D10
Walgherton Ches E 43 H9
Walgrave Northants 28 A5
Walhampton Hants 10 E2
Walk Mill Lancs 50 F4
Walkden Gtr Man 43 B10
Walker T&W 63 G8
Walker Barn Ches E 44 E3
Walker Fold Lancs 50 E2
Walkerburn Borders 70 G2
Walkeringham Notts 45 C11
Walkerith Lincs 45 C11
Walkern Herts 29 F9
Walker's Green Hereford 26 D2
Walkerville N Yorks 58 G3
Walkford Dorset 9 E11
Walkhampton Devon 4 E6
Walkington E Yorks 52 F5
Walkley S Yorks 45 D7
Wall Northumb 62 G5
Wall Staffs 35 E7
Wall Bank Shrops 33 F11
Wall Heath W Mid 34 G4
Wall under Heywood Shrops 33 F11
Wallaceton Dumfries 60 E4
Wallacetown S Ayrs 66 D6
Wallacetown S Ayrs 66 F5
Wallands Park E Sus 12 E3
Wallasey Mers 42 C6
Wallcrouch E Sus 12 C5
Wallingford Oxon 18 C3
Wallington Hants 10 D4
Wallington Herts 29 E9
Wallington London 19 E9
Wallis Pembs 22 D5
Walliswood Sur 19 H8
Walls Shetland 96 J4
Wallsend T&W 63 G8
Wallston V Glam 15 D7
Wallyford E Loth 70 C2
Walmer Kent 21 F10
Walmer Bridge Lancs 49 G4
Walmersley Gtr Man 44 A2
Walmley W Mid 35 F7
Walpole Suff 31 A10
Walpole Cross Keys Norf 37 D11
Walpole Highway Norf 37 D11
Walpole Marsh Norf 37 D10
Walpole St Andrew Norf 37 D11
Walpole St Peter Norf 37 D11
Walsall W Mid 34 F6
Walsall Wood W Mid 34 E6
Walsden W Yorks 50 G5
Walsgrave on Sowe W Mid 35 G9
Walsham le Willows Suff 30 A6
Walshaw Gtr Man 43 A10
Walshford N Yorks 51 D10
Walsoken Cambs 37 D10
Walston S Lanark 69 F9
Walsworth Herts 29 E9
Walters Ash Bucks 18 B5
Walterston V Glam 14 D6
Walterstone Hereford 25 F10
Waltham Kent 21 G8
Waltham NE Lincs 46 B6
Waltham Abbey Essex 19 A10
Waltham Chase Hants 10 C4
Waltham Cross Herts 19 A10
Waltham on the Wolds Leics 36 C4
Waltham St Lawrence Windsor 18 D5
Walthamstow London 19 C10
Walton Cumb 61 G11
Walton Derbys 45 F7
Walton Leics 36 G1
Walton M Keynes 28 E5
Walton Mers 42 C6
Walton Pboro 37 E7
Walton Powys 25 C9
Walton Som 15 H10
Walton Staffs 34 B4
Walton Suff 31 E9
Walton Telford 34 D1
Walton W Yorks 51 E10
Walton W Yorks 51 H9
Walton Warks 27 C9
Walton Cardiff Glos 26 E6
Walton East Pembs 22 D5
Walton-in-Gordano N Som 15 D10
Walton-le-Dale Lancs 50 G1
Walton-on-Thames Sur 19 E8
Walton on the Hill Staffs 34 C5
Walton on the Hill Sur 19 F9
Walton-on-the-Naze Essex 31 F9
Walton on the Wolds Leics 36 D1
Walton-on-Trent Derbys 35 D8
Walton West Pembs 22 E3
Walwen Flint 42 E5
Walwick Northumb 62 F5
Walworth Darl 58 E3
Walworth Gate Darl 58 D3
Walwyn's Castle Pembs 22 E3
Wambrook Som 8 D1
Wanborough Sur 18 G6
Wanborough Swindon 17 C9
Wandsworth London 19 D9
Wangford Suff 39 H10
Wanlockhead Dumfries 60 B4
Wansford E Yorks 53 D6
Wansford Pboro 37 F6
Wanstead London 19 C11
Wanstrow Som 16 G4
Wanswell Glos 16 A3
Wantage Oxon 17 C10
Wapley S Glos 16 D4
Wappenbury Warks 27 B10
Wappenham Northants 28 D3
Warbleton E Sus 12 E5
Warblington Hants 10 D6
Warborough Oxon 18 B2
Warboys Cambs 37 G9
Warbreck Blackpool 49 F3
Warbstow Corn 4 B3
Warburton Gtr Man 43 D10
Warcop Cumb 57 E9
Ward End W Mid 35 G7
Ward Green Suff 31 B7
Warden Kent 21 D7
Warden Northumb 62 G5
Wardhill Orkney 95 F7
Wardington Oxon 27 D11
Wardlaw Borders 61 B8
Wardle Ches E 43 G9
Wardle Gtr Man 50 H5
Wardley Rutland 36 E4
Wardlow Derbys 44 E5
Wardy Hill Cambs 37 G10
Ware Herts 29 G10
Ware Kent 21 E9
Wareham Dorset 9 F8
Warehorne Kent 13 C8
Waren Mill Northumb 71 G10
Warenford Northumb 71 H10
Warenton Northumb 71 G10
Wareside Herts 29 G10
Waresley Cambs 29 C9
Waresley Worcs 26 A5
Warfield Brack 18 D5
Warfleet Devon 5 F9
Wargrave Wokingham 18 D4
Warham Norf 38 A5
Warhill Gtr Man 44 C3
Wark Northumb 62 F4
Wark Northumb 71 G7
Warkleigh Devon 6 D5
Warkton Northants 36 H4
Warkworth Northants 27 D11
Warkworth Northumb 63 C8
Warlaby N Yorks 58 G4
Warland W Yorks 50 G5
Warleggan Corn 4 E2
Warlingham Sur 19 F10
Warmfield W Yorks 51 G9
Warmingham Ches E 43 F10
Warmington Northants 37 F6
Warmington Warks 27 D11
Warminster Wilts 16 G5
Warmlake Kent 20 F5
Warmley S Glos 16 D3
Warmley Tower S Glos 16 D3
Warmonds Hill Northants 28 B6
Warmsworth S Yorks 45 B9
Warmwell Dorset 9 F6
Warndon Worcs 26 C5
Warnford Hants 10 B5
Warnham W Sus 11 A10
Warninglid W Sus 11 B11
Warren Ches E 44 E2
Warren Pembs 22 G4
Warren Heath Suff 31 D9
Warren Row Windsor 18 C5
Warren Street Kent 20 F6
Warrington M Keynes 28 C5
Warrington Warr 43 D9
Warsash Hants 10 D3
Warslow Staffs 44 G4
Warter E Yorks 52 D4
Warthermarske N Yorks 51 B8
Warthill N Yorks 52 D2
Wartling E Sus 12 F5
Wartnaby Leics 36 C3
Warton Lancs 49 B4
Warton Lancs 49 G4
Warton Northumb 62 C6
Warton Warks 35 E8
Warwick Warks 27 B9
Warwick Bridge Cumb 61 H10
Warwick on Eden Cumb 61 H10
Wasbister Orkney 95 E4
Wasdale Head Cumb 56 F3
Wash Common W Berks 17 E11
Washaway Corn 3 C9
Washbourne Devon 5 F8
Washfield Devon 7 E8
Washfold N Yorks 58 F1
Washford Som 7 B9
Washford Pyne Devon 7 E7
Washingborough Lincs 46 E4
Washington T&W 63 H9
Washington W Sus 11 C10
Wasing W Berks 18 E2
Waskerley Durham 58 B1
Wasperton Warks 27 C9
Wasps Nest Lincs 46 F4
Wass N Yorks 52 B1
Watchet Som 7 B9
Watchfield Oxon 17 B9
Watchfield Som 15 G9
Watchgate Cumb 57 G7
Watchhill Cumb 56 B3
Watcombe Torbay 5 E10
Watendlath Cumb 56 E4
Water Devon 5 C8
Water Lancs 50 G4
Water End E Yorks 52 F3
Water End Herts 19 A9
Water End Herts 29 G7
Water Newton Cambs 37 F7
Water Orton Warks 35 F7
Water Stratford Bucks 28 E3
Water Yeat Cumb 56 H4
Waterbeach Cambs 29 B11
Waterbeck Dumfries 61 F8
Waterden Norf 38 B4
Waterfall Staffs 44 G4
Waterfoot E Renf 68 E4
Waterfoot Lancs 50 G4
Waterford Hants 10 E2
Waterford Herts 29 G10
Waterhead Cumb 56 F5
Waterhead Dumfries 61 D7
Waterheads Borders 69 E11
Waterhouses Durham 58 B2
Waterhouses Staffs 44 G4
Wateringbury Kent 20 F3
Waterloo Gtr Man 44 B3
Waterloo Highld 85 F11
Waterloo Mers 42 C6
Waterloo N Lanark 69 E7
Waterloo Norf 39 D8
Waterloo Perth 76 D3
Waterloo Poole 9 E9
Waterloo Shrops 33 B11
Waterloo Port Gwyn 40 D6
Waterlooville Hants 10 D5
Watermeetings S Lanark 60 B5
Watermillock Cumb 56 D6
Waterperry Oxon 28 H3
Waterrow Som 7 D9
Water's Nook Gtr Man 43 B9
Waters Upton Telford 34 D2
Watersfield W Sus 11 C9
Waterside Aberds 89 F10
Waterside Blackburn 50 G3
Waterside Cumb 56 B4
Waterside E Ayrs 67 B7
Waterside E Ayrs 67 F7
Waterside E Dunb 68 C5
Waterside E Renf 68 E4
Waterstock Oxon 28 H3
Waterston Pembs 22 F4
Watford Herts 19 B8
Watford Northants 28 B3
Watford Gap Staffs 35 E7
Wath N Yorks 51 B9
Wath N Yorks 51 C7
Wath N Yorks 52 B2
Wath Brow Cumb 56 E2
Wath upon Dearne S Yorks 45 B8
Watley's End S Glos 16 C3
Watlington Norf 38 D2
Watlington Oxon 18 B3
Watnall Notts 45 H9
Watten Highld 94 E4
Wattisfield Suff 31 A7
Wattisham Suff 31 C7
Wattlesborough Heath Shrops 33 D9
Watton E Yorks 52 D6
Watton Norf 38 E5
Watton at Stone Herts 29 G10
Wattston N Lanark 68 C6
Wattstown Rhondda 14 B6
Wauchan Highld 80 E1
Waulkmill Lodge Orkney 95 H4
Waun Powys 32 E4
Waun-y-clyn Carms 23 F9
Waunarlwydd Swansea 14 B2
Wauncluda Carms 24 E3
Waunfawr Gwyn 41 E7
Waungron Swansea 23 F10
Waunlwyd Bl Gwent 25 H8
Wavendon M Keynes 28 E6
Waverbridge Cumb 56 B4
Waverton Ches W 43 F7
Waverton Cumb 56 B4
Wavertree Mers 43 D6
Wawne E Yorks 53 F6
Waxham Norf 39 C10
Waxholme E Yorks 53 G9
Way Kent 21 E10
Way Village Devon 7 E7
Wayfield Medway 20 E4
Wayford Som 8 D3
Waymills Shrops 34 A1
Wayne Green Mon 25 G11
Wdig = Goodwick Pembs 22 C4
Weachyburn Aberds 89 C6
Weald Oxon 17 A10
Wealdstone London 19 C8
Weardley W Yorks 51 E8
Weare Som 15 F10
Weare Giffard Devon 6 D3
Wearhead Durham 57 C10
Weasdale Cumb 57 F8
Weasenham All Saints Norf 38 C4
Weasenham St Peter Norf 38 C4
Weatherhill Sur 12 B2
Weaverham Ches W 43 E9
Weaverthorpe N Yorks 52 B5
Webheath Worcs 27 B7
Wedderlairs Aberds 89 E8
Wedderlie Borders 70 E5
Weddington Warks 35 F9
Wedhampton Wilts 17 F7
Wedmore Som 15 G10
Wednesbury W Mid 34 F5
Wednesfield W Mid 34 E5
Weedon Bucks 28 G5
Weedon Bec Northants 28 C3
Weedon Lois Northants 28 D3
Weeford Staffs 35 E7
Week Devon 7 E6
Week St Mary Corn 4 B3
Weeke Hants 10 A3
Weekley Northants 36 G4
Weel E Yorks 53 F6
Weeley Essex 31 F8
Weeley Heath Essex 31 F8
Weem Perth 75 C11
Weeping Cross Staffs 34 C5
Weethley Gate Warks 27 C7
Weeting Norf 38 G3
Weeton E Yorks 53 G9
Weeton Lancs 49 F3
Weeton N Yorks 51 E8
Weetwood Hall Northumb 71 H9
Weir Lancs 50 G4
Weir Quay Devon 4 E5
Welborne Norf 39 E6
Welbourn Lincs 46 G3
Welburn N Yorks 52 A2
Welburn N Yorks 52 C3
Welbury N Yorks 58 F4
Welby Lincs 36 B5
Welches Dam Cambs 37 G10
Welcombe Devon 6 E1
Weld Bank Lancs 50 H1
Weldon Northumb 63 D7
Welford Northants 36 G2
Welford W Berks 17 D11
Welford-on-Avon Warks 27 C8
Welham Leics 36 F3
Welham Notts 45 D11
Welham Green Herts 29 H9
Well Hants 18 G4
Well Lincs 47 E8
Well N Yorks 51 A8
Well End Bucks 18 C5
Well Heads W Yorks 51 F6
Well Hill Kent 19 E11
Well Town Devon 7 F8
Welland Worcs 26 D4
Wellbank Angus 77 D7
Welldale Dumfries 61 G7
Wellesbourne Warks 27 C9
Welling London 19 D11
Wellingborough Northants 28 B5
Wellingham Norf 38 C4
Wellingore Lincs 46 G3
Wellington Cumb 56 F2
Wellington Hereford 25 D11
Wellington Som 7 D10
Wellington Telford 34 D2
Wellington Heath Hereford 26 D4
Wellington Hill W Yorks 51 F9
Wellow Bath 16 F4
Wellow IoW 10 F2
Wellow Notts 45 F10
Wellpond Green Herts 29 F11
Wells Som 15 G11
Wells Green Ches E 43 G9
Wells-Next-The-Sea Norf 38 A5
Wellsborough Leics 35 E9
Wellswood Torbay 5 E10
Wellwood Fife 69 B9
Welney Norf 37 F11
Welsh Bicknor Hereford 26 G2
Welsh End Shrops 33 B11
Welsh Frankton Shrops 33 B9
Welsh Hook Pembs 22 D4
Welsh Newton Hereford 25 G11
Welsh St Donats V Glam 14 D6
Welshampton Shrops 33 B10
Welshpool = Y Trallwng Powys 33 E8
Welton Cumb 56 B5
Welton E Yorks 52 G5
Welton Lincs 46 E4
Welton Northants 28 B2
Welton Hill Lincs 46 D4
Welton le Marsh Lincs 47 F8
Welton le Wold Lincs 46 D6
Welwick E Yorks 53 G9
Welwyn Herts 29 G9
Welwyn Garden City Herts 29 G9
Wem Shrops 33 C11
Wembdon Som 15 H8
Wembley London 19 C8
Wembury Devon 4 G6
Wembworthy Devon 6 F5
Wemyss Bay Invclyd 73 G10
Wenallt Ceredig 24 A3
Wenallt Gwyn 32 A5
Wendens Ambo Essex 30 E2
Wendlebury Oxon 28 G2
Wendling Norf 38 D5
Wendover Bucks 28 H5
Wendron Corn 2 F5
Wendy Cambs 29 D10
Wenfordbridge Corn 4 D1
Wenhaston Suff 39 H10
Wennington Cambs 37 H8
Wennington Lancs 50 B2
Wennington London 20 C2
Wensley Derbys 44 F6
Wensley N Yorks 58 H1
Wentbridge W Yorks 51 H10
Wentnor Shrops 33 F9
Wentworth Cambs 37 H10
Wentworth S Yorks 45 C7
Wenvoe V Glam 15 D7
Weobley Hereford 25 C11
Weobley Marsh Hereford 25 C11
Wereham Norf 38 E2
Wergs W Mid 34 E4
Wern Powys 32 D5
Wern Powys 33 D8
Wernffrwd Swansea 23 G10
Wernyrheolydd Mon 25 G10
Werrington Corn 4 C4
Werrington Pboro 37 E7
Werrington Staffs 44 H3
Wervin Ches W 43 E7
Wesham Lancs 49 F4
Wessington Derbys 45 G7
West Acre Norf 38 D3
West Adderbury Oxon 27 E11
West Allerdean Northumb 71 F8
West Alvington Devon 5 G8
West Amesbury Wilts 17 G8
West Anstey Devon 7 D7
West Ashby Lincs 46 E6
West Ashling W Sus 11 D7
West Ashton Wilts 16 F5
West Auckland Durham 58 D2
West Ayton N Yorks 52 A5
West Bagborough Som 7 C10
West Barkwith Lincs 46 D5
West Barnby N Yorks 59 E9
West Barns E Loth 70 C5
West Barsham Norf 38 B5
West Bay Dorset 8 E3
West Beckham Norf 39 B7
West Bedfont Sur 19 D7
West Benhar N Lanark 69 D7
West Bergholt Essex 30 F6
West Bexington Dorset 8 F4
West Bilney Norf 38 D3
West Blatchington Brighton 12 F1
West Bowling W Yorks 51 F7
West Bradford Lancs 50 E3
West Bradley Som 16 H2
West Bretton W Yorks 44 A6
West Bridgford Notts 36 B1
West Bromwich W Mid 34 F6
West Buckland Devon 6 C5
West Buckland Som 7 D10
West Burrafirth Shetland 96 H4
West Burton N Yorks 58 H1
West Burton W Sus 11 C8
West Butterwick N Lincs 46 B2
West Byfleet Sur 19 E7
West Caister Norf 39 D11
West Calder W Loth 69 D9
West Camel Som 8 B4
West Challow Oxon 17 C10
West Chelborough Dorset 8 D4
West Chevington Northumb 63 D8
West Chiltington W Sus 11 C9
West Chiltington Common W Sus 11 C9
West Chinnock Som 8 C3
West Chisenbury Wilts 17 F8
West Clandon Sur 19 F7
West Cliffe Kent 21 G10
West Clyne Highld 93 J11
West Clyth Highld 94 G4
West Coker Som 8 C4
West Compton Dorset 8 E4
West Compton Som 16 G2
West Cowick E Yorks 52 G2
West Cranmore Som 16 G3
West Cross Swansea 14 C2
West Cullery Aberds 83 C9
West Curry Corn 6 G1
West Curthwaite Cumb 56 B5
West Darlochan Argyll 65 F7
West Dean W Sus 11 C7
West Dean Wilts 10 B1
West Deeping Lincs 37 E7
West Derby Mers 43 C6
West Dereham Norf 38 E2
West Didsbury Gtr Man 44 C2
West Ditchburn Northumb 63 A7
West Down Devon 6 B4
West Drayton London 19 D7
West Drayton Notts 45 E11
West Ella E Yorks 52 G6
West End Bedford 28 C6
West End E Yorks 52 F5
West End E Yorks 53 F7
West End Hants 10 C3
West End Lancs 50 G3
West End N Som 15 E10
West End N Yorks 51 D7
West End Norf 38 E5
West End Norf 39 D11
West End Oxon 17 A11
West End S Lanark 69 F8
West End S Yorks 45 B10
West End Suff 39 G10
West End Sur 18 E6
West End W Sus 11 C11
West End Wilts 9 B8
West End Wilts 16 D6
West End Green Hants 18 E3
West Farleigh Kent 20 F4
West Felton Shrops 33 C9
West Fenton E Loth 70 B3
West Ferry Dundee 77 D7
West Firle E Sus 12 F3
West Ginge Oxon 17 C11
West Grafton Wilts 17 E9
West Green Hants 18 F4
West Greenskares Aberds 89 B7
West Grimstead Wilts 9 B11
West Grinstead W Sus 11 B10
West Haddlesey N Yorks 52 G1
West Haddon Northants 28 A3
West Hagbourne Oxon 18 C2
West Hagley Worcs 34 G5
West Hall Cumb 61 G11
West Hallam Derbys 35 A10
West Halton N Lincs 52 G5
West Ham London 19 C11
West Handley Derbys 45 E7
West Hanney Oxon 17 B11
West Hanningfield Essex 20 B4
West Hardwick W Yorks 51 H10
West Harnham Wilts 9 B10
West Harptree Bath 16 F2
West Hatch Som 8 B1
West Head Norf 38 E1
West Heath Ches E 44 F2
West Heath Hants 18 F2
West Heath Hants 18 F5
West Helmsdale Highld 93 H13
West Hendred Oxon 17 C11
West Heslerton N Yorks 52 B5
West Hill Devon 7 G9
West Hill E Yorks 53 C7
West Hill N Som 15 D10
West Hoathly W Sus 12 C2
West Holme Dorset 9 F7
West Horndon Essex 20 C3
West Horrington Som 16 G2
West Horsley Sur 19 F7
West Horton Northumb 71 G9
West Hougham Kent 21 G9
West Houlland Shetland 96 H4
West-houses Derbys 45 G8
West Huntington York 52 D2
West Hythe Kent 13 C10
West Ilsley W Berks 17 C11
West Itchenor W Sus 11 D6
West Keal Lincs 47 F7
West Kennett Wilts 17 E8
West Kilbride N Ayrs 66 B5
West Kingsdown Kent 20 E2
West Kington Wilts 16 D5
West Kinharrachie Aberds 89 E9
West Kirby Mers 42 D5
West Knapton N Yorks 52 B4
West Knighton Dorset 8 F6
West Knoyle Wilts 9 A7
West Kyloe Northumb 71 F9
West Lambrook Som 8 C3
West Langdon Kent 21 G10
West Langwell Highld 93 J9
West Lavington W Sus 11 B7
West Lavington Wilts 17 F7
West Layton N Yorks 58 F2
West Lea Durham 58 B5
West Leake Notts 35 C11
West Learmouth Northumb 71 G7
West Leigh Devon 6 F5
West Lexham Norf 38 D4
West Lilling N Yorks 52 C2
West Linton Borders 69 E10
West Liss Hants 11 B6
West Littleton S Glos 16 D4
West Looe Corn 4 F3
West Luccombe Som 7 B7
West Lulworth Dorset 9 F7
West Lutton N Yorks 52 C5
West Lydford Som 8 A4
West Lyng Som 8 B2
West Lynn Norf 38 C2
West Malling Kent 20 F3
West Malvern Worcs 26 D4
West Marden W Sus 11 C6
West Marina E Sus 13 F6
West Markham Notts 45 E11
West Marsh NE Lincs 46 A6
West Marton N Yorks 50 D4
West Meon Hants 10 B5
West Mersea Essex 31 G7
West Milton Dorset 8 E4
West Minster Kent 20 D6
West Molesey Sur 19 E8
West Monkton Som 8 B1
West Moors Dorset 9 D9
West Morriston Borders 70 F5
West Muir Angus 77 A8
West Ness N Yorks 52 B2
West Newham Northumb 62 F6
West Newton E Yorks 53 F7
West Newton Norf 38 C2
West Norwood London 19 D10
West Ogwell Devon 5 D9
West Orchard Dorset 9 C7
West Overton Wilts 17 E8
West Park Hrtlpl 58 C5
West Parley Dorset 9 E9
West Peckham Kent 20 F3
West Pelton Durham 58 A3
West Pennard Som 15 H11
West Pentire Corn 3 C6
West Perry Cambs 29 B8
West Putford Devon 6 E2
West Quantoxhead Som 7 B10
West Rainton Durham 58 B4
West Rasen Lincs 46 D4
West Raynham Norf 38 C4
West Retford Notts 45 D10
West Rounton N Yorks 58 F5
West Row Suff 38 H2
West Rudham Norf 38 C4
West Runton Norf 39 A7
West Saltoun E Loth 70 D3
West Sandwick Shetland 96 E6
West Scrafton N Yorks 51 A6
West Sleekburn Northumb 63 E8
West Somerton Norf 39 D10
West Stafford Dorset 8 F6
West Stockwith Notts 45 C11
West Stoke W Sus 11 D7
West Stonesdale N Yorks 57 F10
West Stoughton Som 15 G10
West Stour Dorset 9 B6
West Stourmouth Kent 21 E9
West Stow Suff 30 A5
West Stowell Wilts 17 E8
West Strathan Highld 93 C8
West Stratton Hants 18 G2
West Street Kent 20 F6
West Tanfield N Yorks 51 B8
West Taphouse Corn 4 E2
West Tarbert Argyll 73 G7
West Thirston Northumb 63 D7
West Thorney W Sus 11 D6
West Thurrock Thurrock 20 D2
West Tilbury Thurrock 20 D3
West Tisted Hants 10 B5
West Tofts Norf 38 F4
West Tofts Perth 76 D4
West Torrington Lincs 46 D5
West Town Hants 10 E6
West Town N Som 15 E10
West Tytherley Hants 10 B1
West Tytherton Wilts 16 D6
West Walton Norf 37 D10
West Walton Highway Norf 37 D10
West Wellow Hants 10 C1
West Wemyss Fife 70 A2
West Wick N Som 15 E9
West Wickham Cambs 30 D3
West Wickham London 19 E10
West Williamston Pembs 22 F5
West Willoughby Lincs 36 A5
West Winch Norf 38 D2
West Winterslow Wilts 9 A11
West Wittering W Sus 11 E6
West Witton N Yorks 58 H1
West Woodburn Northumb 62 E4
West Woodhay W Berks 17 E10
West Woodlands Som 16 G4
West Worldham Hants 18 H4
West Worlington Devon 7 E6
West Worthing W Sus 11 D10
West Wratting Cambs 30 C3
West Wycombe Bucks 18 B5
West Wylam Northumb 63 G7
West Yell Shetland 96 E6
Westacott Devon 6 C4
Westbere Kent 21 E8
Westborough Lincs 36 A4
Westbourne Bmouth 9 E9
Westbourne Suff 31 D8
Westbourne W Sus 11 D6
Westbrook W Berks 17 D11
Westbury Bucks 28 E3
Westbury Shrops 33 E9
Westbury Wilts 16 F5
Westbury Leigh Wilts 16 F5
Westbury-on-Severn Glos 26 G4
Westbury on Trym Bristol 16 D2
Westbury-sub-Mendip Som 15 G11
Westby Lancs 49 F3
Westcliff-on-Sea Southend 20 C5
Westcombe Som 16 H3
Westcote Glos 27 F9
Westcott Bucks 28 G4
Westcott Devon 7 F9
Westcott Sur 19 G8
Westcott Barton Oxon 27 F11
Westdean E Sus 12 G4
Westdene Brighton 12 F1
Wester Aberchalder Highld 81 A7
Wester Balgedie Perth 76 G4
Wester Culbeuchly Aberds 89 B6
Wester Dechmont W Loth 69 D9
Wester Denoon Angus 76 C6
Wester Fintray Aberds 83 B10
Wester Gruinards Highld 87 B8
Wester Lealty Highld 87 D9
Wester Milton Highld 87 F12
Wester Newburn Fife 77 G7
Wester Quarff Shetland 96 K6
Wester Skeld Shetland 96 J4
Westerdale Highld 94 E3
Westerdale N Yorks 59 F7
Westerfield Shetland 96 H5
Westerfield Suff 31 D8
Westergate W Sus 11 D8
Westerham Kent 19 F11
Westerhope T&W 63 G7
Westerleigh S Glos 16 D4
Westerton Angus 77 B9
Westerton Durham 58 C3
Westerton W Sus 11 D7
Westerwick Shetland 96 J4
Westfield Cumb 56 D1
Westfield E Sus 13 E7
Westfield Hereford 26 D4
Westfield Highld 94 D2
Westfield N Lanark 68 C6
Westfield Norf 38 E5
Westfield W Loth 69 C8
Westfields Dorset 8 D6
Westfields of Rattray Perth 76 C4
Westgate Durham 57 C11
Westgate N Lincs 45 B11
Westgate Norf 38 A4
Westgate Norf 38 A5
Westgate on Sea Kent 21 D10
Westhall Aberds 83 A8
Westhall Suff 39 G10
Westham Dorset 8 G5
Westham E Sus 12 F5
Westham Som 15 G10
Westhampnett W Sus 11 D7
Westhay Som 15 G10
Westhead Lancs 43 B7
Westhide Hereford 26 D2
Westhill Aberds 83 C10
Westhill Highld 87 G10
Westhope Hereford 25 C11
Westhope Shrops 33 G10
Westhorpe Lincs 37 B8
Westhorpe Suff 31 B7
Westhoughton Gtr Man 43 B9
Westhouse N Yorks 50 B2
Westhumble Sur 19 F8
Westing Shetland 96 C7
Westlake Devon 5 F7
Westleigh Devon 6 D3
Westleigh Devon 7 E9
Westleigh Gtr Man 43 B9
Westleton Suff 31 B11
Westley Shrops 33 E9
Westley Suff 30 B5
Westley Waterless Cambs 30 C3
Westlington Bucks 28 G4
Westlinton Cumb 61 G9
Westmarsh Kent 21 E9
Westmeston E Sus 12 E2
Westmill Herts 29 F10
Westminster London 19 D10
Westmuir Angus 76 B6
Westness Orkney 95 F4
Westnewton Cumb 56 B3
Westnewton Northumb 71 G8
Westoe T&W 63 G9
Weston Bath 16 E4
Weston Ches E 43 G10
Weston Devon 7 H10
Weston Dorset 8 G5
Weston Halton 43 D8
Weston Hants 10 B6
Weston Herts 29 E9
Weston Lincs 37 C8
Weston N Yorks 51 E7
Weston Northants 28 D2
Weston Notts 45 F11
Weston Shrops 34 C1
Weston Shrops 34 F1
Weston Staffs 34 C5
Weston W Berks 17 D10
Weston Beggard Hereford 26 D2
Weston by Welland Northants 36 F3
Weston Colville Cambs 30 C3
Weston Coyney Stoke 34 A5
Weston Favell Northants 28 B4
Weston Green Cambs 30 C3
Weston Green Norf 39 D7
Weston Heath Shrops 34 D3
Weston Hills Lincs 37 C8
Weston-in-Gordano N Som 15 D10
Weston Jones Staffs 34 C3
Weston Longville Norf 39 D7
Weston Lullingfields Shrops 33 C10
Weston-on-the-Green Oxon 28 G2
Weston-on-Trent Derbys 35 C10
Weston Patrick Hants 18 G3
Weston Rhyn Shrops 33 B8
Weston-Sub-Edge Glos 27 D8
Weston-super-Mare N Som 15 E9
Weston Turville Bucks 28 G5
Weston under Lizard Staffs 34 D4
Weston under Penyard Hereford 26 F3
Weston under Wetherley Warks 27 B10
Weston Underwood Derbys 35 A8
Weston Underwood M Keynes 28 C5
Westonbirt Glos 16 C5
Westoncommon Shrops 33 C10
Westoning C Beds 29 E7
Westonzoyland Som 8 A2
Westow N Yorks 52 C3
Westport Argyll 65 F7
Westport Som 8 C2
Westrigg W Loth 69 D8
Westruther Borders 70 F5
Westry Cambs 37 F9
Westville Notts 45 H9
Westward Cumb 56 B4
Westward Ho! Devon 6 D3
Westwell Kent 20 G6
Westwell Oxon 27 H9
Westwell Leacon Kent 20 G6
Westwick Cambs 29 B11
Westwick Durham 58 E1
Westwick Norf 39 C8
Westwood Devon 7 G9
Westwood Wilts 16 F5
Westwoodside N Lincs 45 C11
Wetheral Cumb 56 A6
Wetherby W Yorks 51 E10
Wetherden Suff 31 B7
Wetheringsett Suff 31 B8
Wethersfield Essex 30 E4
Wethersta Shetland 96 G5